D1880670

THE ZODIAC

AND THE SALTS OF SALVATION

THE ZODIAC
AND THE SALTS OF SALVATION

PART ONE

BY

DR. GEORGE WASHINGTON CAREY

THE RELATION OF THE MINERAL SALTS. OF THE: BODY TO THE SIGNS OF THE ZODIAC

(FOURTEENTH AND MEMORIAL EDITION)

PART TWO

AN ESOTERIC ANALYSIS AND SYNTHESIS OF THE ZODIACAL SIGNS AND THEIR PHYSIO-CHEMICAL ALLOCATIONS

BY

INEZ EUDORA PERRY

©Reserved

All rights reserved. No part of this work may be reproduced, stored, adapted, or transmitted in any form or by any means, electronic, mechanical, photocopying, micro-filming recording or otherwise, or translated in any language, without the prior written permission of the copyright owner and the publisher. The book is sold subject to the condition that it shall not, by way of trade or otherwise, be lent, resold, hired out, or otherwise circulated without the prior publisher's written consent in any form of binding or cover other than that in which it is published.

The views and opinions expressed in this book are author(s) own and the facts reported by them have been verified to the extent possible, and the publishers are not in any way liable for the same.

ISBN: 978-93-5128-765-0(HB)

First Published in 1932
Indian Reprint in 2017

Published by

Kalpaz Publications
C-30, Satyawati Nagar,
Delhi – 110052
E-mail: kalpaz@hotmail.com
Website: kalpazpublications.com
Ph.: +91-9212142040

CONTENTS

Part One

CONTENTS *(Continued)*

PART TWO

Part One

INTRODUCTION TO PART ONE

BY

INEZ EUDORA PERRY

DR. GEORGE W. CAREY'S booklet, *"The Relation of the Mineral Salts of the Body to the Signs of the Zodiac,"* has seen many editions; but it was not until 1906 that I secured my first copy, and, mentally hungry for *truth,* eagerly devoured its pages.

Such actual meat and drink it was to me, so fascinatingly interesting, that I was convinced at once of its immeasurable value to humanity. That realization became intensified, year after year, as constant experience and intensive research work furnished conclusive proof. I believe that the day is not far distant when Dr. Carey will be acclaimed as one of the world's greatest benefactors.

In this chaotic and materialistic age he discovered and published a priceless key, that which unlocks the door to mental as well as physical health. *The understanding and use of this key will accomplish the physio-chemical process whereby mankind may regenerate.* This means the slow but sure rise from physical and mental degeneracy, disease, unhappiness, and death to that glorious state which is the heritage of every one—*perfection.* Thus will be consummated the Scriptural injunction, "Be ye therefore perfect even as your father in heaven is perfect." Matt. 5:48.

The great majority of people will be startled, if, indeed, not actually shocked, by the statement which fifteen years of earnest research and experience causes me to make. Duty and a sincere wish to help humanity are also contributing factors, but there is another and more powerful reason. Our solar system is entering, once again in the cycles of the ages, the sign of Aquarius, the Son of Man, and those who know the Truth, or any part of it, must write, speak, and live it. Aquarius is the humanitarian, or human sign, and the planet (vibration) Uranus is the ruler of this division of the zodiac, which is the path of the solar system.

Therefore, as this is the *Age of Truth, those who work with and for it* are *working in harmony with natural law,* while those who follow the opposite course will wonder why they are not prospering. To prosper means to have sufficient for one's necessities, to be physically and mentally comfortable.

It is only *truth* that matters; *opinions* do not count. Dr. Carey was not interested in the latter, he was an iconoclast. He felt impelled to make scientific statements no matter how they were received.

My method (and purpose) is the same as his. I aspire to give out facts as I know and have proved them to be.

Therefore, please consider, carefully and earnestly, the following statement which should be written in letters of flame:

A knowledge of, and the practice of, the process necessary to the attainment of perfection is absolutely impossible without a thorough understanding of physiological chemistry. This Dr. William Schuessler furnished in his Biochemic System of Medicine, and the perfect key was supplied by Dr. Carey in his allocation of the biological salts with the zodiacal signs.

The truth of the foregoing statement is as definite and real to me as the fact that I live, move and have my being. I wish it could be made even more emphatic so that it would be engraved forever on the minds of those who read it.

Dr. Schuessler's system is the only true system of medicine, for it is the method of supplying the blood with its component parts. The Bible most truly states a great chemical fact (Leviticus 17:11) in the following words: "For the life of the flesh is in the blood—for it is the blood that maketh an atonement for the soul."

As the blood is the life of the flesh, it naturally follows that, as man is a trinity (body, or flesh, soul and spirit), the quality, condition, or health of his body determines that of his soul, which corresponds in exact degree.

The word "atonement" means at-one-ment or harmony. If the blood were chemically perfect, the highly differentiated and attenuated nerve and *glandular* fluids, which constitute the soul, would also be perfect. It is only when the blood is chemically perfect that the full quota of Spirit, otherwise God-power, can enter the body, for "Like attracts like."

Introduction to Part One

The study of Schuessler's Biochemistry enables us to become acquainted with the different kinds of material or basic substances which the Great Chemist and Architect of the Universe created as a medium for the Spirit, which is Life.

Spirit manifests imperfectly when material is deficient.

Deficiency means dis-ease, lack of ease, inharmony, imperfection.

Dormant, unhealthy, or imperfect brain cells do not make for an efficient brain. Thought corresponds to the nature and condition of the brain cells, for they constitute our thought machine, and the quality and value of that which it brings forth depend entirely on its condition.

Herein lies the explanation of all the trouble in the world, sin, crime, disease, death, unhappiness, insanity, fear, cowardice, lack of positivity, differences in opinions and the wars of nations and peoples.

Each one of us represents a consensus or aggregate of vibrations, a sum total of those present in Nature at the time we come into birth. Indeed, it is what makes birth possible. A certain rate of vibration is manifesting at that particular time and a corresponding result is produced.

"Whatsoever a man soweth, that shall he also reap." Sowing and reaping, reaping and sowing constitute birth and death. If we were not responsible for the kind of life we live, we would not then be accountable for the form of death which we attract.

Is it not, then, equally logical that a reincarnating ego must, because of the vibratory law of attraction, come to birth in an environment and into conditions which are decided by this self-same law? Otherwise justice would not exist. Justice is conformity to divine law. It is the working out, the expression or administration of law—doing the *right* thing because it is the *best*.

In Greek mythology, which constitutes the sacred and secret writings of that people, we find this statement which, it seems to me, agrees perfectly with the foregoing. "Amphion built the walls of Thebes (the human head) by charming (producing a harmonious vibration) the stones (mineral elements) into their places by the music of his lyre." (The lyre is a certain marvelous organ in the head.)

It is a poetical way of stating that the human head, which is the *beginning* of the human body, is formed according to a vibratory law, *for by it the very mineral atoms are grouped together and cells formed.* The meaning of Thebes is head. It was originally a physiological term.

Showing the chemical correspondence of the mineral salt Kali phos, or phosphate of potassium, to the highest part of the head, the cerebrum, alone elevates Dr. Carey to the heights where honor and gratitude should forever be accorded him. For this salt is the dynamic material which generates *spiritual electricity*, and ensouls the physical form with life.

And this is only one of his twelve astounding allocations. For astrology, that *synthesizer* of all knowledge, both cosmic and microcosmic, in the universe and in man, reveals to us why Kali phos is the Aries salt. This substance, through which the Most High manifests in man, is the cause of actual life in his form.

And to the degree in which the cerebro-spinal nerves are supplied with it, will energy or life manifest in and through him. The light of intelligence (Spirit or Father) will burn brightly if this substance, which alone can feed it, is sufficiently and adequately furnished.

Therefore: a *perfect* supply of the right chemical elements means *perfect cells, a perfect brain, perfect thought, perfect acts, perfection*—A GOD-MAN!

In contributing the foregoing I bespeak my deep and lasting gratitude to Dr. George W. Carey for the chemical light which he has thrown on dark places. Reader, *Truth* is the water of life! May you drink deeply, and begin to learn how to live forever!

"And let *patience* have its perfect work, that ye may be PERFECT and ENTIRE and LACK NOTHING."—James 1:4.

THE BIRTH OF THE AUTHOR, "THE SAINT GEORGE" OF BIOCHEMISTRY

BY

EDITH F. A. U. PAINTON

Time, September 7th, 1845, 4:45 P. M.

ENTER—R. L. U.—SAINT GEORGE

It was on September seventh, in eighteen hundred forty-five,
The planets of the heavens were wonderfully alive;
Luna was well in Scorpio, with Sol in Virgo's light,
While Venus was exalted, just between, in Libra bright.

Said Luna, "Listen, Venus! although we are semi-square,
It's up to you and me to send to Earth a spirit rare;
That dark star's out of tune, and needs a strong, awakening soul
Like those that you, fair Queen of Art, do beautifully control!

"Let's send down to the Earth today—today, but ne'er again—
One of those Alchemists of life they call September men!
A genius, Venus—listen from your Occult House, I pray,
A genius of that Virgin soil that must all Science sway."

The Goddess of Love answered, "I know, but take one peep—
Uranus's opposition is a thing to make me weep!
And his house rises soon—so—heavens! what could we ever do?
A genius we might send, but Oh! what MUST we send him through?"

"Naught cares a genius," Luna smiled; "send him through hottest hell,
He'll smile, and take his way unmoved, declaring all is well!
I've picked the man—with heart of gold—an OR of vital force,
And at the proper hour, we'll speed the soul upon its course!"

Still Venus hesitated—"But Mercury, what of him?
He's in his night-house, don't you see, where all his force is dim!

And Jove opposed, you see"— "Be still," said Luna, "he
Is close behind Old Sol, in Seventh, where Messengers should
be!

"And as for Jupiter, of course I'd rather he would smile,
But if he won't—he'll have to frown another little while;
We'll fix him in Third House to make a man of broadest
mind,
A Father of Big Thought, a chief and leader of his kind!"

"But Luna—can you think it safe? The Dragon is at rest,
Its Head within religion's house where all is at its best;
Its Tail down in the lower mind—O what a power today!
But this Saint George would saunter forth this heavenly beast
to slay!"

A deep bass growl from distant space rolled through the home
of spheres,
And Venus drew near Luna, seeking solace for her fears.
"Hush! don't let grim old Saturn hear, or He'll retard the
plan,
And cast his gloom o'er all our works in every way he can!"

"Eclipse for Saturn and his frowns," said Luna, full of scorn,
"Let Mars and Neptune in first house the leading aspects
form;
While Uranus, defying both, will leap o'er all that bars,
And lure to earth to plead for us a student of the stars!"

"He is the one to ever rule the true Aquarian born,
So what care we for Saturn's chill, or Mar's malignant scorn?
He'll draw unto the Earth, I'm sure, a Saint George full of
fire,
To slay the world's conventions with a sword of purpose
dire!"

Hark! A swift war-like commotion through the stellar
spaces ran,
As all the heavenly planets overheard the little plan;
"We will not have this rebel loosed on earth," protested they,
"We will not countenance such revolt. Man must our laws
obey!"

They all recalled the many lives they'd helped him live before,
They all looked back on ages past, and then—they sternly
swore,

The Birth of the Author

Not once again could they be blamed for such peculiar dope
As now boiled in Life's crucible to mold this horoscope!

"We've met in trines; we've fought; we've joined; we've met
in terms of sex;
We've formed all sorts of aspects that can human souls per-
plex;
But if he goes to earth again, just count our force not there!
For if we're to come to orb, we'll all act on the square!"

Then all reversed their motion, and walked backward, one by
one,
Endeavoring to escape the thing the karmic gods had done;
But, retrograde or not, the word went forth to shake the earth,
And Gee-OR-Gee, (the Gold in Earth) came to the hour of
birth!

And ever since, the planets as they grace his horoscope,
Have kept their faces towards him, walking backward, void
of hope,
For he upsets all theories, and their age-old thought he jars,
Preaching a New Age Eternal, in defiance of the Stars!

He came to slay the Dragon, and to span the Bridge of Time;
To find the chemicals of life, and blend their force sublime,
To unlock earth's grim secrets, facing revolution's strife,
And scaling highest heaven to demand immortal life!

Los Angeles, California, February 19, 1916.

Note. Mrs. Painton will be remembered by many of the older astrologers and especially by the Fellows of the American Academy.

IN MEMORIAM

Dr. George Washington Carey was born in Dixon, Illinois, on September 7th, 1845, and was one of a large family of children. His father's name was John Carey, and bore the relation of grand-nephew to John Quincy Adams. On his mother's side, a grandfather served with General Marion during the Revolution. His mother's name was Ruth Odell. When George Carey was about a year and a half old, the Careys left Illinois and came by covered wagon to Oregon, a journey of six months. The motion picture entitled "The Covered Wagon" gives an extremely realistic presentation of the main features of that trip and Dr. Carey greatly enjoyed seeing it.

He had very little schooling, but his parents were well qualified to teach him the fundamentals. His father was well known for his humorous verses which embodied much of Irish wit. As a child George was very delicate, his parents being doubtful that he would grow to manhood. His earlier years were spent on a farm, the evenings enlivened by music. Later on, he became leader of the village orchestra.

In his early forties he became the first Postmaster of Yakima, Washington, and held the position for several terms. Hearing of the science of biochemistry, he resigned to devote his life to its study.

Together with a number of physicians, Dr. Carey founded the College of Biochemistry in Yakima, Washington, and a few students enrolled and graduated, among them being the College founders; but, as this was many years ago, not much interest in the subject was aroused, and the project was given up because of lack of support.

Dr. Chapman was one of those taking the course, and the book which he wrote on biochemistry has been a popular household work.

Today this science is coming before the world, seemingly by leaps and bounds. Schools devoted to the teaching of biochemistry in a practical way are starting up in many states of the Middle West, and entire families are learning how to supply their blood deficiencies. After years of almost heartbreaking pioneering, of almost utter discouragement, on the part of its advocates, the science is now fast becoming recognized. In 1928, I believe, the Eclectic College of Chiropractic of Los Angeles added biochemistry to its curriculum.

Most people are not aware that biochemistry is an ancient Sanscrit science. Once again the cycle has appeared, upon whose wave it is borne. When Dr. Carey wrote his work on *The Biochemic System of Medicine,* its first press recognition was in a Health Magazine published by biochemic physicians in India. It stated: "We are glad to see that a western brother is helping to bring back the ancient science of biochemistry."

The book referred to above is now in its twenty-third edition. Years ago, when Dr. Carey wrote this treatise, he was financially unable to publish it, and sold the copyright to the Luyties Pharmacal Company, of St. Louis. Old Dr. Luyties, the founder of the firm, as well as Dr. Boericke, had interviewed Dr. William Schuessler, the originator of biochemistry, in Oldenburg, Germany. They learned his method of preparing the cell salts or mineral constituents of the blood, and presented it in this country. Since Dr. Carey's death in 1924, the last edition of his book was re-edited by a Dr. Arthur Perry, and it has lost its old familiar aspect. The writer of this article is now preparing a new and up-to-date edition combining with the science of astrology. This will enable anyone to work out his or her own individual chemical plan from the birth data.

It was Dr. Carey, who, in one of those strange and rare moments which come to those who seek, ascribed to each sign of the zodiac its corresponding chemical element or salt (salt is an old term for "earth"), and wrote *The Relation of the Mineral Salts of the Body to the Signs of the Zodiac,* the most unique work of the century and the most valuable.

It has been regrettable that so many have copied this work, plagiarists who have never mentioned his name as the distinguished author. Recently a Chicago magazine carried an advertisement, much of which was copied, word for word, from one of his circulars, no credit given and no quotation marks used.

Because the work was never copyrighted by Dr. Carey is no excuse for not giving the author credit for it. It is for the purpose of emphasizing this, and securing for him permanent recognition, that this fourteenth edition is combined with some new writings of my own, and copyrighted.

And as it is the fourteenth in the series, it means a new product, the mystical fruit of a new age, the Aquarian, concerning which Dr. Carey often wrote and spoke. It is a new product, because *for the first time* it is *definitely* stated *to be the Key to Physical Regeneration and Spiritual Illumination.*

The fourteenth letter of the Hebrew alphabet is N, spelled Nun in that language. Its literal interpretation is *fish,* (fruit or progeny.) In the Biblical story, Joshua was the son of Nun, and Joshua is the origin of the Latinized form, *Jesus.* Therefore Jesus also means *fish.* It is common knowledge that the *fish* has been the esoteric symbol for two thousand years, at least, for the Son of Man. This will be dealt with at great length under Virgo, the sixth lesson or chapter.

This edition, then, is symbolic of all that the letter N means,—the *new man,* for it gives information relative to the necessary material required to produce, or *create* that *new man.* Dr. Carey also gave to the world the formula for bioplasma, which is a combination of the twelve inorganic salts of the blood, combined in the proportion which he considered necessary to create healthy, or chemically perfect blood.

Those who are familiar with his book, *The Biochemic System of Medicine,* feel that he improved greatly the application of Schuessler's system. More and more information is being constantly obtained, so that still further contributions will be made to this invaluable science. As the Scriptures state—"*All* things *work together* for *good,*" and until we learn what they are and apply them, we can not hope to arrive at the perfect state.

Some years after becoming interested in biochemistry, Dr. Carey edited a small magazine dealing with this subject, and containing also humorous articles and poems from his pen. His *Chemistry of the Cosmos* found many appreciative readers, as it contained unusual poems as well as articles of a scientific nature. One which was especially valued was entitled *It,* and dealt with the one universal esse from which all things originate and to which they eventually return.

His explanation of slang phrases is very interesting as well as instructive, for he brings out the fact that they are based on truth and that the Cosmic Mind or planetary vibration, impinging (the same as radio waves) on the human brain at a certain time causes mental electricity to etch in a certain manner on the wax-like brain cells. Hence thoughts are produced relative to particular subjects.

In just this way public or mass interest is aroused along definite lines. Great truths are thus expressed in a manner attractive to the great majority of minds, stepped down, we may say, into a vernacular which is "catchy," while the idea back of it all is comprehended only by a few.

Not only was Dr. Carey deeply interested in life's chemical mysteries, but his searching mind longed to solve the greatest of all, that of physical regeneration and spiritual illumination, and the plan or process necessary for its attainment. Hiram Butler's theory appealed to him and he began his researches along that line, finding at last that God, Word, seed, fish, Jesus and progeny are words synonymous in meaning, and when understood from their etymological derivation, will unlock the door of the Inner Mystery. He discovered that *esse,* the *substance of being,* the *elixir of life*—in other words the brain or life substance—is the protoplasmic seed material which is found to be the possession of every human being. The Herculean task or *great work* which everyone must perform, eventually, is the purification and perfection of this material, for it then *becomes* the Christ or Holy Oil.

The astounding revelation of what this means came to Dr. Carey when he had passed his seventieth year, and he went forth bravely to give it to the world. He found, at a late day, what he had been searching for all his life, the greatest secret of all. It is not hidden from anyone, but each hides it from himself because of mental inability to grasp it.

And thus he set his feet, at last, upon the rung of the ladder which leads back home to God or good. To find that rung and set one's feet thereon is the day of all days for every human being. *Then one must begin the climb.* Literally, it means that one is endeavoring to BECOME a Christian, to make a new being of one's self. To become a Christian does not refer to a *belief* that a certain man was killed by a mob in order that our sins might be forgiven. In fact that is utter nonsense, for it would make null and void the law of cause and effect, and contradict point blank the declaration that we must "Work out our own salvation." It truly must be worked out, for it is a definite process, physiological and mental, and hence moral.

The climb to the heights is not the work of *one* lifetime, but of *many*, for the simple reason that it is too great a task to accomplish in a few short years. "Know the truth and the truth shall *set you free*," the Bible states. Yes, free from pain, sickness, sorrow and *death*, for truly death is "the last enemy to be overcome." Death, aside from accident, is the result of dis-ease, inharmony in the chemical elements of the blood, hence cell starvation. Therefore we will overcome death when we know enough *to live*. One link of the chain of bondage (ignorance) falls off at a time, until we are free.

Dr. Carey's initial attempt to give out information relative to the subject of occult physiology and the process of redemption and salvation was a book entitled *The Tree of Life*.

It was this publication which gave me my first insight into the real nature of the Scriptures and occult works in general. I realized that they were a compilation of scientific facts about mankind, physiological, anatomical, chemical, and metaphysical. Later on, after beginning the study of esoteric astrology, I realized that this noble science synthesized them all. I found it a veritable treasure house of facts, and dug deeply and am still digging in this mine of wealth.

In his seventy-second year Dr. Carey offered me a partnership, which was accepted and purchased. Like his, my interest was, is, and will be entirely along these lines.

In 1923, the work of the Los Angeles office was taken over by me and he sailed for Australia, his plan being to spend some time there. However, the long and tiresome trip and arduous work in a new field was more than he should have attempted. He mapped out too much work, too many lectures. He felt he must not lose a moment, that the great message must be given without ceasing, humanity's need was so great and the time so short. It was short for him, as he was nearing his eightieth year, and short also for those who had not yet turned to higher things. Earth is preparing once again for great changes, as the solar system nears the constellation of Aquarius. The 2160 years required for it to pass through its atmosphere is termed the Aquarian Age or the Age of the Son of Man. Humanity *must* begin to look upward, for it will be *forced* to by this very vibration. The mind must begin to expand and the animal-man at last make a decided effort to purify himself of his animal nature and become really humane.

Then will humanity work with Nature and not against

her, and thus, indeed, will the very earth be made new. "And there shall be a new heaven and a new earth."

Dr. Carey and I together revised and enlarged *The Tree of Life,* and as co-authors published *God-Man, The Word Made Flesh,* together with a large physiological chart giving much data on occult physiology, and indicating the positions of the seven great nerve centers or chakras, otherwise the Seven Churches of Asia. This work has seen three editions. It is temporarily out of print awaiting the completion of a mass of new material which will be added to it.

Dr. Carey also published two other books, *The Chemistry of Life,* and *The Chemistry and Wonders of the Human Body.*

Returning to the states from his trip to Australia, he went to San Diego to lecture, and on the 17th day of November, 1924, stepped forth from his physical vehicle. His wish that it be cremated was fulfilled. The Grand Army, of which he was a member, had charge of the services.

To those who ask the question, "Why did not the cell food and his belief in physical regeneration cause him to live longer," I will say that the answer has already been given. He found the key to physical regeneration only after he had passed seventy. The process is not of *one* life, one incarnation, but of many. Only those unfamiliar with this subject ask that question. He lived, at that, longer than the average person, even though beginning life with a very sensitive, delicate body. Constantly engaged in strenuous work, he accomplished more at seventy years of age along that line than the average man of fifty, and he traveled and lectured up to the very last.

Dr. Carey's mentality was of a mercurial type, Mercury and the Sun having been in Virgo at birth, therefore he was critical and analytical. When lecturing, he would make a tremendously iconoclastic statement relative to some astounding fact and, without explaining, soar on his Mercury wings to more loftv heights. Resting for a moment, his audience would be blinded by another flash from the mighty sword of Truth; but he left it to them to fill in the intervening space, and very few could. His flights into mental ether where facts are born were so lofty that his journey was a lonely one. His was a truly scientific mind which nothing but facts could satisfy, and he demanded facts of others.

In his early forties he gave up smoking and never took liquor in any form whatsoever, as he realized what effect they both had on the delicate tissues, membranes and glands of the body which the Scriptures call "THE TEMPLE OF GOD." In this incarnation he did the best he could to utilize and work out the truths he had contacted.

Many people all over the country tell me that the information which Dr. Carey gave forth in his writings and lectures have been the means of opening up an entirely new vista of life to them, and they bless him for it. We, too, bless him, and radio our gratitude to him in the realm of the unseen where he is waiting. When the time is ripe and the astrological moment arrives which will produce the vibration necessary for his reappearance in the objective, may he come forth again in physical manifestation to go on with the work he loved so well. *Requiescat in pace!*

THE NEW NAME

"And I will write upon him the name of my God." "And I will write upon him my new name."—Revelation.

Man struggling up to the sunlight,
  Up from the mire and clay,
Fighting through wars and jungles,
  And sometimes learning to pray—
And sometimes a king with a scepter,
  And sometimes a slave with a hod;
Some people call it Karma,
  And others call it God.

A beggar ragged and hungry,
  A prince in purple and gold,
A palace gilded and garnished,
  A cottage humble and old—
One's hopes are blighted in blooming,
  One gathers the ripened pod—
Some call it Fate or Destiny,
  And others call it God.

Glimmering waters and breakers,
  Far on the horizon's rim,
White sails and sea-gulls glinting
  Away till the sight grows dim,
And shells, spirit-painted with glory,
  Where seaweeds beckon and nod—
Some people call it Ocean,
  And others call it God.

Cathedrals and domes uplifting,
  Spires pointing up to the sun,
Images, altars and arches,
  Where kneeling and penance are done—
From organs grand anthems are swelling,
  Where the true and faithful plod—
Some call it Superstition,
  While others call it God.

The Zodiac and the Salts of Salvation

Visions of beauty and splendor,
  Forms of a long-lost race,
Sounds of faces and voices,
  From the fourth dimension of space—
And on through the universe boundless,
  Our thoughts go lightning shod—
Some call it Imagination,
  And others call it God.

Acids and alkalies acting,
  Proceeding and acting again,
Operating, transmuting, fomenting,
  In throes and spasms of pain—
Uniting, reacting, creating,
  Like souls "passing under the rod"—
Some people call it Chemistry,
  And others call it God.

Vibration of Etheric Substance,
  Causing light through regions of space,
A girdle of Something, enfolding,
  And binding together the race—
And words without wires transmitted,
  "Ariel"—winged, spirit-sandaled and shod—
Some call it Electricity,
  And others call it God.

Earth redeemed and made glorious,
  Lighted by Heaven within,
Men and angels face to face,
  With never a thought of sin—
Lion and lamb together,
  In flowers that sweeten the sod—
Some of us call it Brotherhood,
  And others call it God.

And now the sixth sense is opened,
  And we have rent the veil,
And we no longer wander,
  We have ransomed the "Holy Grail."
Through all of life's phases and changes,
  Along all new paths to be trod,
We will recognize only one power—
  One present, Omnipotent God.

Note: There have been so many requests for this much admired poem from the pen of Dr. Carey that it is believed its publication herein will be appreciated by his friends.

RELATION OF THE MINERAL SALTS OF THE BODY TO THE SIGNS OF THE ZODIAC

BY

DR. GEORGE W. CAREY

BIOCHEMISTRY

Acid and Alkali acting,
  Proceeding and acting again.
Operating, transmuting, fomenting
  In throes and spasms of pain—
Uniting, reacting, creating,
  Like souls "passing under the rod"—
Some people call it Chemistry,
  And others call it God.

BIOCHEMISTRY means that chemistry of life, or the union of inorganic and organic substances whereby new compounds are formed.

In its relation to so-called disease this system uses the inorganic salts, known as cell-salts, or tissue builders.

The constituent parts of man's body are perfect principles, —namely, oxygen, hydrogen, carbon, lime, iron, potash, soda, silica, magnesia, etc. These elements, gases, etc., are perfect *per se*, but may be endlessly diversified in combination as may the planks, bricks or stones with which a building is to be erected.

A shadow can not be removed by chemicals; neither can disease be removed by poison. There is nothing (no thing) to be removed in either case; but there is a deficiency to be supplied. The shadow may be removed by supplying light to the space covered by the shadow.

So symptoms, called disease, disappear or cease to manifest when the food called for is furnished.

The human body is a receptacle or a storage battery, and will always run well while the chemicals are present in proper quantity and combination, as surely as an automobile will run when charged and supplied with the necessary ingredients to vibrate or cause motion.

The cell-salts are found in all our foods, and are thus carried into the blood, where they carry on the process of life, and by the law of chemical affinity keep the human form, bodily functions, materialized. When a deficiency occurs in any of these workers through a non-assimilation of food, poor action of liver or digestive process, dematerialization of the body commences. So disease is a deficiency in some of the chemical constituents that carry on the chemistry of life and not an entity.

Having learned that disease is not a thing, but a condition due to lack of some inorganic constituent of the blood, it follows naturally that the proper method of cure is to supply the blood with that which is lacking. In the treatment of disease the use of anything not a constituent of the blood is unnecessary.

Dr. Charles W. Littlefield, analytical chemist, says:

"The twelve mineral salts are, in a very real sense, the material basis of the organs and tissues of the body and are absolutely essential to their integrity of structure and functional activity. Experiments prove that the various tissue cells will rapidly disintegrate in the absence of the proper proportion of these salts in the circulating fluid. Whereas the maintenance of this proportion insures healthy growth and perpetual renewal.

"These mineral salts are, therefore, the physical basis of all healing. Regardless of the school employed, if these are absent from the blood and tissues, no permanent cure is possible."

ESOTERIC CHEMISTRY

In this strenuous age of reconstruction, while God's creative compounds are forming a new race in the morning of a new age, all who desire physical regeneration should strive by every means within their reach to build new tissue, nerve fluids and brain cells, thus literally making "new bottles for the new wine." For be it known to all men that the word "wine" as used in Scripture, means blood when used in connection with man. It also means the sap of trees and juice of vegetables or fruit.

The parable of turning water into wine at the marriage of Cana in Galilee is a literal statement of a process taking place every heart-beat in the human organism.

Galilee means a circle of water or fluid—the circulatory system. Cana means a dividing place—the lungs. In the Greek, "a place of reeds," or cells of lungs that vibrate sound.

Biochemists have shown that food does not form blood, but simply furnishes the mineral base by setting free the inorganic or cell-salts contained in all food-stuff. The organic part, oil, fibrin, albumen, etc., contained in food is burned or digested in the stomach and intestinal tract to furnish motive power to operate the human machine and draw air into lungs, thence into arteries; *i.e.*, air carriers.

Therefore, it is clearly proved that air (spirit) unites with the minerals and forms blood, proving that the oil, albumen, etc., found in blood, is created every breath at the "marriage in Cana of Galilee."

Air was called water or pure sea, viz: Virgin Mar-y. So we see how water is changed into wine—blood—every moment.

In the new age, we will need perfect bodies to correspond with the higher vibration, or motion of the new blood, for "old bottles (bodies) can not contain the new wine."

Another allegorical statement typifying the same truth reads, "And I saw a new Heaven and a new Earth," i.e., a new mind and a new body.

Biochemistry may well say with Walt Whitman: "To the sick lying on their backs I bring help, and to the strong, upright man I bring more needed help." To be grouchy, cross, irritable, despondent or easily discouraged, is *prima facie* evidence that the fluids of the stomach, liver and brain are not vibrating at normal rate, the rate that results in equilibrium or health. Health cannot be qualified; *i.e.*, poor health; or good health. There must be either health or dishealth; ease or disease. We do not say poor ease or good ease. We say ease or disease, viz., not at ease.

A sufficient amount of the cell-salts of the body, properly combined and taken as food—not simply to cure some ache, pain or exudation—forms blood that materializes in healthy fluids, flesh and bone tissue.

We should take the tissue cell-salts as one uses health foods, not simply to change not-health to health, but to keep the rate of blood vibration in the tone of health all the time.

THE ULTIMATE OF BIOCHEMISTRY

The microscope increases the rate of motion of the cells of the retina and we see things that were occulted to the natural rate of vibration of sight cells. Increase the rate of activity of brain cells by supplying more of the dynamic molecules of the blood known as mineral or cell-salts of lime, potash, sodium, iron, magnesia, silica; and we see, mentally, truths that we could not sense at lower or natural rates of motion, although the lower rate may manifest ordinary health.

Natural man, or natural things, must be raised from the level of nature to super-natural, in order to realize new concepts that lie waiting for recognition above the solar plexus; that is, above the animal or natural man.

The positive pole, or *being*, must be "lifted up" from the kingdom of earth, animal desire below the solar plexus, to the pineal gland which connects the cerebellum, the temple of the Spiritual Ego, with the optic thalamus, the third eye.

By this regenerative process millions of dormant cells of the brain are resurrected and set in operation, and then man no longer "sees through a glass darkly," but with the eye of spiritual understanding.

To those who object to linking chemistry with astrology, the writer has this to say:

The Cosmic Law is not in the least disturbed by negative statements of the ignorant individual. Those investigators of natural phenomena, who delve deeply to find truth, pay little heed to the dabbler who says, "I can't understand how the zodiacal signs can have any relation to the cell-salts of the human body." The sole reason that he "cannot understand" is because he never tried to understand.

A little earnest, patient study will open the understanding of anyone possessed of ordinary intelligence, and make plain the great truth that the UNIverse is what the word implies; *i.e., one verse.*

It logically follows that all parts of one thing are susceptible to the operation of any part.

The human body is an epitome of the cosmos.

Each sign of the zodiac is represented by the twelve functions of the body and the position of the Sun at birth.

Therefore the cell-salt corresponding to the sign of the zodiac and function of the body is consumed more rapidly than other salts; and an extra amount is needed to supply the deficiency caused by the Sun's influence at that particular time.

Space will permit only a brief statement of the awakening of humanity to great occult truths. However, the following from India will indicate the trend of new thought: "Doctor Carey's remarkable researches in the domain of healing art have left no stone unturned. His discovery of the zodiacal cell-salts has added a new page in the genesis of healing art," writes Swaminatha Bomiah, M.B., Ph.D.Sc., F.I.A.C., in an article in *Self-Culture Magazine,* published at No. 105 Armenian St., G. T., Madras, India.

THE TWELVE CELL-SALTS OF THE ZODIAC
ARIES: "THE LAMB OF GOD"

March 21 to April 21.

Astrologers have for many years waited for the coming discovery of a planet to rule the head or brain of man, symbolized in the "Grand Man" of the heavens by the celestial sign of the zodiac, regnant from March 21 to April 21. This sign is known as Aries—the Ram or Lamb.

Angles of planets cause effects or influences. The priesthood of the middle ages, wishing to control the ignorant masses, personified the influence of planetary aspects, positions or angles, and transposed the letters so they spelled angel. Upon this one "slippery cog" the stupendous frauds of ecclesiasticism were built.

With the false teachings of the Church ingrained into the fiber of the brain of man, is it strange that for years before the advent of a new planet, with its added angle (influence), the brain cells of earth's inhabitants should be disturbed, as the effects of the coming storms disturb the fluids and mechanism of the weather forecaster's laboratory?

The coming of Christ and the end of the world has been preached from every street corner for several years, and thousands, yea, millions, are pledging themselves to try to live as Christ lived or according to their concept of His life.

No great movement of the people ever occurs without a scientific cause.

The optic thalamus, meaning "light of the chamber," is the inner or third eye, situated in the center of the head. It connects the pineal gland and the pituitary body. The optic nerve starts from this "eye single." "If thine eye be single, thy whole body will be full of light." *The optic thalamus is the Aries planet* and when fully developed through physical regeneration (see *God-Man; The Word Made Flesh*), it lifts the initiate from the kingdom of earth, animal desire below the solar plexus, to the pineal gland that connects the cerebellum, the temple of the Spiritual Ego, with the optic thalamus, the third eye.

By this regenerative process millions of dormant cells of the brain are resurrected and set in operation, and then man no longer "sees through a glass darkly," but with the eye of spiritual understanding.

I venture to predict that the planet corresponding to the optic thalamus will soon be located in the heavens.

"The new order cometh."

In ancient lore Aries was known as the "Lamb of God," or Gad, which represents the head or brain. The brain controls and directs the body and mind of man. The brain itself, however, is a receiver operated upon by celestial influences or angles (angels) and must operate according to the directing force or intelligence of its source of power.

Man has been deficient in understanding because his brain receiver did not vibrate to certain subtle influences. The dynamic cells in the gray matter of the nerves were not finely attuned and did not respond—hence sin, or falling short of understanding.

From the teachings of the chemistry of life we find that the basis of the brain or nerve fluid is a certain mineral salt known as potassium phosphate, or Kali phos.

A deficiency in this brain constituent means "sin," or a falling short of judgment or proper comprehension. With the advent of the Aries Lord, God, or planet, cell-salts are rapidly coming to the fore as the basis of all healing. Kali phosphate is the greatest healing agent known to man, because it is the chemical base of material expression and understanding.

The cell-salts of the human organism are now being prepared for use, while poisonous drugs are being discarded everywhere. Kali phosphate is the especial birth salt for those born between March 21 and April 21.

These people are brain workers, earnest, executive and determined—thus do they rapidly use up the brain vitalizers.

Aries gems are amethyst and diamond.

The astral colors are white and rose pink.

In Bible alchemy Aries represents Gad, the seventh son of Jacob, and means "armed and prepared"—thus it is said when in trouble or danger, "keep your head."

In the symbolism of the New Testament, Aries corresponds to the disciple Thomas. Aries people are natural doubters until they figure a thing out for themselves.

TAURUS—"THE WINGED BULL" OF THE ZODIAC

APRIL 21 TO MAY 21.

The ancients were not "primitive men." There never was a first man, nor a primitive man. Man is an eternal verity—the truth. Truth never had a beginning.

The Winged Bull of Nineveh is a symbol of the great truth that substance is materialized air, and that all so-called solid substances may be resolved into air.

Taurus is an earth sign, but earth (soul) is precipitated aerial elements. This chemical fact was known to the scientists of the Taurian age (over 4000 years ago); therefore they carved the emblem of their zodiacal sign with wings.

Those born between the dates April 21 and May 21 can descend very deep into materiality or soar "High as that Heaven where Taurus wheels," as written by Edwin Markham, who is a Taurus native.

What can be finer than the following from this noted Taurian, he who has sprouted the wings of spiritual concept:

> "It is a vision waiting and aware,
> And you must bring it down, oh, men of worth,
> Bring down the New Republic hung in air
> And make for it foundations on the Earth."

Air is the "raw material" for blood, and when it is drawn in, or breathed in, rather, by the "Infinite Alchemist," to the blood vessels, it unites with the philosopher's stone, mineral salts, and in the human laboratory creates blood.

So, then, blood is the elixir of life, the "Ichor of the Gods."

The sulphate of sodium, known to druggists as Nat. sulph., chemically corresponds to the physical and mental characteristics of those born in the Taurus month.

Taurus is represented by the cerebellum, or lower brain, and neck.

A deficiency in Natrium sulphate in the blood is always manifested by pains in the back of the head, sometimes extending down the spine, and then affecting the liver.

The first cell-salt to become deficient in symptoms of disease in the Taurus native is Natrium sulphate.

The chief office of Natrium sulphate is to eliminate an excess of water from the body.

In hot weather the atmosphere becomes heavily laden with water and is thus breathed into the blood through the lungs.

One molecule of the Taurus salt has the chemical power to take up and carry out of the system two molecules of water.

Blood does not become overcharged with water from the water we drink, but from an atmosphere overcharged with aqueous vapor drawn from water in rivers, lakes or swamps, by heat of the sun above seventy degrees in shade.

The more surplus water there is to be thrown out of the blood, the more sodium sulphate required.

All so-called bilious or malarial troubles are simply a chemical effect or action caused by deficient sulphate of soda.

Chills and fever are Nature's method of getting rid of surplus water by squeezing it out of the blood through violent muscular, nervous and vascular spasms.

No "shakes" or ague can occur if blood be properly balanced chemically.

Governing planet: Venus.

Gems: Moss-agate and emerald.

Astral colors: Red and lemon yellow.

In Bible alchemy, Taurus represents Asher, the eighth son of Jacob, and means blessedness or happiness.

In the symbolism of the New Testament, Taurus corresponds to the disciple Thaddeus, meaning firmness, or led by love.

THE CHEMISTRY OF GEMINI

MAY 21 TO JUNE 21.

One of the chief characteristics of the Gemini native is expression. The cell-salt *Kali muriaticum* (potassium chloride) is the mineral worker of blood that forms fibrin and properly diffuses it throughout the tissues of the body.

This salt must not be confused with the chlorate of potash, a poison (chemical formula $KClO_3$).

The formula of the chloride of potassium (Kali mur) is KCl.

Kali mur molecules are the principal agents used in the chemistry of life to build fibrin into the human organism. The skin that covers the face contains the lines and angles that give expression, and thus differentiates one person from another; therefore the maker of fibrin has been designated as the birth salt of the Gemini native.

In venous blood fibrin amounts to three in one thousand

parts. When the molecules of Kali mur fall below the standard, the blood fibrin thickens, causing what is known as pleurisy, pneumonia, catarrh, diphtheria, etc. When the circulation fails to throw out the thickened fibrin via the glands or mucous membrane, it may stop the action of the heart. Embolus is a Latin word meaning little lump, or balls; therefore to die of embolus or "heart failure" generally means that the heart's action was stopped by little lumps of fibrin clogging the auricles and ventricles of the heart.

When the blood contains the proper amount of Kali mur, fibrin is functional and the symptoms referred to above do not manifest. Gemini means twins. Gemini is the sign which governs the United States.

The astral colors of Gemini are red, white, and blue. While those who made our first flag and chose the colors, personally knew nothing of astrology, yet the Cosmic Law worked its will to give America the "red, white, and blue."

Mercury is the governing planet of Gemini. The gems are beryl, aquamarine, and dark blue stones. In Bible alchemy, Gemini represents Issachar, the ninth son of Jacob, and means price, reward, or recompense. In the symbolic allegories of the New Testament, Gemini corresponds to the disciple Judas, which means service or necessity. The perverted ideas of an ignorant dark-age priesthood made "service and necessity" infamous by a literal rendering of the alchemical symbol, but during the present Aquarian age, the Judas symbol will be understood and the disciple of "service" will no longer have to submit to "third degree methods."

CANCER: THE CHEMISTRY OF THE "CRAB"

June 21 to July 22.

Cancer is the mother sign of the zodiac.

The mother's breast is the soul's first home after taking on flesh and "rending the Veil of Isis."

The tenacity of those born between the dates June 21 and July 22, in holding on to a home or dwelling place is well illustrated by the crab's grip, and also by the fact that it carries its house along wherever it goes in order that it may be sure of a dwelling.

The angles (angels) of the twelve zodiacal signs materialize their vitalities in the human microcosm. Through the operation of chemistry, energy creating, the intelligent molecules of Divine substance make the "Word flesh."

The corner stone in the chemistry of the crab is the inorganic salt fluoride of lime, known in pharmacy as *Calcarea flourica.* It is a combination of flourine and lime.

When this cell-salt is deficient in the blood, physical and mental disease (not-at-ease) is the result. Elastic fiber is formed by the union of the fluoride of lime with albuminoids, whether in the rubber tree or the human body. All relaxed conditions of tissue (varicose veins and kindred ailments) are due to a lack of sufficient amount of elastic fiber to "rubber" the tissue and hold it in place.

When elastic fiber is deficient in tissue of membrane between the upper and lower brain poles—cerebrum and cerebellum—there results a "sagging apart" of the positive and negative poles of the dynamo that runs the machinery of man.

An unfailing sign or symptom of this deficiency is a groundless fear of financial ruin.

While those born in any of the twelve signs may sometimes be deficient in Calcium fluoride, due to Mars or Mercury (or both) in Cancer at birth, Cancer people are more liable to symptoms indicating a lack of this elastic fiber-builder than are those born in other signs.

Why should we search Latin or Greek lexicons to find a name for the result of a deficiency in some of the mineral constituents of blood? If we find a briar in our flesh, we say so in the plainest speech; we do not say, "I have the briatitis or splintraligia."

When we know that a deficiency in the cell-salts of the blood causes the symptoms that medical ignorance has dignified and personified with names that nobody knows the meaning of, we will know how to heal scientifically by the unalterable law of the chemistry of life. When we learn the cause of disease, then, and not before, will we prevent disease.

Not through quarantine, nor disinfectants, nor "Boards of Health" will man reach the long sought plane of health; not through affirmations of health, nor denials of disease will bodily regeneration be wrought; not by dieting or fasting or "Fletcherizing" or suggesting, will the elixir of life and the philosopher's stone be found.

The "mercury of the sages" and the "Hidden Manna" are not constituents of health foods.

Victims of salt baths and massage are bald before their time, and the alcohol, steam and Turkish bath fiends die young.

"Sic transit gloria mundi."

When a man's body is made chemically perfect, the operations of mind will perfectly express.

Gems belonging to the sign of the breast are black onyx and emerald; astral colors, green and russet-brown.

Cancer is represented by Zebulum, the tenth son of Jacob, and means dwelling place or habitation.

Matthew is the Cancer disciple.

LEO: THE HEART OF THE ZODIAC

JULY 22 TO AUGUST 23.

The Sun overflows with divine energy. It is the "brewpot" that forever filters and scatters the "elixir of life."

Those born while the Sun is passing through Leo, July 22 to August 23, receive the heart vibrations, or pulses, of the Grand Man, or "Circle of Beasts." All the blood in the body passes through the heart. So the Leo native is the recipient of every quality and possibility contained in the great "alchemical vase," the "Son of Heaven."

The impulsive traits of Leo people are symboled in the pulse, which is a reflex of heart throbs.

The astronomer, by unerring law of mathematics applied to space, proportion, and the so-far-discovered wheels and cogs of the uni-machine, can tell where a certain planet must be located before the telescope has verified the prediction. So the astro-biochemist knows there must of necessity be a blood mineral and tissue builder to correspond with the materialized angle (angel) of the circle of the zodiac.

The phosphate of magnesia, in biochemic therapeutics, is the remedy for all spasmodic impulsive symptoms. This salt supplies the deficient worker or builder in such cases and thus restores normal conditions. A lack of muscular force, or nerve vigor, indicates a disturbance in the operation of the heart cell-salt, magnesia phosphate, which gives the "Lion's spring," or impulse, to the blood that throbs through the heart.

Leo is ruled by the Sun, and the children of that celestial sign are natural sun worshipers.

Gold must contain a small per cent of alloy or base metal before it can be used commercially. Likewise the "Gold of Ophir"—Sun's rays, or vibration—must contain a high potency of the earth salt, magnesia, in order to be available for use in bodily function Thus through the chemical action of the inorganic (mineral and water) in the organic (Sun's rays and ether) does the volatile become fixed, and the Word become flesh.

Leo people consume their birth salts more rapidly than they consume any of the other salts of the blood; hence they are often deficient in magnesium. Crude magnesia is too coarse to enter the blood through the delicate mucous membrane absorbents, and must be prepared according to the biochemic method before being taken into the blood.

Gems of Leo are ruby and diamond.

Astral colors, red and green.

The eleventh child of Jacob, Dinah, represents Leo and means *judged*. Simon is the Leo disciple.

VIRGO: THE VIRGIN MARY

AUGUST 23 TO SEPTEMBER 23.

Virgin means pure. Mary, Marie, or Mare (Mar) means water. The letter M is simply the sign of Aquarius, "The Water Bearer."

Virgin Mary means pure sea, or water.

Jesus is derived from a Greek word, meaning fish. Out of the pure sea, or water, comes fish. Out of woman's body comes the "Word made flesh." All substance comes forth from air, which is a higher potency of water.

All substance is fish, or the substance of Jesus.

This substance is made to say, "Eat, this is My body; drink, this is My blood."

There is nothing from which flesh and blood can be made, but the one universal air, energy, or Spirit, in which man has his being.

All tangible elements are the effects of certain rates of motion of the intangible and unseen elements. Nitrogen gas is mineral in solution, or ultimate potency.

Oil is made by the union of sulphate of potassium (potash) with albuminoids and aerial elements.

The first element that is disturbed in the organism of those born in the celestial sign Virgo is oil; this break in the function of oil shows a deficiency in potassium sulphate, known in pharmacy is Kali sulphate.

Virgo is represented in the human body by the solar plexus and bowels, the solar plexus being the great receiving station of energy from the back brain, while the bowels complete the chemicalization of the food products ready to be assimilated by the blood.

The letter X in Hebrew is Samech or Stomach. X, or cross, means crucifixion, or change—transmutation.

Virgo people are discriminating, analytical, and critical.

The microscope reveals the fact that when the body is in health little jets of steam are constantly escaping from the seven million pores of the skin. A deficiency in Kali sulph molecules causes the oil in the tissue to thicken and clog these safety valves of the human engine, thus turning heat and secretions back upon the inner organs, lungs, pleura, membrane of nasal passages, etc. And does it not seem strange that medical science, that boasts of such great progress, can invent no better term than "bad cold" for these chemical results?

Kali sulph is found in considerable quantities in the scalp and hair. When this salt falls below the standard, dandruff, or eruptions, secreting yellowish, thin, oily matter, or falling out of the hair, is the result.

Kali sulph is a wonderful salt, and its operation in the divine laboratory of man's body, where it manufactures oil, is the miracle of the chemistry of life.

Governing planet, Mercury.

Gems, pink jasper and hyacinth.

Astral colors, gold and black.

In Bible alchemy Virgo is represented by Joseph, the twelfth son of Jacob, and means: To increase power, or "son of the right hand."

Virgo corresponds to the disciple Bartholomew.

LIBRA: THE LOINS

SEPTEMBER 23 TO OCTOBER 23.

This alkaline cell-salt is made from bone ash or by neutralizing orthophosphoric acid with carbonate of sodium.

Libra is a Latin word, meaning scales or balance. Sodium, or Natrium phosphate holds the balance between acids and the normal fluids of the human body.

Acid is organic and can be chemically split into two or more elements, thus destroying the formula that makes the chemical rate of motion called acid.

A certain amount of acid is always present in the blood, nerve, stomach and liver fluids. The apparent excess of acid is always due to a deficiency in the alkaline Libra salt.

Acid, in alchemical lore, is represented as Satan (Saturn), while sodium phosphate symbols Christ (Neptune). An absence of the Christ principle gives license to Satan to run riot in the Holy Temple. The advent of Christ drives the evil out with a whip of thongs. References to the temple in the figurative language of the Bible and New Testament always symbol the human organism. "Know ye not that your bodies are the Temple of the Living God?"

Solomon's temple is an allegory of the physical body of man and woman. Soul-of-man's-temple—the house, church, Beth or temple made without sound of "saw or hammer."

Hate, envy, criticism, jealousy, competition, selfishness, war, suicide and murder are largely caused by acid conditions of the blood, producing changes by chemical poisons and irritation of the brain cells, the keys upon which the soul plays "Divine harmonies" or plays "fantastic tricks before high heaven," according to the arrangement of chemical molecules in the wondrous laboratory of the soul.

Without a proper balance of the Venus salt, the agent of peace and love, man is fit for "treason, strategems and spoils."

The people of the world never needed the alkaline of Libra salt more than they do at the present time, while wars and rumors of wars strut upon the stage of life.

The Sun enters Libra September 23rd, and remains until October 23rd.

Governing planet, Venus.

Gems, diamond and opal.

Astral colors are black, crimson, and light blue.

Libra is an air sign.

In Bible alchemy, Libra represents Reuben, the first son of Jacob. Reuben means Vision of the Sun.

In the symbolism of the New Testament, Libra corresponds to the disciple Peter.

Peter is derived from Petra, a stone or mineral.

"On thee, Peter (mineral), will I build my church;" viz., beth, house, body, or temple.

INFLUENCE OF SUN ON VIBRATION OF BLOOD AT BIRTH

SCORPIO

OCTOBER 23 TO NOVEMBER 22.

From Scorpion to "White Eagle" may seem a very long journey to one who has not learned the science of patience or realized that time is an illusion of physical sense.

The zodiacal sign Scorpio is represented in human material organism by the sexual functions.

The esoteric meaning of sex is based on mathematics, the body being a mathematical fact. Sex in Sanscrit means Six.

"Six days of Creation" simply means that all creation, or formation, from self-existing substance, is by and through the operation of sex principle—the only principle.

Three means male, father, the spirit of the male, the son; this trinity forms or constitutes one pole of Being, Energy or Life—the positive pole.

The negative pole, female trinity; female spirit of mother and daughter.

Thus two threes or trinities produce six or sex, the operation of which is the cause of all manifestation. Those who understand, fully realize the truth of the New Testament statement, "There is no other name under heaven whereby ye may be saved (materialized and sustained) except through Jesus Christ and Him crucified." By tracing the words Jesus and Crucify (also Christ) to their roots a wonderful world of truth appears to the understanding.*

The possibilities of Scorpio people are boundless after they have passed through trials and tribulations, viz.: crucifixion or crossification.

*Explained in *God-Man; The Word Made Flesh.*

One of the cell-salts of the blood, Calcarea sulphate, is the mineral ("stone") that especially corresponds to the Scorpio nature. Crude Calcarea sulphate is gypsum or sulphate of lime.

While in crude form, lime is of little value; but add water, and thus transmute it by changing its chemical formation, and plaster of Paris is formed, a substance useful and ornamental. Every person born between October 23 and November 22, should well consider this wonderful alchemical operation of his esoteric stone, and thus realize the possibilities in store for him on his journey to the "Eyrie of the White Eagle."

Scorpio people are natural magnetic healers, especially after having passed through the waters of adversity, since heat is caused by the union of water and lime.

Scorpio is a water sign, governed by Mars. Mars is "a doer of things," also fiery at times; therefore, it is well that the Scorpio native take heed lest he sometimes "boil over."

In Bible alchemy, Scorpio is represented by Simeon, the second son of Jacob. Simeon means "hears and obeys." In the symbolism of the New Testament, Scorpio corresponds to the disciple Andrew, and means to create or ascend.

The gems are topaz and malachite; astral colors, golden-brown and black.

A break in the molecular chain of the Scorpio salt, caused by a deficiency of that material in the blood, is the primal cause of all the so-called diseases of these people. This disturbance not only causes symptoms called disease in physical functions, but it disturbs the astral fluids and gray matter of brain cells, and thereby changes the operation of mind into inharmony. Sin means to lack or fall short; thus chemical deficiencies in life's chemistry cause sin.

When man learns to supply his dynamo with the proper dynamics, he will "wash away his sins with the blood of Christ"—blood made with the "White Stone."

Calcium sulphate should not be taken internally in crude form; in order to be taken up by absorbents of mucous membrane, the lime salt must be triturated, according to the biochemic method, up to third or sixth. By this method lime may be rendered as fine as the molecules contained in grain, fruit, or vegetables.

Blood contains three forms of lime: lime and fluorine for

Cancer sign; lime and phosphorus for Capricorn sign, and lime and sulphur for Scorpio.

Lime should never be used internally below the third decimal trituration.

THE CHEMISTRY OF SAGITTARIUS

NOVEMBER 22 TO DECEMBER 22.

The mineral or cell-salt of the blood corresponding to Sagittarius is Silica.

Synonyms: Silicea, silici oxide, white pebble or common quartz. Chemical abbreviation, Si. Made by fusing crude silica with carbonate of soda; dissolve the residue, filter and precipitate by hydrochloric acid.

This product must be triturated as per biochemic process before using internally.

This salt is the surgeon of the human organism. Silica is found in the hair, skin, nails, periosteum, the membrane covering and protecting the bone, the nerve sheath, called neurilemma, and a trace is found in bone tissue. The surgical qualities of silica lie in the fact that its particles are sharp cornered. A piece of quartz is a sample of the finer particles. Reduce silica to an impalpable powder and the microscope reveals the fact that the molecules are still pointed and jagged like a large piece of quartz rock. In all cases where it becomes necessary that decaying organic matter be discharged from any part of the body by the process of suppuration, these sharp pointed particles are pushed forward by the marvelous intelligence that operates without ceasing, day and night in the wondrous human Beth, and like a lancet cut a passage to the surface for the discharge of pus. Nowhere in all the records of physiology or biological research can anything be found more wonderful than the chemical and mechanical operation of this Divine artisan.

The bone covering is made strong and firm by silica. In cases of boils or carbuncle, the biochemist loses no time searching for "anthrax bacilli" or germs, nor does he experiment with imaginary germ-killing serum; he simply furnishes nature with tools with which the necessary work may be accomplished.

The Centaur of mythology is known in the "Circle of Beasts

that worship before the Lord (Sun) day and night," as Sagittarius, the Archer, with drawn bow. Arrow heads are composed of flint, decarbonized white pebble or quartz. Thus we see why Silica is the special birth salt of all born in the Sagittarius sign. Silica gives the glossy finish to hair and nails. A stalk of corn or straw of wheat, oats or barley will not stand upright unless it contains this mineral.

Sagittarius people are generally swift and strong; and they are prophetic—look deeply into the future and hit the mark like the archer. A noted astrologer once said: "Never lay a wager with one born with the Sun in Sagittarius or with Sagittarius rising in the east lest you lose your wealth."

The Sagittarius native is very successful in thought transference. He (or she) can concentrate on a brain, miles distant, and so vibrate the aerial wires that fill space that the molecular intelligence of those finely attuned to Nature's harmonies may read the message.

Governing planet, Jupiter.

Gems, carbuncle, diamond and turquoise.

The astral colors are gold, red and green.

Sagittarius is a fire sign and is represented in Bible alchemy by Levi, the third son of Jacob, meaning "joined or associated."

In the symbolism of the New Testament, Sagittarius corresponds to the disciple James, son of Alpheus.

* * * * * * *

The Chicago Evening Post, Wednesday, August 19, 1914, in commenting on "Signs of Wrath and Portents from the Heavens," says among other things: "And in England today are men with the modern scientific mind who say that we cannot disregard utterly the idea that the movements of the heavenly bodies have their effect upon men."

CAPRICORN: THE GOAT OF THE ZODIAC

DECEMBER 22 TO JANUARY 21.

Circle means sacrifice, according to the Kabbala, the straight line bending to form a circle.

Thus we find twelve zodiacal signs sacrificing to the Sun, symbolized by the devotion and sacrificing of the twelve disciples of Jesus.

Twelve months' sacrifice for a solar year.

Twelve functions of man's body sacrifice for the temple, Beth or "Church of God"—the human house of flesh.

Twelve minerals—known as cell-salts—sacrifice by operation and combining to build tissue.

The dynamic force of these vitalized workmen constitute the chemical affinities—the positive and negative poles of mineral expression.

The Cabalistic numerical value of the letters g, o, a, t, add up twelve.

Very ancient allegories depict a goat bearing the sins of Israelites into the wilderness.

In the secret mysteries of initiation into certain societies, the goat is the chief symbol.

In alchemical lore the "Great Work" is commenced "in the Goat" and is finished in the "White Stone." Biochemistry is the "stone which the builders rejected," and furnishes the key to all the mysteries and occultism of the allegorical Goat.

Those persons born between the dates December 22 and January 21, come under the influence of the Sun in Capricorn—the Goat. Capricorn represents the great business interests—trusts and syndicates—where many laborers are employed. Thus Capricorn symbols the foundation and framework of society—the commonwealth of human interests.

The bones of the human organism represent the foundation stones and framework of the soul's temple (Solomon's temple).

Bone tissue is composed principally of phosphate of lime, known as Calcarea phosphate or Calcium phosphate. Without a proper amount of lime no bone can be formed, and bone is the foundation of the body.

A building must first have a foundation before the structure can be reared. Thus we see why the "Great Work" commences in the Goat. Lime is white—hence the "White Stone."

In the second chapter and seventeenth verse of Revelation may be found the alchemical formula of the "White Stone."

"To him that overcometh will I give to eat of the hidden manna, and I will give a White Stone, and in the Stone a new name written which no man knoweth saving he that receiveth it."

In the mountains of India, it is said, a tribe dwells, the priests of which claim that man's complete history from birth to death is recorded in his bones. These people say the bones are secret archives, hence do not decay quickly as does flesh and blood.

When the molecules of lime phosphate fall below the standard, a disturbance often occurs in the bone tissue and the decay of bone, known as caries of bone, commences. Phosphate of lime is the worker in albumin. It carries it to bone and uses it as cement in the making of bone.

So-called Bright's disease (first discovered in a man named Bright) is simply an overflow of albumin via kidneys, due to a deficiency of phosphate of lime.

When the Goat salt is deficient in the gastric juice and bile, ferments arise from undigested foods; acids from the latter find their way to synovial fluids in the joints of legs or arms or hands, and often cause severe pains; but why the perfectly natural chemical operation should be called rheumatism passeth understanding.

Non-functional albumin, caused by a lack of lime phosphate, is the cause of eruptions, abscesses, consumption, catarrh and many so-called diseases.

But let us all remember that disease means not-at-ease, and that the words do not mean an entity of any kind, shape, size, weight or quality, but an effect caused by some deficiency of blood material, and that only.

Phosphate of lime should never be taken in crude form It must be triturated to sixth X, according to the biochemic method, in milk sugar in order to be taken up by the mucous membrane absorbents, and thus carried into the circulation.

Capricorn people possess a deep interior nature in which they often dwell in the "solitude of the soul."

They scheme and plan and build air castles and really enjoy their ideal world. If they are sometimes talkative, their language seldom gives any hint of the wonderland of their imagination. To that enchanted garden the sign, "No Thoroughfare," forever blocks the way.

The Capricorn gems are white onyx and moonstone. The astral colors are garnet, brown, silver-gray and black.

Capricorn is an earth sign.

In Bible alchemy, Capricorn represents Judah, the fourth son of Jacob, and means "the praise of the Lord." In the symbolism of the New Testament, Capricorn corresponds to the disciple John.

THE SIGN OF THE SON OF MAN: AQUARIUS

JANUARY 21 TO FEBRUARY 20.

O age of man! Aquarius,
  Transmuter of all things base,
"Son of Man in the Heavens,
  With sun-illumined face."
Our journey was long and weary,
  With pain and sorrow and tears,
But now at rest in thy kingdom,
  We welcome the coming years.

Those born between the dates of January 21 and February 20 are doubly blest, and babies to be born during that period for many years to come will be favored of the gods.

The solar system has entered the "Sign of the Son of Man," Aquarius, where it will remain for over 2000 years. According to planetary revolutions the Sun passes through Aquarius once every solar year; thus we have the double influence of the Aquarius vibration from January 21 to February 20.

Air contains seventy-eight per cent of nitrogen gas believed by scientists to be mineral in ultimate potency. Minerals are formed by the precipitation of nitrogen gas. Differentiation is attained by the proportion of oxygen and aqueous vapor (hydrogen) that unites with nitrogen.

A combination of sodium and chlorine forms the mineral known as common salt. This mineral absorbs water. The circulation or distribution of water in the human organism is due to the chemical action of the molecules of sodium chloride.

Crude soda can not be taken up by mucous membrane absorbents and carried into the circulation. The sodium molecules found in the blood have been received from vegetable tissue which drew these salts from the soil in high potency. The mineral, or cell-salts, can also be prepared (and are prepared) in biochemic or homeopathic potency as fine as the trituration of Nature's laboratory in the physiology of plant growth. Then they are thoroughly mixed with sugar of milk and pressed into tablets ready to be taken internally to supply deficiencies in the human organism. A lack of the proper amount of these basic mineral salts (twelve in number) is the cause of all so-called disease.

Common table salt does not enter the blood, being too coarse to enter the delicate tubes of mucous membrane absorbents, but this salt does distribute water along the intestinal tract.

Aquarius is known in astrological symbols as "The Water Bearer." Sodium chloride, known also as Natrium muriaticum, is also a bearer of water, and chemically corresponds to the zodiacal angle of Aquarius.

The term angle, or angel, of the Sun may also be used, for the position of the Sun at birth largely controls the vibration of blood.

So, then, we have sodium chloride as the "birth salt" of Aquarius people.

The governing planets are Saturn and Uranus; the gems are sapphire, opal and turquoise; the astral colors are blue, pink and Nile green. Aquarius is an air sign.

In Bible alchemy Aquarius represents Dan, the fifth son of Jacob, and means "judgment," or "he that judges." In the symbolism of the New Testament, Aquarius corresponds to the disciple James.

PISCES: THE FISH THAT SWIM IN THE PURE SEA

FEBRUARY 20 TO MARCH 21.

Nearly everyone knows that Pisces means fishes, but few there be who know the esoteric meaning of fish. Fish in Greek is Ichthus, which Greek scholars claim means "substance from the sea."

Jesus is derived from the Greek word for fish; Mary, mare, means water; therefore we see how the Virgin Mary, pure sea, gives birth to Jesus, or fish. There are two things in the universe—Jesus and the Virgin Mary—spirit and substance. So much for the symbol or allegory.

From the earth viewpoint we say that the Sun enters the zodiacal sign Pisces February 20 and remains until March 21. This position of the Sun at birth gives the native a kind, loving nature, industrious, methodical, logical and mathematical; sympathetic and kind to people in distress.

In the alchemy of the Bible we find that the sixth son of Jacob, Naphthali, which means "wrestling of God," symbols Pisces, for the Pisces natives worry and fret because they can not do more for their friends or those in trouble.

The phosphate of iron is one of the cell-salts of human blood and tissue. This mineral has an affinity for oxygen, which is carried into the circulation and diffused throughout the organism by the chemical force of this inorganic salt. The feet are the foundation of the body. Iron is the foundation of blood. Most diseases of Pisces people commence with symptoms indicating a deficiency of iron molecules in the blood; hence it is inferred that those born between the dates February 20 and March 21, use more iron than do those born in other signs.

Iron is known as the magnetic mineral, due to the fact that it attracts oxygen. Pisces people possess great magnetic force in their hands, and make the best magnetic healers.

Health depends upon a proper amount of iron phosphate molecules in the blood. When these oxygen carriers are deficient, the circulation is increased in order to conduct a sufficient amount of oxygen to the extremities—all parts of the body—with the diminished quantity of iron on hand. This increased motion of blood causes friction, the result of which is heat. Just why this heat is called fever is a conundrum; perhaps because fever is from Latin fevre, "to boil out," but I fail to see any relevancy between a lack of phosphate of iron and "boiling out."

The phosphate of iron (Ferrum phosphate), in order to be made available as a remedy for the blood, must be triturated according to the biochemic method with milk sugar up to the third or sixth potency in order that the mucous membrane absorbents may take it up and carry it into the blood. Iron in the crude state, like the tincture, does not enter the circulation, but passes off with the fæces, and is often injurious to the intestinal mucous membrane.

The governing planet of this sign is Jupiter.

The gems are chrysolite, pink-shell and moonstone.

The astral colors are white, pink, emerald-green and black.

Pisces is a water sign.

In Bible alchemy, Pisces represents Naphthali, the sixth son of Jacob, and means "wrestlings of God." In the symbolism of the New Testament, Pisces corresponds to the disciple Philip. The birth of Benjamin is given in that wonderful allegory, the thirty-fifth chapter of Genesis. Benjamin is, therefore, the thirteenth child of Jacob.

The Zodiac and the Salts of Salvation

See article, "13, the Operation of Wisdom," in *God-Man; the Word Made Flesh.*

"The heavens declare the glory of God;
And the firmament sheweth his handiwork.
Day unto day uttereth speech,
And night unto night sheweth knowledge.
There is no speech nor language,
Where their voice is not heard.
Their line is gone out through all the earth,
And their words to the end of the world.
In them hath he set a tabernacle for the sun,
Which is as a bridegroom coming out of his chamber,
And rejoiceth as a strong man to run a race.
His going forth is from the end of the heaven,
And his circuit unto the ends of it;
And there is nothing hidden from the heat thereof."

Psalms 19:1-6 Vs.

PART TWO

An Esoteric Analysis and Synthesis of the Zodiacal Signs and Their Physio-Chemical Allocations Together With Additional Scientific Findings

BY

Inez Eudora Perry

INTRODUCTION TO PART TWO

In presenting the following findings, the author wishes to say that she does so, not with fear and trembling but with the strength of conviction which truth alone gives. It matters little whether they are accepted or rejected. Into these pages goes a knowledge of the chemical condition of the average human brain, gained from sixteen years' experience along the lines of health. So it is self-evident that a few earnest students will realize the value of this information.

The author, however, has already received her own personal reward for the years of investigation and research work. All her life she has aspired for truth above all things. She has aspired to know facts, to solve the problem of the old injunction "Man, know thyself." This in itself became such a joyous, fascinating occupation that it was like going out into the green sanctuary of Nature and being alone with Nature's God, the *Spirit* within one's self. And this, together with the great appreciation manifested by the many earnest students who have already accepted some of these truths, constitutes an adequate reward.

Dr. Carey brought forth his mental and spiritual progeny, the key whereby humanity may solve its chemical, physical and mental problems, before the influx of the finer ethers which are now permeating our atmosphere and endeavoring to awaken dormant brain cells to action. Therefore, his invaluable message was slow in being accepted. Now, however, there is more and more interest being manifested. Part One of this book will thus be read and studied with greater appreciation.

The world is more ready to accept that which has previously seemed absurd and impossible because of the quickening of comprehension which is now going on. We are merging into the atmosphere of the Aquarian Age. This means, both astrologically and astronomically, that our entire solar system is beginning to pass into the division of the universe which is occupied by the sign Aquarius. Approximately 2160 years are required for the transit.

As Aquarius is "the sign of the Son of Man" it deals not only with humanity as a whole but with the *real man within man*. The Son of Man, the Higher Self, is that real man, or mankind made new.

There is a trend, then, a veritable cosmic urge that is truly very definite and powerful. This is the reason back of, and the cause of the appearance of all the "new" and unusual ideas, happenings, fashions, inventions, etc. It is also the cause of all of the terrible and abnormal crimes with which the papers are constantly filled; the *perversion* of truth which is everywhere being manifested. Nature and Nature's God now demand an expansion of consciousness in man. This is the *beginning* of a realization of the laws of God, their acceptance, the practice of them, and the effort to climb upward.

Thought is the father of action, and with individuals not attuned to the Aquarian vibration actions are spasmodic, unnatural and thus negative and destructive. This is because the high vibration and shorter etheric waves breathed into the lungs do not find therein the *materials* capable of producing the same vibration in the blood. If these materials were present they would produce a corresponding wave length in the blood and thus work harmoniously and constructively under the Aquarian vibrations. Disorganization, disruption and spasmodic reaction take place in the bodies of persons chemically starved in those *"mothers"* or materials which *Father Spirit* demands *at this time*. The Sacred Book expresses it perfectly in these words: "Ye must make new bottles for the new wine *or the old bottles will burst*." We must reconstruct our bodies and brain cells with the desired and required material, in order that they may be able to do the work now demanded of them. Otherwise we will find the fuse blowing out exactly as it does when the lamp and the current do not correspond.

There must be, therefore, an endeavor to investigate new (new only to this age) scientific findings. The greater the aspiration for truth the easier it will be. If you find joy and satisfaction in the study of these pages I shall always be glad and happy to learn of it and help you still further with any additional explanation.

As this is the Aquarian Age, its *spirit* is back of all, and will assist and protect *those who speak the truth*.

Chapter I

THE ANALYSIS AND SYNTHESIS OF ARIES AND KALI PHOS.

"(Gad) A troop shall overcome him, but he shall overcome at last."
—Genesis XLIX.

In order to obtain facts, it is absolutely essential first to trace to their origin the meanings of the words used in expressing the problem under consideration. Therefore, their etymology must be studied. This is the infallible key by means of which knowledge of anything may be obtained.

In his book, *The Study of Words,* Richard Chenevix Trench, D.D., quotes the following from an unmentioned writer: "In a language like ours, where so many words are derived from other languages, there are few modes of instruction more useful or more amusing than that of accustoming young people to seek for the etymology or *primary meaning* of the words they use. There are cases in which more knowledge of more value may be conveyed by the history of a word than by the history of a campaign." To make the foregoing statement more emphatic we would add that accurate information is unobtainable otherwise.

Mr. Trench even more sympathetically states: "Many a single word also is itself a concentrated poem, having stories of poetical thought and imagery laid up in it. Examine it and it will be found to rest on some deep analogy of things natural and things spiritual, bringing those to illustrate and to give an abiding form and body to these. For certainly in itself there is no study which may be made at once more instructive and entertaining than the study of the use, origin, and distinction of words."

Elsewhere in his book he deplores the lack of interest in that which is worth while, at the same time analyzing the word "pastime."

He says, "The world, out of its own use of this word, renders judgment against itself. For it is concerned with amusements and pleasures which do not really *satisfy* the *mind* and fill it with the sense of an abiding and satisfying joy; they serve only, as this word confesses, to pass away the time, to prevent it from hanging, an intolerable burden, on man's hands; all which they can do at the best is to prevent men from discovering and attending to their own internal poverty and dissatisfaction and want."

So important is this subject that one more quotation from his invaluable book must be made. He says: "I shall urge on you something different, namely, that not in books only, but often in *words contemplated singly*, there are boundless stores of moral and historic truth, and no less of passion and imagination, laid up—that from these, lessons of infinite worth may be derived, if only our attention is aroused to their existence. I shall urge on you how well it will repay you to study the words which you are in the habit of using or of meeting, be they such as relate to highest spiritual things, or our common words of the shop and market, and of all the familiar intercourse of life. It will indeed repay you far better than you can easily believe. I am sure that, for many a young man, his first discovery of the fact that words are *living powers*, are the vesture, yea, even of the body, which thoughts weave for themselves, has been like the dropping of scales from his eyes, like the acquiring of another sense, or the introduction into a new world; he is never able to cease wondering at the moral marvels that surround him on every side, and ever reveal themselves more and more to his gaze."

The above statements are true. A New World verily appears to the student of words—the world of *Knowledge*. For words, as well as letters and numbers, are the containers and the expressions of definite values. The reason—satisfying information given herein has been obtained by the study of words.

Because the sun rises in the east, bringing with it light and heat, it has from time immemorial been termed the *creator*, and each nation and people has had its own revered, yet intimate name for this giver of life.

There are two periods in a year when the days and nights are of equal lengths, and they are termed equinoxes. The first, occuring on March twenty-first, is the Spring equinox; exactly six months later we have the Fall equinox.

The Sun, then, crossing the equinoctial line, or equator, on the twenty-first of March, is said to bring the first day of

Spring, for there is an awakening, a spring-ing up and therefore a *resurrection* of all Nature. Indeed, very, very few realize anything at all of the sacred out-pouring, a flood-tide of heavenly power, of spiritual electricity which charges not only the earth but all human beings who are able to receive it. Each human being is a battery, an aggregation of cells, and the law governing its *charging* is exactly the same as that with which electricians are familiar. It *must* have the necessary *material* to *attract electricity*, the proper *kind* and the right *quantity*. A knowledge of the cell-salts, such as is contained in Schuessler's *Biochemistry*, solves the problem.

Few are so dull as to escape entirely the glamour and glory of the days when the first faint misty green appears, when mating birds fly hither and thither, and virgin earth prepares to pour out her bountiful gifts that man may be fed from her bosom.

But what does it mean to those who sense its approach and to whom its arrival brings keenest joy and a deep and abiding satisfaction? They are being *resurrected*, for their *minds* are actually expanding under the influence of that same God-power; the brain substance is being acted on by Cosmic Electricity outpoured from the cerebrum of the Grand Man.

This is the time, then, to begin one's labors, for the charged battery must begin to *work*—to be utilized. Would that humanity could realize this mighty fact! But human batteries are functioning poorly, the currents are weak, the cells actually corroded. The great reservoir of unlimited electrical power is ever present in the universe—Spirit is never deficient. The trouble lies only in the human battery. It can not contact what it has no power to attract. This is the mysterious chemical secret that has been hidden from man by his own ignorance, and it is this secret which this chapter will reveal, for it is Kali phos which is the casket that holds this priceless gem.

The terrific *impetus* back of all natural phenomena at this time is the reason that this period of the year is termed Spring. The rabbit is one of the symbols of Spring and of Easter, as it jumps or springs in moving about. The story of the universe and of man has been brought down through the ages under many forms, among these being animal symbols. Those born at this time of the year usually walk with a springing step.

At this season we find the Sun actually *springing* or climbing up into the heavens until it reaches its highest point, that of the Summer solstice. This is the longest day of the year. The Sun is said to be at its greatest declination, resting, as it were, before going on its journey, but pausing to accomplish something special. The date is approximately June twenty-first.

Six months later we have the Winter solstice, when the sun reaches its lowest point, and on December twenty-first, approximately, again appears to rest. The Summer solstice is, therefore, ninety degrees away from the Spring equinox, and the same number of degrees from the Fall equinox; while the Winter solstice is ninety degrees from both the Spring and Fall equinoxes. These facts are very important to remember and must become fixed in the mind, as these four points constitute the *cardinal cross* of Nature and of the human body as well. The signs having to do with these points of the cross are Aries, Cancer, Libra and Capricorn.

Signs that are ninety degrees away from each other are said to be *square*. This is also an important point to fix in the mind in order to read one's chart correctly. The word square is used for the same reason that both practical and theoretical Masons employ it. When understood, the problem of *squaring one's circle is solved;* for the four signs of one's *cross* form four squares. In making the bodily correction represented by each square one automatically eliminates the cross, and squares the circle. *This constitutes the great work.*

Truly, this is the cross upon which each one is crucified.

And most emphatically is it a *cross of matter*, a *chemical cross.* The story of each one's individual cross will be given in a forthcoming book on *The Biochemic System of Body Building and Astro-Chemical Analysis.*

The Spring equinox, therefore, is the return or springing up of creative energy, while the Fall equinox is the falling or going down, the decreasing or diminishing of the power of the sun or energy. Autumn is derived from the Latin *auctus* meaning enriched, thus bringing out the idea of harvest time, the *gathering in* of the increase of the year.

The out-pouring time of Nature takes place in what is termed the first month of the astrological year, which begins March twenty-first, and lasts until April twenty-first. During this time the sun is transiting or passing through the constellation of Aries, the Lamb or Ram of the zodiac. It is really termed the April month or sign, as it covers two weeks of the latter and only one of the former.

The process going on during this period in Nature and in man is again brought to our attention by the interpretation of the word April. It is derived from the Latin *aperio* and means to uncover, to lay bare, to expose to view, therefore to *open,* to *render accessible.* Thus *the great creative power of Nature is rendered accessible* at this time, which is not only a time but a certain definite place in Nature and in man's body.

From time immemorial the signs of the zodiac have been allocated with the parts of the human body. Whatever other interpretations were given, the physiological application came *first.*

Astrology deals with the body (anatomy) of the Grand Man (the universe) and by analogy, with the body of man. This is a fact that has for the most part been lost sight of, because the mighty science of the macrocosm and the microcosm has been perverted into fortune telling. No wonder so few are interested in it; no wonder so many laugh at and deride it, for they have good reason to. Astrologers, so-called, are for the most part not working for or with Uranus. However, the number of those who are doing so is slowly and surely increasing.

One of the oldest and most common forms in which the signs of the zodiac have been brought down through the ages is in the figure of man, with the glyph of Aries and a gamboling or up-springing Lamb above his head. On the right, from the neck, a line or arrow points to a reclining bull and the symbol of Taurus; on the left from the shoulder is a pointer to two seated children and the symbol of Gemini, and so on to the two fish *crossed* underneath the feet. The latter gives us the story of the Cross and the religion or scientific story of the fishermen, irrefutable evidence of the one purpose of astrology, which is *to give mankind complete information relative to the process,* chemical and physiological, whereby perfection and illumination may be attained.

From an understanding, then, of the word Aries, the first or *head* sign of the zodiac, we obtain its physiological allocation. It is of Latin derivation and means ram. The Latin lexicon also gives *battering-ram,* prop or beam as other derivatives, all having the same basic idea. The ram, as an animal, is known to butt or bat with its *head,* when engaged in conflict. But the word ram comes to us from the Sanskrit, and means *high*. Ram in a Hindu name is evidence that one bearing it is of *high* caste.

The top of the head is the highest part of the body, and man differentiates himself from an animal by *elevating* his head, or *walking upright*. In Hebrew, the top of the head is named *calvary*, for its literal meaning is *bare skull*. It is truly the *place of ascension*.

There are many references in the Scriptures to lofty elevations. One says: "Look toward the holy mountain from whence cometh thy help." As the Bible and all ancient and sacred writings are physiological, the above quotation refers to the upper brain or cerebrum, in which is the marvelous All-Seeing Eye, or center of understanding.

The brain of man is the organ of mind. If the latter functions well, he is helped and all is well, for he helps himself by doing that which brings about the best result. There are also many statements in this same book calling our attention to the Eye Single and the All-Seeing Eye, also the Candle of the Lord and the Imperishable Sacred Lamp.

Each nation and people has had its own name for that period of the year when the Sun passes through the sign of the Ram. The Egyptians termed it the God Amen-Menthu, the Lamb of Gad, which "taketh away the sins of the world," Gad being one of the twelve tribes of Israel.

The sun in the sign of the Ram was looked on by the ancients as the God Aries. The Lamb of the Mysteries of Atys; the Lamb of the Festival of Cybele; the White Lamb of the Trojans; the Redemption of the Lost Sheep; The Golden Fleece of Jason and the Argonauts; the Lord of Hosts. As Aries represents the Vernal or Spring equinox, when the Sun crosses the line from Pisces, the sign of the Fishes, into the sign of the Ram, it is, as Dr. Wakeman Ryno says, "crucified or crossified on the equinoctial line which constitutes the redemption of earth, a saving power; the ice and cold winter disappear, water flows, the buds and blossoms start, and the earth is rejuvenated—the *sin* of cold winter is taken away."

Allocating this with the cerebro-spinal system, with which Aries deals, an outpouring of energy takes place, flowing downward into the form to rebuild and rejuvenate it. This is exactly what occurs in the body of the Grand Man. It was termed "the sign of Baal Gad by the ancients, or Lord of

Felicity, because he presided over the happiest and most prosperous time of the year."

The word Gad is derived from the Hebrew, and the word sun from the Coptic, according to Dr. Taylor, and both mean the same thing. "God or Gad, being the never-translated name in the ancient Tsabaism, or star-worship of the constellation of the Ram, or Lamb of God, the Rama, the Great, the Elevated," and thus corresponding to the human head.

The Greek word Thebes means head. There was an old city by that name, the capital of Ancient Egypt. It was the *seat of marvelous learning and the greatest art,* and was said to have been destroyed by Alexander. This part of the human anatomy, the cerebrum, is, indeed, the storehouse of man, but it is the super-conscious and not the subconscious, as has been so long erroneously taught.

By studying the sacred and secret writings of all nations and peoples, one realizes that Easter was not new to the Piscean Age, nor to the *supposed* dawn of the Christian religion, but belongs to all time and to all peoples, for it signifies both a cosmic and a microcosmic process, literally a renewal of life. An understanding of this fact, constituting, as it does, a logical and wholly natural explanation, is one of the first steps necessary to an entirely new viewpoint of the Bible.

Realization of this eliminates all controversy which at the present time is becoming more and more pronounced. Bishops and ministers alike are unable to give logical and satisfactory elucidation of the Scriptures, and this has largely constituted the reason so many people remain away from church. Humanity is beginning to think for itself, for this is the age of knowing, not blind belief.

Thus we find from the foregoing the meaning of the *opening* month of the year, in man as well as in Nature. We find there is a perfect system of analysis, synthesis and allocation which links up space, time, activity, and mankind, yes, even the most secret part of the body. And, as Dr. Wakeman Ryno says: "What silly trash this would be (quoting from Daniel 7:9) taken exactly as it reads; what a beautiful illustration it becomes when taken as an astronomical allegory of the Sun and Moon in their passage through the constellation of Aries the Ram as the opener of the *growing* months of the year after the winter; 'the judgment was set (the equinox—equal) the books were opened'—(the Spring)."

Let us now consider another science, that particular branch of physiology which is termed embryology. Here we at once find a perfect allocation with Nature's work in the Spring. The *cerebro-spinal system is the first part of the organism developed and from it the whole form materializes.* The cerebrum and cord constitute most truly *The Tree of Life,* for they *bear* or produce the rest of the body. The cerebro-spinal system has, as ancient Sanskrit writings inform us, "its *roots* in *heaven* and its branches in the earth."

The cerebrum is man's potential or embryological heaven, his *heave-N*, for his work is to perfect this heaved-up place. The letter N is the *key* to the secret process. In Hebrew it literally means Jesus.

This statement constitutes the subject matter of another book, *God-Man, the Word Made Flesh,* soon to be re-published with much additional information. It is, however, impossible to leave earnest searchers for truth without some satisfaction, and for the enlightenment of such the explanation is: Jesus is a germ of *life,* a psycho-physical germ-cell, just as real, definite and tangible as any other physical germ, although more ethereal and delicate,—the fruit, progeny and product of a chemically perfect, therefore a highly refined and purified body. An imperfect and impure body can not produce or create this perfect thing. As the Bible states, in Job 14:4: "Who can bring a clean thing out of an unclean? Not one."

When that *little one,* that leaven which shall "leaven the whole lump" or body of man, is at last created in the manger (or solar plexus), it follows a path planned for it. It enters the Jordan, and ascends by this River of God to the cerebrum via certain glands. Then, indeed, will N have been added to the brain, which, as the poet Milton has said, "Is its own place and in itself can make a hell of heaven, a heaven of hell."

The roots of the Tree of Life are three nerves which ascend from the fructified germ cell. These later on form five, and constitute the outline of the five ventricles of the brain. The optic *thalami* is the matrix from which the roots branch out and upward, and it is also the center from which springs the spinal cord, that sacred Euphrates (River of God), which goes down to water the earth. From it, buddings form on either side, and thus the right and left sympathetic nerves grow, constituting the Tree of Knowledge of Good and Evil.

Much more can be written on the above subject, but it will be fully considered in the book *God-Man, the Word Made Flesh*. The above statements serve to prove, however, that astrology and physiology are inseparable, and that in the former we will eventually find every physiological mystery revealed.

Aries, then, relates to the cerebrum and cord, which constitute the Father, the Most High, the Creator or Progenitor of the body, otherwise God and the River of God. "And a river went out of Eden." Therefore the head may be termed truly the *Fountain-Head of Life*. In the New Testament the River Jordan is the same as the Euphrates, and means *descender*, for the River of God does come down from above, our physiological heaven.

Genesis, the first book of the Old Testament, deals with the creation of man's body. The first chapter has to do with the formation of the animal cell or lowest form of life, the amœba or germ cell, without which no human or other form is created. It does not refer to the actual animals themselves. In the light of this explanation the second chapter is logical and not contradictory, for the animals (animal cells) are brought together *into man*. Man's body is an aggregate of animal cells.

"There is a *spirit* in man, and the inspiration (inbreathing) of the Almighty giveth it *understanding*." Differentiation between forms in the different kingdoms of Nature depends on *breath*. The plant breathes and polarizes itself as the plant. The animal breathes, and its breath takes on a certain vibration, thus polarizing it as the animal or negative breath (ani-mal) .

But the breath of man is polarized as that of a human being, and as he was formed in the likeness and image of God, he possesses something *more* than the animal. As the rate of vibration of the cells of his body increases in proportion to the result of purification and obedience to God's laws of right living, he no longer desires, but *inspiration* takes its place.

Space can not be given in this chapter to go into detail relative to the discovery I have recently made that the Erotes are the *keres of life in man*. However, this much must be said: the name given to the upper brain or cerebrum contains the *secret of life*, for cere is kere in Greek, and it is to the literature and sculpture of that classic race we must turn for indisputable information relative to the source of life.

The skull is the Cup of Life and contains the Essence of Life, and we find much information in ancient writings relative to it. In Ha Idra Rabba Quadisha, or The Greater Holy Assembly, we find many statements. In fact the entire work deals intimately with it. From it the following have been selected as examples: "Therefore He carved out (that is, hollowed out) a space which He might flow in," meaning that the Creator formed the skull, a bowl, in which *precipitated Spirit* might accumulate, thus creating the cerebrum or *high* brain.

Again: "The Absolute desire within himself *to create the essence of light.*" The word essence is derived from the Latin verb esse, which means *to be*. Therefore essence means the *substance of being,* or the *material necessary for existence.* Light means life and also Spirit, for the latter produces both light and life. A deficiency in any of these means deficiency in *all.*

The great majority of people in the world have sufficient Spirit to keep them going for only a few years. Spirit or Father works with *mother* or *material.* One must equal the other for perfection to exist.

In Chapter IV we read: "Concerning the Dew or Moisture of the Brain, of the Ancient One, or Macroprosophus: And from that skull distilleth a Dew upon him which is external, and filleth His *head daily.*" "And *from* that Dew which floweth down from his head, the dead are raised up in the world to come." "Concerning which is written, Cant. V:2: My *head* is filled with *dew.*" "And by that Dew are nourished the holy supernal ones." "And this is the *manna* which is prepared for the just in the world to come."

What an astounding mass of information we have here. We find that macroprosophus is the ancient name for the cerebrum, the spiritual brain, the actual Father or Creator. Also that Dew is a very old term for brain substance, and a very fitting one, since dew is a moist precipitation from above, found on the earth or ground. The words "and filleth His head daily" link up directly with the Bible statement in John 6:58: "I am the *living bread* which *cometh down* from Heaven." And again: "Give us this day our *daily bread.*" As the earth (mother) attracts the dew or Spirit, so each person is *responsible* for the creation of his or her own bread. Chemistry alone explains this, which we will consider later.

And how wonderful the promise accompanying the following: "And *from that dew* which floweth down (into the body) from His head the *dead* are raised to life in the world to come."

World means the body, the earth world below the heaven world, in other words, the skull and the torso. This explains why we have deteriorated through the years. We have been really dying daily instead of becoming more alive. There has been insufficient dew or brain esse to feed the body—not enough "daily bread." This means both physical and spiritual starvation. The body is in itself a graveyard, because it contains so many dead bodies—corpuscles.

We are also given another word having the same meaning—manna, for its interpretation in the Hebrew language is *man making*. The manna, or heavenly bread, forms man and also feeds him.

Please read the following until it is indelibly etched upon your mind: *The brain or cerebrum is the first and most important gland in the body. The essence it creates flows through all the glands, but each gland consecutively differentiates its fluid.* It is of a neuter or neutral nature when first formed, and *would continue to be so if mankind did not take from it*—or rob it. We object to having some of our possessions stolen from us by thieves, but never dream that the worst thief is the one who robs himself of his most precious treasure—the *golden essence of life*. This is, indeed, the treasure that we are commanded to *"lay up* in heaven."

To any who become impatient for the chemical allocation, let me say with all kindness that it can never be understood unless all the foregoing statements are linked up with it indissolubly. It is the hidden or esoteric which alone throws light on the exoteric.

Of the optic thalamus the Kabbala informs us: "Therefore it is called the open eye, the holy eye, the excellent eye, the eye of Providence, the eye which sleepeth not, neither slumbereth, the eye which is the guardian of all things, the eye which is the subsistence of all things."

Do we not say "Yes, I *see*" when we *understand* or get a point? Truly we are spiritually blind when we cognize but little. And who is to blame? None but ourselves.

The organ referred to above, the optic thalamus, occupies the central portion of Aries, or the third ventricle—to be correct, the middle decan (ten degrees). While the sign as a whole is ruled by Mars (energy) it has a co-ruler, the Sun. Thus the Sun is *exalted* in Aries, meaning that, at last, the inner sun, or thalamus, is receiving what has been so long kept from it. The Lord is now truly receiving the bread and wine for the supper in the *upper chamber*.

How much the well-being of the lower brain or cerebellum depends on the cerebrum is also explained in the Greater Holy Assembly (which in itself refers to the upper brain, the place where All Things, Essence, are assembled): "Since there is not subsistence in the *inferior* brain except by the *preservation* of the superior brain,"—cerebrum. We must here quote from Malachi, third chapter, eighth verse: "Will a man rob God? Yet ye have robbed me. But ye say, Wherein have we robbed thee? *In tithes and offerings.*"

As the general interpretation of money is that which serves as a common medium of exchange or measure of value in trade, we find its figurative origin in the brain substance of man. It is in very truth his most precious treasure, the mental rule or medium by which he measures values and makes exchanges in his earthly (bodily) dealings. It is truly the coin of the realm.

This is further borne out by the ancient interpretation of Mercury, interpreted as mind, and physiologically as brain and nerves. From its root we obtain the word merchandise. Mercury is said to rule trade, for trading is done by means of merchandise or money. The brain substance is the merchandise or money which, continually laid *up* or restored, becomes an ever increasing asset which actually produces for us more than compound interest. But if the principal is drawn on constantly, through sexual excesses or other forms of depletion, there is no possible means by which any interest can accrue. Conservation indeed makes for efficiency. In ancient days an image of Mercury was placed at the cross-roads to *point the way* for travelers. Mental treasures are the only ones incapable of being stolen by any but ourselves. The mind travels, and is *supported* on all its journeys by the money it possesses.

In their sculptures the Greeks have left to posterity much that is invaluable. The caduceus borne aloft by the hand of

Mercury is used today as the symbol of *healing* by the American and British medical corps, but who can say how many of its members have even the faintest conception of its real meaning.

The word caduceus is derived from the verb *cado,* meaning TO FALL. Therefore the whole story of the FALL and RISE of man is contained in it, for the winged pole represents the cerebro-spinal system; the pole, the spine, and the two wings are the two hemispheres of the brain or the Tree of Life, while the two serpents twined around it are the right and left sympathetic systems, the Tree of Knowledge of Good and Evil, and also the *two thieves.*

The motor system represented by these nerves, in its present deficient and hence imperfect condition, has deteriorated and been perverted into an e-motional system. And this is the condition of humanity in general. E-motion means a waste of motion, a lack of conservation. All *unnecessary* motion constitutes waste, and when the nervous system is so depleted that there is no control over it, one is said to be uncontrolled or carried away by emotion. Where perfection exists no emotion will manifest, and by this is not meant spasmodic control, but harmony. One does not need to exclaim, to weep, to shout or to jump about to express what one *thinks*—but the eyes and face can express deep sympathy and understanding.

To prove that the Hindus know of a Tree of Life we find in their literature the following: "The fruit and sap of the Tree of Life bestows immortality." Among the most ancient traditions of the Hindus is that of the Tree of Life called *Soma* in Sanskrit, the juice of which imparts immortality. Their legend of Elysium or Paradise says: "In the sacred mountain Meru, which is perpetually clothed in the golden rays of the sun, and whose lofty summit reaches into heaven, no sinful man can exist. It is guarded by a dreadful dragon. It is adorned with many celestial plants and trees, and is watered by *four rivers* which thence separate and flow to the four chief directions." These rivers correspond in number to those given in Genesis.

When all students realize that mind can not function without a brain, and the latter is not formed unless the necessary *material* is present it will at last be understood that both Spirit and matter are absolutely necessary in order to accomplish healing.

The word healing has not been understood, for it means to be made whole, perfect, entire. We may be *helped* in many ways and by many things, but to be healed means that all *the work* necessary for perfection has been completed. The mechanic gets busy with the machine that is not running properly, removes old parts, and puts in new. The human body is the only machine which has the power to *rebuild* itself daily, and will do so when the needed material is supplied. There are many more references in Sacred Writings to manna, dew, honey, nectar and ambrosia, food of the gods, elixir of life, sacred Soma juice, Amritam or amrita, all referring to the creative *esse or brain substance.*

Eliphas Levi, in his work on *Transcendental Magic,* says: "*The human head is formed upon the model of the celestial spheres;* it attracts and *radiates,* and *in the conception of a child this* is what is *first formed* and first manifests. Hence *the head is subject in an absolute manner* to astral influence, and evidences its several attractions by its diverse protuberances. The final word of phrenology is to be found, therefore, in scientific and purified astrology."

We find much in the above quotation—that Aries, the upper brain, is a celestial sphere, that it corresponds to heaven and is therefore man's heaven. The Scriptures substantiate this by saying, "The kingdom of heaven is *within you.*" Therefore, within Aries are all of the lights, planets or rates of vibration, in other words gods or *ruling* powers. And it is these which link up with, receive vibrations from, and are affected by, the planets or heavenly bodies without. If the vibrations set up in the head are too slow, because of chemical deficiencies, and therefore unable to respond to those perfect etheric waves from the celestial head or head of the Grand man, then symptoms arise which are the visible manifestation of inharmony and dis-ease.

Not only does the shape of the head bear evidence of this, as Eliphas Levi states, but everything representing the present status of the individual is indelibly etched upon the subtle cere-brum or brain *esse.* For the Spirit brings with it the photographic plate of its existence in its former physical body as it *impregnates* with its *Spirit* the ova which is at the same time being impregnated by the animal spermatozoa.

It is to be hoped that there will be astrologers who will appreciate Mr. Levi's statement relative to "a scientific and purified astrology," for it deals with the mind and body of man.

A study of the word cere-brum gives us the following: cere means wax, and from the same root we have the word cere-al or seed. The letter Beth in Hebrew means womb or matrix of creation. The rest of the word is a Latin neuter ending, signifying that the word has a neuter meaning. Truly is the cerebral substance of a neutral nature, as it contains or consists of all things. The English explanation of the word wax used as a verb means to assume, by degrees, a specified state or condition, and this is true of the brain as an organ.

Wax is a substance secreted from the abdominal rings of bees, and possesses properties which render it a most convenient medium for preparing figures and models. It melts at low heat and *takes the minutest impressions*. It sets and hardens at such temperature that no ordinary climatic changes affect its form, even when cast in thin laminæ. Thus we see why the brain substance is termed wax-like, for electricity, that needle of thought or Spirit, must have a subtle substance upon which to etch its patterns, otherwise termed convolutions.

In the Sanskrit literature, Brahmarandhra is Spirit or *the bee*. Therefore the wax of the brain substance is the excretion of that Spiritual Bee, and truly is it filled with what the Bee produces, the Honey of Life. This links up directly with the Bible statement in reference to "the land flowing with milk and honey," and to which those who obey God's laws are promised a safe return, a veritable return to the Garden of Eden *within one's self*.

The word cere-al deals with seed, which is a wax-like glutenous substance, and the source of all life. In Greek mythology the goddess (female refers to substance or material) Ceres was the daughter (product) of Saturn and Ops (meaning the sower of seed and the earth in which seed is planted), and thus refers to the process of production, or, as Greek literature informs us, to agriculture, which means to till a field.

The Bible states that, "man purchases a *field* (body) with thirty pieces of silver," and the same idea was brought out by the ancients in their statements relative to the heavenly bull (the sun in Taurus) plowing the earth. The Adam man

(Taurus) signifies Spirit cabined and confined in an animal body (bull), which latter plows the earth blindly in rage, or yoked to reason (Aries) cultivates the soil (mineral elements) and thus re-creates himself. In doing this the Adam man is eliminated and only one manifests—God-man.

In order to link up chemically with the sign Aries, we must again repeat that it is, astrologically, the first of the three fire signs. Therefore it has to do with the first manifestation or appearance of life, Spirit confined within the physical vehicle, and especially in a *particular part, its own house.* Here it is possible for it to perform its own particular task.

Aries, then, is the house of God, or the Spirit in man. It houses or contains the brain, the organ of thought.

If the mind is able to function clearly it will *throw light* on every subject—it will illuminate and thus reveal all things to man. The only material which is so chemically constituted that it has the power to produce light or fire, is Kali phos, or potassium phosphate. It produces the *highest rate of vibration* of any of the twelve basic mineral elements of the body.

Here it must be explained why there are not sixteen considered. The four additional, which are oxygen, hydrogen, nitrogen and carbon are not minerals. Their presence in the body depends entirely on the presence of the twelve minerals. For instance, we do not consider oxygen, for its presence in the body depends entirely on the Ferrum or iron content of the blood. This wonderful magnetic salt is the chemical attractor of oxygen and is its only means of entering the body. It is equally true that the *quantity* of oxygen one is able to inspire depends wholly on the amount of iron in the blood stream. Therefore, it is unnecessary to consider this gas as a constituent of the body, for it will take care of itself when the blood is supplied with iron.

Let us return, then, to our consideration of this most wonderful material, Kali phos. It is the *mater*-ial or *mother* (*mater* is Latin for mother) of *light,* for it contacts and links up with the invisible fire in Nature, and actually harnesses it within the human body. As it produces a higher rate of vibration than any other salt, it is proof that the physical body can respond *with safety to no higher rate.*

Therefore, if the body is subjected to the vibrations of radium or those of X-ray, the cells of the body receiving them will be burned. As it has been stated by physicians that this ray will kill *living* cancer cells it is absolutely true that it will also destroy healthy cells by burning. It is well known that scientists who spend their lives experimenting with both radium and X-rays are very low in vitality and, in many instances, suffer from cancer. Their own cells have been burned, and putrify after burning.

Potassium must be used as a healing agent instead, in all three of its forms or combinations, namely, Kali phos, Kali mur, and Kali sulph, together with its opposite pole salt, Ferrum or iron. Thus there will be plenty of oxygen for the fire of purification to consume.

In the study of practical chemistry, we find that when some of this potassium salt is thrown on water, it instantly generates such a powerful electrical current that the hydrogen is separated from the oxygen, takes fire and burns with its characteristic violet flame in the released oxygen. Thus the two gases hydrogen and oxygen disappear. They have returned into the invisible, having been chemically released. If the imagination is active, it is easy to picture in the mind's eye (the optic thalamus) the inverse operation, the process whereby the Great Chemist and Architect of the Universe invisibly unites or forges the two gases, oxygen and hydrogen, and precipitates them in the form of water. The unification is done by electricity, the hidden fire.

Greek mythology tells us of the mighty Vulcan who forges the thunderbolts. Indeed, that literature is a compilation of scientific facts relative to nature and man, transmitted to us in beautiful and poetic language. The Bible contains the same facts but in noble and stately prose. Truly there is only one story of importance, the story of the process whereby humanity may ascend from the depths to the heights—*perfection.*

Potassium is a soft, brilliant, bluish-white metal melting at sixty-two and five-tenths degrees to a liquid resembling mercury. In astrology Mercury is "the Messenger of the Gods" or ruling powers. Therefore we see how applicable the comparison is, for potassium is truly the food by which the gods, or gray matter, are nourished.

The sensory nerves are the wires connected with the great generator of electrical energy, the cerebrum, the house of God or Aries. These ramify throughout the entire body, supplying electricity whereby all of its work is done.

It is important to remember, that not only does this electrical system run the body, but it is actually the *subtle* substance with which thinking is done. For electricity is both energy and substance, although unseen by our eyes, which are incapable of responding to this high rate of vibration as yet.

As potassium is a *carrier of fire,* perhaps it will be well to explain, at this point, what this research work has revealed relative to carbon-monoxide poison. Since the advent of the automobile a new cause of death has been added to the many already tabulated, and the newspapers frequently state that so-and-so was found dead in his car, the motor running and the garage doors closed, thus shutting out the purifying oxygen. As chemistry states, *potassium has a tendency to unite directly with carbon-monoxide to produce a dangerously explosive body* It is my belief therefore that the sensory cells of the brain *expand* violently and thus *burst,* causing death.

The spectrum of potassium is characterized by two sharply defined lines, one in the red and the other in violet. The wave length of the former is 0.0007680, and that of the latter 0.0004095. As red-violet or true magenta is the color of Aries, the above is conclusive proof that the potassium of Aries and the iron of Pisces forge together the closing links in the zodiacal circle of life. (See article on allocation of color with the zodiac elsewhere in this book).

In Sir Thomas Vaughan's works (sixteenth century) translated by A. E. Waite, the earnest student will find a mine of mineral wealth. He says: "Within this fantastic *circle* (the head) stands a Lamp, and it typifies the Light of Nature. This is the Secret Candle of God, which He hath tinned in the elements: it burns and is not seen, for it shines in a dark place. Every natural body is a kind of black lantern; it carries this Candle within it, but the light appears not; it is eclipsed with the *grossness* of matter. The *effects* of this light are apparent in all things; but the Light itself is denied, or else not followed. This Light or Fire is nowhere to be found in such abundance and purity as in that subject which the Arabians call *Halicali,* from Hali (Summum) and *Calop* (Bonum); but the Latin authors write it *Sal Alkali.*

"This substance is the catholic (universal) *receptacle* of Spirits. It is *blessed and impregnated* with light from above, and was therefore styled by the magicians 'a sealed house, full of light and divinity.' "

In Arabic, potassium is given as Al-gali, from which the

word *alkali* is derived. Studying the word, al-kali we find it means, literally, *Father* (al or el in Hebrew means God or father) and Kali, a Sanskrit word for fire. In the Vedic, an older form of the word means *mother*. Thus the true interpretation of alkali is father-mother, or positive and negative *combined* or harmonized, therefore a neutral substance. Indeed it is a chemical fact that it *is* alkaline.

Vaughan refers to the above as "*mineral doctrine*," which is very unique and absolutely true. We will be well on our way in the study of the chemistry of the body when we begin to realize that this is, indeed, a most necessary *doctrine* and must be *religiously followed*.

Again Vaughan says: "For in Genesis he hath discovered many particulars, and especially those secrets which have most relation to this *Art*. For instance, he hath discovered the *minera of man*, or that substance out of which man and all of his fellow-creatures were made." He elsewhere mentions the *sperm* of the world, as the *first essence*, which allocates perfectly with the first explanation herein of the brain substance, from the word cere-brum, or seed substance. *Sperm* means *seed*. Hali-Cali (potassium) is also termed "the casket which *holds* the *Light*, and *links* us up with God and Nature."

Sufficient proof has been given thus far, in these pages, that potassium is a most subtle substance of very high vibration, capable of holding within itself *the fire of life*, electricity, prana, or Spirit. Reviewing the information relative to the astrological interpretation of Aries and its definite relation to the cerebro-spinal system, we see that Dr. Carey's allocation of Kali phos to the zodiacal sign Aries has been indubitably proved.

Well may the wondrous cerebral substance be termed Proteus, for it truly is the Ancient of Days. In Greek mythology Proteus was a many-formed deity. Being composed of *everything*, he could revert back to anything, take any shape he wished, just as by chemical or electrical vibration all chemical substances will eventually be found to revert back to one.

The word protoplasm is derived from the same root word as Proteus. If any one doubts that Kali phos or potassium phosphate is the chief substance in the gray nerve cells let him read the information furnished by any dictionary, encyclopædia or work on the physical body. Perhaps it will be well to explain what is said relative to protoplasm:

Proto, meaning *first,* and plasm, meaning *form,* is the name for the viscous (sticky or *glutinous*) *material* of a vegetable or animal cell. Please be advised that the word glutinous is derived from the same root as gluten, a nutritious substance; a proteid; the sticky, albuminous part of wheat (ceres) flour." It is, therefore, *seed,* a more or less granulated substance that forms the principal portion of an animal or vegetable cell.

"Protoplasm was previously termed *sarcode,* or *flesh.* The protoplasm of most cells appears under the high power of the microscope as a *network* (spongioplasm or reticulum) containing a more fluid substance (hyaloplasm) in its *meshes.* Chemically it is a mixture of eighty to eighty-five per cent water, and fifteen to twenty per cent solids (chiefly proteids), with small quantities of fat, albumoses, globulins, and peptones.

"It also contains small quantities of carbohydrates like glycogen, inosite, and *mineral salts, especially those of potassium, which cause it to yield an alkaline reaction.* Protoplasm has been called by Huxley, owing to its presence in all organized bodies, 'the physical basis of life,' and some have held that *its phenomena show* that the *difference* between organized and unorganized cells is simply complexity of *chemical constitution.* It is therefore a *highly complex substance regarded as a mixture of different chemical substances.*

"Protoplasm is contractile and irritable and *reproduces* by self-division."

The above statement that protoplasm is *contractile* is absolute proof of the presence of Magnesium phos, the *moving* or motor salt, Calcium fluoride, the builder of elasticity, and Potassium phosphate, the electrical salt. We are here informed positively that the *chief* salt is potassium, for electricity, spirit, or the fire of life must ensoul all matter.

In Gray's Anatomy we find that the soft, jelly-like material termed cytoplasm found in the nucleated mass of protoplasm contains, among other things, *mineral salts;* "chief among which are the phosphates and chlorides of potassium, sodium, and calcium." (1924 Edition).

Scientists have for some time known the above facts, and there is no longer any reason or excuse why the medical profession *en masse* should not adopt and utilize henceforth the findings of Dr. William Schuessler relative to Biochemistry—the "inorganic system." The opinions of so many dietitians, naturopaths and others, that the mineral tablets or cell-salts used to supply blood deficiencies *can not enter the blood or be utilized, are absolutely untrue,* and would not be uttered if these salts were faithfully and conscientiously tested for one year.

In the first place, those making such a statement as this, for instance—"the salts are inorganic, and the body can use only what is organic," show their ignorance of the interpretation and derivation of words, for organic does not mean that a mineral is changed, but that several have been combined with fluidic materials. They can not be changed, even by *fire.* Another fact not recognized is that the chemist is able to pulverize or triturate them into as fine particles as they are found in plants. Think how much it means, when one uses the chemical term Kali, to know that it is the same in Latin and German, and is thus traced directly to the Sanskrit. Thousands of Hindus worship the *goddess* Kali as the most powerful deity in Nature—Fire—which is at the same time the Creator, the Preserver, and the Destroyer. Fire creates, it preserves, and yet it can destroy.

Most scientists agree that there can be no life without potassium, and at least we realize that it is the *visible means* whereby life is manifested. It is indeed Proteus.

Since potassium feeds the gray matter of the brain, it at one and the same time nourishes the Spirit in that brain. Sir Thomas Vaughan says: "Be ye transmuted from dead stones into living philosophical stones, a conversion of body into spirit, and spirit into body, from corruption into a perfect mode, *wherein the body would be preserved continually.* The medicine is, however, in *heaven* itself and not to be found elsewhere, yet not meaning thereby that it is *remote* in *place* or time, but rather *in that center* which, *being within us*—is a center that can be found everywhere."

In the form of oil we find that potassium sulphate permeates all parts of the body. The marrow of the bones is thickened oil or fat stored there to feed and preserve them. Each and every cell in the body is surrounded by and bathed in an oily, salty fluid for the same purpose. Potassium, in the form of potassium chloride or Kali mur, spins threads of fibrin or flesh fibers. Therefore all tissue, ligaments, structure of all the organs, glands, skin, etc., are made of it. Then wise Mother Nature adds to some of these fibers a large proportion of potassium phosphate to form electrical wires through which positive currents may pass and thus enable physiological processes to go on. Potassium, in all of its combinations, is then a conveyor or medium of life or fire; for fire is life, and life is Spirit.

In his book, *The Biochemic System of Medicine*, Dr. Carey says: "The gray matter of the brain is controlled entirely by the inorganic cell-salt, potassium phosphate. This salt unites with albumin, and by the addition of oxygen creates nerve fluid, or the gray matter of the brain. Of course, there is a trace of other salts and organic matter in nerve fluid, but potassium phosphate is the chief factor, and has the power within itself to attract, by its own law of affinity, *all things* (Proteus) needed to manufacture the *elixir of life*." And we know that this *esse* (the substance of being) actually creates the child in utero.

He further says: "Therefore, when nervous symptoms arise due to the fact that the nerve-fluid has been exhausted from any cause, the phosphate of potassium is the only true remedy, because nothing else can possibly supply the deficiency. The ills from too rapidly consuming the gray matter of the brain can not be overestimated, and if all who are inclined to nervous disorders would carry Kali phos with them, in tablet form, a large amount of sickness and suffering would be prevented. Let the overworked business man take it and go home good-tempered. Let the weary wife, nerves unstrung from attending to sick children or entertaining company, take it and note how quickly the equilibrium will be restored and *calm and reason assert her throne*. We find this potassium salt largely predominates in nerve fluid, and that a deficiency produces well-defined symptoms. The beginning and end of the matter is to supply the lacking principle, and in molecular form, *exactly as nature furnishes it in vegetables, fruits, and grain*. To supply deficiencies—this is the only law of cure."

There is one point which must be thoroughly understood, and, in order that it may be, it will be referred to in each of these twelve chapters, as follows:

The principle involved in this method is that of *body building*. Many reasons combine to make the body unable to obtain a sufficient supply of the twelve inorganic salts. Therefore supplementing the *moderate* diet of *natural* food, *simply prepared,* with the different kinds of salts which each individual requires day after day, month after month, and year after year, is the actual method by which disease is eliminated and the blood kept well nourished. In this way there is never any deficiency.

Most people seem unable to understand this, and so cease taking the salts when symptoms no longer appear. The salts are taken *not* to cure symptoms, but to build up such a good body that *symptoms can not arise.* A person takes food *every* day, and seems really to understand that the body must have nutriment. One does not say, "I ate yesterday and so I won't need food again for a long time." People like to eat too well ever to think of saying that, but they soon forget their mineral salts when no symptom or pain is present to remind them. Taking them in a desultory way is merely *patching up instead of daily building a new body automatically.* This is the *basic plan for physical regeneration.* "Be ye *perfect,* as your Father in heaven is perfect."

Among the many outstanding symptoms which deficiency in potassium phosphate causes are: Extreme nervousness, insanity, paralysis, hysteria, fainting, mental and physical exhaustion, strange fancies and forebodings, softening of the brain and spinal cord, nervous headache, hungry feeling after eating food, etc. The writer, however, does not deal with symptoms, but furnishes the individual plan whereby the body may be entirely made over.

This plan is founded on the *natural zodiac,* wherein the planets are placed in the degrees of the signs in which they were at a person's birth. Allocating the mineral salts with these signs will give the correct analysis and indicate the tendencies to deficiencies. This being known, one can then give a list of the symptoms, mental as well as physical, which may at any time tend to appear, until the blood is more nearly supplied with the needed salts. And as Shakespeare so truly said:

> "And so from hour to hour we ripe and ripe,
> And then from hour to hour we rot and rot,
> And thereby hangs the tale."

If our chemical needs are supplied we *will* ripen, physically and spiritually, but continued deficiencies in "the dust of the earth," result in the other unattractive and undesirable condition.

In *The Gospel of Buddha* we read the following: "But

to satisfy the *necessities of life* is not evil. To keep the body in good health is a *duty*, for otherwise *we shall not be able to trim the lamp* of wisdom and keep our minds strong and clear." Truly does Kali phos, or phosphate of potassium feed this lamp.

And from the same ancient source, the Sanskrit, we obtain the following physiological information: "The living brain is constituted of gross sensible material (Mahabhuta) infused with prana. Its *material* has been *worked up* so as to constitute a suitable vehicle for the *expression of consciousness* in the form of mind—Antahkarana." (From *Serpent Power*, p. 127). Potassium phosphate is the vehicle of consciousness.

CHAPTER II

THE ANALYSIS AND SYNTHESIS OF TAURUS AND NATRIUM SULPH.

"I come from a land in the sun-bright deep
  Where golden gardens glow—
Where the winds of the North becalmed in sleep
  Their conch-shells never blow."

—From: Moore's *Song of the Hyperborean.*

ON the twenty-first of April, approximately, the Sun enters that part of the heavens wherein is the constellation of the Bull. Dr. Wakeman Ryno writes of it as follows: "This sign has been the inspiration, in all ages, of more myths and stories than all the other twelve signs put together. Taurus was worshiped as a healing god, because he represented the *growing strength* of the Sun, and healing, from 'Helios' the Sun. In the Greek we have the word Theos, which is the basis of our English words theology and theological. He is Taur, Thor or Theuth; the Golden Calf of Horeb, of the Bible story; he is Hesperia, where Hercules conquered the Oxen of Geryon; he was Amen-Apis of the Thebans."

Helios is also Apollo, and every nation and every people has had its own particular term for this divine giver of life, light and heat.

Taurus is the first of the earth triplicity. As two weeks of May and one of April are concerned with its labor, we find the true interpretation of the sign in the word May, the source of which is a Sanskrit root, Mag, meaning to *move*. The word Maia is derived from the same root. She it was to whom the ancients offered gifts on the first day of May, and even to the present day children celebrate May-Day night by exchanging baskets of gifts, hanging them on door knobs. They also delight in May-pole dances and playing pranks of a more or less harmless and foolish nature.

The parts of the body with which this sign allocates are the ears, face around lower jaw, cerebellum, neck, throat, liver and gall-bladder.

The word cerebellum differs from cerebrum in its ending only. The first part of the word, cere, means seed. Bellum is a Latin word meaning war or antagonism, contention. Thus contention or antagonism. It *should* not be; but, because it is the *animal* brain, the bull-headed god of the Age of the Golden Calf, it represents that stage in the evolution of humanity when it is torn by animal passions. Microprosophus (of the Kabbala) is not co-operating with Macroprosophus; in other words, the animal man, Adam, "is ever contending *against God*," for passion can not hear the voice of reason. Seed (cere) essence is destroyed. The word Taurus or Torus also means any round swelling or protuberance—a projecting part or cushion. It is a well known anatomical fact that the cerebellum has such a protection, and is seen in any chart. Indeed it is colored red on the charts so as to be outstanding.

The sub-conscious mind functions through the lower brain or cerebellum. To be sure this is contrary to what psychologists teach, but the following is proof of its functioning process.

Naturally the cerebrum, being the spiritual brain, is the organ of consciousness. It is Rama, the Most High. In the Greek it is Athens, and the goddess Athena means wisdom. It is from this Greek word that we derive the term *attic*. An attic is the top-most room in a house. Delicate wit is termed "attic wisdom." Therefore the cerebrum is the first house or first compartment in the physical dwelling. When this part of the brain is chemically perfected and hence all knowledge is obtained, consciousness or Spirit manifests as the Christ Consciousness.

The term *sub* means *under*, and is derived from the Latin. Therefore, the sub-conscious brain in which the sub-conscious mind functions is situated *under* the brain pertaining to consciousness or the cerebrum. It is, we may say, the basement or cellar brain, where the things stored become damp and full of moths. How beautifully true is the Biblical injunction: "Lay up treasures in heaven (re-read the first chapter) where moths do not corrupt and where thieves do not break through nor steal."

Again, when it is understood that Aries or the cerebrum is the God-brain and Taurus or the cerebellum (the contending brain) in the animal, it becomes perfectly clear.

The state of mind, then, which each one of us manifests

in our imperfect state becomes the divine Bull by being *yoked* to our higher consciousness. When a statement presented to us is understood do we not say "Yes, *I am conscious of that fact.*" And is it not equally true that, when we are unable to cognize another we say, *"No, I am not conscious* that *that* is a fact" This, then, is summed up in the statement that *we are not fully conscious.*

No one can be fully conscious who is living in the animal passions, and to whom they are attractive. To the degree in which we are able to master them, to transmute or use that same energy (Taurus) in mental work—in the house of consciousness, the cerebrum, do we merge from the subconscious state to that of the conscious, or spiritual. The animal is the sub-human and the cerebellum is the animal brain. Taurus must be yoked—controlled—guided by wisdom. Many contend that the solar plexus is the sub-conscious brain; but an understanding of anatomy and physiology proves that this great center which is a collection of twelve great nerve ganglia and hence a zodiac in itself, is a receiver of energy, and hence one of feeling and sensation, not of thought.

It is indeed true that, as long as we live in the animal brain and are carnally minded, we are *spiritually moldy* and full of moths; and eventually the form itself goes back into the ground to be consumed.

"The last enemy to be overcome is death."—Bible; and "The wages of sin is death." Therefore, when we no longer *fall short or are deficient,* which is the true meaning of *sin,* we will no longer die, for it will be physiologically and chemically impossible.

Taurus, or the Bull, is said to plow the earth, preparing the soil that it may *bring forth.* Here we must recall the parable of the sower who *went forth* to sow. The Adam man is the sower. He is given, has made, and contains the seeds of all things, as also does the earth.

But upon what kind of ground will these seeds fall—on fertile or barren? Ponder well on a mighty fact: *The corpuscles of the body are its seed.* I am not referring to the seed of *procreation,* for that is a different kind. But I will give you another point, equally mighty: The animal man actually *robs his body of its corpuscles (one tenth, to be exact) in forming the germs of procreation.* This is a fact which science will one day admit.

The Bible states that "Man purchases a field with thirty pieces of silver." The field (and the term "thirty pieces of silver") is understood by studying the thirty degrees of Scorpio which allocate with the organs of procreation. It is only by means of these organs that progeny may be had. The body or form is purchased, and with the *coin of the realm,* for it has its *origin* in Aries, the cerebrum, which is the *first gland in the body.* This heavenly treasure, the Gold of Ophir, becomes perverted from its original and Paradisiacal use and is changed to silver after flowing *out of* the Garden of Eden—the cerebrum.

The middle decan of Aries, allocating with the optic thalami, is the place of the sagittal or All-Seeing Eye, the seat of knowledge where we interpret all that we see, hear, smell, taste and touch. So the last decan of Taurus is also concerned with the senses, and especially with eyesight. As the nerves from the head contact or *cross* at the base of the brain, a chart will often indicate trouble with sight. The reason for this is that there is interference with circulation, and the special nerves having to do with this function are unable to carry nutritive blood to the center in sufficient quantity, or to bring away the waste products. As a result we often find cataracts forming on the eyes. The middle decan of Aries is, therefore, the positive pole pertaining to the vision, and the last decan of Taurus is the negative end.

Referring to our interpretation of the sign with which we are dealing, we must again note that it means *to move.* After the outpouring of Divine Fire at the Spring equinox and until April 21st, *action* begins. Nature starts to manifest *visibly* or bring forth *objectively.* Here again we check accurately with the anatomy and physiology of the cerebellum, for it is the *motor* brain, the mechanical brain. It *does* things. It receives the electricity which Aries, the cerebrum, generates. For cosmic electricity—Spirit—starts the motor, and the medulla oblongata relays it so that it may start on its long journey down into Egypt (the torso, or place of darkness). The energy thus sent is received by the solar plexus, consisting of twelve large nerve ganglia, which, in turn, broadcasts it to the organs. If the solar plexus is weak because chemically deficient, it is not only unable to receive sufficient of this great influx, but is also unable to supply the organs. It can not give what it does not possess. Then, again, the trouble may originate in the cerebellum itself and that organ may be unable both to receive and dispense energy. Stop and consider, please, all of the allocations that we have thus far synthesized: the meaning of the period which constitutes Taurus (May—the doing, or moving month) and the cerebellum (the motor, the brain which *acts*).

Here we must dwell, for a time, on the chaotic condition in which we find humanity today. We find everything perverted—religion, science, law, medicine, sex, finance, amusements. Nothing has escaped, with the exception of mathematics. We are indeed fortunate that two and two still make four, and that no one contradicts.

It is a self-evident fact that, if all the parts of a machine are in perfect order, properly co-ordinated and contacting power, it will work *perfectly. The human mechanism is subject to the same law.* If a motor stops and starts, the result is spasmodic action, not action which is harmonious. Thus, spasmodic thought results in inharmonious acts, and to the degree in which it thus manifests chaos results.

With both cerebrum and cerebellum extremely deficient chemically, is it then any wonder that human thought and action are unsettled, inharmonious and spasmodic? It can not be otherwise. This is the solution, then, for it explains why wars exist, why there is no agreement, no harmony among nations, and why social, civic, religious and racial inharmony is rampant.

The spirit or God confined in an unhealthy, deficient brain, poisoned with the waste products of gluttony and wrong living, is utterly unable to produce harmonious thought. The lower brain in an equally imperfect condition can not give birth to a vibration or current of energy that is as constructive as is necessary. For the most part the energy generated is used in a negative or destructive way. Thoughts are imperfect and spasmodic, and the *acts* which follow are equally so.

The Gold of Ophir mentioned in the Scriptures is the manna or dew referred to in Aries, and is the first substance with which Spirit (the Erotes of Life) links up, *uniting* the *elements* and bringing order out of chaos. The word Ophir means in Hebrew a fruitful region. In Smith's *Bible Dictionary* (1915, Appleton) we find that Baron von Wrede made a small vocabulary of Himyaritic words in the vernacular tongue, and among these he gives *ofir* as *red*. As this color is associated with Aries, *energy* and fire, it allocates perfectly.

In addition we have, on leaving off the letter O, *fir*, which is the fir or evergreen tree which from time immemorial has been used as a symbol of the Tree of Life.

As the word pine is also used interchangeably, we find that the pine cone has been employed as a symbol of the pineal gland in the head, and indeed the word itself literally means *pine god*. The evergreen is a symbol of the renewal and hence continuity of life. Likewise this wonderful and so-called mysterious gland in the head is the *creator* and *renewer of life*. Al and el in Hebrew mean God. Fine gold is refined gold and there are many references in the Scriptures to the Gold of Ophir being of this nature. The cerebrum is truly a mine, a cave, in which is cloistered that most precious of all substances which has always been likened to gold.

In this Garden of Eden, coiled around the trunk of the pine tree or Tree of Life we find the *serpent*, which is symbolical of energy, the head issuing forth from the midst of its branches. In many very ancient illustrations we find that the serpent has three heads, the middle being more elevated.

This is in keeping with the physiological correspondence, for those on either side stand for the right and left sympathetic systems which constitute the two *thieves* of the Scriptures. Here the Gold of Ophir changes, takes on a different vibration and becomes silver. The Spiritual Man is represented by gold, the feminine counterpart by silver, while the Adam man is copper. Both gold and silver are said to be noble metals, because not easily oxidized. Gold is the fire of life, while silver is the water of life. The adi nerve is associated with the pituitary body or gland in the head, while the pengala connects with the pineal gland. The Sun rules the pineal and the Moon the pituitary. These constitute the *male and female which God joined together in the Garden of Eden*, otherwise Aries, the cerebrum.

The nerve-fluid from these two glands meets and crosses at the point or place in the head where Taurus begins. It is Golgotha—Place of the Skull. This is the cross on which animal nature brings suffering. We must refer to the sign *opposite* Taurus, its *complement*, that of Scorpio, as it is here that we find much of the animal energy of Taurus expressed.

There is a curious reference in the Bible to Scorpio which ecclesiastics do not seem to deal with: "In Sodom and Egypt where our Lord was also crucified."

Not only do these nerves cross at the base of the brain but at the second lumbar vertebra also, for the fire and water of life go downward into Scorpio and are literally thrown away. This causes the *real man*, the *Spirit*, to be crucified, defrauded by the animal nature of material with which to express divinity.

But when the fire and water of life are not used *prodigally*, —when *Adam no longer sacrifices his own son (substance) but offers up the animal instead*, these divine fluids, gold and silver, the noble metals (because high born) return to their source. *They ascend by going over the cross* from Taurus into Aries, when the father and son, the creator and the product of that creation, again merge or blend into one another.

The right and left sympathetic systems are thieves, for until the emotions become controlled through the proper supply of the necessary chemical elements, the *real* function of this part of the body is unable to manifest. The real function is *motion and not e-motion*. The e-motional life robs the body of nerve energy and of the highly specialized nerve or soul fluid. Summing up this statement and referring to our zodiacal sign which deals with emotion—Leo—it is made plain that the conservation of nerve energy and of soul fluid *recreates that body which initiates it*.

We must understand, then, that the story which Taurus gives us is relative to motion, work, doing. Therefore in order that such may result, it is self-evident that there is in Nature a certain substance that creates motion (which is *energy manifesting)*. Natrium or sodium is said to be a *reducing agent*. In other words it *steps down* chemical action and lowers the rate of vibration. It has the power to decompose water. In the form of Natrium sulph or sulphate of sodium, the addition of the sulphur causes a little different action.

Sulphur has been known from the remotest times. It forms an essential part of human and animal tissues and exists to a considerable extent in plant life, in that the human body must obtain it through food. When digestion and assimilation fail because of Calcium starvation it must be derived from the highly triturated tablets of this mineral. Natrium sulph is electro-negative, in this instance. It is linked with sodium and thus especially active in water.

The brain or Aries essence is a proteid, in fact this Ancient of Days in the Greek myth was Proteus—the first substance. It is a well-known chemical fact that sulphur is the only visible mineral substance found in proteid, which proves that it performs a *linking function*. Thus it serves to link up the brain substance or Proteus with the next chemical agent or Natrium, in order that a more substantial substance may result. There are twelve steps in this reduction or stepping-down process, corresponding to the twelve signs of the zodiac. Therefore the "heavenly dew" is brought into a different state or condition, becoming more earthy or tangible.

One particle of Natrium sulph has the power to attract twice its bulk of water *containing waste products* and to throw it out of the blood. As waste products consist in the average human body of unhealthy or acid residue, they can truthfully be compared to sulphuric acid. Indeed we find strange and sinister chemical products in a very foul and unhealthy human body.

The sodium, then, takes some of the fluid from the essence, mixes it with sulphur and begins the process of reduction, seeking to make a denser substance. A form is to be created. Spirit is to be clothed with matter.

We have said that Natrium sulph is a reducing agent in chemistry, and it indeed is. Those born when the Sun is transiting Taurus are lymphatic types, for they are deficient in sodium sulphate. They will find many of the symptoms which appear at intervals during their lifetime listed under this salt in Schuessler's *Biochemic System*. They are also set forth in Dr. Carey's work. When this salt is supplied and taken faithfully it will gradually eliminate all these ills.

When the nature and use of Natrium sulph is understood, people will then know why they take on weight and increase in size in spite of strict dieting. It is because the lymphatic system slowly becomes engorged with excess fluid derived from the atmosphere through the breath. Air goes directly into the arterial blood, for the word artery means air-carrier. Air is humid or moist, and when it carries in suspension a great quantity of water the blood becomes quickly overcharged. Particularly is it difficult for the Taurian born to live in comfort in the tropics, and especially in localities where there is great humidity.

I am positive that Dr. Carey has given us the correct explanation of a chill. He says, in his *Biochemic System:* "There is not a 'medical authority' (?) in existence who has given us a true definition of this phenomena. Their so-called explanations are meaningless and glittering generalities. I explain a chill (ague) thus: When the blood becomes overcharged with water, of course the various tissues of the body must suffer from lack of proper nourishment. This sets up a panic.

"Now, as the water-carriers are not present in sufficient quantities to throw out the excess in the natural way, nature does the next best thing—causes a *spasm* of the vascular, nervous and muscular systems, and thus, by violent effort, throws out the excess of water; hence the profuse perspiration which follows the chill. Where Natrium sulph is not given to supply the workmen, and thus keep out an excess of water, the chill will recur in about forty-eight hours, simply because that much time is required again to overcharge the blood with water."

Thus we see that kindly Mother Nature actually wrings the water out of the blood, when the needed material which would eliminate water comfortably is not at hand.

We also learn in his book that malarial conditions or symptoms are not caused by microbes from a swamp—he was not at all interested in the germ theory as the *cause* of disease. Deficient material for Nature to *work* with and a general toxic condition constitute the reason for physical and mental dis-ease and inharmony. When a person suffering from malaria visits a mountain resort he is relieved, simply because he is breathing the air from a cool, dry stratum, and is above the point where water is held in suspension by heat. A large supply of oxygen is also obtained, but here again, if the Ferrum or iron content of the blood is low, it is not able to enter.

We find the month of May to be a humid month, for the reason that Nature, Aries, is *reducing*—taking water from the fire—impregnated air—and precipitating it into the fire-impregnated earth, so that the work of production or growth may take place. Thus we see the formation of buds and the trees clothed with their first faintly green spring garments. It is perfectly legitimate for humanity to think of new garments in the Spring, for does not Mother Nature, the eternal feminine, clothe herself anew at this time? We should ever seek to know this cosmic mother of ours, to work understandingly with her.

During the Spring period a great many people feel lazy and debilitated and are thus unable to appreciate what is going on in Nature and what she is endeavoring to accomplish in human bodies. The blood is very deficient in the needed workmen (minerals) and the system is full of physical rubbish. Nature is endeavoring to work—and against odds. We could accomplish marvelous things if we could only work with her.

The human body, like the earth, may actually become dry, parched and barren because of lack of water. It may also become flooded with water and the corpuscles drowned. Many people suffer from drowsiness when the attention is not occupied, in spite of having had sufficient sleep, due to excess water in the brain cells. Sleeping sickness is an exaggerated form of this, and thought is actually *drowned,* indeed, temporarily submerged.

There is a great need for all three sodium or Natrium combinations. A few of the many indications or symptoms which inform us of a need for this reducing agent are: Irritation due to biliousness; tendency to suicide with wildness and irritability from an excessive secretion of bile and from too much fluid which is of an acid nature in the cells; headache on top of the head; biliousness; vomiting of bile; dizziness; tongue dirty, greenish-gray or greenish-brown color; bitter or metallic taste in the mouth; violent pains at the base of the brain; spinal meningitis; conjunctivitis; lightning-like pain through the ears; enlargement of the liver; diabetes; asthma; dropsy; gout; fistulous abscess of long standing; drowsiness; debility; heavy, anxious dreams, nightmare, etc.

It must be understood that the above are only a *few* symptoms from the long list which the book on this subject gives us. All symptoms are worse in the morning and in rainy or damp weather, this being what is termed "a modality."

The Biblical story of the ten captive tribes refers to the remaining ten signs of the zodiac and the allocating parts of the body which are truly captives, forced into bondage by the animal man, Adam, Taurus, the Bull or cerebellum. The animal mind, the emotions, wastes in the pleasures of the prodigal son, the man, the substance, the daily bread from heaven, while the ten tribes or parts of the body slowly starve. In this state they represent the ten tribes of Jacob. But when at last they become nourished and sustained by the conservation of this Alkahest or cerebral honey, they become the tribes of Israel, which means *warriors of God*—serving the most high, the God-brain, the cerebrum.

Our own poet, Edwin Markham, refers to this constellation in the words "High as that Heaven where Taurus wheels" and says:

> "It is a vision waiting and aware,
> And you must bring it down, oh men of worth,
> Bring down the New Republic hung in air,
> And make for it foundations on the Earth."

Another of our modern day writers, G. A. Gaskell, who has given us *A Dictionary of the Sacred Language of All Scriptures and Myths,* a most enlightening work for students, interprets Taurus as "A symbol of the second period of the cycle of life. It signifies the *divine out-going activity* in the creation of forms. The Bull of the West represents the matrix of forms on the Buddhic plane, or the productive energy of Buddhi. It pertains to the period of involution when Spirit is descending into matter and giving it the potencies of forms and qualities afterwards to be evolved in natural phenomena and in the souls of humanity."

Taurus is a symbol of the *second* period of the cycle of life, for it is the second sign and house of the zodiac, receiving the out-going electrical energy of Aries, and utilizing it in the formation of the human body. Earth, Taurus, has received the baptism of fire and water from the pineal and pituitary; and Mercury, the guide of travelers and the Messenger of the Gods, *descends.*

CHAPTER III

THE ANALYSIS AND SYNTHESIS OF GEMINI AND KALI MUR OR CHLORIDE OF POTASSIUM

"A noiseless, patient spider,
  I mark'd, where, on a little promontory, it stood, isolated;
Mark'd how, to explore the vacant, vast surrounding,
  It launched forth filament, filament, filament, out of itself;
Ever unreeling them—ever tirelessly speeding them.

And you, O my soul, where you stand,
  Surrounded, surrounded, in measureless oceans of space,
Ceaselessly musing, venturing, throwing—seeking the spheres to connect them;
  Till the bridge you will need be formed—till the ductile anchor hold;
Till the gossamer thread you fling, catch somewhere, O my soul."

—*Walt Whitman.*

THE spider is a creature of air as well as of earth. Standing, as our poet so beautifully expresses it, on a material foundation, it launches forth into space fairy-like threads, spun from the substance of its own body, a thick, viscous fluid, secreted by certain glands in the abdominal region. Air currents lift this aerial raft, bearing its creator on its way, and, eventually, by means of this silken cable, it ties up at another port.

The student of Esoteric Biochemistry revels in the perfect analogy existing between the above lines, the metaphysical, physiological and astrological interpretations of Gemini, and its allocation with potassium chloride or Kali mur by Dr. George W. Carey. For the entire story has to do with offshoots, threads, fibers, filaments—or offspring.

In the preceding chapters we have considered the outpouring of energy into undifferentiated matter, the creative *esse* of life, and its impregnation by fire. It manifests in nature as the Spring time and in the human body by the generation of electrical energy in the cerebrum (Aries).

Then, by the addition of Natrium sulph to Kali phos, a different chemical product results. The *work* at last begins, a protuberance appears, Aaron's rod buds and the back-brain or cerebellum forms.

The Sun in its journey now enters the sign of Gemini, which occurs, approximately, on May 21, and as there are two weeks of June and only one of May in this period, it is termed the June month.

The word is derived from the Latin verb *jungo,* and means a joining or joint, therefore a fiber or shoot. It is a thread, a filament branching off from the main stalk, whose source is the bud (gemma) or swelling brought forth by the Sun in Taurus. We have an identical interpretation in the word *bulb,* a protuberance, derived from the same root as Bull, which is the animal glyph for that sign. In the term *gemmation,* we have direct evidence of the true meaning of Gemini, as it refers to a new organism developed from a *projection.* It may be separated off or remain attached, the shoots of a plant being an example of the latter, and human progeny of the former. This last differs in that it takes place within the body.

Juno, as consort of Jupiter, refers to this sign, Gemini and Sagittarius (Jove's house) constituting the two ends of one pole—that of growth and travel. Under the name Juno Lucina the goddess of childbirth is represented, which again checks the original interpretation and the glyph of the twins. In India, they were popularly termed Mithuna, the Boy and Girl, while in Arabian astrology they are Al Tau'aman, a term replete with esoteric significance. Al or El meaning God; Tau, meaning cross; and Amen or Aman signifying concealed or hidden.

As the inner meaning of Taurus (Tau and Rus) is *dew cross* corresponding with Golgotha, "the place of the skull," "this Manna (man) or brain *esse* comes down *to form man,* which is an anatomical fact. Thus the *Divine Man or Spirit in us* actually becomes suspended on a *cross of matter.* Its body constitutes that cross (tree of nerves). The oldest glyphs brought down from times remote picture man crucified on a tree. Later, much of the true interpretation was lost because of the change from tree to cross.

It must be understood that the *two nervous systems constitute the living physiological trees* upon which each and every human being is crucified, for through them all of the functions of the body are carried on. They register in themselves, the kind of life each person lives, for every thought reacts instantly on them. The brain and nerves have a chemical formula, as do all parts of the body, and not until they are chemically perfect will absolute self control be possible. This is the reason why the story of Freemasonry is not relative to character building, *but to body building;* character will take care of itself when the brain cells are chemically perfect.

On page 167 of Part 1 of the *Secret Doctrine,* Madam Blavatsky quotes the following: "*Lead the life necessary* for the acquisition of such knowledge and powers, and Wisdom will come to you naturally." As the Sun is exalted in Aries and the Moon in Taurus, neither one, the same writer informs us, can accomplish anything in the great work without Mercury, who truly is the messenger of the gods, the mind-fluid, the bearer or *carrier* of light or electricity.

The cerebro-spinal system is the generator and carrier of physio-chemical electricity, which is energy or life. This explains why Mercury is associated with Gemini as its ruler, meaning that all the activities with which this sign and house have to do are of a *Mercurial nature,* and must thus be interpreted.

The different rates of vibration by means of which all Nature's work is accomplished have received the names of planets, in order that humanity may study them and the effects they produce, not only in nature, but in the human body. Metaphysically, Mercury is mind; physiologically, the cerebro-spinal system—the nerves; chemically it is quicksilver, an oily or fatty substance, the *argentum vivum* or living *philosophical silver,* for we learn that the true interpretation of *quick* is *living.*

The root of the word Mercury is the Latin word *merx,* meaning *goods* or merchandise, and when the various offices and attributes ascribed to "him" are analyzed, a vast treasure house of information is available.

In ancient times this god was identified as the Greek Hermes, son of Jupiter and Maia. He was the messenger of the gods, the inventor of the lyre, god of oratory, conductor of the souls of the dead to the lower world, and patron (father) of merchants and *thieves.*

As messenger, Mercury (mind and the sensory nerves) utilizes the electrical energy of thought and the subtle nerve fluids created by Father Jupiter, the giver of all good things. In action he may do this positively and hence beneficially, or negatively and destructively. In any case Mercury stands for *merchandise, wares or goods,* utilized in commerce or exchange by the mind in the body. As god of oratory he refers to the mental power necessary to become a good speaker, one who voices truth.

The reference to the lyre is concerned with a very mysterious organ in the brain having that name and which is the real source of the singing voice. It is the positive pole, while the negative is the place where sound is emitted, or the vocal cords in the throat.

The explanation of Mercury as *father* of merchants and thieves is the same as that given above. Mind, the father of thought, can actually rob the body by becoming the prodigal son as the Bible states, and wasting its substance or merchandise in riotous living.

The brain *esse* and thought power or electricity constitute the true merchandise of every human body and the *great work* is to perfect it so that it will be able to attract the highest form of ether (Akasha) into the body. We become thieves when we make no effort to do this, stealing not only from ourselves, but from others as well. To rob another or one's self of this most precious merchandise is truly the *sin against the Holy Ghost.*

In the Scorpio division of the zodiac, astrology gives us complete information relative to thieving. The body is the rightful owner of all that is created in it and when this sentence is understood, the Biblical statement relative to "inheriting the earth" will at last become clear. To inherit means *to hold possession of.*

Death is the separation of Spirit from the body—there is insufficient material for it to work with or function through, its *piece of real estate is of poor quality,* its mineral or chemical formula is imperfect, so much so that it can not support life. Hence it leaves.

When the chemical formula created by the Divine Chemist for the perfect man is complied with, then indeed will the great work have been accomplished.

The cerebro-spinal substance is thought material, creative *esse,* manna, elixir of life, the ambrosia of the gods, the Gold of Ophir and the treasure of the Kingdom of Heaven, which becomes *argentum vivum*—quick or living silver, in the human body.

And thus we find the true interpretation of merchandise perverted along with everything else, for the words Mercury and mind are derived from the same root. Our minds must have *goods* with which and through which to *express.* The old slang phrase "you haven't got the goods" is accurate even though it can not be termed "attic wisdom," delicate wit.

As the mind (Mercury) can be capable of recognizing facts or their absence while surrounded by a mass of mental rubbish in the literature of today, or of any age, even so is the *chemical* Mercury endowed with the same power. It is an amalgam, and can separate gold and silver from other ores—truly releasing them from their bondage with impurities. It is also a solvent of metals. Its work in nature is analogous with that of the human body.

Again, we have another and perfect correspondence in the thermometer and the barometer, whose tubes are filled with mercury which measures air temperature and pressure. Mercury expands and rises in the tube under the influence of heat vibrations. It was invented and named by man for the simple reason that it was patterned from his own spinal canal which contains living (quick) silver. The lower or negative bulb is the sacral (sacred) ganglia, the upper and positive being the cerebrum.

Another mechanical device patterned from the spinal canal is the syringe, the Latin word for which is *syrinx*. One end is attached to a *source* of *supply*, the cerebrum, and pressure applied to a bulb at the lower end releases the fluid. Even so in the human body Euphrates, the River of God, is robbed of the Water of Life.

Gemini is a *neutral* sign, and the three others, Virgo, Sagittarius, and Pisces, constitute the neutral, harmonious, or as I have named it, the purification cross. It has been understood by most students of astrology that beginning with Aries as positive and masculine, every alternate sign is feminine. But I have found it much more satisfactory and very illuminating to consider every third sign as neuter. When the fact is recalled that there are neuter planets it is only logical to differentiate the signs in the same way, and I wish to make the emphatic statement that the true astrological story will never become clear unless the four signs above mentioned are studied from this viewpoint.

The information which actually proves this to be true can be obtained by studying the nature and use of the four mineral salts which Dr. Carey allocated with them, namely: Kali mur, Silicea, Kali sulph and Ferrum phos. After carefully studying every point in each of the twelve chapters you will readily see on reconsidering the information given relative to the purification cross, that the amazing story it tells is none other than that of purity, harmony, and perfection, and therefore is neuter.

In his *Dictionary of Sacred Language of All Scriptures and Myths,* G. A. Gaskell says of Gemini: "A symbol of the third period of the cycle of life. The 'twins' signifying the higher and lower selves, or the Individuality and Personality on the mental plane. These are the two centers of consciousness in the soul for the higher and lower activities. In the constellation Gemini are the two stars Castor and Pollux, which are symbols of the personality and the individuality, in accordance with the story of the Dioscuri."

While the above definition is one of the best we have had, it is rather misleading in the light which physiology throws on it. There is really but *one* self, and that is the Spirit, the individual.

When the physical vehicle, the brain, is *chemically perfect,* then Spirit, the individuality, manifests as such unhampered. Its manifestation is limited and colored by the imperfect vehicle in and through which it endeavors to function. It is cramped, chaotic and spasmodic. It harms the body and injures others. This, in its various and varied manifestations, we term personality or lower mind. A concrete example of this is the difference between the vibrations produced by a perfect musical instrument and one dilapidated and utterly incapable of producing anything but discordant sounds. Both keyboards are manipulated by a gifted artist, the Spirit.

Mr. Gaskell quotes from Smith's *Classical Dictionary* relative to Dioscuri, the Twins, or Castor and Pollux, the two principal stars of Gemini. "They were the sons of Leda. Pollux and Helen only were children of Zeus, and Castor was the son of Tyndareus, also the daughter Clytemnestra." The fact that their mother was mortal makes them half-human, half-divine, and emphasizes the dual nature of the brothers.

The key to the real meaning of Castor and Pollux is in their etymology. Castor is derived from the Latin word *castus,* meaning pure, spotless, abstinence from sensual pleasure, chastity; while Pollux means to defile or pollute.

Thus Spirit utilizes the wares of the body or physical merchandise in perfecting it, and in making it spotless and pure. If the substance of the body is otherwise employed it defiles and pollutes. It is needless to say that the great majority of human beings come under the negative interpretation of Gemini. They are living in the lower mind. Gradually we will learn, through the suffering which inevitably results from misuse of the cerebro-spinal substance and electrical energy the great lesson which must be driven home to each one.

Madam Blavatsky says, on page 122 of Part II, S. D., "But the variant of the Leda allegory which has a direct reference to mystic man is found in Pindar only, with a slighter reference to it in Homeric hymns. Castor and Pollux are, in it, no longer the Dioscuri (of Appolodorus III, 10, 7) but become the highly significant symbol of the dual man, the Mortal and the Immortal. Not only this, but as will now be seen, they are also the symbol of the Third Race, and its transformation from the animal man into a God-man with only an animal body."

In the Greek allegory we read: "Pollux will either remain immortal, living eternally in Olympus; or, if he would *share* his brother's fate in all things, he must pass half his existence underground, and the other half in the golden, heavenly abodes.

This semi-immortality which is also to be shared by Castor is accepted by Pollux. *And thus the twin brothers live alternately, one during the day, and the other during the night.*"

In all esoteric writings references to day have to do with the higher mind, living the life which leads to illumination, while the night symbolizes the life of spiritual darkness.

Exoterically Gemini deals with short journeys, letters, mail carriers, messenger boys, telegrams, and methods of communication, children and relatives, all of those things which have underlying them the idea of threads (of thought), fibers, twigs, emanations—that which branches off from a parent.

In the Vedas the Twins are called "the Physicians of Heaven," and this probably refers to the influence of Mercury whose caduceus is, to this day, used as the official insignia of our army medical corps and among physicians generally.

The explanation of caduceus is one with which real students must become thoroughly conversant, as there is no one thing which so clearly links us up with, and at the same time gives us the physiological key to what we have termed religion.

The word is derived from the Latin cadus meaning a vessel or jar, also from the verb cado meaning to fall. A dead body is termed a cadaver and is derived from the same root. Webster's *Dictionary* informs us that caduceus is derived from cadere—meaning *to fall.* Summing up our various interpretations, we find that the human body is a vessel or jar containing the Water of Life. When a *living* body *falls lifeless,* it is termed a cadaver. It is a desert, a deserted place from which the Water of Life has departed.

The inner meaning of caduceus, then, is concerned with the fall of man. If this is the negative interpretation, since it obviously deals with destruction, then in its positive analysis we find the plan for the rise or ascent of man. In other words, this is his *return to the Father*—which consummation is the at-one-ment. As the word *ment* is derived from the Latin *mentis* meaning mind, right here we have the complete explanation, *one mind,* mind forever manifesting harmoniously, benevolently, the Christ Mind. The vehicle has been perfected, therefore there is no longer any antagonism, no mental chaos caused by mind—Spirit—*searching for material with which to manifest. The Father now has sufficient Mother (mater-material) with which to produce harmony.*

This brings us to our physiological allocation, and to the consideration of those parts assigned by the ancients to Gemini, the bronchial tubes and lungs, the shoulders, arms and hands. Some astrologers include the nerves, which is correct if one considers their basic formation as fibers, for other salts must be present in order that they may respond to either sensory or motor impulses. The sensory nerves must be studied under Aries, the motor under Leo. All nerves are essentially filaments. To the above list I add the skin and glands, especially, but it must be remembered that *all flesh* is constituted of fibers or filaments, so there is very little of the body which does not have flesh filaments for its basis. These constitute man's garment.

Referring to the interpretation of June from the Latin word meaning joint or joining, we must bear in mind the fact that the nerves and bronchial tubes constitute that part of the body which first *branches off,* after the formation of the cerebrum, cord and cerebellum.

The bronchi are the *branches* which convey air to the lung cells which we may term the twigs and leaves. Without lungs there would be no marriage in Cana of Galilee, no turning of the water of life into wine. For here is where oxygen, spirit or prana, combines with the blood for the arterial system, producing a combination of earth, air, fire and water of which so very, very little is really known. How amusing it becomes, then, to the student of synthesis, when he reads that this *supposed* turning of water into wine in an ancient city in times remote may today serve as a reason for even ministers of the gospel voting against prohibition. They say, "at least give us wine, for since Jesus himself made it to serve to wedding guests, it must be quite all right."

The word Cana means *reeds* in Hebrew, while Galilee means circle. Their combination clearly refers to the lungs and their function of combining air and blood, which is the *Water* of Life. It becomes the *wine* of life when Spirit is added.

Is it not now clear how utterly perverted the whole subject of beverages has become? A clean, healthy, pure body nourished by *this* brand of wine, the Wine of Life, makes for a clear intellect and a brain without cobwebs, which is the necessary qualification for understanding. Thus we have a good foundation for wisdom. On the other hand, a stomach filled with any other kind of wine results in a befuddled brain and the entire absence of reason. We have as yet so little sense that it behooves us not to drown it.

We link up again with Mercury as ruler of Gemini when we dwell on the fact that air, breath, oxygen and Spirit energize and make active the mind for which Mercury stands. The following quotation from the scriptures gives us a clear-cut picture of it: "There is a Spirit in man, and inspiration (inbreathing) of the Almighty *giveth* it *understanding.*" The *kind* of air and the amount we inbreathe depends on our physical chemistry, but that is another story and is told in Chapter Twelve. Our mental power is our metaphysical merchandise or money which *needs must have brain substance through which to manifest* and which constitutes our physiological coin—real treasure.

That astro-physio-chemical book, the Bible, also tells us that "The blood is the life of the flesh," for it carries not only nutriment to every cell, *but air as well.* Every corpuscle is a *water-air* creature, truly a salt water habitant, a human fish.

The eager, open-minded searcher for truth will find many questions relative to religion answered in these pages. This book, however, serves only as an introduction to others which will follow, and which will go still deeper into those subjects concerning which there is so much controversy today.

Truth is very simple and easily understood, when the brain is in good condition, for there is a clear and logical explanation for every problem. But the cerebral cells as well as all other cells must be supplied with the proper mineral food, and kept free from acid accumulations and poison. It is a *process,* like everything else, and time is required.

Before dealing with the mineral allocation, let us see if we can find anything in the physiological story which has been brought down through the ages. In C. A. Gaskell's *Classic Myths,* we note that the Three Fates (Clotho, Lachesis and Atrophos) were the *spinners* of the *thread* of *human destiny.* They were provided with shears with which to cut it off when they pleased, and, according to Hesiod, were the daughters of Night. Clotho held the *distaff,* Lachesis *spun* the *thread,* and Atrophos cut it off when it was ended.

In Funk & Wagnall's *New Standard Dictionary* we are informed that the Fates dwelt in the deep abyss of Demogorgon, and with unwearied fingers *drew out the threads of life.* Demogorgon was said to be the genius of the soil or earth, fabled to be the *life and substance of plants.* He was depicted as a little old man covered with moss who lived underground.

Gemini is the branching-off month or period of the year, as has been heretofore explained. It has to do, in utero, with the branching-off of the nerves from the head, to form the body. Thus it does not require much imagination to see that the story of the Three Fates is concerned with the three decans of Gemini. The distaff refers to the base of the brain, where seventy-five per cent of the nerves of the head concentrate and cross, appearing to *wind* upon themselves. In some mythological pictures the thread is represented as first appearing at the feet of Jove and his heavenly spouse. Clotho, the *youngest* of the three fates is allocated with the first decan of the sign Gemini, and is holder of the distaff. Lachesis spins or draws out the thread, while Atrophos *divides* it so that it may form the great nerve branch in either leg.

While the interpretation of the story is that Atrophos cuts off the thread, much research into the etymology of the word *shear* reveals the fact that it also means "the parting or fork of the human body" hence the limbs. The nerves do not terminate at the end of the spine but continue to the end of the extremities, after *branching off.* It is also true that life ceases when *nerve action ends*. An archaic interpretation of *shear* is to make an incision or cleft.

It is also true that fate or destiny of each individual depends on the extent and degree to which the Spirit in man is able to control, direct and manifest the *threads of life* through the cerebro-spinal nervous system. The electricity of life truly flows through them.

The Three Fates were termed the Parcæ by the Romans, while the Greeks called them the Mœræ, meaning to divide, to apportion. Other interpretations are a tree-*shoot,* a cutting —a *lot* of anything. From this latter, no doubt, arose the idea of casting lots, or one's lot or fate—destiny. There is, then, every evidence, from its synthetic analysis, that the branching off of the nerves from the base of the brain, the formation of the air passages and the growth of blood vessels and arteries to form the torso and extremities must be studied under Gemini.

"In the astronomical story of Gemini we find that in the feet of the Twins, a brilliant white star named Almeisan or Al Maisan is described by Al Biruni as *winding,* as though the stars of this station were *winding* around each other, or curving from the central star. In Babylonia this star marked the tenth ecliptic constellation, Mash-mashu-sha-Risu, the Twins of the Shepherd, and may have been the Babylonian lunar mansion Khigalla, the *Canal*." This information is available in *Star Names and Their Meanings,* by Richard Hinckley Allen.

There is every evidence that the Canal represented by stars in the constellation of Gemini refers to the spinal canal.

"In the human body and blood, fibrin is distinguished from albumin and casein by its separation, in a solid state, into delicate *filaments* in any fluid in which it is dissolved, shortly after the fluid is taken from the organism. It is clearly shown by biochemistry that, without the inorganic salt potassium chloride, *no fibrin can be made;* and it is further shown that the normal amount of fibrin can not be held in proper solution in the blood without the proper balance of that cell-salt. Fibrin results from the union of certain fibrin-plastic substances (albuminoids), *but this union does not take place* in the *absence of the chloride of potash molecules.*

"In venous blood the fibrin amounts to three in 1000 parts. Arterial blood contains less, and lymph a still smaller amount.

In inflammatory exudations we find fibrin in the serous cavities—such as pleura and peritoneum—and on the mucous membrane, as in croup, diphtheria, catarrh, etc. In all inflammatory conditions, Ferrum phos (the Pisces salt) should be given with Kali mur, for iron particles carry oxygen which becomes deficient when the proper balance is disturbed by the outflow of fibrin. It is quite clear to my mind that fibrin is created or produced by the action of the chloride of potash, with the assistance of oxygen, on certain albuminoids." *Dr. Carey's Biochemic System.*

The definition of Fibrin is: "A whitish proteid from the blood and the serous fluids of the body. It is seen in elastic fibrillar masses." It is not recognized as fibrin in the blood but as coagulum from which fibers or *filaments—threads*—are *spun.* The definition of fiber is "an elongated, *thread-like structure* of organic tissue."

Potassium chloride is the mineral sylvite termed in Latin, *sal digestivus,* the digestive salt. The word "digest" is derived from the Latin dis—apart, and gerere—to carry. Its meaning therefore is to *carry apart in different directions*, to separate, divide. It will be clearly seen what a significant allocation Dr. Carey made when he assigned to Gemini, the *branching-off sign* of the zodiac, this salt which has the power *to carry apart in different directions.* But it must be remembered that his allocations of the salts to the signs were made automatically, and he did not (in this incarnation, at least) check up with esoteric astrology. It is evident, however, that he recalled, from a past incarnation these accurate chemical correspondences.

As we study anatomy and physiology, it is evident that with the exception of the bones, fibrin is necessary in the formation of the nerves, ligaments, veins, skin, tissue—in fact, all *flesh.* From a deep realization of this fact, I have named potassium chloride *the spinning salt,* for it *spins the threads from which the seamless garment of flesh is woven.*

Let us refer to Mercury as the Messenger of the Gods, or ruling powers from Mt. Olympus, the cerebrum. Let us picture for ourselves the character of the message that Mercury held in itself from the past. From what pattern did it reconstruct the garment which serves in this incarnation? What is the texture of our Mercury—what of the garments commonly known as mind and body? Is the mind capable of boring like a gimlet into a subject, revealing hidden treasures of truth?

Is it able to stand, towering like an impregnable fortress of strength against the blows of adversity and sorrow which sooner or later come to test each one of us? Do we find *reason* tottering and mental confusion resulting when difficult situations arise? Are we fearful and panicky, lonely, homesick and discouraged? Are we stiff, lame and rheumatic as the years go by? Do we find some symptom more or less constantly manifesting, until, finally, there is no mental or physical rest, and life becomes merely a painful existence, death at last coming as a blessed relief?

Such, then, is the Mercury we brought with us into incarnation. It was *intended* by the Great Chemist to be *argentum vivum* or *living* silver, but we were prodigal sons in our past incarnations; and in the depths to which we descended this silver became polluted. That which is so quick to attract to itself became an amalgum which indeed chained us to the *mire* and *filth* of earth.

Mercury's wings seem to have been broken. Instead of soaring into the higher realm of mind which is the result of the *expansion* of a purified and *living* silver in the spinal canal (our physiological thermometer and barometer), Mercury has been coagulated with lead by Saturn. Heavy, instead of light, are those winged feet. Mind (Mercury) functions very, very slowly and crudely (Saturn) and we drag ourselves along as though weighted down with *lead,* Saturn's allocating metal. Is it strange, then, that lead coagulates mercury, and is the only metal having the power to do so?

What is the process whereby we may free our mercury from the burden of impurities it bears—*both* the tangible, physical mercury and the intangible, abstract Mercury of mind? By exactly the same process used by the chemist—by raising its vibrations and *vaporizing* it. Remember—our Mercury is a true creature of the *air*—the *height* is its *home.* Gemini is an air sign. Mercury originated in Aries, it was GOLD there, but in the LOWER regions it became ARGENTUM VIVUM, living silver or the WATER OF LIFE.

Its passage-way, the spinal canal, is both the River Euphrates and the Jordan. By this process of vaporization all incumbrances fall away. In metallurgy we are informed that when minute quantities of either gold or silver can not be extracted from a mass, they are mixed with mercury, to which the precious particles are attracted. It *picks up* just as the mind does, either that which is valuable or valueless. The mercury is separated and vaporized, and the gold or silver is released.

Thus we find that Mercury is a symbol of Mind, free at last of all that would prevent its soaring into those realms where only pure Spirit is at home. When the brain is at last completely purified and perfected, which means that it is formed of the *ultimate chemical atoms*, this will be possible. Why do we delay this Divine Messenger on his journey back to Olympus? Obviously because we have not known that road or the *direction* in which it lies. Perhaps until recently we had not wished to journey; or dreamed, ever so vaguely, of the golden glory and the peace beyond words to be found at the journey's end.

And so, once more, let us take up the *threads* of Gemini and review. again, the ancient story of the Caduceus of Mercury. Although it is used as the symbol of healing by the American and British Medical Corps, how many physicians among them know of its immemorial metaphysical and physiological tradition? About as many as those having knowledge of the real interpretation of Freemasonry, of Astrology or Christianity.

A cut made from a photograph of a beautiful bronze Mercury accompanies this article, in order that it may be studied in connection with it.

Mercury, as has been explained, means mind, also that through which mind expresses in the physical body, namely, the cerebro-spinal system or semi-fluidic material which constitutes *soul*. Spirit must have a medium through which to impress the dense physical atoms. It is our psyche, the tender mother substance which can be more easily manipulated. Spirit is not soul, neither is soul Spirit; but how often we find these terms used interchangeably. They should not be. The Scriptures state that body, soul and Spirit exist, the first two being detachable and subject to dissolution.

Mercury, poised on winged feet on the lips of Gaia or Mother Earth, the right arm lifted and forefinger pointed directly overhead, is crowned with a winged hat. In the left hand and grasped by a handle extending from the middle pole or wand, is the caduceus, resting against the forearm and in the hollow made by the elbow. A very short distance from the top of this wand are two wings. Twined around the pole with their bodies meeting and crossing at four points are two serpents, their heads turned inward and toward it.

Study carefully the position in which the caduceus is held. Ordinarily the natural way of holding a thing is outward or forward a little away from the body. The reader will note that the arm is *forced backward* and away from the body, instead, an unnatural and awkward position.

This was planned as a means of attracting one's attention to its *relation* to the *back* of Mercury, for the wand is the *spine,* and we find this fact expressed in Hindu literature as the *stick of Brahm.* Brahmarhandra (Spirit or *the Bee*) enters the body through the Door of Brahm (suture in the skull) and leans on his *stick.* The *backbone* is the *support* of the body, and there is much more to this statement than appears on the surface, for does not lack of *character* mean a *weak back bone?* In terms of Masonry it certainly does, in spite of the French pronunciation of the Pass-word. In Hebraic literature the back bone is the Rod of Moses. Thus we learn that the same story, the fall and rise of man, is universal among all nations and peoples.

The meaning of spine is *thorn,* and that is exactly what it looks like, the skull forming its head and the coccyx its point. As flesh is torn and bruised on contacting a thorn, *so does the point of our own individual thorn in the flesh* bleed us of the Water of Life and torture us to madness. (See Pisces). The spinal canal is humanity's Euphrates and its Jordan.

The wings on the hat of Mercury represent the two hemispheres of the brain, our *thinking cap.* The two serpents are symbolical of the right and left sympathetic systems, and correspond to the two *thieves* of the Bible story. For when life is lived negatively, they steal from us.

The winged pole of Mercury is the *Tree of Life,* while the serpents correspond to the *Tree of Knowledge of Good and Evil.* One is the sensory system, the other the motor, the latter planned to work in harmony with the former, *doing the work* pertaining to *motion.* Perverted—it becomes E-MOTION, *energy wasted, substance lost.*

All around us today we see its effect, humanity as a whole

floundering in chaos—a sea of emotion. Why was the symbol of the Lion allocated with Leo, away back in the morning of time? Why is it *the only beast of prey* symbol in the entire circle of the zodiac? Because it has to do with the process of SELF-CONTROL, the taming of the beast in man, the EMOTIONS WHICH TEAR US TO PIECES AND CONSUME US. Bear this in mind when reading the chapter dealing with Leo and note its interesting chemical explanation.

The heads of the two thieves and the heads of the serpents *cross* or are *crucified at the base of the brain*—the cerebellum —Taurus. (See previous lesson). The four points of contact are important centers *within* the canal.

Lest there be any to whom the foregoing explanation is not yet clear, let it be further stated, that under the winged hat is the nectar and ambrosia of the gods—*that which nourishes.* It is the electricity of life which runs the body, and with which we think. It forms the protoplasmic basis of *all* the fluids of the body *including the pro-creative.* This fact will ere long be scientifically accepted. See Lesson Ten, Capricorn, for further information relative to this statement.

No wonder then, that Mercury was said to be a patron of merchants and thieves, the former supposed (devoid of perversion) to deal legitimately with *goods,* the latter taken by stealth, *without reimbursing.* Here we note the distinction between the positive and the negative mind, one functioning constructively, the other destructively. As the positive mind, Mercury expands under the rapid vibrations (heat) of Spirit; as the negative, he is cold, congealed—stagnant.

In the study of Schuessler's *Biochemic System,* as set forth by Dr. Carey and other writers, we note how the symptoms arising from deficient Kali mur check with the last statement of the foregoing paragraph, for the *spinning* process stops, the threads thicken, tangle; and the parts feel enlarged, congested, swollen. The thread or fiber takes up too much room. This is the true explanation for swellings, glandular enlargements, etc., etc.

Thick blood or embolus results from need of this salt, causing the heart to work harder, as more energy is required to circulate the blood. Biochemistry states that Kali mur is a specific for *children's* diseases, for they have to do with disturbances in the fibrin, and are usually accompanied by exudations through the skin, as in scarlet fever, measles, chickenpox, or in swollen glands, and throat irritation such as diphtheria, tonsilitis, mumps, etc. And to the degree in which iron or Ferrum phos (the *squaring* Pisces salt) is deficient, fever will manifest.

Inflammatory rheumatism has to do with the fibers or threads of flesh deficient in this Gemini salt, and is augmented by the need for more oxygen due to iron deficiency. The brain becomes congested because the blood is thick and circulation slow, causing it to feel dull and heavy. One is unable to think clearly. The *thread* of thought is broken. It must be repeated that the *basis* of all fibrin is Kali mur; but, as there are many different uses for it, the fibers are differentiated by the addition of other minerals, or inorganic salts. *When these salts are put together—combined with the protoplasm formed by the cerebrum, they become organic*—which merely means *put together—as bricks with mortar.*

Joseph of the Bible story is the Mercury of astrology. Is not his coat of many colors symbolical of the countless shades and hues of *thought?* The mental as well as the physical garment is SEAMLESS. Religion, so absolutely and entirely perverted down the ages, begins now to blossom forth as a new and wondrous story, and we realize at last that each individual has his own *Tree of Life,* his own Garden of Eden. No one but himself can destroy that tree. No one but himself can cultivate it or supply it with nutriment, so that in time it may bear twelve kinds of *perfect* fruit (the twelve divisions of the body). This process means THE OVER-COMING OF DEATH. Barring accidents, no one dies except from dis-ease, and even the former will be done away with as the cerebral centers having to do with intuition are perfected, for one will then be forewarned.

It is very interesting to note that both Castor and Pollux have dual and seemingly contradictory interpretations. For while it is a fact that Castor is derived from castus, meaning pure, while Pollux means to taint or pollute, yet, at the same time when we analyze the Latin derivation, polluere, (literally meaning *to wash forth*) we divide the word into POLL and LUX. Here we have the *basis* of another interpretation. Poll is the Middle English word for top of the head, which physiologically is the *source of light* or understanding, while *lux* means light. We have here the source of the compound word HEAD-LIGHT. It is the light of the higher understanding which enables us to *become purified*.

The word *cast* means to throw violently, to cast off, to shed, etc. It also means to expurge. This conglomeration of dual meanings for both Castor and Pollux substantiates the statement that each alternately goes to a higher vibration (living in heaven one day) and to a lower (living in the earth the next day).

When the information embodied in the sign Gemini is acquired, humanity will strive more and more to live positively, creatively and no longer destructively, thus dividing its merchandise, the bread which comes down from heaven daily TO FEED it. Mercury, the Great Physician, will at last fulfill his divine mission, which is *to heal all diseases*. Do not become confused by this statement and say, "Yes, I know that mind can heal," and forget the fact that on the *mater-ial* plane of expression the *cerebro-spinal system is Mercury also*. One can not get along without the other. BOTH require sustenance—food corresponding to their own individual needs.

Other symptoms arising from lack of this salt are: hawking of thick, white mucus; sick headache from sluggish liver—want of bile; thick, white mucus from the eyes; granulated eyelids; earache, with swelling of glands and gray or white-furred tongue; catarrhal condition of the middle ear, cracking noises; dullness of hearing from throat affections or swelling of the middle ear; stuffy colds in the head; thick, white discharge from the throat; catarrh; faceache from swelling of gums or cheek; canker of the mouth; ulcerated sore throat (this salt is a specific for all throat troubles when used with Nat. mur and Ferrum phos); mumps; poor appetite from sluggish liver; gastritis; constipation; typhoid; smallpox; cancer; peritonitis; cystitis; gonorrhea; syphilis; leucorrhea, when discharge is thick and white; pneumonia; pleurisy; coughs; embolism (thick blood); poor circulation; rheumatism; all swellings; rheumatism of the joints; chief remedy in epilepsy; acne; boils; chronic swelling of the feet and legs; creaking of the muscles; all swellings; eczema, with white, floury scales; erysipelas; children's diseases; glandular swellings; typhoid and typhus fever; rheumatic fever. Pains are increased and aggravated by motion.

Faith without *works* is *dead,* and in all work *material* is required. We can *never* separate ourselves from this fact, for it is purely scientific. It is the basis for the following statement taken from the ninth chapter and the twelfth verse of Matthew:

"THEY THAT BE WHOLE NEED NOT A PHYSICIAN."

and again,

"PHYSICIAN, HEAL THYSELF."

Chapter IV

THE ANALYSIS AND SYNTHESIS OF CANCER AND CALCIUM FLUORIDE

"I am constant as the northern star,
Of whose true-fix'd and resting quality
There is no fellow in the firmament.
The skies are painted with unnumber'd sparks;
They are all fire, and every one doth shine;
But there's but one in all doth hold his place."
—*Shakespeare.*

WHEN the Sun reaches its highest northern limit and begins to go backward toward the south, it is transiting the constellation of Cancer, the crab, which is the fourth sign of the zodiac; and, indeed, like the crustacean whose name it bears, its return is sideways. Its journey begins approximately June 21, and continues until July 22. Physiologically it pertains to the breast, stomach and spleen, and governs expansion and contraction, elasticity and tenacity. It is ruled by the Moon whose expansive and contractile nature is expressed by the terms waxing and waning, and is the most fertile or productive of the twelve zodiacal signs. As this silver orb is mistress of the night, so Nature's most occult work—THAT OF THE FORMATION AND FERTILIZATION OF SEED—is carried on under cover of darkness and with the utmost secrecy.

In ancient lore, Cancer is termed the house of physical conception, while Capricorn, the opposite sign, is concerned with *Spiritual* conception. Porphyry tells us that "the Egyptians employed every year a talisman in remembrance of the world; at the summer solstice (when the Sun is in Cancer) they marked their houses, flocks and trees with red, supposing that on that day the whole world had been set on fire."

It was also at the same period that they celebrated the Pyrrhic (fire) dance. "And," says Olney, "this illustrates the origin of purification by fire and water; for, having denominated the tropic of Cancer, 'Gate of Heaven and of heat or celestial fire,' and that of Capricorn, 'Gate of deluge or of water,' it was imagined THAT THE SPIRITS OR SOULS WHO PASSED THROUGH THESE GATES, ON THEIR WAY TO AND FROM HEAVEN, WERE *SCORCHED* OR *BATHED* (italics mine); hence the baptism of Mithra, and the passage through the flames, observed throughout the East."

Cancer pertains to fluids, and is said by students of astrology to be one of the signs of the water triplicity. In my personal research work into this noble science, I have been able to glean many new (to this age only) and startling facts by interpreting the signs Pisces, Scorpio and Cancer as *fluidic.* This suggestion may be illustrated by the following: the fluids of Cancer are the mother's milk (breast); the chyle (digested food elements of the stomach); and the white corpuscles (spleen). All have to do with nutrition. Therefore none of them *represent* water, although they contain more or less of it. The mother's milk nourishes the child, chyle furnishes food for the *blood corpuscles to which the spleen gives birth.* In another book soon to be published, entitled *New Facts About the Glands,* THE REAL FUNCTION OF THE SPLEEN will be revealed for the first time, I believe, in *this* age. Without astrology its secret would not have been discovered.

Fecundity means to be *capable* of bearing fruit, or the ability to produce. But *this does not mean exclusively impregnation of ova.* A far greater mystery than this awaits unveiling.

A most important point must be constantly emphasized—that each sign of the zodiac as well as each planet HAS ONE BASIC INTERPRETATION which must instantly be recalled whenever a sign or planet is considered. This will give a solid foundation on which and from which to build up one's analysis. For the most part, I regret to say, these have not heretofore been obtainable from works on astrology as they had not been discovered. Allocation, analysis and synthesis reveal them.

Max Müller informs us that Plato had much the same interpretation of Cancer and Capricorn as the Egyptians, in that he termed them "the two mouths, the former *through which souls descend,* the latter *through which they ascend.*" When this chapter and the one on Capricorn have been thoroughly digested by the readers of this book they will understand THE REAL STORY THAT ASTROLOGY TELLS. THAT STORY CONCERNS THE UNDERSTANDING, PURIFICATION, MASTERY AND PERFECTION OF THE HUMAN BODY and NOTHING ELSE.

To accomplish this is to become one with all that is, hence to know and understand the Universe, for Gad has overcome at last. "Be ye *perfect* even as your Father in heaven is perfect." The names of the months, their derivation, the etymology of the signs, the analysis of the symbols, and the planetary interpretations, *all* actually trumpet forth their clarion call to humanity freely to help themselves to this information.

While Max Müller did not enlarge on the statement he made or analyze it in any way, nevertheless therein lies the key to a great mystery which has been safely hidden for æon upon æon. "The 'Sons of God,' became the 'fallen angels' after perceiving that the daughters of men were fair," says Madam Blavatsky, in *The Secret Doctrine*.

To understand the foregoing statement it will be necessary to re-read the chapter on Aries, the cerebrum, the *Most High*, the House of Gad or God, THE HOUSE OF SPIRITUAL SEED-ESSE. It will dawn on you that Seed-Esse is the *substance* of "The Sons of God," ITS CREATION, ITS PROGENY. That which Cancer manifests is of the MOTHER nature, the fluidic, which is truly the *Daughter of Earth*, as well as *Mother*.

Returning to the mystery we are considering, *of what do these souls which descend consist?* Remember our fruitful Taurus, *the earth full of seeds*, made alive and fed by the manna or bread from heaven—Aries. These are the souls—in very truth the NUCLEI with which the heavenly Crab—Cancer—is daily, hourly, yes, minute by minute, fed. Ever tirelessly reaching out its claws, ceaselessly moving up, down and sideways, it seizes upon each microscopic Spirit (soul-seed) and sweeps it into its mouth-like stomach. For this crustacean, the crab, uniquely has its teeth in that organ.

As the basic idea back of fertility is that of SEED, and as we have already proved that Aries has to do with *Spiritual Seed*, or *Seed Essence*, we have arrived at the SQUARE, for Cancer is ninety degrees from Aries.

Something has consummated; a work has been done; and

we must now measure it. Aries and Cancer must WORK ON THE SQUARE with each other. In plain words, CONCEPTION HAS TAKEN PLACE. The word conception is derived from the Latin *concipio* and literally means, to *take together*, to *hold together.* Consider, now, is not that what the Crab does? It is impossible to make it loosen its hold. Even though the leg be torn from the body, its claw will not relax. *There* is *tenacity* for you. Memory is tenacity of *thought,* and it is well known by astrologers that the fluid-like substance which Cancer represents is also associated with the *brain.* Here again we link up with the seed essence, the *esse* or substance of *being*—of Aries.

It is well to state at this point even though we have not yet considered the chemical side of Cancer, that DEFICIENCY IN CALCIUM FLUORIDE CAUSES ONE TO BE *FORGETFUL.* THE THREADS OR FILAMENTS OF THOUGHT ARE *NOT* ELASTIC. Kali mur builds or fashions these threads, but Calcium fluoride must be blended with and into them to make them ELASTIC and capable of expanding and contracting. This is a true chemical statement and *physiologically* correct as well. Get out your Gray's Anatomy and read about the *webs* in your brain, scientifically termed the Arachnoid (spider) membrane interposed between the *pia mater* and the *dura mater* of the brain and cord.

It is well known that the brain disease termed lunacy becomes intensified during certain periods of the moon; and, as Luna is the ancient name of the moon, we now have the key to this symptom. The brain fluid or ocean of the Great Mother is disturbed, the spider-like membranes are starved.

The symbol for the sign Cancer has never been explained, but the two tiny, hook-like characters lying parallel to each other but with the hook ends at opposite corners are really the Hebrew letter YOD. As yod is the tenth in the Jewish alphabet it stands for that which is *complete,* and, as it is the smallest of all letters in that language, it allocates with SEED or LIFE GERM, *which is the most minute cell capable of reproduction.* It corresponds to I, Y and J in English. *Gray's Anatomy* states that the perfected life germ is no larger than the *dot* over the letter I.

Even Papus, who is one of our very best authorities on the Kabbala, seems unaware of the wonderful physiological interpretation which throws a great flood of light on the Tarot. The very first interpretation and the initial key to all occult writings brought down through the ages is PHYSIOLOGICAL. When this is understood, the other six keys will turn much more easily in the lock of *truth*.

It is well to state at this point that some of the modern writers on the Kabbala have confused and perverted it. *Since the mind functions through the brain*, it is obvious that the physiological *key* is the first and most important. *The six are automatically perfected when the physiological work is accomplished* and not otherwise. The study of physiology and chemistry will alone enable us to live metaphysically.

In *Sepher Yetzirah* or *The Book of Creation*, we find this statement relative to the number ten: "Ten are the numbers of the ineffable Sephiroth, ten and not nine, ten and not eleven.

"Learn this wisdom, and be wise in the understanding of it, investigate these numbers, and draw knowledge from them, FIX THE *DESIGN* IN ITS PURITY, and pass from it to its Creator seated on his throne." The *design* of anything in nature is the seed, for in it is hidden the prototype.

A study of the tenth card of the Tarot reveals the fact that it has to do with force potential in its manifestation, the union of male and female in nature. Astronomically it corresponds with the zodiacal sign Virgo, in that it is the universal or COSMIC MOTHER, although the potential force itself—fecundity—is represented by the Moon. Both stand for the Virgin, the immaculate Mother, for remember *there is no lust connected with the coming together of the two yods, the male and female germ cells* IN EACH INDIVIDUAL BODY, for *such has wholly to do with the* BIRTH OF CORPUSCLES. In plainer words the cells of the body can not be reproduced unless this takes place. Virgin means pure, unadulterated, hence *no deficiency in the natural or original material.*

Therefore the great secret hidden in the sign Cancer is that of NATURE'S POWER TO REPRODUCE, otherwise the body would not be able to RECREATE ITSELF DAILY. Again I repeat that it has to do—not with procreative germs, but with the ceaseless *formation of corpuscles within the spleen*. In so far as I am aware, this information has not previously been available in this incarnation. Deep meditation on the esoteric meanings of the zodiacal signs is the only method whereby information relative to occult physiology may be obtained. Astrology alone is the treasure house of arcane knowledge.

It has been my very good fortune to obtain "*Researches into the Primitive Constellations of the Greeks, Phœnicians, and Babylonians,*" by Robert Brown, F.S.A. In this book I have found conclusive proof that my statement that Cancer is the sign related to the physiological functions having to do with the *implanting* of the *nucleus* or SPIRITUAL SEED *within* and the *formation of each corpuscle of the body* is true. EROS or heavenly sprite, the spark or flame of life thrown off from the forge of Vulcan—in other words descending from its abode in higher realms into Aries, the cerebrum—is carried into the middle decan of Cancer, the spleen, deep within its center. Here, like the crab, it *reaches out* from all sides of itself and seizes upon all sorts of materials which may be said to represent every degree and rate of vibration associated with the circumference of its reach, for it is able to take *from all directions.* Every kind of building material is required to form a *seed,* for in itself it is a consensus of all that exists.

The proof referred to above is that on an old Euphratean Planisphere representing the Babylonian creation scheme, the sign Cancer is named Su-kulna or "THE SEIZER OF THE SEED," also "Workmen of the River-bed and Ship of the Canal of Heaven." The Canal of heaven in astrology is the Milky Way. And to enlarge on this interpretation, reviewing the statement made heretofore, CANCER, THE CRAB, SEIZES THE NUCLEI OR ELECTRIC SEED—SPIRITS ENGENDERED IN ARIES—AND FORMS CORPUSCLES WHICH ARE MINIATURE CRABS.

Again, it is by means of these corpuscles that the human body is kept alive, and daily recreated. No apology is made for this repetition, for it is necessary in order to clarify this most important and mysterious process. The corpuscle is the boat or ark containing the DIVINE GERM—or MOSES.

As the nucleus in the corpuscle is HIGH BORN, having been created or precipitated in Aries, the cerebrum, *the body built around it,* as the corpuscle is perfected in the spleen, can well be termed an *enclosure.* Therefore the following quotation from "*Primitive Constellations,*" by Robert Brown contributes still further proof of the correctness of my discovery:

"The Pole Star is Dugga-Kaga-gilgatil. The primary meaning of *gil,* as is also shown by the form of the cuneiform ideograph, is *'an enclosure.' Til* means *'life.'* DUGGA-GILGATIL means 'THE HIGH-ONE-OF-THE-ENCLOSURE-OF-LIFE,' and there is much reason to believe that 'the Enclosure-of-Life' of which the Pole-star was lord, is the famous 'Oblong' formed by the four stars in the pan of the Little Bear, familiarly termed 'the little dipper.' This particular Oblong, and the connection between Oblongs and the Quarters or 'Divisions' (Regiones) of the heavens, have been always referred to; and, as has been noticed, the modern votaries of Polaris mark out an 'oblong space' the side walls of which 'run from north to south,' so that it fronts the Pole-star in the same manner as the celestial oblong of Ursa Minor fronts the star *a* Draconis. Here, as so frequently, terrestrial ritual is based upon, and is a 'pattern' of 'things in the heavens.' "

"IT IS NATURAL TO SUPPOSE THAT THERE IS SOME SPECIAL PLACE IN THE UNIVERSE WHICH IS, IN AN OCCULT AND PECULIAR MANNER, THE ABODE OF THE ESSENCE AND SPIRIT OF LIFE; and it is equally natural to locate this spot in the heights of the north, ever crowned by the unsinking stars."

"A study of the interpretation of the Egyptian scarabeus which is this nation's symbol for Cancer, and of the tortoise of Indian Astrology, furnishes us with further proof. The former, or Egyptian beetle, lays its egg in a ball of excrement, and may be seen on sandy slopes in hot sunshine, compacting the pellet by pushing it *backward* up hill with its hind legs and allowing it to roll down again, eventually reaching a place of deposit. Whatever the Egyptians understood by its actions, they compared its pellet to the globe of the sun, as it rolled across the sky. The scarabeus was much used in Egyptian religions, appearing sometimes with outstretched wings or WITH A *RAM'S* HEAD AND HORNS AS THE VIVIFYING SOUL."

Here we note additional proof of and reference to the close association of Aries and Cancer, or their mutual work "on the square" represented by the distance between them, or the angle of ninety degrees.

In many works we find reference to Aries, Cancer, Libra and Capricorn, the signs constituting the cardinal or *creative* cross, as "the gates of heaven," for they include the solstices and equinoxes. Physiologically these signs have to do with *creative* functions, as explained heretofore.

In *Smith's Bible Dictionary* (1915, D. Appleton & Co.), we find a curious reference to the sign Cancer as Tammuz, the name given in ancient Hebrew literature to the Sun when in this sign. " 'Ezekiel, the prophet, as he sat in his *house* surrounded by the elders of Judah, was transported in spirit to the far distant temple at Jerusalem (Aries). The hand of the Lord God was upon him, and led him to the door of the *gate of the House of Jehovah, which was toward the north* (Cancer); and beheld there the women sitting, weeping for Tammuz.' Jerome, in his note on Ez. 8:14, adds that, according to the Gentile fable, *Tammuz had been slain in June.*"

This is descriptive of the heat of the Sun decreasing (slain) by its ceasing to be in a vertical position overhead. Smith also states that Tammuz may be a name of Adonis, the Sun-god. Why, I ask, are these references made in Jewish literature to supposed heathen deities? Is it not because they pertain to the same thing? And indeed, this is true of *all* sacred literature.

Additional proof of the most important phase of creation accomplished by means of the combined efforts of Aries, contributing the spiritual or creative germ (seed), and Cancer, using the seed as a nucleus and building around it the ocean of semi-fluidic substance necessary for its material form, is furnished by a study of the constellations in the three decans of Cancer.

In the first ten degrees we find Ursa Minor, the Little Bear, or, in ancient astrological lore, THE LESSER SHEEP-FOLD. It is commonly known as the Little Dipper, the end star of the handle being North Star, Polaris.

Spencer, in his Færie Queen, refers to it as the Wagoner, and again as a timepiece. He refers to Polaris as a guide:

> "By this the northern wagoner had set
> His sevenfold teme behind the steadfast starre
> That was in ocean waves never yet wet,
> But firme is fixt, and sendith light from farre
> To all that in the wide deep wandering arre."

"In the early days of Greek navigation it was used as a guide and was paralleled in the deserts of Arabia, through which travelers direct their course by the Bears in the same manner as is done at sea," says Richard Hinckley Allen in his *Star Names and Their Meanings.*

Mrs. Sigourney, in her poem, *The Stars,* writing of Polaris, describes:

> "The weary caravan, with chiming bells,
> Making strange music 'mid the desert sands,
> Guides by thy pillar'd fires its nightly march."

and Keats in his *Robin Hood:*

> "........the seven stars to light you,
> On the polar way to right you."

Richard Allen also says that "Delitzsch writes that even today the group of stars is known as a BIER in Syria; Flammarion attributing this title to the slow and solemn motion of the figure around the pole. This seems to have originated in Arabia; and from it comes the titles even now occasionally heard for the quadrangle stars—the BIER and the GREAT COFFIN. With the early Arab poets, these stars were an emblem of laziness."

Analyzing the above, it is clear that the charge of laziness coincides well with the slow movements of the crab, while the Arabian interpretation of Bier and Great Coffin is intimately related to Cancer's mysterious CREATION OF BODIES, the *miniature* ones or the corpuscles. The root of *corpus* means BODY. As the word coffin is derived from the Greek *kophinos,* meaning *basket* or *chest,* it is clear that it indeed does refer to the *enclosing* of a minute body (a nucleus from the cerebrum or Aries) within the casket or chest. This process consists of a network or delicate web formed in the BOSOM of Mother Nature. Thus within the spleen is formed the TRUE PHYSIOLOGICAL SEED (THE CORPUSCLES OF THE BODY). THE SPLEEN ALLOCATES WITH THE MIDDLE DECAN OF THIS SIGN.

Students may ask wherein lies the proof for the statement that the spleen pertains to the middle decan. It is to be found in the allocation of that gland with Saturn, according to ancient tradition. As Saturn's interpretation is always SEED, we have to find in the sign Cancer (because of the fact that the spleen is located close to the stomach) the place where the exact vibration of Saturn and Capricorn is located. This can be found by dividing each decan into four parts of two and one-half degrees each, and allocating them with the signs of the zodiac.

To explain to those not familiar with this process (which is not new, although I did not know it when I discovered and used it), the ancients had a separate zodiac for each *month,* which revealed much more, as it brought out each minute point in detail. Illustrating with Cancer, the first two and one-half degrees are strongly Cancerian. The next two and one-half are related to Leo, the next two and one-half to Virgo and with the degrees allocating with Libra, complete the first decan.

As Scorpio rules the first two degrees and one-half of this vibration, *this constitutes the explanation for the assignment of rulers to the decans.* Ultimately this is how we will slowly rediscover all astrological information; and, in doing so, obtain our proofs of its correctness.

Proceeding with the division of the middle decan of Cancer, the first two and one-half degrees allocates with Scorpio, next with Sagittarius and the following two and one-half degrees with Capricorn. As the *middle* decan of a sign is its *matrix,* naturally this would constitute the logical place for this deeply-hidden process. Here the Great Mother, brooding in darkness, the Womb of Nature, lays both her cosmic and physiological eggs—THE CORPUSCLES.

Before presenting still more proof from ancient writers, I wish again to call attention to the fact that I have not dealt with or referred to PROCREATIVE GERMS OR CORPUSCLES, for they are entirely different and must be considered under Scorpio. The particular function of the latter sign has to do with ANIMAL OR ANIMALIZED CORPUSCLES, this being another revelation which much research has uncovered, and WHICH CONSTITUTES IRREFUTABLE EVIDENCE OF THE ORIGINAL AND FUNDAMENTAL PURPOSE OF ASTROLOGY. At the same time it reveals the secret of LIFE, DEATH, and IMMORTALITY IN AND OF THE FLESH.

Returning to our study of the constellations in the decans, we find Ursa Major or the Great Bear associated with the wonderful Arcturus, the GUARDIAN AND KEEPER, and interpreted by the ancients as the GREATER SHEEPFOLD.

As a sheepfold is where sheep are *housed*, this constitutes another proof of the co-operation between these two "gates of heaven." Aries is the creator of the sheep or *nuclei*, the Spiritual germ-seeds; and Cancer, the place where these "sheep" are housed.

Arcturus is derived from two Greek derivatives, *arktos*, meaning bear, and *ouros*, keeper. A family of *crustaceans* is termed Arcturidæ. The word bear really has the same meaning as the verb *to bear*, bring forth, support, sustain. Therefore we note the idea of sustenance, which again allocates with the underlying idea of Cancer, the breast, stomach and spleen. Perhaps we now have a better understanding of what was really meant by the Biblical statement, "Feed my lambs," John 21:15. It should be interpreted physiologically. In other words, furnish the nuclei of your corpuscles with sufficient material so they will remain. Thereby is Spirit supported, or kept within the body.

Innumerable other proofs are available, but we have space for only a few more. When Egypt began to be influenced by Greece, we find this constellation regarded as the *CAR* OF OSIRIS and shown on some of the planispheres by an ARK or BOAT. The corpuscle *carries* the spiritual germ or nucleus (Osiris) surrounded by fluid. As Cancer is ruled by the Moon whose Egyptian name was Isis, the allocation is complete. We find, too, that the Moon *carries* or reflects the light from the Sun, which means that it is *its* reflection in the ambient ether or akasha.

Popular names for this constellation are: the BROOD HEN, the significance of which is undeniable; Ship of Saint Peter, the Ladle or Big Dipper (its common name today); while in southern France it is known as the Casserole or Saucepan. All, with the exception of the Ship of Saint Peter, pertain to nutriment.

To the Mohammedan, Cancer was Al Fass, the Hole in which the earth's axle found its bearing (*bear*-ing). The Persians called it Ihlilgji, or Date-palm *Seed* or Fruit. The early Danes and Icelanders knew the Lesser Bear or Ursa Minor as the Smaller Chariot (carrier) or *Throne* of *Thor*, which is another proof of the correctness of my findings, since Thor is the *spark* or electrical seed-germ from Aries and becomes enthroned in Cancer, the spleen. Their descendants also call it Fiosakonur ā lopti, the *Milkmaids* of the Sky, which allocates with the breast under this sign.

Prof. Whitney quotes from the sixty-second verse of the first chapter of the Surya Siddhānta:

"The mountain which is the SEAT of the gods;"

and again:

"The 'seat of the gods' is Mount Meru, situated at the north pole."

As the sign Cancer is in the north and the stars in this constellation revolve around the Pole-star, the seat of the gods refers respectively to corpuscle and nucleus. It is well known that Polaris is 1° 14′ distant from the exact pole.

"It is the Load-star or Lodestar of the early English authors. The Chinese had several names for it—Pih Keih; Ta Shin; Tien Hwang and Ta Ti, The Great Imperial Ruler of Heaven. In earliest Northern India the star nearest the pole was known as Grahadhāra, or the 'Pivot of the Planets,' Arcturus, the brightest star in this constellation, has been mentioned from earliest times and we find in Job 38:32, the following reference: 'Canst thou guide Arcturus with his *sons?*" says Richard Allen.

Early fable attributes the *guardianship* of Cancer to Mercury, which, without the explanation given of the true function of the spleen would not be clear. It depends upon Mercury (mind and nerves) whether the *keres of life* (in other words, the Spiritual seed) shall be dragged down into hell or allowed to return to heaven. In that sense Mercury *is* its guardian.

In Chaldean and Platonist philosophy Cancer *was also said to be the Gate of Men, through which souls descended from heaven into human bodies.* Here we have the word soul used when it should have been spirit, for soul is of strictly physical formation, being the brain and glandular *esse,* formed by Spirit or electricity (fire) contacting or drawn down into matter (mother) and producing moisture or the fluidic essence termed *soul.* This fire draws moisture out of the earth, and when the nature of all twelve mineral salts is understood, as explained in these articles, it is made clear *why* one salt will attract moisture to *use* it while another will attract to *eliminate;* why one salt attracts and holds fire, while another cools and allays inflammation, etc.

The great mystery embodied in Cancer is the *Descent* of

the *Demiurge* or Artificer, in other words, the "Supreme Architect" of the Freemasons. That we may not lose sight of the physiological explanation, the *electron* or *nucleus* which is Osiris in its *car* or *casket,* is the CORPUSCLE FORMED BY MOTHER ISIS in the *spleen.* Gray's Anatomy states that the function of this organ is not known. I have now given you its *exoteric physiological use,* but it will be explained in my next book, *The Truth about Birth and Its Control,* and in *New Facts about the Glands.*

In the *Book of Dzyan* (Tibetan Book of Wisdom) it is stated that "Darkness radiates Light, and Light (Aries) drops one solitary ray into the waters, into the Mother Deep. The ray shoots through the virgin-egg; the ray causes the eternal egg to thrill, and drop the non-eternal (periodical) germ, which condenses into the world (physical) egg." And again:"The mystery of apparent *self-generation* and evolution through its own creative power repeating *in miniature* the process of Cosmic evolution in the egg, both being due to heat (sun in Leo) and moisture *under the efflux of the unseen creative spirit*" (seed germ from Aries) is undeniably true of the spleen's work in creating and fructifying human eggs or corpuscles.

Statements in sacred books relative to"the *churning* of the ocean" are symbolic of the mother liquor or nutritive fluid from which *all* forms proceed. Not only does it apply to the *churning* motion of the stomach, but to the other *fertile* parts which allocate with Scorpio and Pisces.

Cancer is the MOST productive, the most important of the three fluidic signs, for without it no corpuscles can be formed. Therefore, no possible creation or RECREATION of the human body could take place.

The Moon is "the Cow of Plenty," in Hindu literature, and when EXALTED IN TAURUS is serving its DIVINE purpose of CONSERVING ITS SACRED AMRITAM OR SOMA JUICE. This in plain English means the CREATIVE FLUID FROM ARIES. Perhaps this statement may serve to throw light on the Biblical reference to "the land flowing with milk and honey." Remember, in the chapter on Aries it is proved that there are MAMMILLARY GLANDS IN THE CEREBRUM. These fluids reappear later on in Cancer, ruling the BREAST, STOMACH and SPLEEN. They have taken on a lower vibration and more of a physiological or dense character. They now become of earthly sustenance, where before they were HEAVENLY. The astrological Milky Way has its physiological analogy in the descent of the brain or cerebral milk from the mammillary glands in the head, the positive pole of creation. In Cancer these glands constitute the negative pole.

Madam Blavatsky says, most truly, "The Law of Analogy is the *first* key to the world problem, and these links have to be studied co-ordinately in their occult relations to each other."

There is no doubt concerning the function of the spleen referred to in the following quotation from the Stanzas of Dzyan: "The great Chohans (Lords) called the Lords of the Moon, of the airy bodies: 'Bring forth men, (they were told), men of your nature. Give them their *forms within.* She, (Mother Earth or Nature) will build *coverings* without. For Males-Females will they be. *Lords* of the Flame, also.' Thus the *lunar spirits (Aries sparks),* became the creative Elohim of FORM, or the Adam of dust." There are innumerable other statements—indeed an entire book could be written on the sign Cancer—but we will add one more, and from the same source, Madam Blavatsky: "The Ark, in which is preserved the germs of all living things necessary to re-people the earth, represents the survival of life, and the supremacy of Spirit over matter, through the conflict of the opposing powers of nature. In the Astro-Theosophic chart of the Western Rite, the Ark corresponds with the navel, and is placed at the sinister side, the side of the woman (the moon) one of whose symbols is the left pillar of Solomon's temple—Boaz, pituitary, in the head. The *umbilicus is connected with the receptacle in which are fructified the germs of the race.*"

Man is the integral part of the race—one body, while the corpuscles within him, and of which he is built up, constitute the germs of the race, the seed-germ being the nucleus.

The Demiurge is the Logos, the WORD which was in the *beginning,* hence THE SEED. "THE SEED IS THE WORD OF GOD."—Luke 8:11.

Before dealing with the chemical correspondence, a few references taken from G. A. Gaskell's *Dictionary of the Sacred Language of Scriptures and Myths*" must be given, as they link up metaphysically with the physiological interpretation of this sign:

"Cancer is a symbol of the *fourth* (it is the fourth sign) period of the cycle of life. It signifies the lower mind (preceding sign, Gemini) energized from the astral plane.

"The crab or the tortoise (Indian sign of Cancer) is a symbol of the lower nature into which the soul *descends in evolution*." We here note that he uses the word *soul* when it should be Spirit.

Again, in writing of the HIGHER aspect of the MOON (exalted in Taurus), he says: "a symbol of Buddha as *containing* the transmuted results of the experience of the lower self." Also: "When the spiritual monad, or Individuality, quits the lower nature, it passes into the energized higher mental vehicle, or causal-body, and from thence unites with the Higher Self. Fortified by this union, it passes upward through the Buddhic plane (moon) and becomes merged in Love eternal on the plane of Atma."

In its lower aspect "the moon is a symbol of the lower self —the personality. This includes the astral principle of the lower nature, namely *desire*, and also the form or matter side of nature, which was developed in the lunar cycles on the lunar globes. The Sun is Spirit, matter is the Moon." Prasna Upanishad, 1. 5.

Plutarch, in *"Face in the Moon's Orb,"* says: "For the moon herself, out of desire for the sun, revolves round and comes in contact with him because she longs to derive from him the generative principle." Mr. Gaskell interprets the above as: "The lower self, attracted to the Higher Self, evolves through the life cycle: for the *soul longs for* REGENERATION and immortal union with the Higher Self in the causal body, WHEREIN THE TWO SELVES BECOME ONE."

In his *Sermons*, A. McLaren says: "If the unseen is ever to rule in men's lives it must be through their thoughts. It must become intelligible, clear, real. It must be brought out of the flickering moonlight of fancy and surmises, into the sunlight of certitude and knowledge."

Because the great majority of humanity is living in its desire nature we see personality overshadowing—yes, almost entirely darkening—the Individuality. We find insanity increasing by leaps and bounds; incompetency, in vast degree.

In a recent issue of *The Literary Digest* (May 23, 1931), we are given sufficient proof of the truth of the foregoing statements: "In Mississippi alone the cost of caring for one feeble-minded person is $714. As there are about 600,000 such defectives in the country, the cost of their care, in segregation, would be enormous."

Officials think they have solved the problem by endeavoring to pass a general or country-wide law for sterilization. This will be about as *morally* effective as the use of contraceptives in birth control. In neither instance is the real problem dealt with. No training or teaching has been formulated which will *prevent* incompetency. This lack in itself constitutes a crime.

Recalling the fact that Gemini deals with children (the sparks) the SONS of GOD, Aries, we now find them in Cancer clothed with material forms, corpuscles or bodies. They have actually been caught in nets, in the salt water, the MARE or mary of the human body, and now have *web-like* forms.

We will consider the allocation of this sign with Calcium or lime fluoride. In Dr. Carey's *Biochemic System of Medicine* we note the following: "It occurs in nature as mineral fluor-spar, beautifully crystallized, of various colors, in lead veins, the crystals having commonly the *cubic*, but sometimes the octohedral form, parallel to the faces of which latter figure they always cleave. Some varieties, when heated, emit a greenish, and some a purple, *phosphorescent light*.

"To know that a certain inorganic cell-salt is indicated by certain symptoms, is one thing; but to know the process by which it *works* to accomplish certain results, is quite another thing. The fluoride of lime is found in the enamel of teeth, connective tissue and the elastic fiber of all muscular tissue. A lack of *elastic* fiber in muscular tissue causes falling of the womb, varicose veins,* and a general 'sagging-down' feeling. When a deficiency in this lime-salt, and consequently a deficiency of elastic fiber, occurs in the connective tissue between the cerebrum and the cerebellum, an abnormal process of thought occurs, causing groundless fears of financial ruin."

A contribution which I humbly offer as the result of years of experience and research, is the following: as all web or

*Natrium mur is also required, as indicated by Venus in Aquarius in many charts.

spider-like formations in the body must contain this salt, it is obvious that the Arachnoid (spider-web) membrane which envelops the brain and cord must require a large proportion of calcium fluoride in its composition.

The following from *Gray's Anatomy* is conclusive proof: "The Arachnoid consists of bundles of white *fibrinous* and *elastic tissue, intimately blended together.* Its outer surface is covered with a layer of low *cuboidal mesothelium.* The inner surface and the trabeculæ are likewise covered by a somewhat low type of cuboidal mesothelium, which in places are flattened to a pavement type. Vessels of considerable size, but few in number, and according to Bochdalek, a rich *plexus of nerves derived from the motor root* of the trigeminal, the facial and the accessory nerves, are found in the Arachnoid."

The outstanding fact in the above statement is that "the Arachnoid CONSISTS OF WHITE, FIBRINOUS AND ELASTIC TISSUE, intimately *blended together,*" all of which is characteristic of Calcium fluoride, as was previously quoted from Dr. Carey's *Biochemic System.* As this salt is known to be a natural FLUX, or substance which promotes the *fusing* of minerals and metals, it will be at once realized that, unless this salt is present in sufficient quantity, the fibrinous and elastic character of tissues change, losing these properties. The result is a prolapsed condition, a general flabbiness, a good example being a piece of rubber from which the *elasticity* has departed.

Here we must again call to mind the fact that as Cancer is ruled by the moon, which is known to be closely associated with the brain, many very peculiar mental conditions are noted in Biochemistry as arising from deficiency in Calcium fluoride.

The following are outstanding examples: fear of poverty, HOLDING ON LIKE THE CRAB to every cent, scarcely "LETTING GO" to purchase even bare necessities. One of the earliest symptoms of need of this salt is FORGETFULNESS, which means lack of mental elasticity. When fear is present, whether in respect to one's finances or other matters, it indicates decreasing mental tenacity. One loses one's grip or positivity.

As Aries, the cerebrum, forms an angle of ninety degrees with Cancer (indicating that these two are *associated* in work which must be done "on the square"), when Calcium fluoride and Kali phos become very deficient there is an actual SEPA-

RATION which takes place, and it becomes extremely difficult, and in severe cases impossible, to *express* one's self. Indeed, ideas are conspicuous by their absence.

It is quite common to meet people who are at a loss for words. When conversing, they hesitate, repeat, and some minutes pass before they are able to state what they have in mind. It seems to me that words are actually held in leash by elastic threads. When they begin to lose elasticity, they are unable to contract so tightly. The memory fails to contact them, the electricity of thought is unable to flow freely along its natural grooves.

Imagine, if you can, these spidery filaments, which in health are quiescent, beginning to reach out hungrily for the mineral substance which is their food—calcium fluoride. Is it not easy to understand how creepy, crawling sensations within the brain are indicative of need of this salt? Particularly within the last few years has this symptom been common, and those having it say they fear insanity. A contraction of these fibers causes a feeling of tightness and constriction.

The old slang phrase, "You have cobwebs on the brain," is a physiological fact; and indeed, as Dr. Carey stated in his article on that subject, such expressions are based on truth, but clothed in common vernacular.

On re-reading the description of the Arachnoid, quoted from *Gray's Anatomy,* please note carefully this sentence: "Its outer surface is covered with a layer of low CUBOIDAL mesothelium." Cuboidal means formed like a cube, which is a solid bounded by SIX equal squares and having all its angles right angles. It is the third power of a quantity. THE PRODUCT OF THREE EQUAL FACTORS.

This wonderful Cancer-sign salt, then, *must* have the power to produce or create a *triune* product, since each and every element in nature moves in a certain direction and at a certain rate (vibration), and not until the element changes are direction and rate of motion or vibration affected. Calcium fluoride then, has the VIBRATION OF A TRINITY. Six or sex consists of *two threes*, or two trinities, a masculine, we may say, and a feminine. It will be seen how well this applies to the sign, for THIS IS THE WORK IT DOES. Cancer is feminine, prolific, the most fertile of the twelve zodiacal signs and parts of the human body. But remember, students of astrology, you will not understand WHY, unless you recall the discovery that the SPLEEN forms one of the *three* organs associated with this sign, and in it corpuscles are created.

Even the symbol of this fourth sign of the zodiac, the crab or scarabæus, bears out the cuboid description in the three-fold or triune stages through which the tiny crab and beetle pass before full development is attained. As man is animal, human, and divine, he corresponds to the three different individual germ-states or seeds upon which the triune nature depends.

Let us again review the *fact* that his spiritual seed-germ is precipitated in Aries, the cerebral essence, the BREAD from HEAVEN. In Taurus it starts on its journey; and, on arriving in the spleen, becomes a human germ or corpuscle (not a procreative germ) by uniting the material sent down by the pituitary gland with the FEMALE GERM WHICH THE SPLEEN PRODUCES.

Thus is SOUL created, an earthly product. The soul or corpuscles must be nourished by the chyle formed by the digestion of *food* and when, for any one of several reasons, this is interfered with, these individual and diminutive bodies become weak and unable to do *their* work. For man's body is a collection of bodies. And again, his permanent or Spiritual body, his Erotes, are the collection of sparks from the celestial fire.

The third or animal phase which each must pass through is concerned with a very great mystery which will be dealt with in the second volume of *God-Man,* also in *New Facts About the Glands.* But we must realize that the differentiation of a *corpuscle* necessary to produce a procreative germ cell can only be accomplished in the testes and ovaries, as considered in Chapter Eight.

The above should prove indubitably that the symbol of the crab or scarabæus was well chosen—it, too, represents three different stages of development. It is also interesting to note that the beetle or scarabæus buries its eggs in the material which is to serve as shelter, warmth and food for them. In the human body, the immortal egg or spiritual germ is *buried* in the same way when it reaches Scorpio.

As the beetle or scarabæus buries its eggs in excrement we find here an analogy to Capricorn, or the sacrum, the great nerve ganglia controlling sexual activities. In ancient writings dealing with occult matters, the Pelican is said to be buried in horse dung. Only students of facts will recognize the similarity of expression. Physicists know that the lower part of the spine is termed the *cauda equina* or tail of the horse, and the sacrum is in this region, near the back passage. In Greek mythology this is the Augean stable which required a thorough cleansing. It is absolutely true when interpreted physiologically. The esoteric meaning of Pelican is Christ.

No doubt some readers will instantly say, "What sacrilege!" It is well, therefore, to state here and now, that Christ is a Greek word meaning *oil,* a HIGHLY REFINED OIL, the *esse* or sum total of a *perfect* physical mechanism. It is the "water" in the Jordan. Is it, then, any wonder that the symbol refers to immortality, and not to an individual?

The following quotation taken from Madam Blavatsky's *Glossary* furnishes us, with further evidence that the sign Cancer is productive and productile, and truly THE HOUSE OF THE GREAT MOTHER HERSELF, since ALL THINGS are nourished by her. It deals also with seed, for it creates and nourishes human seed, the *corpuscles.*

"In Egypt the Scarabæus is the symbol of *resurrection, and also of rebirth;* of resurrection for the mummy or rather of the highest aspects of the PERSONALITY which animated it, and of rebirth of the Ego, the 'Spiritual body' of the lower, human soul. Egyptologists give us but half of the truth, when in speculating upon the meaning of certain inscriptions, they say, 'the justified soul, once arrived at a certain period of its peregrinations (simply at the death of the physical body) should be united to its body (i.e., the Ego) never more *to be separated from it.'* (Rouge) What is this so-called body? Can it be the mummy? Certainly not, for the emptied mummified corpse can never resurrect. It can only be the eternal, spiritual vestment, the Ego that never dies *but gives immortality to whatsoever becomes united to it.* 'The delivered Intelligence retakes its luminous envelope and (re) becomes Daimon' as Prof. Maspero says, is the *spiritual* Ego; the personal. For Kama Manas, its direct ray, or the lower soul, is that which aspires to become OSIRIFIED, *i. e.,* to unite itself with its 'god'; and that portion of it which will succeed in so doing, will *never more be separated from it* (the god), not even when the latter incarnates again and again, descending periodically on earth in its pilgrimage, in search of further experiences and following the decrees of Karma. KHEM,

'THE SOWER OF THE SEED,' is shown on a stele in a picture of Resurrection after physical death, as the CREATOR AND SOWER OF THE GRAIN OF CORN, WHICH, AFTER CORRUPTION, SPRINGS UP AFRESH EACH TIME INTO A NEW EAR, ON WHICH A SCARABÆUS BEETLE IS SEEN POISED; and Deveria shows very justly that 'Ptah is the inert, material form of Osiris, who will become Sokari, (the eternal Ego) to be reborn, and afterwards by Harmachus,' or Horus in his transformation, the *risen god*. The prayer so often found in the tumular inscriptions, 'the wish for the resurrection in one's LIVING SOUL' or the Higher Ego, had ever a Scarabæus at the end, standing for the personal soul. The scarabæus is the most honored, as the most frequent and familiar, of all Egyptian symbols. No mummy is without several of them; the favorite ornament on engravings, household furniture and utensils is this sacred beetle, and Pierret pertinently shows in his *Oivre des Morts* that the secret meaning of the hieroglyph is sufficiently explained in that the Egyptian name for the Scarabæus, KHEPER, SIGNIFIES TO BE, TO BECOME, TO BUILD AGAIN."

While sufficient is given in the above statement to prove that this sign has to do with RE-CREATION, it has not given us the real, physiological interpretation which would clarify it. No one will ever be permanently united with his Higher Self or Ego, until the physical corpuscles to which Cancer gives birth in the spleen, cease being tormented, starved and destroyed because of the ignorance of the personality.

Two outstanding statements to remember are that Cancer is THE SOWER OF THE SEED, and that the symbol, the scarabæus, signifies *to be* (existence), to become, TO BUILD AGAIN. *Only through the continued maintenance of the health of the corpuscles is life in the physical body made permanent, and victory gained over the grave.* THIS IS ONE OF MY MOST IMPORTANT PRONOUNCEMENTS. It is truly the KEY TO PHYSICAL REGENERATION.

In *The Pathway of the Soul,* by Van Stone, we read: "This serpentine force fashioned the universe and fashioned man. It created him, and yet he in his turn could use it for creation *if he would only cease from generation.*" It is true that the enormous amount of energy expended in procreation

ALSO EXPELS THOUSANDS OF PERVERTED CORPUSCLES. (See Chapter Eight).

Reviewing and allocating, now, our Biochemical facts with the statement from *Gray's Anatomy*, we find that Calcium fluoride possesses a vibration or rate of motion capable of building up *cuboidal* formations. We find that the Arachnoid or brain webs consist of bundles of white, fibrinous and elastic tissue, their outer surface covered with *cuboidal* mesothelium. Is any additional testimony required to substantiate Dr. Carey's allocation of Calcium fluoride with the zodiacal sign Cancer which truly fructifies the germs of the race?

There is yet further evidence:

The word crustacean has the same Latin root as crust. Crustacean in Greek means *crystal,* having the power to crystallize or harden. It also means a hard coating or covering, a *shell,* a horny substance. Crusta Petrosa means the *cement* of a tooth. It is therefore true that Calcium fluoride is of the nature of cement but having the peculiar property of elasticity. Both the beetle and the crab have hard shells. The body corpuscles are also encased in shells but another Calcium combination is required to harden them, Calcium sulph of Scorpio or plaster of Paris.

Biochemistry teaches us that the enamel of teeth and the finger nails require this salt, and some is also utilized by the bones. When Calcium fluoride is deficient, the skin is rough. chapping and cracking; fissures tend to form in certain parts, as between the toes, around the fingers, anus, back of the ears or in the corners of the mouth. The skin has become deficient in this rubbery-tissue material—the elastic substance. Hard growths, tumors of a *fibroid* character; blurred vision; cataracts; osseous lumps or growth on the jaw or cheekbones; loose teeth; receding gums; thin and brittle enamel; tongue has a *cracked* appearance; elongation of the uvula; hemorrhoids; apparently increased quantity of urine (due to a relaxed condition of the muscular fibres); hardening of the testicles; dragging pains in the groin; prolapsed uterus; varicose veins; digestive disturbances; spleen trouble; valvular heart trouble; forgetfulness and fear of poverty are some of the outstanding indications of need of this salt. A CRUSTY disposition is another.

There is one more important point which must be dealt with before closing this chapter, and that is relative to the interpretation of FLUORIDE, its nature and its close relation to the Moon by which its allocating sign, Cancer, is ruled.

It is well known that the Moon's light is reflected from the sun. Is it any wonder that the ancients considered it male and not female, for this reason? Luna is its Latin name. In Greek it is Selena, while it is known as Lebanah and Yarcah in Hebrew.

Please bear in mind that the following statements relative to Calcium fluoride are scientifically correct, as they are taken from *A Text Book on Elemental Chemistry, Theoretical and Inorganic*, by George F. Barker, M. D., Professor of Physics in the University of Pennsylvania.

"The mineral known as fluorite, fluor or Derbyshire spar, is a compound of fluorine with calcium, CaF_2. From this mineral hydrogen-potassium fluoride may be prepared, and by the action of heat on this, anhydrous hydrogen fluoride is obtained. By the electrolysis of this substance a colorless gas is obtained, possessed of extraordinary activity. It unites directly with hydrogen even in the dark, and decomposes water, readily setting free OZONIZED OXYGEN." He later says that "the *activity* of fluoride seems to surpass that of all other elements. Fluorite comes from the Latin *fluo*, to flow, because it can be used as a flux in the *reduction* of metals."

A logical deduction from the above data seems to be that as Calcium fluoride is necessary in fusing together all kinds of material to make corpuscles or seeds, it has another important function. It decomposes the water in the atmosphere and thus furnishes the spiritual germ enclosed within the corpuscle with the *ozonized* oxygen or ELECTRIFIED AIR WHICH IS ITS PARTICULAR ENERGIZER. Since the *life* of the corpuscle is the electrical germ-cell within it, it must be *fed* by that which contains electrical energy. Nothing else is logical.

It is interesting to note that the word *flux* also pertains to the menstrual flow, since its appearance is ruled by the Moon. It is well known that the Moon has very much to do with the ebb and *flow* of tides. Many years' experience in this work has proved conclusively that a deficiency in this salt causes many very painful as well as weakening female troubles. The word fluor is the root of fluorescent, and as chemistry informs us, " this salt is *thermo fluorescent*.

It *glows on exposure to moderate heat.* Fluorescent means the property a substance has when illuminated of giving off light of a color different from its own and from that of any incident light (the light falling upon it). Thermo-fluorescent means luminescence exhibited by certain substances after exposure to heat, cathode or solar rays. The light given off is usually of greater wave length than the incident light, and the violet and ultra-violet rays are its best exciters. It is powerfully fluorescent."

Not only does the above scientific statement furnish us with illumination relative to the orb of night, but it conclusively proves Dr. Carey's allocation of Calcium fluoride to Cancer, a *fluidic sign,* ruled by the Moon which affects fluids and itself a TRUE FLUX. And as Calcium fluoride will not combine with oxygen, we find in this fact the reason why it must constitute a large percentage of the material used in forming the corpuscle, so that IT WILL NOT BE DEPRIVED OF OXYGEN, FOR IT, TOO, MUST BREATHE. Indeed, a corpuscle is, in a sense, a fish, as well as an egg, for the kind of air it needs to sustain life must be similar to that which serves to maintain life in the habitants of the sea.

On consulting the *Encyclopedia Britannica,* we find that this salt is found in the *enamel* of teeth, which corroborates Dr. Schuessler's findings. Is it not, then, very *foolish* to deny the efficiency of Calcium fluoride tablets as a restorer of this necessary dental covering? Let us use common sense and at last admit that when a thing needs renovating, THE SAME KIND OF MATERIAL MUST BE UTILIZED TO ACCOMPLISH IT.

"Through astrology we may become cognizant of the relationship existing between the Macrocosm or *body* of the universe and the body of man. In this way we discover *how* and *where* or in what part of man Nature's *forces* are constantly reacting." We begin to realize, then, that when powerful planetary forces impinge upon that part of the anatomy of the Grand Man known as Cancer, CALCIUM FLUORIDE IS TREMENDOUSLY ACTIVE; AND IF IN THAT PART OF THE BODY OF MAN ITS ESSENTIAL SALT, CALCIUM FLUORIDE, IS NOT PRESENT IN SUFFICIENT QUANTITY TO SET UP THE SAME RATE OF VIBRATION WHICH IS THE

PERFECT HEALTH RATIO, THEN DIS-EASE MANIFESTS. One is not then WORKING WITH NATURE, BUT AGAINST HER.

Chemistry tells us that each element has a *fixed* and definite *combining power,* and that the arrangement of the atoms is of as much importance as their *kind* and *number.* The old philosopher doubtless was familiar with chemistry when he said, "God geometrizes and forms man and the universe by number and geometry." The earnest student of astro-biochemistry certainly realizes the truth of this statement.

We find that, in addition to its use as a flux and *welder,* Calcium fluoride is also employed in making *opal* glass. We find a correspondence here in the fact that, as before stated, lack of this salt causes dimness of the crystalline lens of the eyes. It also causes cataracts. It is interesting to note that the word CORNEA, which is the term for the transparent structure forming the anterior part of the *external* layer of the eyeball, means *horny,* and is derived from the Latin word *corneus.* This checks up again with both beetle and scarabæus. Much data has been accumulated proving that when the thirteenth degree of Aries is afflicted by square from Cancer, and indeed, from Libra and Capricorn, it is proof of a degenerating optic nerve, for it lies within the middle decan of Aries which allocates physiologically with the optic thalamus, THE ALL-SEEING EYE, which is really *a continuation of the brain substance itself.*

Will it not be wonderful when parents are familiar with physio-chemical astrology, also with the science of supplying the constituent elements of the blood, for then tendencies to blindness and other weakness will be eliminated by restoring to the brain cells all that is required to perfectly nourish them.

It has also been proved that the last degrees of Taurus, when occupied or negatively aspected by a powerful planet, affect the nerves which cross at the base of the brain, resulting in a disturbance in the circulation and hence partially cutting off the supply of blood to the eyes. This will often cause cataracts to form.

Sixty-five percent of all people *born* in the sign Cancer are physical weaklings from birth. Anyone can verify this from the birth dates of friends and acquaintances. Remember, however, that thirty-five percent are not weaklings. The reason so many (although they may live quite beyond the average) are never well, and almost constantly manifest some symptom or other, is *because they have never had sufficient corpuscles* created by the spleen. THEY ARE UNDER-NOURISHED. In addition, they do not digest or assimilate food well because of the fact that their GREATEST CHEMICAL DEFICIENCIES ARE CALCIUM FLUORIDE, THE CANCER SIGN SALT AND CALCIUM PHOSPHATE, THE CAPRICORN MATERIAL. THE LATTER HAPPENS TO BE THEIR ADVERSARY SIGN.

And because CANCER IS THE NATURAL CONCEPTION SIGN—THE CONCEPTION OF CORPUSCLES, AND of PROCREATION, IT IS UNNATURAL TO BE BORN DURING THAT PERIOD. One is working against Nature, and consequently suffers in health. It is also true, however, that in the process of evolution which none can side-step or gainsay, one works with a certain degree of harmony on a lower plane of Nature when physical conception takes place as the sun transits Cancer. The Ego is brought to birth at the resurrection time of Nature—in the Spring, when cosmic forces are the most powerful and the intake of vital energy by the physical body is very great. Those born at this time usually have a great supply of reserve energy; and, although they are described as delicate looking, are yet surprisingly strong, and have wonderful recuperative powers.

There *must* be many wonderful Egos awaiting birth, and when conception is no longer subject to unbridled lust and two who respect and love each other wish for progeny, they will not only make careful preparation by correcting chemical deficiencies but will choose that time when Nature herself brings ALL THINGS TO BIRTH. How many are there, today, who are even *thinking* about such a plan? The answer gives us the key to humanity's condition. However, the powerful rays of Neptune and Uranus are endeavoring to stir up and shake out the old dead cells of decadent ideas and opinions, and ere long some rays of light will dawn on dark mental horizons. Either that, or the actual snuffing out of the little consciousness which remains will take place.

"Man draws not only health from the elements WHEN IN EQUILIBRIUM BUT ALSO DISEASE WHEN THEY ARE DISTURBED."—Paracelsus.

Cancer and Calcium Fluoride

"The world is too much with us; late and soon
Getting and spending, WE LAY WASTE OUR POWERS;
Little we see in Nature that is ours;
We have given our hearts away, a sordid boon!
This sea that bares her bosom to the moon;
The winds that will be howling at all hours,
And are ungathered now like sleeping flowers;
For this, for everything, we are out of tune;
It moves us not;—Great God! I'd rather be
A Pagan suckled in a creed outworn;
So might I, standing on this pleasant lea,
Have glimpses that would make me less forlorn;
Have sight of Proteus rising from the sea;
Or hear old Triton blow his wreathed horn."

—***Wordsworth.***

Chapter V

THE ANALYSIS AND SYNTHESIS OF LEO AND MAGNESIUM PHOSPHATE

"Lest he tear my soul like a lion, rending it in pieces while there is none to deliver."—Psalms VII:2.

FROM July 22 to August 23 the Sun is transiting his own sign, Leo, wherein he is lord of all. Leo is the Latin word for Lion. This sign is the only one in the circle of the zodiac having a beast of prey for a symbol. We must again review the fact that there is a very definite reason why the ancients assigned certain symbols to the twelve divisions of the Grand Man; for they allocate perfectly when their physiological correspondences are understood. We again realize that a knowledge of the body is *absolutely essential* to the study of astrology.

It was necessary to consult a Latin dictionary in order to obtain the etymology of Leo, which is TO BLOT OUT, TO DESTROY, TO ANNIHILATE. This is entirely in keeping with the *nature* of this animal. "But in what way," some will inquire, "does this Carnivora synthesize with the fifth division of the human body?" The *basic* interpretation of the latter is *motion,* energy manifesting in *action,* and the parts of the anatomy having to do with it are the *heart* and *motor* nerves.

Before completing this explanation, we must consider the interpretation of the name given to the month in which the largest part of this sign falls, namely *August.* It is the hottest period of the year, and the word literally means, *to bring to fruition, to make brown, to sun-burn.*

The Latin verb *augeo,* from which it is derived, means *to make, to increase, to fertilize.* Farmers and horticulturists know that this is the period of the year when everything is *ripened* by the intense heat of the sun. Seed is perfected. Vegetation begins to look brown and parched; it is being consumed. August also means imperial—very great power.

The lion is termed the King of beasts because of its very

great strength and majestic bearing, and the word is often met with in occult literature, an outstanding expression being "in the grip of the lion's paw," which is symbolical of high moral courage and self-control.

It is very evident that the *name* of the month applying to a zodiacal sign gives the key to the KIND OF WORK done, while the *symbol* relates to the NATURE OF THE FORCE DOING THAT WORK. This, in turn, checks up correctly with the chemical element which alone can accomplish it.

Leo is the second of the fire triplicity, and its position in the circle is 120° from the first fire sign, or Aries. It is so placed, in harmonious relation to the latter because the two must *work in harmony*. Again we realize that some knowledge of the anatomy of man is essential. The energy which originates in and is sent forth from Aries, comes to fruition in Leo. In other words, the former is the place of sowing, while the latter—Leo—is the place of reaping.

Reviewing the process, we recall that Aries relates to the cerebrum, and the precipitation therein of spiritual electricity —the fire of life. This vital energy flows into the motor nerves, attracted by their magnetism and is utilized in MOTION.

As the heart is a great mass of nervous muscular tissue concerned in dividing, lifting and circulating the blood, IT RECEIVES FROM THE INNER SUN IN ARIES (the electrical generator) the divine fire, and utilizes it in producing VISIBLE activities, as well as those which go on unseen within the body. To work in harmony with Aries, LEO MUST USE CONSTRUCTIVELY ALL THE ENERGY GENERATED IN ARIES.

Until humanity starts on the path of return, such is *not* the case, and here is where the *negative* interpretation of the lion applies perfectly, for a very great portion of mental power and the energy generated in the inner nucleus IS WASTED IN E-MOTION, the meaning of which is to flow or move *out*, to go forth from.

It is to be greatly regretted that at the present time there seems to be a movement on foot to discourage the teaching of Greek and Latin in our colleges. Naturally there will not be many who will share this opinion, simply because they do not realize that these languages, and especially the latter, reveal the meanings concealed in words. The study of Latin for a year or two enables one to catch automatically, as it were, the secrets hidden in them.

It has been said that August derived its name from the Emperor Augustus. It seems more logical, however, that he received the name not only because it was his birth month but because his rank made it appropriate.

The ancient Roman appellation for this month was Sextilis. Here we find direct reference to one of the subjects which has been attributed to this sign (Leo) and which is one phase of *emotional expression—namely children.*

The earnest student of esoteric astrology will see that this interpretation by some astrologers *as a basic idea* is erroneous. Leo does *not* deal with children *as such,* but with sexual passion, that emotion which is necessary for the procreative act. Animal heat, typified by the Sun in Leo, is the means of procreation. Gemini is the offspring or progeny sign, as its symbol, THE TWINS, plainly indicates. We must continually bear in mind that our basic interpretations must be accurate. It will then be easy to analyze correctly.

In addition to sexual passion, we find love affairs, amusements and speculation attributed to and analyzed under Leo. When we synthesize all the facts assembled relative to this sign, it will be easy to understand how they came to be allocated with it.

It may be very difficult, perhaps, for any except earnest students of esoteric astrology to agree with my statement that the subjects which are related to Leo (sexual passion, amusements, love affairs and speculation) are, in their *ultimate* analysis, negative and therefore destructive.

It is very interesting that Leo (the sign with the BEAST OF PREY symbol) which ordinarily would seem to be one of the easiest signs to analyze, is very difficult to present. The reason is, that the great mass of humanity is still concerned with and living in the E-motional or destructive phase of this sign. For that reason they will continue to deny for some time yet that these Leo subjects are destructive.

They should not be blamed or condemned. What one can not at present contact mentally constitutes no real crime. As one gathers experience, knowledge ultimately accumulates; and there are no exceptions to this rule. Therefore I reach out friendly hands to clasp those of all Leo natives, whether young or old souls, for we are members of one great family, children of the Great Creator, Architect and Chemist of the Universe. We are all on our way down and up the ladder of life. We are unable to contact, physically, any who have reached the top. Their bodies are too refined and pure for our dull eyes to see. Eventually, however, we will see them.

There are, however, several analogies of a scientific nature which may assist those having difficulty in understanding why these Leo subjects are destructive.

First let us recall the exact anatomical and physiological interpretation of Leo. It has to do with the heart and motor system of the universe, and by analogy with those same parts in man. It is one of the four "agents" of the vital forces, the others being Taurus, Scorpio and Aquarius. The heart is a great pump and blood divider. The motor nerves are those white fibers which are magnetically capable of contacting the electricity generated in Aries, and thereby producing MOTION.

MOTION, THEN, IS THE MECHANICAL, POSITIVE AND SCIENTIFIC INTERPRETATION OF LEO—MOTION, NOT E-MOTION.

Why then do we find the BEAST OF PREY, the lion, as the symbol allocated with this sign by the ancients?

We find innumerable references in the Scriptures to both positive (constructive) and negative (destructive) interpretations of the lion. The language is stately and dignified.

In Greek mythology we also find these two aspects dealt with, clothed in picturesque and uniquely poetical language. In fact there is no sacred literature of any nation and people which does not contain such references.

In *Smith's Bible Dictionary*, we read: "Rabbinical writers discover in the Old Testament *seven* Hebrew names for the lion, which they assign to the animal at *seven periods* of its life." This is analogous to the seven cycles or periods in the life of man. These have to do not only with his physical and mental development, but to a corresponding degree with spiritual unfoldment. It would seem logical that this was one reason why the lion was used as a symbol to represent the various stages in a man's life. In other words, they express his degree or rate of vibration at seven different periods of his existence.

The Old Testament is a mass of scientific facts relative to the many epochs in the life of the imperfect being, as the etymology of the words Old Testament reveals. Testament consists of two words derived from the Latin: *testa,* meaning body, and *ment,* from *mentis,* meaning mind. The old or imperfect body and mind are thus considered in its pages, while the New Testament naturally has to do with the perfect product, the perfected man. Here we find only one name for the Lion. It is "the Lion of the Tribe of Judah, he who has attained and is now able to open the book and to loose the seven seals thereof," as stated in Revelation.

The name "lion" is very ancient and is said to be of either Egyptian or Semitic origin. It stands for a carnivorous mammal of the cat family which is often of a tawny, yellowish color. The color of the sign Leo is also yellow.

The Sun creates the most powerful vibrations. Some ancient occult works inform us that ALL of the planets originate from and eventually revert back to it; that they have produced no life or light in themselves, but have derived it from the Sun. On allocating the planets with the organs in the body which they also respectively represent, the above statement is found to be true. The organs in the torso DO derive their life and power from that part of the body which is ruled by the Sun in Aries. This is the optic thalamus, the eye within the chamber, the *Hidden* Sun or electrical generator. By reflection, the visible physiological Sun is the SOLAR (SUN) PLEXUS. This great nerve ganglia broadcasts the energy received from the hidden sun (Aries) *To the Organs.* When the solar plexus receives a "knock-out blow" temporary paralysis results.

As the Sun is King of Heaven because invested with supreme power over the universe, so the lion, AS KING OF BEASTS on earth, is used as a symbol to illustrate the fact that energy or power may be used TO CREATE (to GIVE life) and also to destroy life. The story that Aries and Leo reveal when allocated with the functions of the body, is that of ENERGY DIRECTED OR GUIDED BY WISDOM. Energy *moves* (Leo) up and down and around in the body, doing its work wisely (Aries) while the outer servants of the body (the hands, for example) do constructive work. The antithesis of this is energy misdirected, used destructively.

The following passages quoted from the Bible dictionary are splendid examples of energy used destructively and typified by the ravening lion: "When driven by hunger it not only ventured to attack *flocks* in the desert in presence of the shepherd (Is. 31:4), but laid waste towns and villages, and devoured men. The *lion was a symbol of strength* and sovereignty (as is the SUN). Among the Jews and throughout the Old Testament the lion was the *achievement* of the princely tribe of Judah. On the other hand, its fierceness and cruelty rendered it an appropriate metaphor FOR A FIERCE AND MALIGNANT ENEMY AND HENCE FOR THE ARCH-FIEND HIMSELF."

This is a clear and concise statement and does not leave us in doubt. It must be understood that the term lion, as used in Sacred Scripture, stood for two diametrically opposed characters and conditions. One represented energy creating life and conserving or protecting it; the other, destroying it.

In Psalms 7:2, we find the following: "Lest he tear my soul like a lion, rending it in pieces, while there is none to deliver." The foregoing has direct reference to a physiological fact. The soul of the human body is Isis, the Moon or mother-liquor. It is the pituitary substance which forms the basis of all the glandular fluids.

An important fact to remember is, that the pineal and pituitary glands in the head (Aries) are the male and female *creative* and *recreative* glands, whose office is to rebuild our bodies daily; while the procreative glands (Scorpio) are used destructively by the majority of humanity today, instead of for the purpose of which they were originally intended during *one period* in our evolution. This period has to do with *furnishing bodies* for reincarnating egos, in other words, spirits which must come to birth.

It is a fact that the gamut of emotions which human beings manifest from the cradle to the grave, results eventually in despoiling and pillaging the entire glandular system and also in utterly demoralizing both nervous systems.

Before giving the complete explanation which will prove the above statement to be true, let us examine a few more Biblical quotations: "Mine *eye* is *consumed* of grief; it waxeth old because of all mine enemies."—Psalms 6:7. Note that eye is singular and not used in the plural sense as it is natural to assume it should be. It is not referring to the outer eyes, but to the *saggital* eye deep within the head in the Holy of Holies. It is the Eye Single of which it is written: "If thine eye be single, *thine whole body shall be full of light.*"

The optic thalamus, then, is the eye referred to, and concerning which *Gray's Anatomy* gives us very limited information. Of its higher or spiritual nature nothing is given therein. It is stated, however, that it is a most important nerve *center,* and many of the nerves of special sense have been traced to it. Some specialists on the subject place a question mark after this statement, as they surmise that these nerve origins may be found farther up.

My own researches cause me to conclude that they do not originate in the optic thalamic center. This conclusion seems to be substantiated by the information given in *Gray's Anatomy* that "the optic nerve corresponds rather to a TRACT OF FIBERS WITHIN THE BRAIN than to the other cranial nerves. The optic nerve is peculiar in that its fibers and ganglion cells are probably third in the series of neurons from the receptors to the brain."

It is evident that the thalami and optic nerves branching off therefrom are really continuations of the cerebral arachnoidal fibers. This indeed proves the statement true that "the eyes are the windows of the Spirit." With most of us these windows are still covered with the dust of our animal delusions (desires). We can not see clearly, for the cerebral substance has not yet been clarified and chemically perfected. When this at last has been accomplished, we will not "see as through a glass, DARKLY," but the windows of our heaven shall be open, illumination will have been attained. The cerebrum will be as a ball of living fire.

Our outer eyes constitute in themselves two zodiacs, and a very interesting science will eventually develop which will throw light on the condition of the areas in the two cerebral hemispheres, in addition to those in the body, as now used.

Returning to the analysis of our Biblical quotation, we find that this eye may be actually consumed by grief. Here is direct reference to what may be termed a Saturnine emotion. The lachrymal glands are over-stimulated by emotion; and hence are over active. As this fluid is derived from the brain we can understand why the loss is depleting. It is deflected from its natural course downward to supply the entire glandular system, and the latter does not obtain sufficient. It seems reasonable to assume that intense grief, continuous over a period of time *could* drain away a large part of the cerebral substance or exhaust it so that it would cease to function. This may be one of the reasons why some people (in rare instances) die of grief.

Sorrow has a contracting and crystallizing effect on the nerves, and it is a fact that it very materially limits the supply of energy sent ordinarily to the solar plexus. The functions of all the organs are thus retarded. Particularly do we find trouble arising relative to digestion, liver, kidney and bowel action.

Completing our analysis of the above quotation, "it waxeth *old* because of all mine enemies." If we are true to ourselves, meaning if we study to live and perfect ourselves by doing the RIGHT thing, we will have no enemies, for the latter are OUR DESIRES AND EMOTIONS. Like the lion, the beast of prey, THEY TEAR US TO PIECES AND CONSUME US. It is *physiologically* true.

From Psalms 22:21, we quote the following: "Save me from the lion's mouth; for thou hast heard me from the horns of the unicorns." The last part of the above statement is very curious and deeply occult. The unicorn was a mythical animal whose legendary story is extremely interesting. It has to do with the subject matter of this book. It will be fully considered under Capricorn, the tenth chapter.

We find the same idea concerning emotion set forth in Psalms 57:4: "My soul is among lions; and I lie even among them that are set on fire, even the sons of men whose teeth are spears and arrows and their tongue a sharp sword."

Here we find reference to desires so consuming that the body is literally set on fire. The flames become as teeth to mutilate and consume the flesh. The blood becomes feverish and the heart labors furiously to circulate it as fast as the throbbing nerves demand. Is it any wonder that the sexual act causes severe strain on the heart? It is not uncommon for death to result at its termination. No one can be in perfect health and suddenly die from heart failure as we so often read in the papers. It is a statement of such ignorance as actually to be silly. There are many forms of heart disturbance and they, together with their causes, will be considered later on in this chapter. Any organ (the same as any machine) will suddenly give out when constant and undue strain is put upon it.

Another interesting quotation from Second Timothy 4:17, refers to the result of co-operation between Aries and Leo, when all our actions are directed by the Lord (the Spirit in us): "Notwithstanding the Lord stood with me, and strengthened me; that by me the preaching might be fully known, and all the Gentiles might hear; and I was delivered out of the mouth of the lion." By preaching is meant the admonition of the Higher Self (Aries) to the motion-self (the personality) to cease being emotional, thus delivering the former out of the mouth of the lion.

In the fourteenth chapter of Judges, we read how "Samson went *down* to Timnath and in the vineyards a young lion roared against him. The Spirit of the Lord came mightily upon him and he rent him as he would have rent a kid, and he had nothing in his hands." After a time he returned to the carcass of the lion; and behold there was a swarm of bees and honey in the carcass of the lion. He ate the honey—and "the Spirit of the Lord came upon him and he slew thirty men and *went up* TO HIS FATHER'S HOUSE."

This reference to Samson is remarkable, for in Hebrew we find the name means SUN-LIKE, strong, distinguished, the hero. It is analogous to the vital force generated in Aries going down (exactly as it was said to do) into Leo which was, in the rendering, called Timnath. In Hebrew, this word means PORTION ASSIGNED, OR RESIDENCE. It symbolizes the great motive center which receives electrical impulses from the brain. The power of the spirit within enabled Samson to control the passion which suddenly arose to tempt him and even to subdue it entirely, which the word "slay" implies. That powerful force was TRANSMUTED. This idea is impressed on one rather forcibly by the statement that "he had nothing in his hands." It was not a material weapon which he used, but the electrical power of WILL.

WILL is a higher or celestial attribute, and is required to dominate the senses. It is not will but *desire*, beastly, ravening like the lion, which is the SLAVE of passion. We can not afford to ignore the rest of this quotation, the reference to bees and honey which Samson found in the carcass of the lion on returning to it, also to the power which came upon him after eating.

It will be recalled that the *Bee*, as stated in the chapter on Aries, is a symbol of Prana, in Sanskrit, or the buzzing dancing electrons of Spirit; also that honey is a precipitation of etheric particles, termed ambrosia and nectar of the gods.

That which was found in the lion, heavenly nectar gathered there because *not thrown away in passion,* was reabsorbed by the blood and nerves. This gave the supposed Samson such strength ("the spirit of the Lord came mightily upon him") that he slew thirty men and "returned to his Father's house."

The thirty men are analogous to the thirty degrees of Leo, also of Scorpio, and it is evident that the return of Samson to his Father's house has to do with the return of that same mighty force to the brain, which truly is the Father's (Aries) house. Expressed in scientific and mechanical terms, *energy was conserved.*

There are very curious and subtle references to Leo and Cancer found in the thirty-fourth and thirty-fifth verses of the first chapter of the first book of Samuel: "And David said unto Saul, Thy servant kept his Father's sheep, and there came a lion and a bear and took a lamb out of the flock. And I went after him and smote him and delivered it out of his mouth; and when he rose against me I caught him by the beard and slew him. And David said moreover the Lord delivered me out of the paw of the lion and out of the paw of the bear."

Unless the chapter on the sign Cancer is understood it will be a little difficult, perhaps, to get the full interpretation of the reference to *Bear.* Ursa Major, or the Great Bear or Shepherd in the constellation of Cancer is the reference. Therefore the Biblical story concerns that deeply hidden mystery which Cancer alone reveals and which is of such intense physiological interest.

The meaning of "Thy servant *kept* his Father's sheep," will be clear if the chapter on Aries has been thoroughly digested. Any reference to flocks, sheep, lamb or ram is analogous to this sign. Father also refers to Aries, as it is the house or organ of the Creator. TO KEEP one's sheep literally means that one does not part with or waste the seed essence from the brain.

Taking the lamb out of the flock by a lion and a bear has reference not only to catching one of these seed-electrons (which, as stated before, constitutes a nucleus for a corpuscle, in a crab-like web in the spleen and perfecting a corpuscle, but to the fire of passion (the lion) seeking to create in it the same vibration as itself. This would, if successful, cause the corpuscle to be changed and eventually ejected from the body. The bear means *to create* while lion means to consume.

But we find that the latter did *not* result, for David "went after him and smote him (the lion) and delivered it (the lamb) out of his mouth." And when passion still surged and would not cease, will asserted itself, and he slew the lion.

The result of disobedience to God's laws, as when the will is not yet strong enough to *control* the lion (holding the passions as a dog is held by a leash), is brought out clearly in the fourteenth chapter of the first book of Kings: "It is the man of God who was disobedient unto the word of the Lord; therefore the Lord hath delivered him unto the lion which hath torn him and slain him."

The kind of seed that is sown and the soil in which it falls decides what the reaping will be. Again we have an example of the inevitable working out of the law of cause and effect. If the passions and emotions are controlled (slain, transmuted), creative energy and substance is free to return to the Father's house, the place of its inception. When they are not controlled, the contrary is true.

Because the four signs of the vital cross are separately and collectively concerned in the great work of slaying the lion, they are referred to in Rev. IV, sixth and seventh verses, as "the four beasts," and are described as follows: "The first was like a lion, the second a calf, the third had the face of a man and the fourth *beast* was like a *flying* eagle."

It will be seen that all four are termed beasts, even the one having the face of a man. The latter has been carved in stone, and preserved through the ages as an everlasting memorial or reminder of the negative and positive processes. As Dr. Carey stated in his book *The Chemistry and Wonders of the Human Body:* "A dream of an ancient alchemist solidified in stone, and the awful sphinx sat down in Egypt's sand to gaze into eternity."

Aquarius and Leo, two diametrically opposed signs, are placed *opposite* each other in the zodiacal circle for the very good reason that they, as constellations, are found to occupy the same positions in relation to each other in the *heavens*. They represent therefore, the two ends of one pole of existence. Aquarius has to do with the Real Man, the regenerated being, while Leo points out the struggle with the lion (the beast) which must result in victory or the crucifixion of the Son of man in us.

Countless are the crucifixions constantly taking place!

The calf referred to is Taurus, the lower brain, the animal man, the bull which WILL EVENTUALLY BECOME DIVINE, now plowing up the earth in rage, reaping a crop of tares. He is the *prodigal* son.

The reference to "the beast like a flying eagle" is a very great mystery, but is solved by an understanding of esoteric astrology. It will be explained in the chapter dealing with Scorpio, and we need only state here that it has reference to the seed-electrons or corpuscle-nuclei at last becoming free to ascend (fly as the eagle) to the heights.

When Leo and Aries work in harmony or in trine as their positions in relation to each other in the zodiac indicate, the electrical energy generated in Aries is utilized in a harmonious and positive manner. No energy is wasted when one is mentally balanced. The physical and mental work accomplished is always constructive.

We find the above happy state expressed in the following, taken from I Chronicles 12:8: "The lion-faced warriors of Gad (God) were among David's most valiant troops." Brain cells which function perfectly, assuredly fight for or do the will of the Most High.

The Bible contains innumerable other references, but the above are sufficient for our purpose.

"To misunderstand and confuse the meanings of words, and to misapply the words themselves is a *disease* of memory," says the well-known writer, Max Müller. What store of priceless mental wealth awaits the earnest student who labors constantly to eradicate this disease.

G. M. Gayley, in his *Classic Myths of English Literature*, says: "Allegorical interpretation is akin to the philological in its results. It leads us to explain myths as embodiments in symbolic guise of *hidden meaning* of *physical, chemical,* or *astronomical* FACTS; or of moral, religious, philosophical truth."

It is indeed encouraging to find other writers who, although they do not always interpret their translations, readily admit that great truths of a scientific and philosophical character are concealed in ancient writings.

Mr. Gayley also says: "This method of explanation rests upon the assumption that the men who made the allegories were proficient in physics, chemistry, astronomy, etc., and clever in allegory; but that, for some unknown reason their descendants becoming stupid, knowledge as well as wit deserted the race. In some cases the myth was, without doubt, from the first an allegory; but where the myth was consciously fashioned as an allegory, in all probability it was preserved as such. It is not, however, likely that allegories of *deep scientific* or *philosophical* import were *invented by savages.* Where the myth has every mark of great antiquity, is especially silly and senseless and savage, it is safe to believe that any profound allegorical meaning, read into it, is the work of men of a later generation who thus attempted to make reasonable the divine and heroic narratives which they could not otherwise justify, and of whose existence they were ashamed.

"Among the ancients, Theagenes of Rhegium, six hundred years before Christ, suggested the allegorical theory and method of interpretation. In modern times he has been supported by Lord Bacon, whose *Wisdom of the Ancients* treats myths as 'elegant and instructive fables,' and by many Germans, especially Professor Creutzer."

Wordsworth, in his poem *Excursion,* furnishes us with a delightful word picture of the intensely imaginative Grecian mind:

"In that fair clime the lonely herdsman, stretched
On the soft grass through half a summer's day,
With music lulled his indolent repose;
And, in some fit of weariness, if he,
When his own breath was silent chanced to hear
A distant strain far sweeter than the sounds
Which his poor skill could make, his fancy fetched
Even from the blazing chariot of the sun
A beardless youth who touched a golden lute,
And filled the illumined groves with ravishment."

Mr. Gayley further states: "If we were living, like the Greek of old, close to the heart of nature, such personification of natural powers would be more easy for us to appreciate." And as Ruskin says: "If for us also, as for the Greek, the sunrise means daily restoration to the sense of passionate gladness and of perfect life—if it means the thrilling of new strength through every nerve—the shedding over us of better peace than the peace of night, in the power of the dawn, and the purging of evil vision and fear by the baptism of its dew; —if the sun itself is an influence, to us also, of spiritual good —and becomes thus in reality, not in imagination, to us also, a spiritual power—we may then soon over-pass the narrow limit of conception which kept the power impersonal, and rise with the Greek to the thought of an angel who rejoiced as a strong man to run his course, whose voice, calling to life and labor, rang around the earth, and whose going forth was to the ends of heaven."*

In Greek literature Helios represented the Sun in its daily and yearly course, its physical rather than its spiritual manifestation, Apollo being the name of the latter.

"Apollo brought not only the warm spring and summer, but also the blessings of the harvest. He warded off dangers and diseases of summer and autumn; and he healed the sick. He was patron of music and poetry. He was a founder of cities, a promoter of colonization, a giver of good laws, the ideal of fair and manly youth—a *pure* and *just* god, requiring CLEAN HANDS AND PURE HEARTS of those that worshiped him. But though a god of life and peace, the far-darter did not shun the weapons of war. When presumption was to be punished, or wrong righted, he could bend his bow, and slay with the arrows of his sunlight."—Gayley.

Shelley says of the Sun:

"The sunbeams are my shafts, with which I kill
Deceit, that loves the night and fears the day;
All men who do or even imagine ill
Fly me, and from the glory of my ray
Good minds and open actions take new might,
Until diminished by the reign of night.
I am the EYE with which the universe
Beholds itself and knows itself divine;
All harmony of instrument or verse,
All prophecy, all *medicine*, are mine,
All light of art or nature; —to my song,
Victory and praise in their own right belong."

The story of Phaëton is a very realistic description of the terrible effect of a will too weak to guide the horses of the chariot of the Sun.

It is the story of the destructive phase of energy. As it is the only example I shall quote from Greek mythology, it is well to do so at length:

"Phaëton was the son of Apollo and the nymph Clymene. One day Epaphus, the son of Jupiter and Io, scoffed at the idea of Phaëton being the son of a god. Phaëton complained of the insult to his mother Clymene. She sent him to Phœbus

***Queen of the Air.*

to ask for himself whether he had not been truly informed concerning his parentage. Gladly Phaëton traveled *toward* the regions of sunrise, and gained at last the palace of the Sun. He approached his father's presence, but stopped at a distance, *for the light was more than he could bear.* Phœbus Apollo, arrayed in purple, sat on a throne that glittered with diamonds. Beside him stood the Day, the Month, the Year, the Hours, and the Seasons. Surrounded by these attendants the Sun beheld the youth dazzled with the novelty and splendor of the scene, and inquired the purpose of his errand. The youth replied, 'Oh, light of the boundless world, Phœbus, my father—if thou dost yield me that name—give me some proof, I beseech thee, by which I may be known as thine!' He ceased. His father, laying aside the beams that shone around his head, bade him approach, embraced him, owned him for his son, and swore by the river Styx that whatever proof he might ask should be granted. Phaëton immediately asked to be permitted for one day to drive the chariot of the Sun. The father repented his promise, and tried to dissuade the boy by telling him the perils of the undertaking. 'None but myself,' he said, 'may drive the flaming car of day. Not even Jupiter, whose terrible right arm hurls the thunderbolts. The first part of the way is steep, and such as the horses when fresh in the morning can hardly climb; the middle is high up in the heavens, when I myself can scarcely, without alarm, look down and behold the earth and sea stretched beneath me. The last part of the road descends rapidly, and requires most careful driving. Tethys, who is waiting to receive me, often trembles for me lest I should fall headlong. Add to this that the heaven is all the time turning round and carrying the stars with it. Couldst thou keep thy course, while the sphere revolved beneath thee? The road, also is through the midst of frightful monsters. Thou must pass by the horns of the Bull, in front of the Archer, and near the Lion's jaws, and where the Scorpion stretches its arms in one direction and the Crab in another. Nor wilt thou find it easy to guide those horses, *with their breasts full of fire* that they breathe forth from their mouths and nostrils. Beware, my son, lest I be the donor of a *fatal gift;* recall the request while yet thou canst.' He ended; but the youth rejected admonition, and held to his demand. So, having resisted as long as he might, Phœbus at last led the way to where stood the lofty chariot.

"It was of gold, the gift of Vulcan: the axle of gold, the pole and wheels of gold, the spokes of silver. Along the seat were rows of chrysolites and diamonds, reflecting the brightness of the sun. While the daring youth gazed in admiration, the early Dawn threw open the purple doors of the east, and showed the pathway strewn with roses. The stars withdrew, marshaled by the Day star, which last of all retired also. The father, when he saw the earth beginning to glow, and the Moon preparing to retire, ordered the Hours to harness up the horses. They led forth from the lofty stalls the steeds *full fed with ambrosia,* and attached the reins. Then the father, smearing the face of his son with a powerful unguent, made him capable of enduring the brightness of the flame. He set the rays on the lad's head, and, with a foreboding sigh, told him to spare the whip and hold tight the reins; not to take the straight road between the five circles, but to turn off to the left; to keep within the limit of the middle zone, and avoid the northern and southern alike; finally, to keep in the well-worn ruts, and to drive neither too high nor too low, for the middle course was safest and best.

"Forthwith the agile youth sprang into the chariot, stood erect, and grasped the reins with *delight,* pouring out thanks to his *reluctant parent.* But the steeds soon perceived that the load they drew was lighter than usual; and as a ship without ballast is tossed hither and thither on the sea, the chariot, without its accustomed weight, was dashed about as if empty. The *horses rushed headlong and left the traveled road.* Then, for the first time, the Great and Little Bears were scorched with heat, and would fain, if it were possible, have plunged into the water; and the *Serpent which lies coiled around the north pole, torpid* and *harmless, grew warm,* and with *warmth* felt its *rage revive.* Bootes, they say, fled away, though encumbered with his plow, and unused to rapid motion.

"When hapless Phaëton looked down upon the earth, now spreading in vast extent beneath him, he grew pale, and his knees shook with terror. *He lost his self command, and knew not whether to draw tight the reins or throw them loose;* he forgot the names of the horses. But when he beheld the monstrous forms scattered over the surface of the heaven, the *Scorpion* extending two great arms, his tail, and his crooked claws over the space of two signs of the zodiac, when the boy beheld him, *reeking with poison* and menacing with fangs, his courage failed, *and the reins fell from his hands.* The horses, unrestrained, went off into unknown regions of the sky, in among the stars, *hurling the chariot* over the pathless places, now up in high heaven, now down almost to the earth. The moon saw with astonishment her brother's chariot running beneath her own. The clouds began to smoke. The forest-clad mountains burned—Athos, and Taurus and Tmolus and Œte; Ida, once celebrated for fountains; the muses' mountain Helicon, and Hæmus; Ætna, with fires within and without, and Parnassus, with his two peaks, and Rhodope, forced at last to part with his snowy crown. Her cold climate was no protection to Scythia; Caucasus burned, and Ossa and Pindus, and greater than both, *Olympus*—the Alps high in air, and the Apennines crowned with clouds.

"Phaëton beheld the world on fire, and felt the heat intolerable. Then, too, is said, the people of Æthiopia became black because the blood was called by the heat so suddenly to the surface; and the Libyan desert was dried up to the condition in which it remains to this day. The Nymphs of the fountains, with disheveled hair, mourned their waters, nor were the rivers safe beneath their banks; Tanais smoked, and Caicus, Zanthus, and Meander; Babylonian Euphrates and Ganges, Tagus, with golden sands, and Cayster where the swans resort. Nile fled away and hid his head in the desert, and there it still remains concealed. Where he used to discharge his waters through seven mouths into the sea, seven dry channels alone remained. The earth cracked open, and through the chinks light broke into Tartarus, and frightened the king of shadows and his queen. The sea shrank up. Even Nereus and his wife Doris, with the Nereids, their daughters, sought the deepest caves for refuge. Thrice Neptune essayed to raise his head above the surface, and thrice was driven back by the heat. Earth, surrounded as she was by waters, yet with head and shoulders bare, screening her face with her hands, looked up to heaven, and with husky voice prayed Jupiter if it were his will that she should perish by fire, to end her agony at once by his thunderbolts, or else to consider his own heaven, how both the *poles* were *smoking* that *sustained his palace,* and that *all must fall* if they were destroyed.

"Earth, overcome by heat and thirst, could say no more. Then Jupiter, calling the gods to witness that *all was lost* unless some speedy remedy were applied, thundered, brandished a lightning bolt in his right hand, launched it against the charioteer, and struck him at the same moment from his seat and from existence. Phaeton, with his hair on fire, fell headlong, like a shooting star which marks the heavens with its brightness as it falls, and Eridanus, the great river, received him and cooled his burning frame.

"The Italian Naiads reared a tomb for him, and inscribed these words upon the stone:

'Driver of Phœbus' chariot, Phaëton,
Struck by Jove's Thunder, rests beneath this stone.
He could not rule his father's car of fire,
Yet was it much so nobly to aspire.'

"It was not, however, only by accident, or by the ill-advised action of those whom he loved, that Apollo's gifts of light and heat were turned into misfortunes. Mortals who offended him were leveled by the cruel sunstroke, by arrows of malarial venom, or manifold sickness and death."

A few comments are necessary in order to elucidate certain points in this remarkable account which otherwise might escape the attention of the reader:

The word Phaëton means "shining one," or "son of the Sun" and dictionaries inform us that the word is chiefly used allusively for a rash or venturesome charioteer, also, one who sets the world on fire. It is evident that such a one has not developed will power or discrimination. It is analogous of one possessing tremendous energy (life force) but not knowing how to direct it wisely.

The criticism concerning his birth status as son of the Sun comes from the fact that he had *personally manifested no proof*. He could not bear the light of his father's presence, not being strong or pure enough to link up with and utilize the powerful and consuming rays. There was yet too much dross in his body. Pure gold does not burn. Only poison and waste products, that which is not *chemically pure*, are consumed.

The purple robe of the Sun at dawn is expressive of the colors of Pisces and Aries where two ends of the zodiacal circle of life are forged together. It is not only typical of the rising Sun but of the Dawn of Life in nature (the Sun rising in the east) and in the human body.

It must be recalled that the passage of the Sun across the

sky during the day is analogous to the spiritual life, while the journey of the Moon by night typifies the life of the senses. Therefore the Sun alone (the triumphant Spirit) was capable of driving the flaming car *by day*.

Much emphasis is laid on the fact that constant and persistent effort of the Spirit is required. Immutable law is the force which keeps everything in its destined course. Disobedience of God's laws results in inability to follow the course, together with ever-present danger.

How true the admonition to those in the present stage of evolution, "the middle course is safest and best." There is a subtle meaning in these words which may not be noted, as the general interpretation is, that while we must strive not to fall, we must not soar too high. The idea really embodied, however, is that we must attain equilibrium, we must become balanced, perfect. The chapter on Libra, the Scales, must be studied to clarify this thought.

The fact that the car had too little *ballast* when driven by Phaëton should be clear to all. The word ballast means that which is put into a car or vehicle to *steady* it. Therefore, when used metaphysically it has reference to stability of character, morals, etc., otherwise perfect poise.

We find that some of the zodiacal signs are mentioned, and when these are analyzed it will be clear why they are mentioned. The Bull (Taurus); the Archer (Sagittarius); the Lion (Leo); and the Crab (Cancer) are those referred to. Every sentence is replete with hidden facts.

"Along the seat of the gorgeous chariot were rows of chrysolites and diamonds." In considering this statement we are delighted to find that we are able to check up with another interesting subject, that of precious stones.

In *The Curious Lore of Precious Stones,* by Frederick Kunz, we find many interesting references relative to the chrysolite. The name means GOLDEN STONE and is therefore appropriate to adorn the car of the Sun. He says: "Golden yellow was, of course, the symbol of the Sun and of Sunday. The precious stone was the chrysolite. The animal connected with the color was the lion, doubtless from the association of the zodiacal sign Leo with the mid-summer sun. Of the *seven ages of man* yellow typified *adolescence.* Roman matrons covered their heads with a yellow veil *to show their hope of offspring* and happiness. Because garments of this color were a sign of grandeur and nobility, a golden vestment is assigned to the Queen of Heaven, as a sign of her pre-eminence, as we read in Psalms 14:9: 'Upon thy right hand did stand the queen in gold of Ophir.' Gimma's explanation of this as referring to the Virgin Mary is in accord with the Catholic exegesis of his time."

Whenever we search for FACTS we find them. Please note how many statements relative to the subjects pertaining to Leo we find in the above paragraph. They check correctly with points given before, such as the seven periods in the life of man; adolescence, which is the time when sexual passion is rampant, and which also tallies with the old name of this month, Sextilis; with the *desire* of Roman matrons *for offspring;* and with gold as the color of Leo, or grandeur and nobility. It is embodied in the expression "AUGUST PRESENCE."

Mr. Kunz also states in his very interesting treatise that "the belief in the virtue of the chrysolite to dissolve enchantments and to put evil spirits to flight was probably due to the association of this stone with the sun, before whose life-giving rays darkness and all the powers of darkness were driven away."

The fact that Phaëton was filled with *intense* admiration of the beauty and grandeur of his father's surroundings and that he grasped the horses' reins with delight proves that he had become keyed to a high pitch of *emotion.* Naturally the pendulum was to swing just as far in the opposite direction. This fact constitutes *one* of the several reasons which will be given later on as proof that what is *termed positive* emotion is also of a destructive nature.

Phaëton's mind was not kept steadily on the business at hand, that of driving the car, for he was filled with conflicting emotions.

It was stated that the steeds were "full-fed with ambrosia." This should be clear to those who have understood the first chapter, Aries. The Divine Bee, Bramharandha, produces the honey or ambrosia. Energy was at its *highest.*

But fear followed swiftly after his exuberance and delight: the horses rushed headlong, and left the beaten path. His knees even shook with terror, which is analogous to lack of character. (See Capricorn).

Then the *serpent* (desire), which had hitherto been torpid

and *harmless*, and wound around the *North Pole* (manifesting as *wisdom)*, was aroused by the heat and "its rage revived." An explanation is hardly necessary here but lest there is one reader who is unable to understand, let it be said that the torpid and harmless serpent typified passion restrained and utilized in constructive work, as when Phœbus himself drove his own chariot. It means that desire was again aroused. Then utter panic possessed Phaëton, and he forgot even the names of the horses. In biochemic science, this is a definite modality indicative of MENTAL CONFUSION.

At this point it will be seen that Phaëton gave way wholly to passion, for he now faces the Scorpion itself. In astrologic lore this sign is said to be the HOUSE OF DEATH. However there have been no books which have given the true esoteric reason. Chapter VIII will do so. As the terrible claws reached out toward him and he breathed the poisonous and death-dealing effluvia, HIS COURAGE DESERTED HIM. Is it not true that when courage is gone one is unable to keep on?

And so the earth (body) became hot and at last smoked. The fluids and the glandular substance of a watery nature also began to evaporate from the ever-present animal heat. In a last extremity Earth called aloud to Heaven, exactly as the suffering body calls to the mind, demanding to know the cause of its agony and asking for help. In this instance, we receive proof that the brain itself was about to expire. Jupiter, the beneficent Father, giver of all good things, and metaphysically the Higher Mind, responded; and the electricity from the brain in one heroic effort destroyed desire and with it the body already practically consumed. It was too late to save it.

And as the verse following the quotation states, "He was unable to drive his Father's car." He lacked self-control or mental equilibrium, hence the necessary MATERIAL.

In G. A. Gaskell's *Dictionary of the Sacred Language of All Scripture and Myths,* we find many illuminating references to our subject; "Leo is a symbol of the fifth period of the cycle of life, which is a period of involution on the astral plane, wherein *strong desire* works in the *lower nature through passion, instinct, appetite* and *animal affection.* It is the period of the *involutionary* development of the astral nature of the soul."

The above statements are very clear and therefore require no comment.

Mr. Gaskell quotes from St. Gregory's book, *Morals on the Book of Job:* "Forasmuch as the nature of everything is compounded of different *elements,* in Holy writ different things are allowably represented by any one thing. For the lion has *magnanimity,* it has also *ferocity;* by its magnanimity then it represents the Lord, by its ferocity the devil. Hence it is declared of the Lord, 'Behold the Lion of the Tribe of Judah, the root of David, hath prevailed' (Rev. 5:5). Hence it is written of the devil, 'Your adversary, the devil, like a roaring lion, walketh about seeking whom he may *devour.'* "

It is indeed true that the sun's rays are extremely powerful at this time of the year, coming as they do from a point directly overhead. The process of creating, fructifying and ripening having been accomplished, which concerns evolution, the inverse process now begins, and nature seeks to take back into herself, or *consume.* This is involution. At the Spring outpouring, evolution will once again begin.

In *Buddha-Karita* (Book I. 34), we read: " 'I (Buddha) am born for supreme knowledge, for the welfare of the world—thus this is my last birth.' Thus did he of *lion-gait,* gazing at the four quarters, utter a voice of auspicious meaning."

Mr. Gaskell very clearly interprets the above as follows: "The Self is born in the soul for its supreme illumination, *i.e.,* the *enlightenment* of the incarnate Self. This is the *supreme moment* in spiritual involution when potential perfection is consummated (last birth), and now and henceforward proceeds the fulfillment of the Divine nature, which through the Self is brought to realize itself. So did the Self of FORCEFUL mien, *conqueror of the Quarternary,* foresee his Divine mission." By conqueror of the quarternary is meant the vital cross, the four beasts of the Scriptures, the four physiological parts of the body having to do with the vital forces.

In *Ibid* (page 216), we read: "The two Lion-gods watch, one at each end, the path of the night Sun."

Right here is the proper place to state, before we leave the subject of the chrysolite, that the chemical term for this gem is MAGNESIUM FERRO SILICATE. In some books on chemistry it is termed MAGNESIUM SILICATE. However, the first-named salt, MAGNESIUM, is its chief earth.

This statement will probably astound many when it is learned that Dr. Carey allocated Magnesium phosphate with this sign.

Magnesium is diamagnetic, which means that it possesses the property of being *repelled* by a magnet and of tending to take a position *at right angles* (in other words to form a *square*) to the lines of force in a magnetic field. Phosphorus, water and hydrogen also have this same property.

As electricity is the SOURCE of all magnetism, we find this scientific statement to be back of the placing of the fire signs, Aries and Leo, in trine or harmonious relationship to each other in the circle of the zodiac.

Magnesium is also a reducing agent, which expression has been previously explained. It will be understood that a substance capable of being *repelled* (such as Magnesium) or MOVED out of its place, is required in order TO PRODUCE MOTION. Therefore the all-wise Architect and Chemist of the universe created and used it for that purpose. That which is incapable of being moved or of moving becomes useless. This is true of the body when Magnesium phosphate becomes very deficient. Spasms result.

As it is chemically true that acid attacks Magnesium with ease, we have here the reason why excruciating nerve pain results, when acid is present in the system for a long time. This condition is hastened and intensified by lack of Silicea which is nature's best insulating agent.

Schuessler's *Biochemic System* informs us that this remarkable salt serves to build sheaths and is indeed a protection for certain parts of the body. Both sensory and motor nerves are wound together in bundles like the strands of a rope and encased in a tube or sheath, so that nothing will contact them or prevent the free flow of electrical currents (energy) through them. In the world of electrical science we find this to be a fact and it is equally true when applied in the human body. The Chapter on Sagittarius and Silicea will further explain this.

It is also instructive to note that when Magnesium is heated to redness, it will take fire and burn with a dazzling light. It is very rich in ultra-violet rays, which again proves that it is practically inseparable from Potassium or Kali, the Aries salt. It has been used in late years as a source of light in photography. It also is refractory (resistant) and hence is used for furnace linings.

In combination with sulphur, Magnesium forms what is familiarly known as epsom salts, the cleansing properties of which are well known. The blood can not utilize epsom salt, however. As its effect is to irritate vascular surfaces, causing them to give up their fluidic content, it will be easily seen that its use as a purgative over a long period of time would eventually result in abnormal dryness, just the opposite effect from that desired. The sodiums are the natural agents having to do with the fluids.

The fluoride of the Cancer sign combination, linked with the Magnesium phosphate of Leo, form fluorphosphate of magnesium which will eventually be found to throw chemical light on the close association of the Sun and Moon as rulers of these two signs.

Splendidly true are the words of E. Underhill, in his book, *Mysticism:* "The Green Lion is the First Matter of the Great Work. It is not by the education of the lamb, but by the hunting and taming of the wild, intractable lion, instinct with vitality, full of ardor and courage, exhibiting heroic qualities *on the sensual plane,* that the Great Work is achieved. The Green Lion, then, in his strength and wholeness, is the only creature potentially able to attain Perfection. 'The Green Lion,' says one alchemist, 'is the priest by whom Sol and Luna are wed.' "

"By Green Lion is meant the astral or desire nature, while the lamb refers to Aries or the Most High. Hence it is true that the sensual nature *is* the creature (animal man) which is potentially able to become perfect. Sol (or energy) and Moon (material or substance) are finally united in the permanent or Heavenly Marriage 'which no man can put asunder.' "

The foregoing statement never meant earthly marriage. That it has been thus interpreted is only one more instance of the perversion of truth. How ridiculous the thought that the uniting of man and woman by any human being and for a price could possibly create a permanent or harmonious union.

In much of the teaching given today we find that Heavenly Marriage is interpreted to mean the joining together in wedlock of a man and woman who seem very well suited to each other and supposedly harmonious. That such is absolutely untrue will be admitted by anyone carefully analyzing the entire phase of married life. This will be considered in the chapter on Libra.

By Green Lion is meant UNDYING ENERGY, the ever-present and undiminishing life force; creative force undepleted. This is the yardstick or measuring rod which we must apply in our analysis of marriage.

On page 274 of Volume I, of her *Secret Doctrine,* Madam Blavatsky says: "Everything in the Universe, throughout all its kingdoms, is CONSCIOUS; *i. e.,* endowed with a consciousness of its own kind and on its own plane of perception. We must remember that because WE do not perceive any signs—which we can recognize of consciousness, say, in stones, we have no right to say that NO CONSCIOUSNESS EXISTS THERE. There is no such thing as either 'dead' or 'blind' matter, as there is no 'blind' or 'unconscious' law."

Anyone who has had a few years' experience in the study and use of the twelve mineral salts of the blood as outlined originally by Dr. William Schuessler, even without the astrological allocations, will whole-heartedly endorse this statement. It is astounding what these little mineral workmen do.

Let us consider the action of Magnesium phosphate in the human body. Then we will better understand the symptoms which arise from its need.

As before stated, *all* the nerves are threads or fibers and hence their BASIC material is Kali mur, or chloride of potassium, the SPINNING salt. There must be different kinds of fibers because used for different purposes. So the all-wise Chemist added Kali phos or phosphate of Potassium to those fibers which were to contact *Spirit,* the electrical energy of life. The latter constitute the gray matter.

Other nerves were also required, capable of responding to the sensory impulses and thus producing MOTION. So Magnesium phosphate was combined with certain fibers to make the white or motor nerves. And when it is recalled that the root of the word Magnesium or *mag* is derived from the Sanskrit and means TO MOVE, we again marvel at Dr. Carey's intuition which indeed must have resulted from an intensive study of these subjects in his past incarnation.

It will be recalled that the two opposite renderings of the word lion are MAGNANIMITY and FEROCITY. It is exceedingly curious and yet true that the first word is derived from the same root (MAG) as Magnesium while ferocity has the same root as the chemical term Ferrum or iron. It is also a fact that these two salts work *together*. As no MOTION can be produced without ENERGY, so Ferrum or iron is necessary in order to BEAR ENERGY ALONG ITS WAY, which is interpreted as MOTION.

There are several meanings derived from the Latin *ferre*, i. e., to bear, bring, carry, attack. Iron does all of these. Iron and oxygen attack each other so savagely that the former is eventually consumed. Iron carries oxygen, and oxygen carries iron; without them both, life could not exist for one moment in any body, animate or inanimate. Even Thomas Vaughan quotes Pythagoras as saying in his *Turba:* "Great is the affinity between Magnesia and Iron."

The Latin lexicon states that the word ferocity has a dual interpretation; for it not only means high-spirited or courageous, but fierce, rough, or harsh. And indeed we realize how well these link up with the analysis of the word lion.

On examining the word iron, we find the same situation. This material is used wherever strength is required, and it is well known that iron and steel are used to manufacture machinery and the framework of buildings. All parts of the body need their quota of iron particles for the same reason—to give strength, as will be understood from reading Chapter XII, on Pisces. The negative interpretation is exemplified in the expression, "hard as nails," hard as iron, unfeeling, as manifesting in those of cruel nature.

The term magnanimous is derived from two Latin words, *magnus* for great, and *animus* meaning *mind;* therefore it refers to one who is great of mind, elevated in soul, raised above what is mean or low or ungenerous, courageous, noble-spirited and unselfish.

Mother Nature, working in the human body, lets her wants be known by producing a feeling of discomfort. Health is ease of mind and body. Dis-ease is the absence of ease. Deficiency in Magnesium phosphate causes some very curious and striking symptoms.

When the particles of this salt become very deficient, there is a disturbance in the fibers of nerves and muscular tissue, and their action is no longer rhythmic. Spasmodic action results. Any symptom of this nature calls for this salt. We find some of them are: cramps in the limbs, fingers, neck, in fact any part of the body; lock jaw, spasmodic coughing, sneezing, choking, crying, laughing, hiccough.

This salt is the only true spasmodic remedy; and, when taken in hot water, very soon brings relief. It is also the specific for pain.

Hot applications and hot drinks should be taken to assist relaxation. When swimmers are deficient in this salt, cramp of the limbs will cause much discomfort, especially when the water is quite cold. Angina pectoris is a very painful symptom which calls for large doses of this salt. Neuritis and neuralgia indicate need of it, but there are other salts required in addition.

All troubles of heart and motor system call for Magnesium phosphate. It has been my experience that where Calcium in any one combination (or in all three) is deficient, Magnesium should also be included, for there seems to be a special affinity between it and Calcium. Whenever a person's chemical plan calls for Magnesium, Ferrum should also be taken, because they *need* each other. And indeed, there is never a condition where there is no call for Iron, since it is the attractor of oxygen in the body, the means of purification and the great healer.

"Each inorganic salt knows how to make some constituent of the human organism," says Dr. Carey. This is proof that the giving of serums for disease does not constitute a logical treatment, for the body will manufacture its own serums in its countless laboratories, provided the little mineral workmen are supplied. The cerebrum is the Father that precipitates the heavenly dew, and forms the proteus or fluidic substance needed to work with the salts.

Lack of Magnesium phosphate causes many illusions of the senses and queer mental disorders, as it is closely allied with Kali or potassium.

Other symptoms are nervous headache, with illusions of sight; "seeing double"; seeing colors. It must be remembered that disturbances in the gray matter of the brain also react on the eyes. Headache with chilly sensations up and down the spine may appear; sharp, shooting, darting and intermittent pain; all pain which heat relieves and cold aggravates; pain in the nape of the neck, of sharp character; sensitiveness to light; spasmodic twitching of the eyelids; squinting; pain in eyes; spasmodic earache, relieved by heat; loss of sense of smell. When not caused by a cold, this last is a very unique symptom. Personally I have proved that, to eradicate it, three other salts are required in connection with Magnesium, *i.e.*, Natrium mur, Natrium sulph, and Calcium sulph.

Other symptoms are: twitching of mouth or lips; spasmodic stammering; lockjaw (the gums should also be rubbed with the salt); convulsions in teething children; spasmodic closing of the windpipe (a very unique and rather rare symptom); constricted feeling in the throat; stomach spasms; cramping of the solar plexus; pain accompanying belching of gas; spasmodic retention of the urine; stricture of the male sexual organs; menstrual colic; neuralgia of the ovaries (also apply hot local applications); constrictive cough of asthma; shooting sensation in the limbs, resembling electric shocks; trembling and involuntary motion of the hands; paralysis agitans; epileptic spasms; writer's cramp; yawning, with spasmodic straining of the lower jaw.

The modalities indicative of need of this salt are: symptoms relieved by heat, pressure and rubbing; aggravated by cold, cold air, etc. It must be remembered that the fundamental interpretation of the function of this salt is, that it is concerned with VITALITY, therefore activity, the circulation of blood, nerve force, glandular fluids, etc., etc.

After setting forth the analysis of the sign Leo, in conjunction with that of the lion as its symbol, we have proceeded to synthesize them with the chemical element doing the leonine work.

It now remains to prove that what has been termed positive emotion is also ultimately detrimental. It has been generally accepted that so-called negative emotion is injurious. Let us analyze both.

First let us recall the etymology of the word E-motion, which is, to flow forth, to *go out* from. The mind and body are concerned, as has been proved, with MOTION. E-motion, then, implies disturbance, waste or loss of that which produces MOTION. Any skilled mechanic will agree. Any unusual noise around machinery, be it ever so slight, is at once noticed, and a careful examination results immediately, for it is evident that something is wrong. Imperfect insulation of electrical wires, or any imperfection in the manufacture or the installation of apparatus, results in a loss of electrical power, *e. g.*, one is unable to obtain continuous light, or the electrical iron will not heat sufficiently. There are innumerable other illustrations.

There is, then, nothing the matter with electrical energy (power). The trouble lies with the *material,* that with which energy WORKS. Each and every part of a machine, be it ever so tiny, is constituted of substance, and it must be present, otherwise one of two things results. Either *no* energy or power manifests, or it comes and goes, is spasmodic in its action.

All of the above must be applied to the human body and the perfect circulation of energy by means of a perfect supply of material to work with. *Then there can be no spasmodic action,* no loss of energy.

Emotion is the spasmodic action of energy. The BALANCE POINT (which the chapter on Libra considers) is quivering and the least thing sends it up or down. When the mind is BALANCED (the result of body and brain being balanced, which takes a tremendously long time to accomplish) it will be impossible to be emotional; for this latter typifies an unbalanced state.

In analyzing the two phases of emotion, we find that what has been interpreted as negative, is constrictive or contracting in nature; such as fear, sorrow, worry, etc., etc. Everything contracts, and the entire nervous system gets "tied up in a knot." The solar plexus, that great receiving and broadcasting station for the torso, instantly contracts, resulting in none of the organs receiving sufficient energy. The supply of electricity is at once limited.

When a person born with the Sun in Capricorn is thus affected, digestion stops and dangerous symptoms may result, especially if a very hearty meal has been eaten. This is often the cause of acute indigestion.

Those born when the Sun is transiting the sign Pisces have the solar plexus for their weakest organ, and so are doubly handicapped. This subject could be considered indefinitely, but we have not sufficient space in this work. It will be fully covered in a future publication on *The Biochemic System of Body Building* and *Astrological Allocation.*

However, it will be understood that these emotions retard and sometimes actually shut off energy temporarily. Death may result.

It has been thought that joy is always beneficial, because of the fact that it seems to stimulate one physically as well as mentally. That such is not the case will become clear to those who have gained some understanding of the work done in the body by the chemical laborers.

Please remember that there is no *quickening* or retarding of energy in a BALANCED BODY. The heart neither almost stops beating with fear, nor moves spasmodically and furiously from sudden joy or the passion of so-called love. Love is EASE, balance, harmony, for it is UNDERSTANDING OF THE LAW, hence the living of the law.

Therefore, as a result of the impulse of joyous emotion, the brain strives to generate and liberate throughout the body an extra amount of energy. Or it endeavors to quicken the energy that it has. If it were a NORMAL condition, or permanent state, when every cell is vibrating at the highest rate, there would be no reaction of a negative nature, for there would be no wear and tear or any spasmodic flow of high-tension current. The effect is identical with that produced by the crossing of wires. A higher current is generated, with the result that the fuse is burned out.

It is true that joy has been known to kill, and this is proof of the sudden and intense strain brought to bear on nerves imperfectly supplied with material. They sometimes *snap*.

The point I am endeavoring to make clear is, that all the emotions which have been considered as beneficial *strain* the nerves and heart. This is physiologically true. Therefore let the fact again be considered that the study of physiology, anatomy, biochemistry and astrology will clear up all doubts anyone may have on this subject. The analysis of the sign Libra alone gives indubitable proof. It must always be remembered that astrology is the consideration of the *body* of the universe and, by analogy, the anatomy, therefore, of man.

We approach, now, the bowels of the earth, that center where the rays of Leo are garnered in, the with-drawal into the womb of man and nature of those forces sent out at springtime. Involution is beginning!

"There was no heavy heat, no cold,
  The dwellers there wax never old,
Nor wither with the waning time,
  But each man keeps the age he had
When first he won the fairy clime.
  The night falls never from on high,
Nor ever burns the heat of noon;
  But such soft light eternally
Shines, as in silver dawns of June
  Before the sun hath climbed the sky."

—*Andrew Lang.*

Chapter VI

THE ANALYSIS AND SYNTHESIS OF VIRGO AND KALI SULPH

"Thou Virgin Mother, daughter of thy Son,
Humble and high beyond all other creatures."
—*Dante, Divina Commedia*, last Canto.

ON the twenty-third of August, approximately, the Sun enters the zodiacal sign Virgo, which is the Latin word for Virgin. The name "Virgin Mary" had its origin in this constellation, which is truly the Divine Mother.

The Hebrew term for Virgin is Bethulah; *beth*, meaning "house or place" and *ulah*, meaning "pure water." The Latin word for pure water or sea is *mare*. Changing the letter E to Y we have the name Mary. The term "Virgin Mary" will thus be seen to have a double significance, since both names have practically the same meaning—purity.

The word Bethlehem is derived from the same Hebrew root, but instead of house or place of water, its interpretation is "house or place of *bread*." However, it will be recalled that Jesus was born in Bethlehem. In Scriptural writings Bethlehem is referred to both as "the Bread of Life" and "the Water of Life."

To mentally register the full meaning of the word VIRGIN, one should consider all the synonyms used, namely: a male or female who has had no sexual intercourse; chaste, pure, undefiled, unsullied, not corrupted, fresh, new, *unadulterated*.

When the complete significance of this word (Virgin) is realized, it will perhaps be clear to students of astrology why the sign Virgo is interpreted as THE HOUSE OF HEALTH. For no one possesses health until the body is in a pure, unadulterated state, and until all the synonyms used to interpret the word Virgin are manifested. It must also be borne in mind that the *first* interpretation given in dictionaries, "a male or female who has had no sexual intercourse," is outstanding in importance.

When studied from a chemical standpoint, it will be seen how applicable is the term "unadulterated" as the definition of a pure body. Health exists when all of the chemical constituents of the blood are present, since they are the ORIGINAL ELEMENTS FROM WHICH the Divine Chemist created it.

The word adulteration means "some of the original elements missing." Could we have any better description of disease? It is clear, concise and outstanding; we are not left in doubt as to its meaning. All humanity is therefore living in a state of adulteration. We find many Biblical references to the term "an adulterous nation."

To be perfect, is to be pure, unadulterated.

As stated before, we find scarcely anything, with the exception of some of the sciences, like mathematics, which has not been perverted. There is no better outstanding example of this than in the modern and therefore common interpretation of the word "adultery."

The man-made law relative to adultery is said to mean "the sexual intercourse of two persons either of whom is married to a third person." It is therefore considered unlawful.

The Seventh Commandment reads "Thou shalt not commit adultery." We find adultery referred to in dictionaries as "lewdness or unchastity of thought or act as forbidden by the Seventh Commandment." The Latin word for lewd is "impudicus" and its literal meaning in that language is UNCHASTE, INCONTINENT.

As we can not fail to remember that words have definite meanings, we are therefore unable to deny that the Biblical injunction literally means that humanity must not be unchaste or incontinent.

In the Latin lexicon we find the word continent means: "to keep or bind together, to hold fast, unseparated." Here we link up with the term adulterate, for when anything is adulterated it means that the original elements have not been held fast, are not bound together, but on the contrary have become *separated*. Therefore a LOSS is implied.

Doubtless there will be many who will admit that these interpretations have hitherto been unknown to them, and naturally it will be difficult to become reconciled. We may not *want* them to be true and so we can not do otherwise, at first, than rebel against facts. We are very slow in learning what God's laws are relative to mankind, and extremely so in interpreting them correctly.

Many years ago I made the declaration to myself that I wanted TRUTH, FACTS, and I did not care how much they hurt. If my *idea* or opinion of a thing was wrong, then I wanted the correct explanation. I am never satisfied until I have found it. Everyone has ideas and opinions, but they are very often incorrect. When the higher faculty begins to work, we intuitively know when a statement is untrue.

No one accepts truth until he has been forced to do so by means of experience gained through suffering. There is only one right and perfect method to gain health, happiness and peace. No matter how long we sidestep this issue, or how stubbornly we resist, ultimately we are forced to give in. A child may not *want* to believe that he will be burned by placing his hand against a hot stove, but the fact is not changed.

The word "adult" is derived from the same root as adulteration, and is "one who has *attained full size and strength*—maturity." A grown person may indeed appear to be an adult, but in the light of the above interpretation, when he is deficient in the original elements, he is merely *adulterated.*

Until humanity as a whole turns its attention to the science of attaining and preserving health, it will indeed be difficult for any great number to be interested in anything but opinions. Indeed, a great deal of time will actually be spent in arguing against facts. A common question having its inception in the mass mind is: "If continence is the law of God, and if it were obeyed, the earth would eventually become depopulated."

It is true that the law of God (good or ultimate perfection), is that of continence. But until the triune being, animal-human-spiritual man attains to perfection (purity—the original state) by ridding himself of all that pertains to the animal, he is not keeping that law. It is a definite and long drawn-out process. As continence means NO LOSS OF ORIGINAL ELEMENTS, therefore no adulteration, this process of purification deals with *all stages and degrees of loss.* It can not be otherwise.

The MINIMUM loss, when correctly analyzed, really pertains to the fall of man into generation. It represents an actual sacrifice of cerebral *esse* by a man and woman in order that a body may be furnished for an incoming ego. It is solely for the continuance of the race, and as such is the means whereby evolution may go on.

Reincarnation of the spirit again and again into a new body should mean a better physical vehicle each time. But so slow have we been in learning, that very little improvement seems to have been made. Many pass out in infancy. Is it not true of the average person that he or she is well past middle life before even diet is considered?

The unconsciously facetious statement was made in a juvenile composition recently that "a beast is an imperfect animal. Man is the only perfect beast." This would seem to be true in more than one instance since Uranus entered Aries in 1927, so chaotic has the human brain become.

It is a fact generally recognized, that the true animal obeys the law of God relative to procreation. Death, as the inevitable result of the fall of man into generation, will gradually be eliminated by a *reversal* of method.

The animal has its seasons when, from instinct, it prepares to perpetuate its kind. It does not seek to cohabit BECAUSE OF LOVE OF SENSATION, as does humanity. The detrimental effect resulting from man's fall into generation became intensified a thousand fold by this perversion, caused by the hypnotic power of the sensation created by the act. Thus humanity became almost hopelessly enmeshed in the coils of this serpent of desire.

"The serpent beguiled me and I did eat," said Eve, the negative, material, magnetic part of the human body, otherwise the procreative substance. The loss of the creative *esse* which originates in the cerebrum, the Father's house, as has been stated in the first chapter, eventually results in death. As the meaning of Eve in Hebrew is LIFE, it is evident that the beguilement of sensation results in the loss of life itself.

A study of the revelations of this remarkable sign, Virgo, will solve the problem of religion. It will at the same time answer the question relative to the real purpose of astrology.

As Virgo is the sixth sign in the natural zodiac, it has to do with sex or creation, but on a plane higher than any with which we have been dealing.

Reviewing a point mentioned in the previous chapter on Leo, we find that the consuming fire of the Sun in August represents the first step in a different cosmic and physical process. It signifies the INDRAWING of energy *into* the earth, *i. e.*, its concentration into the earth's matrix, or womb of the Divine Mother (Virgo), if it is not wasted through emotion.

It is stated in works on astrology that Virgo is an earth sign, female, but barren. As there are said to be male (positive), female (negative) and neuter planets, it has been evident to me for some time that the zodiacal signs must be divided in like manner. Gemini, Virgo, Sagittarius and Pisces are thus neutral signs. I have named them the purification cross. This has resulted in much new (to this age) information being gained. The allocating salts also have to do with cleansing.

Virgo was allocated in ancient times with the solar plexus and bowels. We find this plexus to be the *abdominal brain* and therefore a matrix or WOMB. From the latter word we obtain the so-called feminine interpretation, *but* because it is creative ONLY ON A HIGHER PLANE, it must be interpreted as neuter or *barren*. It *is* barren to CARNALITY, therefore represents BARREN EARTH. But it is indeed *fertile* to *spirituality*, which is the source of its name VIRGO, the VIRGIN.

Before going further with the astrological explanation, we must analyze this sign anatomically and physiologically.

The solar plexus lies directly back of the stomach and consists of a group of twelve different nerve ganglia whose arrangement, together with the multitudinous nerves which branch off from it in all directions, is responsible for its name, sun plexus.

It is the largest of the three sympathetic plexuses, and receives the greater and lesser splanchnic nerves of both sides and some filaments from the right vagus. As it supplies the energy required by the organs in the torso, it is evident that anything affecting the sympathetic system will react instantly on the solar plexus.

The most important parts are the semilunar ganglia. These are two large irregularly-shaped masses having the appearance of lymph glands, placed one on either side of the middle line and in front of the crura of the diaphragm close to the supra-renal glands. The one on the right side is placed behind the inferior *vena cava*.

Besides the two semilunar ganglia there are the following: the phrenic; the hepatic; the lienal; the superior gastric; the suprarenal; the renal; the spermatic; the superior mesenteric;

the abdominal aortic, and the inferior mesenteric. Earnest students should have *Gray's Anatomy*, and obtain a thorough knowledge of these ganglia. When this is done it will be easy to verify or disprove the statements made by different writers on occult subjects, especially those having to do with the chakras or esoteric nerve centers. Mistakes often occur in translating ancient Sanskrit writings; also in the statements made by occidental writers who claim to have obtained their information on this subject by psychic means.

One in the latter class has stated that the spleenic or lienal plexus is separate or independent—it is not given as one of the twelve divisions of the solar plexus. It is, however, one of the solar plexus ganglia.

Some information of an unusual nature relative to the spleen will be given in the forthcoming book, *The Truth About Sex and Birth Control.* This publication will include New Facts About the Glands, which was originally planned as a separate book.

Each of the twelve divisions of the solar plexus allocates with one of the signs of the zodiac and hence with a certain part of the body. The plexus itself is a little zodiac.

The spermatic plexus has to do with *procreative seed.* It accompanies the internal spermatic artery to the testes of the male and to the ovaries and uterus of the female. It will be easy to understand, therefore, that every sensual thought instantaneously reaches the solar plexus and is relayed directly to the sexual organs. Thus nerve, blood and glandular circulation and action are at once accelerated. This again reacts on the mind because of the sensations produced.

The solar plexus is the seat of feeling and sensation. Therefore the old and familiar expression "I love you with all my heart" is incorrect. When real or pure love, which is the only feeling worthy of being called love, permeates one's being, it is the out-pouring of the Spirit. Therefore we love *mentally* with the cerebrum. The correct expression for the *affection* which one person experiences for another is, "I love you with all my solar plexus," therefore with the bowels as well, for they are both allocated with Virgo.

Of course this correct expression of one's feelings is not at all attractive, for it is very prosaic. Naturally the poetic appeals to us more. However, we find several references to the prosaic terminology in the Scriptures as any Word Book or Concordance will prove. Some of them are: "Bowels of compassion; bowels of mercy; bowels of affection; Jacob's bowels yearned after his son," etc., etc.

In Philippians 1:8, we read "For God is my record, how greatly I long after you all in the bowels of Jesus Christ."

The interpretation of the word "bowels" is "the interior part of anything," as of the earth; the seat of feeling, etc. As Shakespeare has said: "Thou thing of no bowels," and "his soldiers rushed into the bowels of the battle."

The word intestine means "within, on the inside, internal, inclosed or confined—*subjective,"* the latter interpreted in the Latin lexicon as "placing or *laying under"* which is very applicable. If the intestines were drawn out in a straight line they would cover a space five or six times the length of the body. Is it any wonder that the ancients named the constellation allocating with this part of the anatomy the Great Dragon or Hydra?

In the twelfth chapter of Revelation, first to sixth verse, we read: "And there appeared a great wonder in heaven; a woman clothed with the sun, and the moon under her feet, and upon her head a crown of twelve stars:

"And she being with child cried, travailing in birth, and pained to be delivered.

"And there appeared another wonder in heaven; and behold a great red dragon, having seven heads and ten horns, and seven crowns upon his head.

"And his tail drew a third part of the stars of heaven, and did cast them to the earth; and the dragon stood before the woman which was ready to be delivered, for to devour her child as soon as it was born.

"And she brought forth a man child who was to rule all nations with a rod of iron; and her child was caught up unto God and to his throne."

We find direct evidence in the above passages that the constellation of Virgo is referred to. As it is by nature a neuter sign because BARREN TO CARNALITY (virgin) we may term it neuter-feminine, for the reason that it has to do with mater-ial (mother-substance).

In the esoteric story in the Scriptures, the Virgin Mary gave birth to Jesus. Jesus is the Latinized Greek form of Joshua, who was the son of Nun. As Nun is Hebrew for *fish*, progeny or life-germ, the analogy should be plain, for it is the origin of the religion of the FISHERMEN. Jesus is a Divine Fish or psycho-physical germseed which is formed in the solar plexus center, the semi-lunar ganglia, when this hub of our physical wheel is at last perfected.

The solar plexus is always deficient in power until the cerebrum and cerebellum are perfected, for insufficient is generated to supply it. In addition, none of its own parts are perfect. Therefore it is unable to respond, other than in a spasmodic way, to the energy which it receives from the brain. The solar plexus is both a receiving and a broadcasting station.

The intestinal tract also reflects the state or condition of the body. Most people are troubled more or less with constipation, and admit it. Others, who have one evacuation per day, think this sufficient. Such is not the case. Whenever food is taken into the stomach a bowel movement should occur soon after, for the stomach and intestinal tract are connected. They are one long passage, the two openings of which are the mouth and the anus. Is it, then, any wonder that the breath of the average person is not sweet or that the tongue is coated?

It does not *always* prove true that the intestinal tract is healthy when a person has several movements during the day. The condition termed "running off" of the bowels may exist. This is caused by very great deficiency in the Scorpio cell salt, Calcium sulph, which is plaster of Paris.

This unique material coats all the *vascular* surfaces of the body, exactly as the coarser form of it is used in the arts to make casts and for a *protective* covering for walls. Its use in the human body is exactly the same. When it becomes deficient in the walls of the intestines, they are irritated by the effete material constantly contacting their surface. The result is similar to that of a blister on any exterior part of the body. The delicate vascular fibers give up their water or fluid, and pieces of the scaly wall are found in it.

Naturally this condition results in great weakness if continued. Generous doses of Calcium sulph must be taken in *hot water,* when its soothing effect will be almost instantly noticeable. It at once coats the intestinal surfaces and the irritation is allayed. See chapter on Scorpio for other information relative to this salt.

There are probably very, very few people who have splendidly functioning livers and stomachs. In all the astrological charts coming under my notice either one or the other (and usually both) has been found to function very imperfectly. Constipation is common.

We have conclusive evidence, therefore, that the anatomical parts allocating with Virgo REFLECT the condition of the entire body. We can synthesize this statement with the following analogy: the Sun (energy) in the bowels of the earth REFLECTS energy (broadcasts it also) to the degree in which it RECEIVES it. The human body possesses two lenses. The one in the cerebrum which focuses light vibrations impinging on the brain from above into the optic thalamic center, is the upper, and the celiac ganglia of the solar plexus is the lower.

It will always be found, when the body is studied intensively that there are two centers of a kind, one being above, and positive, the other below and negative.

It can not be repeated too often that the glyphs and symbols of the twelve signs of the zodiac are the repositories of secret lore and invaluable information. Let us study those of Virgo.

For a long time it had been evident to me that the ancient and therefore fundamental idea embodied in this glyph was that of the Virgin and Child (Jesus), but it was not until about three years ago that I found my proof.

It is plain to be seen that the first part of this symbol is the letter M, which from time immemorial has typified WATER. Recalling the statements made relative to the definition of Virgin Mary in the beginning of this chapter, we realize that they are here verified in the cryptic meaning of the letter. In Hebrew M is spelled *Mem,* and in that ancient language means MOTHER, the female, material or substance; also magnetic, the negative, etc., etc. It is one of the three sacred letters which are termed "MOTHERS."

While studying some Phœnician characters one day, my attention was attracted to a certain letter. There was something about it which enthralled me. Suddenly it dawned on me that it was the last part of the Virgo sign, the part attached to the M. This Phœnician character 𐤍 is the letter N and in Hebrew its meaning is FISH or JESUS. If the Virgo symbol is studied carefully, it will be found that the addition of N actually represents a fish standing erect on its tail and with open mouth, thus ♍.

There is no astrological work available which gives any information of the above nature relative to the sign Virgo.

It is my firm conviction that the analysis of this sign is alone sufficient to prove for all time that the sole purpose of astrology is to furnish mankind with the astro-chemical plan for its physical and mental regeneration.

As body and brain improve, intuition will quicken. One will know, intuitively, *when* to take a journey, will automatically, as it were, follow safe paths and will never be subject to injury. No advice will be asked of another, who, in spite of frequent examinations of aspects, suffers financial reverses, poor health, and privately is just as discouraged, at times, as one having no knowledge of astrology. We have all been in this condition, but the study of this mighty science allocated with chemistry, anatomy and physiology will eventually result in the fulfillment of the old injunction, "Man, *know* THYSELF."

We find another fact of an astounding nature derived from the study of the word Christ. Jesus, the new man IN man, *becomes* the Christ, otherwise Jesus Christed. Greek scholars do not interpret the word Christos as a person but as a THING. Christ means anointed or oiled, and the literal interpretation is OIL. If the translators of the Scriptures had not interpreted things as persons, or *parts* of the body as geographical locations, the age-long perversion of religion would not have occurred. The Bible, as stated before, is a mass of scientific facts relative to the BODY of man, as well as the universe.

As man is the universal term for both male and female, it will be realized that when all parts of the body are constantly receiving all of the required chemical elements, and all laws relative to right living are being obeyed, the physical form will then change very rapidly. Eventually this constant good work will result in a perfectly functioning system.

As the solar plexus is anatomically and physiologically a TWELVE part machine, it constitutes a *complete process*. The science of numerology must be considered for a moment, in order to add another point of verification relative to the previous statements. To do this we must refer to the letter M in the Virgo glyph.

M is the THIRTEENTH letter in the Kabbala and when its true meaning, as explained in this chapter, is understood, the age-long superstition relative to thirteen being unlucky will be solved. Until we become TRUE VIRGINS—in other words, until we are no longer *adulterated,* we are and will continue to be UNLUCKY.

To be lucky does not mean sidestepping the result of wrong doing, for inevitably the fiddler has to be paid. It merely has to do with a *seeming* delay in the matter of settlement.

The student should become familiar with *The Tarot of the Bohemians,* by Papus, as it is without doubt one of the best on the subject.

Numerology has not escaped perversion at the hands of some modern writers. A study of the Tarot cards which allocate with the letters of the Hebrew alphabet as given in the above named treatise, will reveal much information which will be recognized at once as verifying the points set forth herein.

The letter M or Mem is the *center* between creation as embodied in the tenth letter Yod, and Ayin, the sixteenth letter of the Hebrew alphabet, which deals with the end of things, meaning rather the end of one phase of life and the beginning of a new. As Ayin is said to be allocated in a certain way with Capricorn, the above explanation will prove true. The god Janus which was the Roman name for January, was pictured as a man with two faces, one looking backward (to the past), the other looking toward the future, thus the beginning and the ending of a thing. As January is the month when the civil year, or New Year begins, it also stands for the ending of the old. This, however, is the exoteric explanation. The esoteric is much more instructive, as will be found by studying chapter ten on Capricorn.

As we have discovered from the analysis of the letter M, the true interpretation of the state or condition represented is one of perfect action. We next consider THAT NEW THING WHICH CAN NOW BE PRODUCED BY MEANS OF PERFECT ACTION,—namely A GOOD THING, ONE THAT IS GOD-LIKE. The product of any machine operating perfectly is the perfect product.

Virgo, then, that strange center in the human body, concerning which so little has been discovered, has now become prepared and capable of producing an entirely new thing—THE NEW MAN, or man made new. For no longer is the supply of energy needed by the twelve divisions of the body diminished; never again can the corpuscles of the body die, for there is never any deficency in material to sustain them.

Virgo is no longer Mary Magdalene, she is now the Widow. The modern interpretation of this word has completely veiled its true significance. It means "to be separated from, to lack," and therefore may have other reference in addition to a female who is separated from her husband.

There are many Scriptural references to this word and in Freemasonry the initiate is the son of the widow. One who has separated from the old life of destruction and has begun a NEW one is an initiate, for the meaning of the latter word is "to commence, to make a beginning with."

A work on *The Physiological Explanation of Freemasonry* is in the course of preparation. In it the physiological interpretation of the thirty-three degrees will be given, also the astrological and numerical or Kabbalistic. It will doubtless surprise those interested in this subject to find that the thirteenth degree in Freemasonry allocates with the first decan of Virgo, and is the Royal Arch of·Solomon. The candidate of this degree becomes the Knight of the Sacred Vault, which is indeed in the bowels of the earth. He is entitled to wear a golden triangle on which is the name Enoch, the meaning of which in Hebrew is "INITIATED."

Indeed, so accurately do the sciences of astrology, chemistry, anatomy and physiology interpret and verify Freemasonry, that they also serve to indicate where it has been grossly perverted.

Further verification of the correctness of my allocation of the thirteenth degree of the Royal Arch to the sign Virgo is found in the statement of the candidate for this degree when he is asked *where* he is. His reply is "I am in the *bowels of the earth* where the light of the sun is not needed."

Virgo is an earth sign allocating with the bowels, and as it is the SUN CENTER (the sun thus being in the bowels of the earth), NO LIGHT IS NEEDED. Why? The answer is BECAUSE THE CANDIDATE REPRESENTS THE SUN ITSELF IN THIS DEGREE. When we find truth, its simplicity astounds us.

We find, then, that the thirteenth, fourteenth and fifteenth degrees of Freemasonry allocate respectively with the three decans of Virgo.

As the middle decan of any sign is its matrix, it is interesting to note in this instance that the Hebrew letter allocating with the fourteenth degree, that of the Perfect Elu, is N or

Jesus. Note, please, that the letter which in Hebrew means Jesus or the new man, actually falls over the womb or matrix of the Virgin. How clearly the Scriptures state what next occurs: "OUT OF DARKNESS COMETH LIGHT." Jesus is truly the light of each individual world or material whorl—the human body. And it is indeed true that when the Light at last appears in our darkness, the path of life is forevermore illuminated; so much so, in very truth, that we are told no outer light from sun or moon is needed.

How wonderfully the vibration of the Aquarian or Air Age is bringing this to the attention of the world! It is only in the last few years that the tops of buildings have been illuminated with colored as well as beacon lights. They represent the struggle of the Spirit in man to make him realize that he also has a *head light,* although he is doing everything possible to destroy instead of perfect the Lamp within his Holy of Holies—the optic thalamus.

Love of sensation has caused man's body to become dulled and semi-paralyzed by the more or less continuous indulgence. This has given rise to the invention of the popular slogan "give me something with a *kick* in it." The reason for this is obvious. NOTHING LESS THAN A KICK WILL PRODUCE ANY SENSATION. Can health of body and brain exist in one using this slogan? The careful study of this expression will throw much light on the long list of sexual perversions so common among humanity.

Sensation wastes energy and actually *consumes* material, as stated in the preceding chapter on Leo.

Resuming comment on the allocation of the thirteenth and fourteenth degrees of Freemasonry with the first and second decans of Virgo, it would seem that the foregoing synthesis should prove indubitably that this *constitutes a definite system by which information on any subject* may be obtained. Personally I have found such to be the case.

The fourteenth degree represents the number five, and the fifth letter in the Tarot is HE or E. The name of the Tarot card bearing the objects and figure symbolizing this letter (containing its interpretation) is THE POPE. As the word Pope is Latin for papa or father, it is evident that it has never referred to any special representative or indeed to any historical personage, but on the contrary to THE NEW MAN WHO IS THE TRUE SON OF THE FATHER

AND BECOMES ONE WITH HIM. The fruit of the perfect solar plexus or womb of creation (Mary) becomes one with the spiritual consciousness (Aries the Father) by working in harmony with it. Read all that Papus has to say of this letter.

Since Neptune, the ruler of the spiritual phase of Pisces, entered the house of the Virgin in October of 1928, a general upheaval and "housecleaning" in respect to all matters pertaining to Pisces, Gemini, Virgo and Sagittarius has been going on. And as Neptune requires fourteen years to transit a sign, great changes will take place. As the vibration of this planet is the highest known, it represents the Christ Consciousness itself. A real purification has begun. We have already begun to note that a change for the better is being initiated relative to cinema.

A broad-minded altruistic person endeavors to start a movement along a certain line. A few co-operate, but the great mass of people are not interested. Years pass when, almost over night and out of a clear sky, great interest is aroused. Newspapers and magazines feature articles on the subject where before they scarcely mentioned it even desultorily. They perhaps even ridiculed it.

The young people of today can not possibly appreciate the older viewpoint, for they were not living in pre-Aquarian atmosphere. Eventually the brain will become steady, and at last, far above the scrap heap of old ideas and opinions, the white wings of TRUTH will be seen, shorn at last of all perversion.

As the Aquarian age is devoid of all that pertains to the animal, liquor, tobacco, drugs and meat as food will gradually disappear. For the outraged body will no longer consent to receive what it has NO USE FOR, being no part of a healthy body.

The letter He, then, stands for the Divine Spirit, the MEDIATING principle, which *attaches* the material body to itself. Man requires no other mediator. Down through the ages (and even today) the majority have worshiped personalities, both mystical and modern, thus losing sight of TRUTH. But already the Divine Virgin is beginning to manifest in the heavens and her breath is already being diffused through the ethers.

In ancient times a Vestal Virgin was a maiden who was

dedicated to the goddess Vesta or Hestia. This supposed being was the custodian of the Sacred Fire. It was lighted afresh annually at the Spring Equinox (Aries). The duty of the virgins was TO KEEP THE FIRE OF THE TEMPLE ALWAYS BURNING, and its extinction was considered a national calamity. The virgins were required to be of spotless chastity.

In the French calendar the Virgo period is termed "the fruit month" which is very appropriate from the esoteric as well as the exoteric viewpoint. It was termed the Holy-month by the ancients, as the nativity of the Virgin Mary fell on the eighth of September, and the exaltation of the Cross on the fourteenth. Using the ancient Sanskrit method of analyzing a sign by the twelve divisional means, the date of the nativity falls over the Aquarian (son of Man) vibration of Virgo, while the exaltation of the Cross falls over that of Taurus, which in itself constitutes the actual physiological cross. In Hebrew tau is the word for cross. Thus another verification is added to the list. As the constellation of Aquarius is represented by the figure of a man with an urn from which the water of life is being poured, it is symbolical of the fact that only by the complete purification of the saline solution of the blood is the VIRGIN state entered into. This constitutes the *birth* (manifestation) of the Virgin, in other words her nativity.

Virgo has many names among nations and peoples. She is Isis, wife of Osiris; Juno, wife of Jupiter; Cybele, consort of Chronus; Venus, wife of Mars (represented especially by the last decan of Virgo) which is ruled by Venus; she is Ceres, wife of Zeus; the Virgin Coronis, wife of Esculapius; the Virgin Maia, mother of Mercury; Rebekah, wife and sister of Isaac; Rachel, wife of Jacob; Ruth, wife of Boaz, and last but far from the least she is the Mother of Christ.

The astrological interpretation of the Virgin is that Virgo is the only one who can give birth to a son and still remain a Virgin. The Virgin of September has a Sun once every year. It is also the time and place for the manifestation of the Divine Son in us when the necessary work has been consummated.

Then only is the Virgin "clothed with the Sun, the Moon under her feet, and upon her head a crown of twelve stars" (Revelation 12:1-6).

As Virgo is Bethlehem (house of bread), it is natural that we understand it to mean THE BREAD OF LIFE. "At the time of the assumption of the Virgin, which takes place on the fifteenth, the sun is so entirely in the constellation of the Virgin that the stars of which it is composed are rendered invisible by the effulgence of its rays," says Dr. Wakeman Ryno.

As the last decan of Virgo is the Taurian, and ruled by the Venus vibration, it constitutes the STABLE wherein the bull is housed and close to the spot (middle decan) wherein the Holy Child is born.

It will be well at this point to read over the chapter on Taurus, and note that the middle decan of that sign is related to Virgo. Falling as it does on the first day of May it is commemorated as May day, sacred to the goddess Maia, the Virgin.

The *free* woman is Virgo, and no human being is ever FREE until he or she has attained to virginity. Therefore slavery still exists and will, for many a long year.

The Eleusinian mysteries were sacred to Ceres (Virgo) and in Greek mythology are said to represent THE ALTERNATION OF DEATH AND LIFE. This statement gives further proof of the correct allocation of health to this sign.

A word which is erroneously used is "HEAL." How often we hear the statement "I was healed of such and such a disease." The word means "TO BE MADE WHOLE" and applies solely to the Virgin state. None are healed until WHOLE or HOLY. Moreover no one can heal another. Each one must do it for himself, just as the Scriptures state. One by one the so-called "healers" pass on, garnered in by the great Reaper whom they have cheated out of that which would have made them whole. They had not been fed "GOOD SEED" and therefore could not produce A PERFECT SEED, "the one and only one," the Virgin's Son.

A story of Proserpina (daughter of Virgo—Ceres) as queen of the underworld (bowels of the earth) is symbolical of the negative interpretation of Virgo, and also of corn, which is the archaic name for seed. It signifies the seed-corn, which, when cast into the ground, lies there concealed and is carried off by the god of the underworld. When the seed sprouts and shoots upward, its appearance is said to symbolize the return of Proserpina to Ceres, the Virgin.

The etymology of the word Ceres is interesting, being derived from the Sanskrit stem "cer or Kri" meaning *"to make."* By metonomy the word comes to signify "corn" in the Latin.

Some of the old Semitic names of Virgo are: "Shepherd-Spirit-of-Heaven; Proclaimer-of-rain; Great-storm-bird and Bird-of-the-*great-seed.*" The latter name will be seen to be exceedingly esoteric, the Great-Seed being "the bread of life." Ab-nam is "The Proclaimer-of-rain" while Imdugudkhu, "The Great-storm-bird" is the crow. Spica, the bright star which the Virgin holds in her hand is Ululu or Siru, meaning "the ear of corn."

The Crow in the constellation of the Virgin is named Sizi in the Euphratean Celestial Sphere and Prof. Sayce gives the translation as "greenish-yellow" which is the color of Virgo, the first half of the sign being yellow and the last half green. It will be noted on studying the accompanying color chart that the yellow-green of the spectrum zodiac falls exactly over Virgo.

In the Euphratean Star-List we find Sakh, which is their name for Spica, the great star interpreted by them as a spike of wheat in the hand of the Virgin. It is spoken of as "the star of *Prosperity.*" It is also called "khi-se" (Propitious-one-of-seed) and "Sema" (Corn-bearer). The creation of the Great Seed is indeed evidence of physiological prosperity.

In Ogygian ages and among the Orientals, Virgo was represented as a sun-burned damsel with an ear of corn in her hand, like a gleaner in the field.

Ovid tells us that Virgo was the maiden who hung herself in grief at the death of her father Icarius and was transported as Bootes to the skies with Icarius and their faithful hound Procyon or Sirius.

Richard Allen, in *Star Names and Their Meanings,* says: "Virgo is the oldest purely allegorical representation of innocence and virtue. She is Cybele, drawn by lions, for our Leo immediately precedes her. Avienus identifies her with Isis, the thousand-named goddess who holds in her hand the wheat ear which she afterwards drops to form the Milky Way. She is also represented as clasping in her arms the young Horus, the infant southern sun-god, the last of the Divine Kings. This very ancient figuring reappeared in the Middle Ages as the Virgin Mary with the child Jesus, Shakespeare alluding to it in *Titus Andronicus* as 'The God Boy in Virgo's lap.' "

"In India, Virgo was Kanya, the Tamil 'Kauni,' or maiden, mother of the great Krishna. In the land of Judæa, Virgo was Bethulah, and being always associated with the idea of abundance in harvest, was assigned by the Rabbis to the tribe of Asher, of whom Jacob had declared *'his bread* shall be *fat,'* " says Richard Allen.

From *Star Names and Their Meanings,* we also quote the following: "In astrology this constellation and Gemini constitute the HOUSE OF MERCURY, Macrobius saying that the planet was created here; the association being plainly shown by the *caduceus* of that god, the herald's trumpet entwined with serpents, instead of the palm branch, often represented in her left hand. The Alfonsine Tables showed her as a very young girl with wings; the Leyden Manuscript and the Hygius of 1488 as a young woman with branch and caduceus; and the Albumasar of 1489 as a woman with a fillet of wheat ears.

"But all these figurings, ancient as some of them are, are modern when compared with the still enduring Sphinx generally proclaimed as prehistoric, perhaps of the times of Hor-she-shu, long anterior to the first Egyptian ruler, Menes; and constructed, according to Greek tradition with Virgo's head on Leo's body, from the fact that the sun passed through these two constellations during the inundation of the Nile."

The Sphinx was mentioned in Chapter V as having the body of a lion and the head of a man, which latter is its opposite sign Aquarius. Thus the Sphinx represents the polar opposites and is typical of the beast of prey and the regenerated being. Personally this interpretation appeals to me more than the one in *Star Names.*

In Latin, the word *spica* means spike or ear of corn, and hence is the name given to the star which is seen in the left hand of the Virgin. In Webster's Dictionary it is also interpreted as a nail or thorn. The Latin meanings, however, are of first importance.

"The Hindus knew Spica as Citra, figured as a lamp or as a Pearl," says Richard Allen, both names significant of Jesus. He also states that the Babylonian name was "Emuku Tin-tir-ki, the *Might* of the Abode of Life," which is equally good.

In Egypt, Spica was the Lute-Bearer; also Repa, the Lord. Two temples were built in Greece, almost touching one another, oriented to follow the shifting places of this star, testifying to its sacred character.

Spica is one of the lunar stars much utilized in navigation, and Mr. Allen states that "it lies but two degrees south of the ecliptic, and ten degrees south of the celestial equator, coming to a meridian on the twenty-eighth of May." It will be seen that this is a position of great power, tending to bring to a climax matters pertaining to Pisces, Sagittarius, Gemini and Virgo.

"A pale violet star on the front of the garment of the Virgin and below the girdle is named Apami-Atsa, or The Child of the Waters. With an adjacent star it was known in China as Ping-Taou, the Plain and Even Way" says Mr. Allen in *Star Names and Their Meanings.*

All the above quotations relative to the stars of Virgo, serve to prove to us that this old, old story of the New Man, which is indeed "The plain and even way," antedates *all* of the Scriptures in existence. It is a very old story, but becomes ever new to each individual as he places his feet at last upon the path which leads Home.

Virgo is indeed the hub of the physical wheel, the branching nerves of the solar plexus forming its spokes. Madam Blavatsky states in her *Secret Doctrine,* referring to the Virgin Mary and this sign: "When the point generates a line it becomes a diameter which stands for the androgynous Logos. When the son separates from the mother he becomes the Father." Thus in the Scriptures Jesus preaches in the Temple, enters the Jordan (separating from the Virgo center) to be baptized in its oil, and *ascends.*

Early Christians symbolized the Holy Ghost (Water of Life from the pituitary gland or Isis), as a shape of fire (cloven tongues like as fire) constituting the breath of the Father-Sun. In the physiological process, the fire descends into the water or the sea (Mare or Mary). Thus it is that Jesus (the little son) is born or formed of the union of fire, or spirit, and water, or Mary.

As mythology informs us, Venus arose from the foam (froth) of the sea at the *wounding of Uranus,* and hence was called by the Greeks, Aphrodite, the foam-born. As Uranus is ruler of Aquarius, the sign of the Son of Man, it is obvious that Venus is analogous to Mary Magdalene, since she rose from the sea as a result of that wounding. It is said of Venus, "In her broidered girdle lurk love and desire, and loving converse that *steals the wits even of the wise.*" Indeed does lust or venality (derived from the same root as Venus) rob the brain of its power.

When Jupiter enters Virgo in 1932 to work with Neptune it will be natural to expect very great disturbances and upheavals of ocean beds, tidal waves, earthquakes, and great landslides. The Hub of the Wheel will seek to readjust itself, and create a real center of balance, since the old has gotten out of alignment.

Madam Blavatsky states that "Jupiter is merely the personification of that immutable Cyclic Law, which arrests the downward tendency of each Root Race, after attaining the zenith of its glory." So, once again, as Jupiter transits Virgo, we will find Divine Mind reasserting itself in its endeavors to fructify the Divine Mother in humanity, so that she may become big with the Divine Child. This constitutes the trinity.

Virgo is the Phœnix, which, when resurrected, again becomes—man's hope of immortality.

In G. A. Gaskell's *Dictionary of the Sacred Language of All Scriptures and Myths,* we find splendid references to the Virgin, all of which add to the foregoing.

"The Virgin: symbol of the purified emotion, or purified lower nature, no longer fructified by the desire-mind." Virgo *is* a barren earth sign, as stated elsewhere in this chapter; and, whether the Sphinx, as Leo, has the head of Virgo or that of Aquarius, the interpretation is the same.

How appropriate is Mr. Gaskell's quotation from Philo Judæus, *De Cherub,* 14, 15: "For the congress of men *for the procreation* of children makes virgins women. But when God begins to associate with the soul, He brings it to pass that she who was formerly woman becomes virgin again. For, banishing the foreign and degenerate and *non-virile* desires by which it was made womanish, He *substitutes* for them native and noble and pure virtues. For it is fitting that God should converse with an undefiled, an untouched and pure nature, with her who is in very truth the Virgin."

The foregoing substantiates our previous statement that even congress between the sexes for the procreation of children robs both bodies of many corpuscles which eventually, in the *natural* order of things, will remain within the body.

It is, as Philo Judæus states, the result of a NON-VIRILE desire. Absolute virility can not exist as long as the body is robbed of even one corpuscle.

Bishop Methodius says, in *Harnack's "History of Dogma"* and quoted by Mr. Gaskell: "Exceedingly wonderful and glorious is virginity. This most noble and fair practice is the flower and first fruits of INCORRUPTION. . . . The state of virginity, WHICH IS THE GOAL OF THE INCARNATION, THOUGH ALL MAY NOT YET REACH IT. We must understand that virginity, while walking upon the earth, reaches the heavens." The meaning of the last statement is "that the purified lower nature (earth) becomes raised and united with the higher nature (heaven)."

Virgo is the Womb of Maya, as Mr. Gaskell says: "A symbol of primordial matter, astral and physical—in which the world-soul is conceived in the period of *involution,* and from which it is brought forth into the manifest existence of the involutionary cycle." It will be observed that Mr. Gaskell agrees with our previous statement that astrologically and physiologically Virgo stands for involution, the indrawing of forces.

"A Divine element, a spiritual quickening, is required for the evolution of anything God-like in our mundane sphere; it is a Virgin Birth. Lower acting upon lower can never produce a higher. It is the downpouring and incoming of the higher to the lower which produces through the lower the Divine manhood *which leaves the brute behind.* This is the sense in which it is true that Jesus was of Divine as well as human parentage."—R. J. Campbell, *"The New Theology."* The initiation of a candidate in a cavern, Jesus being born in a cave, and the thirteenth degree of Freemasonry are all symbolical of the formation of the New Man in us.

In completing our quotations from Mr. Gaskell we give his reference to Virgo as a zodiacal sign: "A symbol of the sixth period in the cycle of life. It signifies the completion of the process of involution resulting in the one perfect matrix of Matter fully permeated and informed by Spirit, and ready to bring forth the qualities and the Christ in many souls during the subsequent six periods of evolution. Christ, the Archetypal Man, who is perfected and dies in involution, is also the Archetypal Virgo who brings forth, as Mother Matter, all things during evolution: 'For in him were all things created, in the heavens and upon the earth, things visible and things invisible.'" Col. 1:16.

The above Biblical quotation is extremely appropriate, for it serves as a perfect link between the physiological, astrological and metaphysical analysis just completed, and their synthesis with Kali sulph or sulphate of potassium which Dr. Carey allocates with the sign Virgo. For in very truth out of this salt ALL THINGS MAY BE OBTAINED, since it is THE MAKER OF OIL ITSELF. As Christ is all, as the Scriptures state, so is oil a *quintessence*. The sixth *contains the five*—and quintessence means the fifth, last or highest essence or power in a natural body; pure and concentrated essence.

As the word essence is derived from the Latin *esse,* which means "to be," it is, therefore, the essence of being (existence). It is the very substance upon which life itself depends. Quintessence is, therefore, the essence refined to the Nth degree. N, it will be recalled, is used in algebra to express the *highest power* to which an equation may be raised.

A very old interpretation of the word essence is medulla or marrow, the PITH of anything. The meaning of pith is a pit or kernel—that which contains the strength or life, the vital or ESSENTIAL PART.

It is very interesting to find that the Middle English word for marrow is MARY. Marrow is the highly vascular, soft tissue which fills the cavities of most bones. As the marrow of the long bones is said to contain 95 percent fat, it will be seen that it is practically a thick oil.

Again we have obtained verification of our original findings from the meanings of the words themselves. Mary, marrow, oil (fat) and Virgo are all synonymous. Let us again recall the statement of Jacob relative to the tribe of Asher, "His BREAD shall be FAT."

In nature, quintessence allocates with ether, which has a powerful attraction for oil, its material counterpart in the human body. Thus combustion is caused. But it must be remembered that oil varies in *quality* in each individual, just as many grades of oil are found in the earth. As compared with oil in other parts of the body, that in the spinal canal is the most refined. But it is a fact that even here it has not attained to the degree of purification which makes it of the nature of the real Christos. This is not accomplished until the chemical formula of the body is that of the perfect or Christ-man. The Lamp in the cerebrum will not become spiritually illuminated until the spinal oil is sufficiently refined. This subject will be further considered in the second volume of God-Man which will be published later.

What is OIL? Who has studied the subject sufficiently to know? Several years ago I had the pleasure of seeing a collection of oil products assembled by the Hollywood High School. There were refined as well as heavy lubricating oils; all sorts of dyes, including special film colors; many forms of medicines and many kinds of perfumes. Can one then doubt my statement that all kinds of products may be obtained from oil, since it is a perfect thing? Eventually it will be so refined that the process will take it beyond the vision of the naked eye.

OIL is a marvelous word, as will be noted if one stops to think about it. It actually *flows oilfully* out of the mouth. Enunciate it slowly and see.

In the Kabbalistic analysis of the word, we find that it totals two, which allocates with the second letter of the Hebrew alphabet or *Beth*. Here again we find additional corroboration of our statement that Virgo is *Bethlehem*.

The letters of the word OIL, when interpreted from the Tarot, are: O or Ayin which means eye, and is analogous to the entrance of the Holy Spirit into matter—its VISIBLE manifestation. I (I, Y and J are the same in Hebrew) means the forefinger or hand of man, and symbolizes potential force. I is also Vishnu, the *Preserver*. L is Lamed, and means an ox goad or the arm. It typifies EXPANSIVE MOVEMENT of a *balanced* nature.

Combining the above interpretations, we find that this three or triune-lettered word means *the visible manifestation* of energy. It is a material constituting a *preserver,* which is of a BALANCED nature and capable of great *expansive* movement. It will be realized at once that this is, indeed, the correct interpretation of oil. It is the "Natura Naturata" (that which follows or proceeds from the Divine Nature) in other words, the PRODUCT OF A PERFECT THING.

Oil is truly a fuel, a solvent, a lubricator and purifier for man's body, as well as for machinery. Its value as a medicine was well known by the ancients. Its recognition as a neutralizer of poison is proved by the following quotation from *The Odes of Horace:*

"Like poison loathes oil."

It has recently been discovered that leprosy can be cured by the use of a certain oil.

In old age, the human body is very low in oil, and hence looks dry and shriveled. Skin, hair, intestinal tract and bones all require their full quota of oil. The fluid of the lymphatic glands (termed lymph), must have sufficient oil. When present, it gives this fluid a beautiful opalescent color.

It is said that the ocean contains enormous quantities of Kali sulph or potassium sulphate in addition to the other three combinations of this salt. Amber or ambergris, found in certain parts of the ocean, is said to be a morbid excretion from the alimentary canal of the sperm whale; but, as it is also found fossil in alluvial soil, I venture to predict that it will eventually prove to be a collection of thick oil, which has been combined with certain other ingredients, and hardened. It is highly electric.

Liebig stated many years ago that potassium is the essential alkali of the animal body and this is true of the human body. In combination with sulphur it forms oil or Kali sulph. It is said that the bodies of *sheep* contain a huge quantity of this salt, which may be the reason why mutton fat is supposed to possess healing qualities. Sheep are said to excrete a very great quantity of potassium in perspiration and one-third of the weight of raw merino consists of potassium compounds. Here again we have proof of the correct allocation of Kali phos to Aries, the sheep sign, as well as to Virgo, the Virgin, which creates the Lamb of God "Which taketh away the sins of the world." As sin means deficiency, and also disease, the statement is clear.

Lack of potassium or Kalium (as it is chemically known), in ALL THREE COMBINATIONS causes VIRULENT AND POISONOUS DISEASES. In particular do those deficient in Kali sulph suffer from them. They are also easily poisoned by tainted food. They should be extremely careful relative to their diet.

As Kali sulph acts as a fuel, deficiency in it will cause a person to feel suffocated, and he suffers greatly under certain atmospheric conditions. As Pisces is the polar opposite of

Virgo, and allocates with Ferrum or iron, the above symptom is usually aggravated when insufficient oxygen is obtained. Combustion can not take place in the absence of air.

An infallible modality indicative of Kali sulph deficiency, is a rise of temperature in the afternoon or early evening. Also a desire for cold air. It also causes severe hot flashes. The period in the life of a female termed the menopause, greatly intensifies these flashes, and many suffer extremely from them. Shifting pains constitute another modality.

Some of the many symptoms which manifest at various times in those born in Virgo, Pisces, Gemini and Sagittarius are: scaly and sticky dandruff; yellow or yellowish-green discharge of the eyes; inflammation of the conjunctiva; earache, with sharp, cutting pain (this salt is a specific for this trouble and especially for children; the ear should be carefully syringed with this remedy every day); deafness from swelling of the internal ear; catarrhal conditions of the head and throat, acute or chronic, with discharge of slimy, yellow or greenish matter (this salt should be given freely for colds, and it generally assists in promoting perspiration); stuffy colds; neuralgia of the face with shifting, intermittent pain, evening aggravation (worse in heated atmosphere, better in cool air); cancer on nose, face, or on any part of the body (injections of Kali sulph and Ferrum should be given frequently for intestinal, also vaginal and uterine cancer; Kali sulph should also be applied whenever possible to reach the location). Other symptoms are: dread of hot drinks; thirstlessness; gastric fever; all abdominal troubles; typhoid or typhus fever; cystitis; sexual disorders; bronchitis; cough which is worse in the evening; pneumonia; whooping-cough; skin hot, dry and harsh; rheumatic pains in joints of a shifting, wandering nature; rattling and gurgling of mucus in the chest; fungoid inflammation of the joints; all sores which exude a thin, yellow, watery matter; skin scaling freely on a sticky base; eczema; blood poisoning; typhoid, and small-pox. Naturally there are other symptoms, but they will be considered in another work. Kali sulph should be given in all children's diseases to aid in formation of new skin.

In closing this chapter it is fitting that some very remarkable points descriptive of this salt should be given.

Potassium sulphate was known as early as the fourteenth century, we find, on consulting the Encyclopædia Britannica, and in the seventeenth was named ARCANUM. As the word ARCANUM is derived from the Latin noun *arca* (a box or chest) also from the verb *arcere* (to enclose) it signifies a SECRET OR MYSTERY, which adds still another verification to our list of proofs. Webster's Dictionary further elucidates the latter by adding that it also refers to a POWERFUL NATURAL AGENT, AN ELIXIR. It is evident that no further proof is required.

The words arc and arch are both derived from this root. which makes all the more interesting our previous reference to the Royal Arch Degree of Freemasonry, as pertaining to the solar plexus.

As the great pyramid of Gizeh was built on a line between Upper and Lower Egypt it also allocates with the solar plexus, the upper part being the visible pyramid and the lower being its shadow. In Hebrew it means "darkness." The initial sign of Upper Egypt was a bent reed, symbolical of an arch. The solar plexus and bowels constitute a place of darkness. This great nerve ganglia is indeed analogous to an arch since it is a receiving and broadcasting station for energy, and paralysis results when it ceases to function.

Kali sulph has another unique name, that of SAL DUPLICATUM, which means the salt which increases or *doubles.* Most interesting and illuminating is the explanation of this term. This salt derived the name DUPLICATUM from the fact that its beautiful crystals have the habit of a DOUBLE SIX-SIDED PYRAMID, and really belong to the rhombic system.

The form in which any salt crystallizes naturally depends on its rate of vibration, and this must continue in order that the shape may persist. Electrical experiments have proved this to be true, as I have personally witnessed. Each stone glows with its own individual light and color. Therefore to crystallize in rhombic form, proves that the vibration of Kali sulph moves *in a circle* "like a spinning top or magic wheel," as Webster states. This last statement is very appropriate, since the solar plexus is indeed the MAGIC WHEEL OF LIFE. Again, the fact that its crystals form a DOUBLE SIX-SIDED PYRAMID gives additional verification, for they total twelve, which allocates with the twelve divisions of the solar plexus.

It is stated that among the rare and precious books which

contain the mysteries of the GREAT ARCANUM, is one entitled *"The Chemical Pathway,"* by Paracelsus. It deals with the mysteries of demonstrative physics and the most secret Kabbala, and is said to be in the Vatican Library. It is to be hoped that its treasures will soon be open to those desirous of obtaining information.

Much more could be written on this subject, for proof upon proof is available, but we will give the following from Sir Thomas Vaughan's splendid work: "This is the SALT which you ought to have in yourselves; this is that SEED which falls to the ground and multiplies to an hundred fold." The Son of the Virgin is that SEED, and the *ground* is the earth sign Virgo, the cosmic and microcosmic earth.

It should be clear to the readers of this book that the human body must possess sufficient Kali sulph to enable the solar plexus to create its perfect double pyramids. Then indeed will the darkness of Egypt flee away, and all sorrow, sickness and death—all the plagues of Egypt—will disappear forever.

"And ye shall serve the Lord your God, and he shall bless thy bread and thy water, and *I will take away sickness from the midst of thee.*" Exodus 23:25.

"I must become Queen Mary, and birth to God must give; if I in blessedness for now and evermore would live."—Scheffler.

CHAPTER VII

THE ANALYSIS AND SYNTHESIS OF LIBRA AND NATRIUM PHOS

"The Scales of Libra will hang obliquely until the horns of the Ram are placed under them."

—*Compt de Gabelis.*

IN the preceding six chapters, the passing of the Sun through the six northern signs has been described, beginning with the Spring equinox. The Fall equinox has now been reached, when the Sun starts on its journey south of the equator. At this time the days and nights are everywhere equal, the same as at the Spring or vernal equinox. The Fall equinox begins approximately on September twenty-second. It must be recalled that although the sign begins in the last week of September, there are two weeks of October included. Therefore it has much more to do with the latter vibration.

The name Libra is Latin for pound. Pound is the unit of weight for the scales. A pair of Scales is the glyph for this sign. As October means eight and is the eighth month beginning with March, the Spring equinox, we must analyze this number.

Eight is made up of 4 plus 4, or two squares, thus □ + □ which constitute the two weights in the scale pans. The idea underlying the analysis of this sign is that of balance—equilibrium. In a cosmic sense it is analogous to the two halves of the year. Physiologically it has to do with the kidneys, adrenal glands and bladder, which constitute the last of the vital organs and the first half or vital part of the body. The seven months beginning with Aries constitute the vital months of the year. There are no vital organs in the parts corresponding to the last five zodiacal signs.

As the well-being of the lower parts of the body depends on the perfect functioning of the vital organs, so does involution depend on evolution, and vice versa. The forces of Nature are now indrawing, after having been focused into the matrix or womb of the earth—Virgo.

At this period of the year, vegetation begins to look lifeless and unattractive, except to those who know what is taking place. It is they who understand Nature in all her moods. She is now beginning an entirely new work, gathering in her forces. As autumn is the harvesting time, she is concentrating them so that they may be ready to pour forth again in the Spring.

Libra is the seventh sign, and the second of the air triplicity, Gemini being the first and Aquarius the third. It is under the rulership of Venus. The first decan is essentially under this vibration, the middle decan under the combined vibrations of Uranus and Saturn, while the last decan is subject to the co-rulership of Mercury. Thus the faults or attributes of this planet (Venus) are modified or intensified by the vibration of the co-rulers.

It is very interesting to note that the last decan of Virgo is under the co-rulership of Venus. The vibration of the latter is affected, and we may venture to suggest becomes more rapid, under the expansive power of the air. There are thus two Venus vibrations joining the circle at this point, the last ten degrees of Virgo and the first ten of Libra. This is also true of the opposite side of the circle, with the exception that Mars is the ruler under which the last decan of Pisces vibrates, and it also rules the dominant first decan of Aries.

As Mars means ENERGY and Venus has to do with MATERIAL, their vibrations cross each other at these two points in the circle, that of the two equinoxes. Energy, working with material, closes the circle of the year and the cycle of life at these two points.

In the Bible story, Mercury is Joseph. He had a *coat of many colors,* which is apropos, since Mercury is mind. There are endless shades of thought, and the mind is colored according to the chemical condition of the brain. When purified and perfected, it is crystal clear. Indeed it is exactly like a diamond, its myriad facets reflecting all the beautiful colors of the rainbow.

Dr. Wakeman Ryno quotes the learned Dr. Bryant as saying: "The names of the gods Berith, in the singular number BER, are still retained in conjunction with the Latin words Septem, Octo, Novem, and Decem, in our Septem-Ber, Octo-Ber, Novem-Ber and Decem-Ber. The gods Beth, Baal,

Berith, were taken from the ancient Tsabaism, or Star-Worship. The two pans of the Balances or Scales were known to the ancient Egyptians as the 'Two Truths.' "

In the Scriptural story of Joseph, it will be recalled that Potiphar's wife endeavored to persuade him to become interested in her, but "he fled out of the *house* leaving his garment in her hand." As Mercury passed out of the house of Virgo, it was through the *Venus* decan. Joseph or Mercury (mind) was not tempted by carnality.

The sign Libra represents the seventh day on which the Lord rested. A day constitutes a period of time as is expressed in the words "Lincoln's day" or "Wilson's day," etc. In Genesis (meaning generation, the forming of the child in utero) we note that the Creator was busily engaged in the work of forming the seven vital organs. When this was accomplished, the Lord ceased from creating, for the organs were thus co-ordinated, and, as seven parts of a machine, were prepared to perform all the functions required of them.

The Sun, resurrected as the Lamb of God in Aries at the Spring equinox , or Easter, after passing through the various stages of growth and fecundity, now prepares to go down (in the West) into the darkness and coldness of winter, for heat is withdrawn into the earth.

The earth herself must regain her balance, which virtually represents the beginning and the end of labor. Thus we have Sunday, the seventh day, or day of REST.

The full Moon at this period of the year is of special importance, for its effect on wild life of the forest is very remarkable. It is said that under the influence of this harmonizing or balancing Moon, animals that are natural enemies will play together or pass by without conflict. They resume their warfare when its influence wanes.

Venus (the ruler of Libra) was said by the ancients to have arisen from the foam of the sea at the time of the wounding of Uranus. As the latter is the ruler of the sign of the Son of Man, it should be obvious what is meant by his "wounding."

The etymology of the name Venus is charm, attractiveness, and sensual love. So perverted is the human mind, that few seem to realize that the linking of these two words is incongruous. Sensual affection is the correct expression. Affection means "to affect" and has to do with feeling which is temporary. It is not the real thing, but counterfeit. A line from Shakespeare is an illustration: "Thou dost affect my manners."

The mount of Venus is a physiological expression and refers to the pubic bone above the genital organs. Venery is also derived from the same root and means sexual intercourse. The word vener is another derivative and means "to hunt or chase." It will be easy to understand how applicable this is, for Greek mythology pictures Venus directing her son Cupid in aiming his "love" darts.

In the old days venison was meat obtained by hunting, but in modern times has come to mean that of deer. We may not want to acknowledge it, but it is nevertheless a fact that the great "hunt" is constantly going on. And while some may wish to think that the female is the sole object, such is not the case. The female seeks the male and will continue to do so until accumulated experience with all types eventually proves that mental and physical BALANCE will never be attained by this means. Aries, the cerebrum, the Place of the Most High, is *opposite* Libra. It is indeed true that the darts of Cupid wound Psyche, which is another name for Isis, or Mary. The soul, or creative fluid, is derived from the pituitary gland ruled by the Moon, by Venus, or Neptune, according to one's stage of evolution. Intimacy with Venus truly "steals the wits, even of the wise."

It is a fact well-known by physicians in general that seven of every ten cases of insanity are due to sexual excesses. Aries and Libra are the positive and negative ends of one pole, and their positions in the zodiac are established for the above reason. When the cerebrum is at last perfected, *mental* BALANCE will result.

Cupid means desire, and cupidity is derived from the same root. It means longing or covetousness. The arrows of Cupid never fail to produce *wounds*.

There is little difference, if any, in the modern understanding of Cupid and Eros. But my researches have uncovered a decided and most amazing difference, which will be fully explained in *The Truth About Sex and Birth Control*. It will be sufficient to state here that Cupid is negative and destructive, while Eros has to do with the positive and constructive phase of creation.

Many of the operas embody the story of the struggle with,

and the victory over carnality. In *Tannhauser*, Wagner's wonderful creation, we find the theme dealing with a cave in Venusberg (the mountain of Venus) wherein the goddess of "love" held her court, enticing persons into it by means of music, revelry and sensuous pleasures, and endeavoring to keep them from ever returning to the *light* of day.

It will be realized from the evidence herein given that it is erroneous to interpret the planet Venus as that of love. It is true, however, that the hypnotism of the common interpretation will remain for some time yet. It will only be dissipated when each and every astrologer gives the correct rendering of Venus.

The seductive form and the beauty and fascination of those born under this planet, inevitably lead to severe tests of their moral equilibrium. But when the vibration of Venus is raised and is no longer that of Mary Magdalene, she is Neptune, *ruler* of the *waters*. Pisces, the home of Neptune, the last sign of the zodiac, is the house of UNDERSTANDING or LOVE, since it is the completion of the process.

Venus ever tends to lead one into excesses. She despoils—robs—a thing which LOVE could never do. The following lines taken from *Classic Myths* perfectly express the nature of Venus:

> "Just a soft hint of singing, to beguile a man from his toil;
> Some vanished gleam of beckoning arm, to spoil
> A morning's task with longing, wild and vain.
> Then if across the parching plain
> He seek her, she with passion burns
> His heart to fever, and he hears
> The west wind's mocking laughter when he turns,
> Shivering in mist of ocean's sullen tears.
> It is the Medicean: well I know
> The arts her ancient subtlety will show,—
> The stubble field she turns to ruddy gold;
> The empty distance she will fold
> In purple gauze; the warm glow she has kissed
> Along the chilling mist;
> Cheating and cheated love that grows to hate
> And even deeper loathing, soon or late."

But the poet goes on to sing of the purified Venus:

> "Thou, too, O Fairer spirit, walkest here
> Upon the lifted hills:
> Whenever that still thought within the breast
> The inner beauty of the world hath moved;
> In starlight that the dome of evening fills;
> Or endless waters rounding to the west:
> For them who thro' that beauty's veil have loved
> *The soul of all things beautiful and best.*"

He ends by voicing a prayer for deliverance from the temptress:

> "Oh, save me from the haste and noise and heat
> That spoils life's music sweet:
> And from that *lesser Aphrodite* there—
> Even now she stands
> Close as I turn, and O my soul, how fair!"

Venus was also termed Lucifer by the ancients, and in *Smith's Bible Dictionary* we find the following relative to this subject: "Lucifer literally means LIGHT-BRINGING. The name is, in Isaiah 14:12, coupled with the epithet 'son of the morning,' and clearly means a *bright star*, and probably what we call the morning star. In this passage it is a symbolical representation of the king of Babylon, in his splendor and *in his fall*. Its application (from St. Jerome downward) to SATAN in his fall from heaven, arises probably from the fact that the Babylonian empire is in Scriptures represented as the type of tyrannical and self-idolizing power, and especially connected with the empire of the Evil One in the Apocalypse."

The name Babylon is derived from the same root as Babel (confusion) which means THE GATE OF THE GOD IL. As Libra is significant of the Fall equinox, it is one of the four gates of God, in other words the two equinoxes and the two solstices. Important changes occur in Nature at these periods, and in the body of man are concerned with the most important organs.

In astrological lore, the Sun is said to be in its *fall* when transiting Libra.

The first and last verses in the quotation from Isaiah, furnish us with a good word-picture which allocates perfectly with our own analysis of Venus.

"How art thou fallen from heaven, O Lucifer, son of the morning! how art thou cut down to the ground, *which did weaken the nations*.

"Yet thou shall be brought down to hell, to the sides of the pit."

It is further explained, as the reader of the entire passage will find, that Lucifer sought to displace the Most High. This is literally and physiologically true. *Procreation* robs the brain and the body of the corpuscles which have been expended in the sexual act. When these corpuscles are THROWN

AWAY in creating pleasurable sensation, the sexual act becomes THE SIN AGAINST THE HOLY GHOST.

Venus must regain her balance, and her work as ruler of Libra is to accomplish this task.

What this means, physiologically and anatomically, must now be explained. Students who are familiar with the expression "THE RING-PASS-NOT" have not known to what it really referred. With the exception, perhaps, of one writer (Madam Blavatsky), the consideration of this subject has been for the most part erroneous. At best it is very incomplete and hence unilluminating. When the ANATOMICAL RING IN THE HUMAN BODY IS THOROUGHLY UNDERSTOOD, THEN ONLY WILL THIS AMAZING EXPRESSION BECOME CLEAR.

First, let us review the fact that from time immemorial astrology has allocated Libra with the kidneys, but further research will eventually prove that the bladder and adrenal glands also come under this sign. My own experience with many charts and in connection with astro-biochemistry, has proved this to be a fact.

The old or archaic name for the kidneys is "reins." Again repeating my favorite expression "study words," let us consider this ancient term, and see what light it will throw on the subject matter.

Webster's Dictionary informs us that the word is derived from the Latin *retinere* and means TO HOLD BACK. It also refers to the strap of a *bridle,* fastened to the curb or snaffle *on each side,* by which the rider or driver governs (controls) a horse or other animal. We can repeat the last three words with profit and understanding, I trust—"or other animal." Mankind is that other animal, else the task of becoming *balanced* would not exist.

Other meanings are: to govern, control, hold in check, restrain, to rule, to guide. In the Latin lexicon we find the direct translation, which gives us an even better rendering: TO HOLD FAST, TO KEEP BACK, TO DETAIN, to retain a conquest.

Allocating these interpretations with our previous analysis of Venus and Libra we find that they link up perfectly, and further illuminate our subject.

To become balanced, mentally and physically, the passions must be held in *check* (LEO the LION) in order that the cerebral *esse,* MARY (VIRGO), will not GO DOWN TO

ITS FALL (SUN IS IN ITS FALL IN LIBRA). They must be REINED IN, held in leash. If the pull on either rein is the same, then the horse is kept in the middle (balance) of the road. It should be realized by now, that not without definite reason have names been given to objects or things, animate or inanimate.

Let it again be stated, that AS LONG AS ONE CORPUSCLE OF THE HUMAN BODY LOSES ITS LIFE, THE BODY IS UNBALANCED. BALANCE IS ONLY ULTIMATELY ATTAINED by the presence IN THE BODY OF EACH AND EVERY CORPUSCLE REQUIRED TO FORM A NUMERICALLY PERFECT BODY.

The term reins is applicable to this part of the human body from an architectural point of view, as the following reference, obtained from Webster, bears testimony: "Reins: The parts between the crown and the spring or abutment, including the loading or *filling behind the vault shell*—analogous to the HAUNCHES OF AN ARCH."

It is not difficult to check up on facts, for what is true in ONE art, is true in ALL. Man's body is a piece of architecture, and therefore terms used in this profession apply equally to the human dwelling. Man's body is also a PIECE OF REAL ESTATE, for it consists of the same earthly elements. But in most instances it is a pretty poor piece of real estate, for it possesses very little value—it is chemically very much depleted.

To the degree in which a person is chemically deficient, is he mentally and physically unbalanced. Therefore, as the mineral elements are restored to the blood and the laws of right living followed so that no surplus waste or indeed any waste accumulates, the left pan of the scale slowly rises until it eventually balances with the RIGHT.

It is interesting to find that the left pan of the scale of Libra, which covers the first fifteen degrees of the sign, includes the vibrations of Scorpio, Sagittarius, Capricorn, Aquarius and Pisces, the last six signs of the zodiac. It will be realized, therefore, when the reader has studied the last six chapters of this work, that the signs they represent, and the work they cover, is indeed THE GREAT WORK, and must be completed BEFORE THE CIRCLE OF LIFE CAN BE ETERNALLY CEMENTED TOGETHER.

Thus the left scale pan represents the first fifteen degrees of Libra and the last six signs, while the right scale pan covers the last fifteen degrees and the first six signs.

As the result of research work, I have discovered and proved that the first fifteen degrees of any sign pertain to the left side and to the middle line of the body, while the last fifteen degrees extend from the middle of the body to the right side. The use of the NATURAL ZODIAC (no degrees of Aries rising), will enable the student to study and understand the human body as well as the mentality, without confusion. It is necessary to emphasize this point. Thus the left kidney must be studied from the first half of the sign, and the right kidney and bladder from the last half.

Therefore, when the Scorpion no longer stings, but becomes instead the WHITE EAGLE, soaring aloft to the heights (Aries, the cerebrum the Most High), the Higher Mind (Sagittarius, the Archer) will begin to function at last, and will direct (aim his arrow) man to the heights. He will thus become the INITIATE (Capricorn)—will *start out* on the path of return—will *travel* the road which the Higher Mind (Sagittarius-Arrow) points out. It becomes *possible* then, and then only, to arrive at a certain stage of that journey which coincides with that of our brother, the Freemason. When he has reached the thirteenth DEGREE, he is no longer UNLUCKY. He is then able to *create his own pay*, and becomes both payer and payee. Thus the NEW MAN, JESUS, is formed within him; he becomes the true Aquarian, ruled by Uranus, the Ancient of Days. The last sign Pisces is the completion of the task. BALANCE (PERFECTION) HAS AT LAST BEEN ATTAINED. A solid-rock foundation has been *built*.

Webster's Dictionary states that the word kidney is of uncertain origin, but that the last two letters, "ey" may have been derived from the Middle English word *eyren*, meaning egg.

This may check with the shape of this organ, but I believe that it really has the same source as the word KIDDLE which comes from Keutel, a Greek term. It means a NET. The word Kidnap means to SEIZE AND DETAIN, which synthesizes with the word NET, (used to gather in anything).

This seems to be a satisfactory analysis of the word, especially when employed in an anatomical sense, for it is true that the kidneys consist of a mass of tubules (small tubes or pipes). In other words, they constitute a *net-work* which *collects* and then discharges the secretion (the urine) into the main cavity of the kidneys. From thence, it is conveyed through the long tube or ureter to the bladder, from whence it is discharged. The analogy of *net* is indeed a correct one, as applied to this organ. It is really a *filter*.

The kidneys are situated in the middle portion of the body; and, when the astrological decans are allocated with the vertebræ, one finds that they are the sixteenth, seventeenth, and eighteenth; also, that when the vertebræ are numbered, beginning with one at the top and ending with the thirty-third, the seventeenth will be found to be the *middle* point of the spine. This number (17) falls exactly over the *middle* decan, and hence over the BALANCE POINT of the scales of Libra. As 17 totals 8, this checks with the two squares or weights in the scale pans.

Another fact of a very interesting and even startling character is, that before the glands testes of the infant descend into the scrotum, they are in alignment with the kidneys. THEY ARE SITUATED EXACTLY AT THE POINT OF BALANCE. It is obvious to the earnest student of the mysteries of life, that THEY WOULD NOT DESCEND (GO DOWN) BELOW THE BALANCE POINT (IN OTHER WORDS BELOW THE ABDOMINAL RING) IF THE INFANT HAD DIVORCED HIMSELF FROM CARNALITY IN HIS PREVIOUS INCARNATION. I do not fear that this statement can ever be disproved.

It is evident to all, of course, that humanity has not reached the stage where this can be accomplished. Nevertheless there are many who have entered the first degrees of preparation for it, as the writer can personally testify. Satiation, and the inevitable physiological reaction, have already begun. It is a fact that the brain cells automatically rebel when subject to sights and sounds which are detrimental and destructive in nature, and it is this which produces the feeling of boredom. There is no longer any "kick" in them.

Students of astrology know that Neptune was transiting Leo for fourteen years, up to the time it entered Virgo, in October of 1928. As this planet has the highest rate of cosmic vibration, and represents the Christ Spirit or Consciousness, also the MOTHER of Christ (material), it is analogous to purification. While Neptune was in Leo for fourteen years, the Powers That Be (Cosmic) endeavored to change and purify all that pertained to that sign. Recall the fact that the old name for Leo, the Sun's house, was Sextilis, and the cause of the dropping of the bars between male and female, which has been general and of such a noticeable character will be understood. It was a test for all. Many ended in becoming wrecks. Some passed out of this phase of life, while others realized what it was all about, and pulled themselves up and out of the abyss. Some few stood the test, and came out with flying colors, simply because the lesson had been learned at some other time when a past test had been made. Now, Neptune is in Virgo, the House of the Virgin (purity), and it will be interesting to watch what will occur.

Gray's Anatomy states that the nerves of the kidneys connect directly with those of the spermatic plexus. In the female, this must be true of the ovaries. This is given as the reason why pain is often felt in these parts of the body, in connection with kidney trouble. The above statement also checks with the arrangement of the zodiacal signs, for Libra joins Scorpio, the testes and ovaries being located in the first section of this sign.

It is curious, but true, that the kidneys, bladder and other pelvic organs of an infant, are in a much higher position, relatively, than those of the adult. Even the internal urethral orifice sinks rapidly during the first three years, then more slowly until the ninth year, after which it remains stationary until puberty, when it again slowly descends until it reaches its adult position. It is therefore true that the organs below the median line (Libra, the Balance) have a natural tendency to drop, to go below the positions which would be natural if the body (and hence all the organs) were in a higher state of development. This is exactly analogous to the Sun (energy) *going down* in the West.

It is true that both male and female sometimes suffer from a prolapsed condition of most of the pelvic organs. Indeed the flesh of the entire body frequently looks prolapsed. While in this condition it looks flabby—as though the flesh were hanging from it. It is not held firmly against the frame, nor does it appear to be solid and healthy.

It is a fact known to students of anatomy, that the ovaries of the female are in alignment with the kidneys until conception takes place. In the light of the information previously given, it is logical to assume that a slight prolapse would begin with puberty.

In the allocation of the number 8 with numerology, we find that Papus' work on *The Tarot* states that 8 EXPRESSES EQUILIBRIUM IN ALL ITS FORMS. Every student should possess a copy of this book. On page 138 will be found the card illustrative of the symbology of this number. Papus describes it as follows: "A woman, seen full face, and wearing an iron coronet, is seated upon a throne. She is placed between the two columns of the temple. The solar cross is traced upon her breast. She holds a sword, point upwards, in her right hand, and a BALANCE (scales) in her left."

The woman is Venus or material. The sword held in the RIGHT hand and pointed upward, is symbolical of the straight and narrow way above; her position between the two columns of the temple signifies her importance in respect to the attainment of equilibrium. Without material, nothing can be created or accomplished. The solar cross on her breast refers to the association with the cardinal or creative cross of the year. The final proof of this figure's relation to Libra is the fact that the Scale is held in her left hand, significant of the GREAT WORK. Material must be ALL utilized constructively, none wasted. It fulfills the function of Eve, the Mother of all creation, but eventually becomes THE PRESERVER OF GOD, THE SON IN HUMANITY.

We thus find Venus eventually responding to the lofty etheric vibration of the air sign Libra, when a new name, that of Neptune, becomes hers by right of attainment. "And I will write upon his forehead A NEW NAME."

Madam Blavatsky says, in the *Secret Doctrine,* "Venus is symbolized by the sign of a globe over the cross, which shows that it presides over the natural generation of man.

"The Egyptians symbolized Ankh (life) by the ansated cross, which is only another form of Venus (Isis) and meant, esoterically, that mankind and all animal life had stepped out of the divine spiritual circle and *fallen* into physical male and female generation."

She also informs us that "Venus equally with Isis was represented with cow's horns on her head, the symbol of mystic Nature and one that is convertible with and significant of the Moon, since all these were Lunar goddesses, the configuration of this planet is now placed by theologians between the horns of the mystic Lucifer."

Venus, Isis and Eve are identical with Aditi and Vach in Hindu literature. They are all "Mothers of all living."

The fact that Libra is ruled by Venus, and constitutes the SIGN OF BALANCE OR HARMONY, should cause the reader to spend much time in consideration of the deeply important secret concealed in these two words Libra and Venus. Indeed is Venus Lucifer, the Light Bearer, the LIGHT OF LIFE, but it also is THE EXTINGUISHER OF THAT LIGHT. Opposite Aries, the place of light, it is in very truth the *adversary*.

Mary, in the House of the Lord, is stolen away from it by Mary Magdalene—Venus. It becomes a pillaged place wherein the Lord finds insufficient for His needs. In other words, the mind becomes literally UNBALANCED. Light—the light of reason and intelligence—to say nothing of intuition, will be restored to humanity (recreated therein) WHEN SEXUAL INDULGENCE CEASES. All are therefore unbalanced and in varying degrees.

The stars in the constellation of Libra were named JUGUM, the yoke or beam of the *balance*. No doubt it was from this ancient Latin term, which means TO BIND TOGETHER OR CONNECT, that the idea of marriage and partnership was associated with this sign.

Here indeed is where perversion arose. Everything pertaining to the twelve zodiacal signs refers to THE ANATOMY OF THE GRAND MAN (THE UNIVERSE) AND HENCE, BY ANALOGY, TO THE BODY OF MAN.

THE PURPOSE OF THE STUDY OF ASTROLOGY, THEN, IS TO CONSIDER THE BODY OF THE UNIVERSE AND THE BODY OF MAN.

There never can be permanent marriage between male and female, which is obvious, since death inevitably separates. Earthly marriage is a man-made law which concerns the sexual life. It is true, also, that a man is not obliged to support his wife if she refuses this life.

Spiritual marriage, on the other hand, is the coming together, the BALANCING OF THE FORCES AND

ORGANS IN EACH INDIVIDUAL HUMAN BODY, and more especially the union of the pineal and pituitary glands in the head, which are respectively male and female sexual glands.

Because India, whose literature teems with the description of this *heavenly* marriage, has utterly lost sight of its divinely spiritual interpretation, her people (for the most part) have become weak, enervated and mentally degenerate.

They have forgotten, if indeed they ever knew, that the cube has six sides, and that there is a trinity of *divine* creative sexual organs in the head as well as in the PROcreative organs in the torso. "As above, so below" is physiologically true.

It is not India alone, however, that is dominated by the sex life. It is true of all nations and peoples. That country, however, has made the mistake (because of the complete perversion of understanding and interpretation of her own secret and sacred literature) of thinking that the procreative act was referred to in these writings as a RELIGIOUS AND HENCE MOST SACRED RITE. Naturally, the interpreters of these ancient writings have further imbued the people with this idea, because their own mentality has always been colored by sexuality. No work on India has brought out this point.

Sex and money, money and sex! These constitute the two chief subjects in the minds of the great majority. It is indeed true that it is impossible to live without money, as long as the commercial and industrial plan of life is what it is today. But the idea back of it all is the RIGHT USE OF A THING. If the subject of money in relation to sex is analyzed, it will be found that, for the *most* part, money is desired in order to live the sex life. We may not WANT this to be true, but nevertheless close observation will result in an honest admission that it is so. The young man seeks to earn money in order to marry; young women desire money with which to purchase attractive garments.

True money, the coin of the realm (heavenly treasure) is BRAIN POWER, which is CREATIVE. The pure and legitimate ORIGIN of our BANKING SYSTEM may be found in the human brain. This is the money we are told not to squander. "LAY UP for yourselves treasures in heaven, where neither moth nor rust doth corrupt and where thieves do not break through nor steal."

If brain *esse*, from which and by means of which mental power and physical strength are generated, is conserved (used wisely and hence constructively), treasure—actual money—is laid up in the heavenly bank. This INCREASES, for the QUALITY of both energy and substance actually improves with each and every conservation. Thus interest is created which eventually doubles and trebles itself. There is much in Scriptural writings to prove this; for instance, the story of the talents. There are numerous references relative to the INCREASE resulting within a specified time from laying up the first fruits in the temple.

No matter how many errors in translation have resulted from the lack of knowledge of translators, there is a vast fund of information of a reliable and scientific nature to be found in the Scriptures.

The derivation of the word MONEY is very interesting. It comes from the Latin verb *moneo,* which means to warn, to teach, to admonish. The Latin lexicon states that this is traced directly to the noun MEN OR MENS which means MIND. My statement that true money is brain power and cerebral *esse* is therefore verified.

The Latin lexicon states that MONETA (derived from moneó), the name of the mother of Moses (goddess of learning or of the fine arts—meaning material or substance used in creative thinking), was also a surname of Juno; and, as the Roman money was coined in the temple of Juno Moneta, the temple became known as Moneta, or a *mint*.

The word coin in Latin is NUMMUS, and has the same meaning as NUMERUS or NUMBER. The comparison is obvious.

Webster's Dictionary informs us that the word COIN is also derived from the Latin word CUNEUS, which means a WEDGE, PEG or SHAFT—hence ARROW. A wedge is a *triangular-shaped figure*. Therefore we again add to our list of verifications, since sagitta, or the arrow, is the symbol of the sign Sagittarius, which relates to MIND. Is it strange, then, that the first characters used to express thought were cuneiform, or ARROW-SHAPED? It is, in very truth, the explanation why the Magi, of times remote, chose the arrow as the symbol of the Higher Mental sign. This will be further considered under Sagittarius.

The triangle, or arrow-head, is also the symbol of FIRE,

and Sagittarius is the third sign of the fire triplicity. There are several other words which serve to bring out interesting and illuminating facts relative to this subject matter, and we must not pass them by.

Coin, which also means WEDGE, is, in addition, a SPIKE. It is because of this meaning that the star in the wheat spike held in the hand of the Virgin, was named Spica. Spica represents the BREAD OF LIFE. The brain substance is the BREAD OF LIFE. Mind functions through the brain.

A SPIKE is used as a fastener—to HOLD TOGETHER. (Silicea, the Sagittarian salt, actually performs this chemical duty in man's body and in nature.) It also marks a *limit or point of attainment*. All of this pertains intimately to Sagittarius. Metaphysically, a PEG is a support or REASON. The sentence "a peg to hang a claim on" is illustrative.

Carrying this fascinating word-study still further, we find that the feminine name PEG, is a diminutive of Margaret, which means PEARL. In mineralogy, margarite is a SILICATE, from which substance and Calcium a pearl is formed. Silicea and Calcium work together, the same as in the building of concrete. A margarita is also a vessel in which the consecrated Host is preserved.

A *mint* is a place where anything is manufactured or fabricated, but in modern time has come to refer especially to the coining of money. It is also termed menta, which means *mind*.

Pecunia is also a Latin term for money and is the root of the word pecuniary. In ancient times its *basic* meaning was PROPERTY, and the word *proper* is a derivative. It refers to that which is TRUE OR REAL, as in opposition to that which is false and unreal. Therefore the expression, PERSONAL PROPERTY, originally meant THE POSSESSIONS OF THE HUMAN BODY. The correct interpretation of person (from the Latin) is a personality or mask worn by an individual, *e. g.*, MANKIND, AS HE APPEARS TO BE.

Pecus is also derived from the same root as pecunia, and means *flocks* or *heads*. In ancient times flocks constituted the principal property of the tribes. And again we recall that flocks usually refer to sheep, which is the symbol of Aries, the HEAD OF MAN. Brain power is its chief asset.

Some of our well-known authors have made use of the word mint in sentences which further elucidate its meaning.

"But thou and I are one in kind,
As molded like in nature's MINT."
—*Shakespeare.*

"Stamped in clay, a heavenly MINTAGE."
—*Sterling.*

Again, the word cattle is Middle English for catel, or chatel, from which our modern expression chattel is derived, and which means property, or CAPITAL. The latter word is derived from the same root as CAPUT which means THE HEAD. And, curiously enough, the word CHAT, besides meaning light talk, also means a SPIKE or twig.

The many years spent in research work for the writing of this book will not have been in vain, if the readers have been convinced of the importance of WORD STUDY.

The poet Milton must have been aware of the reason why Libra, the sign of the Balance, is placed between Virgo and Scorpio, for he says:

"Th' Eternal, to prevent such horrid fray,
Hung forth in heav'n his golden scales, yet seen
Betwixt Astrea and the Scorpion sign."

And Homer's words also prove this true of him:

"Th' Eternal Father hung
His golden scales aloft."

Richard Allen, in *Star Names and Their Meanings,* tells us that "Addison devoted the 100th number of the TATLER —that of the twenty-ninth of November, 1709—to 'that sign in the heavens which is called by the name of the Balance,' and to his dream thereof in which he saw the Goddess of Justice descending from the constellation to regulate the affairs of men; the whole very beautiful rendering of the ancient thought connecting the Virgin Astræa with Libra. He may have been inspired by recollections of his student days at Oxford, where he must often have seen this sign, as a Judge in full robes, sculptured on the front of Merton College."

"In the early solar zodiac of China, Libra is the Crocodile or Dragon, its national emblem. The Persian sphere shows a human figure lifting the Scales in one hand and grasping a lamb in the other, this being the usual form of a weight for a balance in the early East," says Richard Allen. It would be impossible to find a better presentation or picturization of the immortal story, the PLAN FOR MAN. Aries the Lamb, and Libra the Scales are polar opposites. IF THE LAMB IS NOT SLAIN, EQUILIBRIUM RESULTS.

The symbols and planispheres setting forth this information have always existed. How blind we have been!

Mr. Allen also states that "the symbol of Libra was stamped on the coins of Palmyra, as also on those of Pythdoris." If, as many astronomers emphatically state (strangely enough), the signs of the zodiac play no particular part in nature, and have no effect on mankind, why is it that we contact them in so many ways? Why is it that these old planispheres exist? And again, why do we find zodiacs beautifully inlaid in the floors of many State and Municipal buildings? The answer is that they conceal in their symbols, invaluable information for humanity, and the minds of those having charge of the construction of these buildings respond to the archetypal forms which the Cosmic Mind impresses upon their brain cells. Through this means, these symbols are kept before the eyes of humanity until they are at last impressed to study out what they mean.

The stars in the constellation of Libra form a circular mound, which, in Euphratean lore, is termed THE ALTAR; it is also Tul Ku, the Holy Mound. Sometimes it is called a Censer and at other times a Lamp. Strassmaier confirms this in his translation of an inscription, as *die Lampe als Nuru*, or the Solar Lamp. When these stars, termed the Euphratean SUGI or Chariot Yoke, were clearly seen in the heavens, the ancient Chaldeans considered the season to be auspicious for crops.

Mr. Allen informs us that "In classical lore the whole constituted the ancient House of Venus, for, according to Macrobius, this planet appeared at the Creation; and, moreover, the goddess bound together human couples under the yoke of matrimony. From this came the title Veneris Sidus, although others asserted that Mars was its guardian. Cæsius identifies it with the Balance of the Book of Daniel (5:7), in which Belshazzar had been weighed and 'found wanting.'"

A star above the beam of the Balance is of very unique coloring, pale emerald, a color which is almost unknown in the annals of star lore. However, this checks accurately with my allocation of the spectrum to the zodiac, for deep green falls on Libra. As Aries is a living red (cerise or magenta), green would be the correct color for its complement. All that is necessary to do in allocating color with the signs is to bend the spectrum over them.

In G. A. Gaskell's Dictionary we find many interesting statements relative to this sign: "A symbol of the seventh period of the cycle of life, which is the first period of evolution on the astral plane. The first point of Libra represents the balance between involution and evolution, and the commencement of the evolution from homogeneity to heterogeneity of the many forms and qualities."

Mr. Gaskell quotes Swedenborg as saying that "The Celestial Man is the 'seventh day'; all combat then ceaseth and it is sanctified. Every regenerate person is a 'sabbath,' when he becomes celestial; because he is a likeness of the Lord."

Mr. Gaskell writes most sympathetically of Libra as one of the equinoctial signs: It is a symbol of a point of balance and change reached in the soul's development (sun's course), when a line, as it were, is crossed and a new soul-process is entered upon. The process of Involution is commenced when the Logos (sun) manifests on the upper buddhic plane, at the point symbolized by the first point of Aries; and, after the completion of the process in Virgo, the first point of Libra signifies the commencement of the new process of Evolution in which humanity is now taking part. The Zodiac is a symbol of the Great Cycle of Life. As the sun (Logos) passes through the six northern signs, the process of Involution of the qualities is accomplished; and, as it passes through the six southern signs, so Evolution will be completed, and the qualities and souls returned to God who emanated them."

Spirit and matter are equilibrized when the soul is fully purified, and when, at last, Spirit has a sufficient quantity of the finest (super-microscopic) particles with which to complete the Spiritual body. Spirit is the finest of matter; matter is the coarsest Spirit.

Empedocles says: "At one time all the limbs which form the human body united into one by Love, grow vigorously in the prime of life; but yet at another time, separated by evil Strife, they wander each in different directions along the breakers of the sea of life." This means that the chemical deficiencies of the blood cause the organs (limbs) to become diseased and hence they no longer co-ordinate—work together.

"Malkhuth represents the Sabbath or seventh day, the close of the construction or building of the universe, the Rest Day, or harmony of all." I. Myer, Kabbala, (p. 272). This is also analogous to the formation of the child in utero.

Kingsford and Maitland use modern electrical terms to enlighten us still further: "This 'resting' (on the seventh day)—which is *not* annihilation but *repose*—involves the return of Matter (from its dynamic) to its static condition of Substance. The idea represented is that of the cessation of active-creative force, and the consequent return of phenomenal existence into essential being. It is at once the 'rest which remains for the people of God'; the attainment of perfection by the individual, system or race; and the return of the universe into the bosom of God, by re-absorption into the original substance."

There is much information in the above statement, and much study should be given to the last sentence, "Re-absorption into the original substance;" for this is exactly what takes place in the human body. Not only does Nature instantly begin to utilize the physical materials she has created and built up into a physical vehicle, in sustaining and keeping life within it, but she is also constantly striving to purify these materials, *step them up,* as it were, and reconvert them into the original *esse* or cerebral substance. Inversely, she again *steps them down* to form more solid or material parts.

We are now ready to consider the salt which Dr. Carey allocated with this sign, namely Natrium phos or sodium phosphate. It was not difficult for him to decide that it was a BALANCING salt, since it is chemically known to NEUTRALIZE ACID. Therefore it is correctly assigned to the sign of the Scales. Its great function is to change acid to alkali. This will be considered later on.

It is interesting to trace the word Natrium phos or sodium. The Latin lexicon gives it as Natrum or Natron, the latter spelling being used in Egyptian writings. It is remarkable how much information is obtainable from its Latin derivatives.

First we must recall the fact that Venus is the ruling planet (rate of vibration) of Libra. By this we must understand that THE CHEMICAL ELEMENT ALLOCATING WITH THIS SIGN MUST BE ABLE TO PRODUCE

THIS VENUS VIBRATION. Therefore VENUS REALLY STANDS FOR NATRIUM OR SODIUM. It must also be recalled that Natrium sulph is the Taurus salt, which sign is also ruled by Venus.

Review the fact that Venus was called Lucifer, the BRIGHT star of the morning. This statement is now verified by the interpretation of the root verb to which Natron is traced, namely "niteo," which means bright, shining, glittering, splendid; also handsome, trim, elegant. The latter definitions serve to make clear why the ancients applied these characteristics to Libra.

Nitor means to REST, to support oneself upon anything, to give birth to, to climb, to ascend, push up towards a height. Here we note the idea of balance running like a thread through all of these interpretations. One must have reached the heights in order to rest or to attain equilibrium. One who has thus attained, becomes a beacon star to show the way to other travelers on life's road. In other words, he is a *shining light*.

Tracing the English word sodium, we have sodalis, which means associate, or sharer. This again gives us the idea of partnership or marriage, which students of astrology associate with Libra. Again, the word sod, which literally means *green,* (since sod is grass) is the root of sodium. This explains why the color green is associated with Libra. It will be noted in the color chart that this section of the bent spectrum falls over this sign.

The opal seems to be correctly assigned to Libra. George Kunz states, in his *Curious Lore of Precious Stones,* that Plinii says of opals: "There is in them a softer fire than in the carbuncle; there is the brilliant purple of the amethyst; there is the sea-green of the emerald—all shining together in *incredible union.* Some of their refulgent splendor rivals the colors of the painter, others the flame of burning sulphur or of fire quickened by oil."

The word sodden means to be soaked or softened with water, to be saturated. It is also interpreted to mean bloated, parboiled, heavy or dull-witted, mentally unbalanced.

The above analysis of the words Natrium and sodium indubitably proves the correctness of its allocation with the zodiacal sign Libra.

Referring to the points given above, relative to the words

sodden and bloated, it is interesting to know that sodium phos, or Natrium phos as it is termed in chemical language, releases water from the tissues, collects it in its little tubes or cups in the kidneys and then drains it into the ureter which carries it to the bladder. I have noticed that some astrologers assign this latter organ to Scorpio, but it is wrong to do so. All the organs having to do with the collecting of urine have to do with Libra, and the bladder must be considered from the last decan of this sign. This statement is the result of long experience.

It is said that plants imbibe very freely of the potassium salts in the soil, but they contain traces of sodium salts, in some instances in very notable quantities. The carrot is an example of the latter, and there is no more healthful vegetable than this brilliantly colored product of the soil. It furnishes us with a good supply of sodium and lime, the two salts which are required in *greater quantities* than any of the others. One should learn to like this vegetable, and to use it several times during the week. The reason many do not care for carrots, is because of the rather unique flavor which is produced by the association of these two salts.

On heating sodium a vapor is produced which has a peculiar purple color with a greenish fluorescence. It ranks fourth with silver, copper and gold as a conductor of electricity and heat, and is said by Bunsen to be the most electro-positive metal with the exception of potassium, cæsium and rubidium. It is very reactive.

Encyclopædia Britannica states, "Generally speaking, sodium salts closely resemble the corresponding potassium salts, and their method of preparation is usually the same. It combines very *energetically* (effervesces) with moist, non-metallic elements. It is a CONDENSING AGENT. With potassium it forms a liquid alloy resembling mercury, which is employed in high temperature thermometers. It is one of the most useful gastric sedatives and antacids. It is a *constituent of most stomachic mixtures*. Large doses are used to remove fluid in dropsy. It is a diuretic, acting on the kidneys and increasing the flow of water and the output of urea and rendering urine less acid. It increases the flow of bile."

I have purposely mentioned first what the Encyclopædia

has to say of this salt. A few comments are necessary before we pass on to our biochemic treatise.

First, its electrical power is second to potassium, which means that, while it is capable of generating electrical currents, its power is not quite so high. The proof is, that, while it will separate oxygen and hydrogen, it will not at the same time set fire to the latter. It is natural, then, that it should follow potassium, the Aries salt, and in the form of Natrium sulph release water to be utilized in the production of form. As Natrium phos, the opposite pole of Aries, it brings into manifestation the life that Kali phos has contacted. This explains why it is a condenser. "It is a constituent of the stomach fluids." This is an extremely important statement, not only because it is true from the biochemic standpoint, but also for the reason that it serves to forever disprove a statement credited to many physicians, relative to hydrochloric acid being a constituent of the stomach fluids.

Scientists have stated that sodium is an alkaline salt and is a constituent of most stomach fluids. It is a CHEMICAL FACT that acid can not exist in the presence of this salt. And again, ACID OF ANY KIND FORMS NO PART IN HUMAN ECONOMY.

Can anyone imagine the Great Architect and Chemist of the Universe choosing IRRITANTS from which to fashion the temple of God? Nothing could be more contrary to logic. Medical science has contradicted itself here.

We add to our evidence from *Gray's Anatomy* which states, as quoted before, that phosphates and chlorides of sodium, calcium and potassium constitute a large proportion of the material required in cell structure.

Again we ask why the profession has not informed the general public relative to these facts? Also, why has it not *used* them?

The Encyclopædia also emphasizes the fact that sodium increases the flow of urine and renders it, at the same time, less acid. The truth of the matter is that when sufficient Natrium phos is used the urine will become *alkaline*. This eliminates the extremely annoying scalding which invariably results from acid conditions.

Dr. Carey says, in his *Biochemic System of Medicine*, "Acid, like seeming evil, is all-pervading." To accompany his chemical statement is the astrological twin: All humanity is unbalanced, in varying degrees. If balanced, human beings would be PERFECT. The Great Work would have been accomplished.

Acid results from a general deficiency in the sodiums and also from the fermentation of food. This latter condition is general, for the reason that so few eat as they should. No wonder the Bible states "A glutton shall not enter the kingdom of heaven." A balanced or harmonious condition of body and brain is absolutely impossible for such an individual.

Acid causes a terrible gnawing sensation in the stomach. Most people think this is hunger. Such is not the case, for only after a person has gone without food for a long time could this sensation be experienced. Those having acid are almost constantly craving something, hence often rush into a drug store for soda, candy or sandwiches. They are the ones having the proverbial chip on the shoulder. The least thing knocks it off. They are quickly upset, and easily become unbalanced.

When acid results from the fermentation of food, which is due to the inability of the stomach to digest it, its long-continued presence in the system naturally becomes a *secondary* cause for further trouble, and many painful and dangerous symptoms eventually appear. Chief among these is rheumatism. Even the perspiration has a sour odor, and it is highly irritating to the skin. If this condition continues, the kidneys eventually become affected, and stomach or bladder ulcerates. Vision changes, fluctuates from day to day, cloudy today, clearer tomorrow. There is nothing which so quickly reacts on the eyes as acid.

What physician can tell you that it is acid which causes a child or adult to grind the teeth during sleep; that intestinal parasites form in the accumulation of ferment in that long tract; that these often cause convulsions in children and adults, and in the former more frequently at night; that the throat may become so raw and sore from the continued presence of acid, that it appears to be diphtheria (it is termed "false diphtheria" by Dr. Schuessler); and that morning nausea, a yellow coating on the back of the tongue, itching and pimples like flea-bites, are all due to a great deficiency in this salt. I wish to emphasize this point: there is nothing which so quickly changes a good disposition into a quarrelsome, disagreeable one, as acid.

Other symptoms originating from lack of this salt are: headache on the crown of the head, also the forehead; feeling as if the skull were too full; intense pressure and heat, causing one to fear insanity; headache with pain in the stomach, and ejection of sour, frothy fluid, giddiness; inflammation of the eyes, and the secretion there of a golden-yellow, creamy matter. Golden yellow is always the color of the secretions, and the tongue coating, when this salt is needed.

When Natrium phos is deficient, the ears (outer) may become sore and scabby, with a creamy discharge, or they may become hot and burning. There may be: itching of the nose, denoting worms; face red and blotched, blotches coming and going; acid risings; sour taste in mouth; canker sores; tonsils and throat inflamed; dyspepsia; gastric abrasions; superficial ulceration. Sometimes the long-continued presence of acid in the stomach causes it to become partially covered with ulcers, so deep-seated and angry-looking that they seem to be of a cancerous nature. Frequently they DO develop into cancers.

Sometimes diarrhœa results, especially with children; also, jelly-like masses of mucus are passed, sometimes in such quantities as to surprise one, passing in chunks and strings. Injections of this salt should be used daily to rid the tract of this condition, and also to assist in eliminating any parasites which may be present.

Insufficient urination is another symptom indicative of need of this salt, also scalding of the parts; seminal weakness or emissions; increased sexual desire; acid secretions from the vagina, sometimes creamy yellow and sometimes watery; irregularity of the periods, when accompanied by frontal headache; morning nausea, in pregnancy; palpitation and irregularity of heart action (the result of imperfect digestion); trembling around the heart, especially after eating; rheumatism of the joints, cracking and creaking, with pain and soreness; eczema; "rose-rash;" hives; flashes of heat from indigestion; itching of the anus; restless sleep, etc., etc.

In Latin, the word acid is derived from *acidus* and its original meaning is SHARP AND CUTTING, which has naturally given rise to the term. There are some physiological fluids which must be viscid, in order to act as attractors; but it does not mean that they are acid. However, many have been confused on this point.

Since the terms sharp, cutting, disagreeable and unattractive are the negatives of agreeable, pleasant, attractive, charm, beauty and loveliness, the attributes of the purified Venus will be readily seen.

Without sodium phosphate in the blood to supply the cells of the body, the fluids in and around the corpuscles would not only become acid, but the garment or fragile capsule surrounding them would be pierced and the nuclei escape. To be in a balanced state, the proportion of water must be constant, neither too much nor too little, and the corpuscles truly may be drowned in acid fluid.

Therefore to scale the heights and gain the balance, Venus must bid her son Cupid throw away his darts. The sign following Libra, that of Scorpio, tells the story of the DART or SCORPION'S STING.

"Balance, measure and patience, these are the eternal conditions of high success."—Matthew Arnold in Celtic Literature.

CHAPTER VIII

THE ANALYSIS AND SYNTHESIS OF SCORPIO AND CALCIUM SULPH OR LIME SULPHATE

"Behold I give unto you power to tread on serpents and scorpions and over all the power of the enemy; and nothing shall by any means hurt you."

—*Luke* 10:19.

THE Sun enters the zodiacal sign of the Scorpion on October 23 (approximately), and remains until November 22. It is the ninth Alban month. Its old Dutch name was SLAGTH-MAAND, or SLAUGHTER month, the time when beasts were slain and salted down for winter use. In the old Saxon language it was Wind-moneth, or wind-month, when the fishermen ceased their labors until spring. In the French Republican calendar it was BRUMAIRE or fog-month.

Dr. Wakeman Ryno says, in his book, *Amen, the God of the Amonians,* that the following are some of the terms used to designate this sign: "Baal-Zebub, or Lord of flies; King of the bottomless pit; Satan of the Hebrews; the very gate of hell; the place of the tormented; the Persian Esrael, or Angel of Death; The Angel Abaddon of Revelation; the Angel Apollyon of the New Testament; the Angel of the Sphinx (the Eagle)."

This same writer further states that "the constellation of Scorpio was held by the ancients to be a bird of bad omen (the harbinger of winter); thus for *mystical* reasons they adopted the Eagle (Aquilla) as its sign. The sign of Scorpio was also considered as THE VERY GATE OF HELL for the reason that it was at the commencement of the five months of winter with its cold, wet and very disagreeable weather, rendering it necessary to have fires to keep warm; hence all the gods of winter were COLORED RED, IN IMITATION OF FIRE, and *having dominion over the lower world.*"

In the Babylonian creation-scheme, Scorpio was Apin-dua, meaning *Opposite* to the *Foundation* (Aries), which is very apropos, for this sign is said by astrologers to be the house of death, although they have never explained *why.*

As Aries (the cerebrum) is the Father, or beginning (the Creator), it is evident that Scorpio, having to do with PRO-creation, possesses a mighty secret, concerning which the great majority of people are still in ignorance. Mr. Bailey, editor of the *British Journal of Astrology,* is the only modern astrologer who has had the courage to deal intimately with this subject. He states, very emphatically, in his book *Astrology and Birth Control,* that, from time immemorial, the sign Scorpio has been allocated with the organs of pro-creation, *and that their use is solely for procreation.* They have a SPECIFIC function the same as the stomach, liver, spleen, eyes and other parts of the body. Students should obtain the above book, for it is one which will assist greatly in restoring the ancient prestige of this splendid science, which has been so grossly perverted.

One of the Babylonian names for Scorpio is *Uigur ali,* denoting *a creature which belongs to and comes up from the underworld.* It is obvious that this has reference to the ANIMAL or procreative germs.

On ancient planispheres this sign was also termed the King or Beast of Death. Among the figures depicted on a large one, is that of the Mithraic Bull (Taurus), which, in so far as art is concerned, is a reduplication of the Euphratean Bull. He is surrounded by hostile creatures: a dog, which springs up to lick his blood; a large serpent which bites him; and a scorpion which seizes his genital organs. The analogy should be clear to all, and especially to those studying the letters of the *Tarot.* The twenty-first card illustrates how man is beset by animals (animal passions).

On these same planispheres, Scorpio was also *Lugal-tudda,* the THIEF and god of lightning, the giver of fire to man. The torment produced by the sting of the scorpion was likened to the burning of lightning. It was called the River of the Snake, also the *River of the Sheepcote of the Ghost-world.* The latter expression will be referred to and explained later on. The electrical fire manifesting in lightning is analogous to the fire of life which leaves the body at the termination of the sexual act.

"And they had tails like unto scorpions, and there were stings in their tails; and their power was to hurt men five months" (the five months of winter)."—Rev. 9:3, 4, 10, 11.

It is obvious that there is a deeper meaning to the words

"And their power was to hurt men for five months." It is true that humanity may suffer from cold during the last five months of the year, but they are not especially "hurt," unless living conditions are unusual. Of all the interpretations given to this sign, and the names by which it is known in different countries and to many races, none is positive or constructive save that of the Eagle, which is deeply esoteric.

As usual we must make use of anatomy and physiology to understand our subject. As Scorpio is the eighth sign, it allocates with the eighth division of the human body which contains the organs of procreation. A study of the nervous systems furnishes us with the information that the great ganglia at the base of the spinal canal termed the sacral, and the coccygeal, which is at the end of the spine, have to do with the procreative glands.

The largest nerve in the body, the great sciatic, rises from the sacral center, and not only sends important branches to the sexual glands, but other nerves branch to the knees and to the extremities. As the sacral center allocates with Capricorn, and the feet with Pisces, it is obvious that this portion of the body relates to *five* zodiacal signs.

The secret explanation of the word "hurt" is revealed when it is realized that the wrong use of Scorpio, the procreative organs, in sexual excesses or self-abuse, not only actually impairs the activities of these five parts, but very often results in paralysis. Therefore, five-twelfths of the human body is directly and constantly deteriorated as a result of sex life, in addition to the indirect effect on the other seven-twelfths. The extremities become less and less active, the limbs stiff and lame, the back is bent, and one *appears* old even if he is not.

It is obvious that the term THIEF is exceedingly apropos, for the sting of the Scorpion, as interpreted physiologically, most assuredly results, sooner or later, in death for all. The sex act not only steals energy from the five divisions of the body represented by the extremities, but slowly and surely reacts on the brain in exactly the same way. Besides, whether we wish to believe it or not, it is a fact that the basic fluid in all the glands is created in the brain, which is the first gland in the body. The cerebrum is truly the fountain-head of life, and within it is precipitated the mysterious semi-fluidic and wax-like substance which is termed "the gray matter." The infinitesimal mineral particles in this gray matter constitute the lode-stone, or magnet, which attracts humid air and the Spirit of life or akasha into the brain reservoir or claustrum. The function of the latter organ has never been explained, nor is any information given relative to innumerable others in the cerebrum alone.

Referring to the Euphratean term by which Scorpio was known to the ancients, "the River of the Sheepcote of the Ghost-world," we are surprised to find modern confirmation of the above term.

The holidays which are recognized and celebrated today were known in very remote times. They exist today because their origin is based on fact. Important and vital truths concerning humanity are embodied in each one.

Hallowe'en is an example. This day is especially applicable and interesting, because its celebration occurs while the Sun is transiting the house of the Scorpion. It is well known to many that the origin of this festival is "lost in the dim shadows of antiquity." But although the customs and ceremonies differ more or less in each country, yet, at the same time, a basic idea is seen to permeate them all—that ghosts walk abroad, and witches, evil spirits or goblins indulge in their yearly revels on October 31. In ancient times, the celebration continued into the following day, November 1. As these days fall in the seventh degree of Scorpio, this degree has a Capricorn vibration.

Each two and one-half days the *creative* vibration of Nature changes, corresponding to the time the moon remains in each sign of the zodiac. To find these variations in the days of the month (or, to be correct, in each zodiacal sign), the twelve signs of the zodiac must be represented IN each sign. To do this, each decan of a sign is divided up into four parts of two and one-half degrees each. It is most interesting to study the charts of people by this method, and I am convinced that it is the only method by which character as well as the physical condition can be correctly analyzed. The rising sign must not be used. No degrees of Aries must be on the ascendant.

Returning to our subject of Hallowe'en, we find, then, that the CHARACTER AND NATURE of this period is essentially Carpricornian. My researches relative to the name of this latter sign have resulted in finding that it consists of two words, Capri and corn.

The word Capri means GOAT and corn is a general term for seed. Therefore, Capricorn means GOAT SEED, or animal seed. In plain words, it refers to the procreative or venal seed. Corn also means horn.

It has been known from ancient times that the sacral vertebræ allocate with Capricorn, but no explanation of the reason for this has been furnished heretofore. However it has now been found, and will be fully explained on a chart accompanying a book entitled, *The Biochemic System of Body Building and Astro-Analysis*. This is to be published next year.

There is much evidence to show that the festival of Hallowe'en was originally based on *some special fact having to do with procreation*. While it is a fact that none of the pastimes, engaged in at this time, serve in any way to attract the attention to this secret, nevertheless the Encyclopædia Britannica furnishes the following information: "On or about the first of November the Druids held their great autumn festival and lighted fires in honor of the Sun-god, in Thanksgiving for the harvest. Further, it was a Druidic belief that on the eve of this festival Saman, the Lord of death, called together the wicked souls that within the past twelve months have been condemned to inhabit the bodies of animals."

Before commenting on the above, another reference must be given. Richard Hinckley Allen, in his *Star Names and Their Meanings,* states that the Greek word for Graffias, one of the stars in the constellation of the Scorpion, means CRAB. He says "It may be that here lies the origin of the title, for it is well known that the ideas and words for crab and scorpion were almost interchangeable in early days, FROM THE BELIEF THAT THE LATTER CREATURE WAS GENERATED FROM THE FORMER."

To emphasize the above, he adds, in a foot note: "This opinion was held by the learned Saints Augustine and Basil of the fourth century, and confidently expressed by Saint Isidore in his *Origines et Etymologiæ.*"

Without some understanding of astrology from an esoteric and physiological standpoint, the full significance of the two references given above will not be appreciated.

Esoteric and biological astrology are the means whereby one discovers that the CRAB IS ACTUALLY CHANGED INTO THE SCORPION. This means that one-tenth of the corpuscles of the body (all of which rightfully belong to the body) under the vibration of the lower (carnal) mind, are attracted and drawn down into the testes, and are there *changed into animal germs or corpuscles.* These may be termed negative in nature, because they are animal. The true physiological corpuscles are neutral (neuter) in themselves, and can reproduce by their own efforts. In other words, the two sexes are in *harmonious* relationship with each other, and hence can divide and produce "daughter cells" indefinitely, or as required, provided, of course, that the necessary materials are furnished.

The corpuscles are QUEEN BEES, for they are of the same nature. They can reproduce themselves, and, in addition, are capable of developing into a different germ cell. One who is receptive to truth and scientifically minded, will find no fault with this simile.

The above is only one of many mighty physiological secrets which a knowledge of REAL astrology will ultimately reveal. The analysis of words is another means.

Much more on this subject will be given in the forthcoming book, *The Truth About Sex and Birth Control.*

Reviewing the interpretation given to this sign or period of the year by the Dutch, we find that it was termed the SLAUGHTER month. This is significant in the light of the foregoing statements concerning the power of the mind to attract the corpuscles into the glands testes and there convert them into ANIMAL GERMS. In the sexual act, these germs ARE SLAUGHTERED, SINCE IT IS A SCIENTIFIC FACT THAT ONLY ONE SPERMATOZOA IS REQUIRED TO IMPREGNATE THE OVUM. The millions which have been uselessly expended of course die, and, as the Bible states, "Their dead bodies lie around the streets of the city."

The above may not be a pleasant picture, but, if one stops to consider, it will be found to be true. Most people know practically nothing relative to the body and its functions. Unless the study of this most important subject is seriously undertaken, the disastrous effect of wrong living will not be realized. It is particularly important to awaken to these facts at this time, since from October, 1928, until 1942, Neptune, the Purifier, transits the house of health, which is Virgo, the virgin. A UNIVERSAL housecleaning has begun. We can not sidestep it if we will. Our only hope is that the fires of purification will find *some* gold in the midst of all the dross.

This terrible waste of corpuscles scourges the brain, and causes both body and brain to deteriorate slowly or quickly, according to the extent of the sex life. Only those who do not wish it to be true will find this fact difficult to realize.

Degeneration, generation and regeneration—these are the three stages in the lives of the triune being—animal, human, Spiritual man. Real thinkers realize, with horror and regret, that the majority of us are still in the first stage. In the light of physiological fact we can not deny that this is true. A description of each of the stages enables one easily to distinguish between them.

Degeneration means that one cohabits solely for the sake of pleasurable sensation.

Generation means to generate, to become parents, therefore to engage in the sexual act, solely that a child may result.

Regeneration means that there is no longer any thought of sex, *therefore the act is not indulged in.* As the body loses neither creative substance nor electrical energy, body and brain are not robbed of *any* of their corpuscles. Therefore they attain the highest stage of efficiency. Thomas Vaughan states in his remarkable work, that the seed which the body creates must be used to feed and therefore recreate the body which forms it. This is a self-evident fact.

The Scorpion and its sting has been known, from ancient times as the Angel of Death; but the White Eagle is its esoteric symbol, and is emblematical of the Divine promise of life everlasting to "him who overcometh." The wonderful words, "And he shall go no more out," refer to the overcoming of death. Death can not take place when there are sufficient corpuscles to sustain life.

Is it any wonder, then, that the ancients referred to Scorpio as "the gate of hell?" Or that it was called "the thief"—since the wiles of Venus steal away the wits?

We will now consider some of the stars in the constellation of Scorpio, and note how the analysis of each one adds to our accumulation of evidence.

The scorpion is said to be the slayer of the giant-man.

It is very interesting to note that Richard Hinckley Allen, in his *Star Names and Their Meanings,* practically begins his article on Scorpio by saying that "classical authors saw in it the monster that caused the disastrous runaway of the steeds of Phœbus Apollo when in the inexperienced hands of Phaëton." Energy became a consuming fire—body and brain were both destroyed.

A very large and brilliant star named ANTARES is said to represent the heart of the Scorpion. Let us study the word. It consists of two words, ANT and ARES. The former means against, or in opposition to, and Ares is the Roman name for the planet Mars and also Aries. It will be recalled that one of Scorpio's interpretations is "opposite to the foundation," meaning that it seeks to undermine and destroy that foundation which is LIFE itself (represented by the cerebrum or Aries).

It is very evident that ANT-ares refers to Mars in a negative or destructive sense, as ruler of Scorpio *in the present stage of evolution.* As astrology teaches that Mars rules Aries and Scorpio, it is necessary closely to analyze the word Mars.

As ruler of Aries, Mars has already been considered, and its interpretation there is energy used CONSTRUCTIVELY, to create or build up. As ruler of Scorpio it becomes the Angel or means of Death. It does not create, but tears down and destroys.

I therefore contribute the following for the use of students: Mars rules the first seven signs of the zodiac *positively and constructively.* It is energy, and as such creates and operates the seven vital organs of the body, from Aries to, and inclusive of, Libra. Mars rules Scorpio and the other four parts of the body *negatively* and *hence destructively.* It has lost its spiritual vibration, and has become animal. Thus it is said that "Æsculapius stole fire from heaven and chained it to the earth."

Remember that Scorpio is next to Libra the balance sign. If one passes *beyond* the BALANCE POINT (Phaëton was told to keep the MIDDLE course), he sees the claws of the Scorpion reaching out to grasp him, and feels its poisonous breath upon his face. HE MUST NOT GO BEYOND THE "RING PASS NOT."

It is not strange, then, that Mars has been interpreted, up to the present, as "the god of war," for those living in its negative vibration can not interpret it otherwise.

The Chinese call Antares, Ta Who, the GREAT FIRE. It will at once be realized that this is very appropriate. There is no more consuming fire than that of sex.

It is interesting to note, in the Bible Concordance, that there are *seven* different interpretations of the serpent, just as there are seven of the lion (as given under Leo). They deal with the different stages or conditions of the material which is studied under Scorpio.

In Revelation it refers to "the old serpent which is the devil." Ignorance (hence sin or wrong doing) is the negative interpretation, while wisdom is the positive. "Be ye wise as a serpent and harmless as a dove."—Matthew 10:16.

In Isaiah we find direct reference to the esoteric symbol of Scorpio as the FLYING SERPENT. "For out of the serpent's root shall come forth a cockatrice, and his fruit shall be a fiery flying serpent." This plainly means the serpent fire in the sacral and coccygeal region, or base of the spine. Some of this fire (fire of wisdom) is lost in sexual congress. The serpent "must be lifted up." The truth is, that IF IT IS LET ALONE (not lost) IT WILL EVENTUALLY GO UP.

A scientific explanation of the above statement is, that where there is no *break* in circulation there is no LOSS. Circulation means to move, to revolve in a circle. Because humanity, in its present stage of evolution *has* such a break in its glandular circulation, *loss* is inevitable. The Divine Fire of Æsculapius can not ascend, nor can all of the essence created in the cerebrum return to it. It is true of many persons that very little of it returns, and the cerebro-spinal system struggles on and works over-time, as it were, to supply enough to keep the physical mechanism functioning.

Continuing with our verifications of Scorpio, we find that, according to Richard Allen, "The Akkadians called it Girtab, the Seizer or Stinger. IT SEIZES or steals the corpuscles of the body, in very truth, and the vernacular expression "you are stung," is heard not infrequently. It is, together with that other expression mentioned earlier ("Give me something with a kick in it,") representative of our present emotional status.

This same name, Girtab, is given another interpretation—the PLACE WHERE ONE BOWS DOWN. It, too, is particularly apropos, for the reason that one of the three male sexual glands is expressive of the same meaning. I refer to the prostate, which means to prostrate or bow down. The prostate receives the male germ seeds after they have been perfected in the testes. They are stored here until ejaculated. The female uterus, correspondingly, receives the ovum. If fertilized, it remains. If not, it passes out of the body. Both GO DOWN, which is the same as bowing down.

In early planispheres the Scorpion was represented as grasping the Scales of Libra. This definitely proves that the ancients were well aware of the fact that sex unbalances physiological and metaphysical functions. These were intended by the Divine Architect and Chemist to be perfect—therefore balanced.

It is said that Odilo, Abbot of Clugny, appointed November 2, the day following Hallowe'en, as a time set apart to pray for souls in purgatory. Lost human procreative germs! Are they not truly LOST SOULS? *INDEED, THERE ARE NO LOST SOULS EXCEPT THESE.* Each individual has life after life in which to make good, incarnation after incarnation. Our many lives in which the Spirit returns, again and again, into a new baby body to learn to build constructively, are analogous to school days. The pity is, that we have all been so slow in learning.

Richard Allen also gives us this curious information, which, in the light of previous chapters, should be readily understood: "but the alchemists held Scorpio in high regard, for only when the sun was in this sign could the transmutation of iron into gold be performed."

As iron is the allocating salt of Mars, and Mars is energy, the highest use of this chemical is the creation of the most precious and noble metal, that of gold. In its true and esoteric signification, all of the old alchemical stories really referred to the transmutation of the inferior and imperfect products of the human body into perfect ones. However, this transmutation was interpreted as an ulterior process, for only a few were capable of realizing that it had a far different meaning.

The special place of Mars in Scorpio was said to be in its tail and sting. "The claws were especially related to the star Jugum in the Yoke of the Balance (Libra) being associated with Venus, because this goddess united persons under the yoke of matrimony," says Richard Allen. Perhaps this may serve to reveal the reason for so many divorces. At least it is one of the many, and probably the most important.

If one studies the new (to this age) and unique diagram and chart entitled "THE COSMIC EMBRYO," found elsewhere in this book, he will note that each succeeding sign of the zodiac takes less space than the preceding one. The following is what Richard Hinckley Allen has to say of Scorpio: "Although nominally in the zodiac, the sun actually occupies but nine days in passing through the two portions that project upwards into Ophiucus, so far south of the ecliptic is it; indeed, except for these projections, it could not be claimed as a member of the Zodiac." Perhaps this is what the Scriptures refer to in the passage which says: "And except those days should be shortened, there should no flesh be saved; but for the elects' sake those days shall be shortened."

The above no doubt refers particularly to the ten degrees of the first decan of this sign, which covers the part of the human body assigned to the CREATION OF ANIMAL GERMS. If more space in the body had been allotted to this function, it is undeniably true that "no flesh could survive," for the flesh itself would be robbed of many more corpuscles than is now the case.

Another interesting name given to this star "Antares" by the ancient Euphrateans was Bilu-sha-ziri, or LORD OF THE SEED. This proves that Antares really belongs in the first decan of Scorpio, where the seed is created.

Twelve years ago, my researches showed me that the first decan of Scorpio is related to the glands testes, or correspondingly, the ovaries. The middle decan is related to Cowpers' glands in the male, and the glands of Bartholin in the female. The last ten degrees cover the prostate and correspondingly the uterus. This will be found *infallible* when the NATURAL ZODIAC IS USED, for the zodiac is essentially physiological as well as anatomical.

The Euphrateans also called this star Kak-shisa, the Creator of Prosperity, an interpretation which is essentially appropriate. One is very rich, who has much grain in his physiological granary. This simile was probably the origin of the Biblical story of the rich man. He was told to exchange what he had, and give it to the poor (the poor, starved cells). "But he went away sorrowful, for he had much possessions."

"In Egyptian astronomy Scorpio represented the goddess Selkit or Serk-t and was the symbol of Isis in the pyramid ceremonies" says Richard Allen. When it is recalled that the Moon was known by the name of Isis, its real nature, that of fertility, will be recognized. True fertility is considered under Cancer, and is concerned with the *creation* of *corpuscles.* In Scorpio, *a certain number of these are changed to animal germs.*

This function of Scorpio is verified by the belief of the ancient astrologers that Scorpions were generated from crabs. Indeed, the early Fathers of Christianity, Saints Augustine, Basil, and Isidore, confidently expressed their knowledge of this most profound secret. It is obvious that the ancients were well aware of it. This would not have been the case if they had used this mighty science, astrology, other than in relation to the body.

ABSOLUTE PURITY IS THE FOUNDATION OF THE STRUCTURE OF THE REAL CHURCH. The purified body is a Holy Place, a Sanctuary, a Holy of Holies. Otherwise, it is a house in which to abide for a little while. Sometimes it is a mere shack.

Akrab, one of the names of Scorpio, means *Wounding.* It will be recalled that in a previous chapter Venus was said to have arisen from the foam of the sea, at the wounding of Uranus. As the latter is the Son of Man (the Savior) in astrological lore, this story really refers to the saline solution of the blood being robbed of its corpuscles. Aquarius (over which Uranus rules) relates to the blood serum, the saline or vitalizing portion.

No comment should be necessary on the following, quoted from Richard Allen: "Another star in this Euphratean planisphere is Gis-gan-gu-sur, the Light of the Hero, or the Tree of the Garden of Light, *placed in the midst of the abyss* and reminding us of that other tree, the Tree of Life in the midst of the Garden of Eden." It is obvious that it is the Tree of Knowledge of Good and Evil, otherwise positive and negative.

This same star was called the Crown. There is no doubt of its *thorns.* There are two other stars in this constellation, named Al Shaulah and Vicritau, interpreted as "the Two Releasers" which are analogous to the two ejaculatory glands, otherwise called Caput Gallinaginis or Vermontanum, in works on Physiology.

In Hindu lore, we find many of the stars of Scorpio grouped

under one name, that of *Calamity*. Here this name refers to the negative or destructive character of Scorpio. The Euphrateans depicted its positive nature as Prosperity, which thus allocates with its symbol, the White Eagle.

Richard Allen states that "the names and legend that Ellis, in his *Polynesian Researches*, applied to Castor and Pollux, the Reverend Mr. W. W. Gill asserts, in his *Myths and Songs of the South Pacific*, belong here, and are the favorites among the story-tellers of the Hervey Islands. They make one, a little girl, Piri-ere-ua, the Inseparable, with her smaller brother, fleeing from home to the sky when ill treated by their parents; two other stars which follow them are still in pursuit."

Castor and Pollux, it will be remembered, were considered under Gemini, and an analysis of the two names was given. It is quite easy to believe that they were related to the sign Scorpio, as well as to Gemini, since the latter is the lower, or carnal mind, which dwells for the most part on the activity of that part of the body allocated with Scorpio. Indeed, it is quite well known that pollux, or bollus, in common parlance is a name applied to one of the genital organs. The word castrate is derived from the same root as Castor, and means to emasculate by removing the testes.

In describing the scorpion, we find that the dictionaries state that "it is distinguishable at a glance from all other existing members by having the *last six* segments of its body modified to form a highly flexible tail, armed at the end with a *sting* consisting of a vescicle holding a pair of poison glands, and of a sharp spine behind the tip of which the ducts of the glands open. They are *extraordinarily susceptible to heat,* and when they feel it beating down upon them they brandish their tails and strike right and left as if to drive off the unseen enemy."

Since the scorpion really corresponds to, and has to do with, the last five signs of the zodiac and the corresponding parts of the body, the number of its segments is apropos. The statement that it is "extraordinarily susceptible to heat," is another allocation verified by the well-known fact that the sexual organs are equally susceptible. They react instantaneously to the fire of passion. The reaction of the scorpion to heat, as it brandishes its tail and strikes, is equally applicable to the sexual organ.

At this point it will be well to explain the meaning of the symbol of this sign. It consists of the ancient letter "m" with the last stroke extended down below the line and a sting placed at the end.

The chapter on Virgo should be reviewed in order to realize the full significance of this letter. In Hebrew it is spelled MEM, and means mother, the female, creative fluid, sea water (because it contains all the elements which sustain life). The fish in the sea water correspond to the corpuscles in the saline solution of the blood. Naturally, MEM means substance, or material, as stated in the sixth chapter, and when material or substance has become pure it is Virgin Mary.

The sting on the tail should be recognized as Cupid's dart, for he is the hunter whose arrow has ever been known to *wound.*

It is obvious that sufficient has already been written relative to the character of this sign to enable everyone to understand why the sign of the Balance, or Libra, is placed between Scorpio and the sign of the Virgin. The two natures are diametrically opposed to one another. Down through the ages, these three have stared humanity in the face, a veritable picturization of God's plan for mankind. Harmony or balance must eventually exist between Virgo and Scorpio, for not until then will it be possible for the latter proudly to replace the symbol of the Scorpion with that of the Eagle. The glandular fluid will have turned to molten gold and ascended to the heights—the cerebrum—the Place of the Most High.

Many other strange and interesting Scriptural statements relating to this part of the body could be given, but they will be incorporated in forthcoming books on these subjects. But one more will not be out of place, since the Two Releasers, the stars allocating with the part of the body we are considering, correspond to caput gallinaginis which in Latin means "head of the woodcock" and is the physiological term for the glands ejaculating the procreative fluid.

It will be recalled that the cock is mentioned in the Scriptures in reference to Peter's *denial of Jesus.* It is a fact that the word "Gever" in Hebrew means both man and cock.

When the complete interpretation and histology of this barnyard fowl is known, then only will students realize why there are so many references to it in occult literature. Animal glyphs always typify, and are symbolical of, the animal or carnal nature. It is a fact, then, that the "crowing" of this most *electrical* of all animals *exactly* corresponds to, and is analogous to, the physiological action of the caput gallinaginis in man.

Why does chanticleer crow while it is yet dark? It *heralds* the approach of the SUN, that electrical orb, the nature of which exactly corresponds to its own. It senses the coming of the positive rays or vibrations which impregnate all things with new life and energy. And so the cock, master of his own harem, knows that it is his special business to do the same on his own plane.

Madame Blavatsky, in her *Secret Doctrine,* has the following to say of it: "A very occult bird, much appreciated in ancient augury and symbolism. According to the Zohar, the cock crows three times before the death of a person; and in Russia and all Slavonian countries whenever a person is ill on the premises where a cock is kept, its crowing is held to be a sign of inevitable death, unless the bird crows at the hour of midnight, or immediately afterward, when its crowing is considered natural. As the cock was sacred to Æsculapius, and as the latter was called SOTER (SAVIOR), who raised the dead to life, the Socratic exclamation 'We owe a cock to Æsculapius,' just before the Sage's death, is very suggestive. As the cock was always connected in symbology with the SUN (or solar gods) Death and Destruction, it has found its appropriate place in the four gospels in the prophecy about Peter *repudiating* his Master before the cock crowed thrice. The cock is the most magnetic and electric of all birds, hence its Greek name ELECTRUM."

The word chanticleer means SHRILL SINGER, since the bird has a rather hoarse or grating voice. The opposite of harmony is FRICTION, and this latter term is entirely applicable to the cock IN EVERY RESPECT, even to its physiological correspondence. Friction must be initiated in order to enable the ejaculatory glands to produce the spasmodic convulsion necessary to force out the procreative fluid.

All interpretations of the word cock given in the dictionaries, indubitably add to the verifications of our discoveries concerning physiological correspondence. Cock means a leader, boss or master. In Danish it is a lump or heap. Other interpretations are: to contend or fight; a small conical pine; to turn or stick up. All of which goes to prove the magic which the study of words reveals.

How scandalized most ministers of the Gospel would be, to learn the real interpretation of the cock on the church steeple. If asked to explain, they would no doubt reply that the cock is mentioned in the Bible in connection with Peter's repudiation of Jesus. Therefore it is an ever-present reminder to humanity today, to watch out and not deny Him. In the light of the points given above, as well as the story told in each zodiacal sign, it should be clear that this bird was used as a symbol *because it was analogous to a certain part of the human anatomy*.

One or two curious references to the cock are given as further verification: "Nourish a cock, but offer it not in *sacrifice*. This is the eighteenth Symbolic Saying in the *Protreptics* of Iamblichus. The cock was sacred to Minerva (goddess of wisdom) and also to the Sun and Moon, and it would be impious to offer a sacrilegious offering to the gods. WHAT IS ALREADY CONSECRATED TO GOD CAN NOT BE EMPLOYED IN SACRIFICE."

"The Misha says 'they do not rear cocks at Jerusalem on account of the holy things.' " Naturally this does not refer to the city of that name, but to a part of the anatomy.

It is interesting to find that one of the star figures in the constellation of Scorpio is that Ophiucus, struggling with the serpent. Stung in one heel, he crushes it with the other.

Mars, as negative ruler of Scorpio, is said in Greek mythology to be the lover of the goddess of beauty herself (Venus). However, the description of the oldest known statue of the supposed "god of war" is that of a seated Mars with Eros at his feet, symbolical of energy, that great creative power which ensouls the erotes or SPIRITS OF LIFE.

The temple and oldest altar of Mars was situated at the Campus Martinus. His sacred emblems were the shield and spear, which, it was believed, had fallen from heaven. These were carried by the priests at the different festivals held in his honor. The first of these was celebrated in March while the others took place in October. These two periods represented THE OPENING AND CLOSING OF THE CAMPAIGN SEASON. These correspond to the creation of the vital organs and the activities taking place within them. The word campaign means any *organized* action or movement.

In October a special event took place, termed the Lustrum. It was a solemn ceremony of expiation and purification. We would do well ourselves to set aside a day for such a purpose.

Mars, as ruler of Scorpio, is the scourge of mortals, *and in this sign only is it interpreted as having to do with rapine and murder, a veritable slaughter of the innocents.* And it must be understood that this is solely and entirely due to human ignorance. Mars was born to labor from the heights. We can not blame him that mortals have dragged him down into the mire and filth. Mars is actually subject to Minerva, the goddess of wisdom, for only she is capable of forcing him to keep his place ON THE HEIGHTS.

"Dearly beloved, I beseech you as strangers and pilgrims, ABSTAIN FROM FLESHLY LUSTS, WHICH WAR AGAINST THE SOUL." Pet. 2:11.

Mankind must become SELF-REDEEMED. This will be accomplished through knowledge of SELF.

In *Smith's Bible Dictionary,* we find the following in reference to the scorpion: "The Biblical references to the scorpion have clearly no reference to the *animal,* but to some instrument of scourging—probably a whip with iron *points*—unless indeed the expression is a *mere figure.* The punishment of scourging was prescribed by the law in cases of *unchastity.*"

In his very unique and interesting article on medicine, this same author seems to have been awake to the real cause of death and disease, for he further states: "Youthful lusts die out, and their organs, of which the 'grasshopper' is perhaps a figure, are relaxed. The 'silver cord' may be that of nervous sensation, or motion, or even the spinal marrow itself. Perhaps some incapacity of retention may be signified by the 'golden bowl broken'; the 'pitcher broken at the well' suggests some vital supply stopping at the usual source—derangement, perhaps, of the digestion or of respiration; the 'wheel shivered at the cistern' conveys, through the image of the water-lifting process familiar in irrigation, the motion of the blood, pumped, as it were, through the vessels, and fertilizing the whole system; for 'THE BLOOD IS THE LIFE.' "

Such statements as the above prove that the consciousness of Dr. Smith, the author, was striving to "bring through" the true explanation and interpretation of the Bible—which is PHYSIOLOGICAL. No other modern Bible dictionary shows anywhere near the intuition and erudition of Dr. William Smith. His book was first published in 1860-63 in three volumes of nearly 3200 pages. Anyone possessing this original work is indeed fortunate. In recent years, these three volumes have been re-edited and the information contained in them reduced to less than half that number of pages.

"The Three Wise Men," "the payment of taxes," "redemption money," "tithes," "vine and fig tree," as well as innumerable other curious statements, will become intelligible, if studied in the light that the interpretation of Scorpio casts upon these subjects.

Mr. G. A. Gaskell, in his *Dictionary of the Sacred Languages of All Scriptures and Myths*, says of Scorpio: "It is a symbol of the eighth period of the cycle of life, in which the desire nature is predominant in the soul. It signifies the mental emotional procreative function—that which can procreate and re-create mental concepts and states. This is the multiplying function which ties to re-birth, and so Scorpio becomes the sign of the 'fall into generation,' on the physical plane in the middle of the Third Root Race, when mind commenced to function in early human bodies. The present method of the life cycle in which humanity is gaining experience and evolving its nature is still that of the sign Scorpio."

As Scorpio is opposite the sign Taurus, these two signs are complements of each other. Further comments from the pen of Mr. Gaskell are instructive: "A symbol of the lower aspect of the emotion-nature. As seen in the sculptures of the God Mithra slaying the Bull, it signifies that the emotions are active through contact with matter."

Swedenborg says: "By a scorpion is signified deadly persuasion; and by a scorpion of the earth persuasion, that falses are truths in things relating to the church; for a scorpion when he stings a man *induces a stupor upon his limbs.*

"The disciplined qualities of the soul, which possess the power of the Christ—the love of goodness and truth—within them, are able to overcome the lower desires and emotions, and the power of the lower principle; and illusion can not affect them for they have knowledge of truth."

It must be understood that "knowledge of truth" is the result of experience induced by suffering. It is the effect on the body, as well as the mind, that eventually causes a person to cease doing a thing that causes suffering. Thus chemical, physiological, anatomical and astrological information are absolutely essential.

Mr. Gaskell further says: "Now the desire-mind (the serpent) is more insidious than any of the simple lower desires or appetites (the beasts), and thus is able to lead the emotion-nature astray from the higher intuitions, and to divert the vibrations of energy downward to the plane of the desires. And so the emotion-nature is drawn to the sense objects."

Here we have direct reference to Leo, the sign dealing with this subject. But no matter how much these topics are considered by various writers, none actually reveal the real method for remedying the situation. Chemistry alone will solve the problem, for all creation is accomplished because certain elements are able to do certain work.

Therefore, when a particular kind of work is required, the perfect chemical plan must be supplied, otherwise the desired result will not be attained.

"Then the desire-mind represents to the emotion-nature that death or extinction shall not supervene for such behavior; for the Divine nature knows that when the fruits of action are tasted, experience shall be acquired which will be the means by which Godhood will eventually be achieved through cleaving to the good, and shunning evil."—G. A. Gaskell.

"The Tree of the Knowledge of Good and Evil, by which man fell, changed into the Tree of Life by which Satan perished; the fruit of disobedience becoming the fruit of the Tree that is in the midst of paradise: the garden whence the first Adam was driven forth replaced by the garden where the second Adam arose from the dead."—J. M. Neal, Com. Psalms, Vol. 1, p. 139.

In the above quotation the reference to two Adams is a little confusing to the average reader. Adam in Hebrew, means man or red earth, because of the color of the flesh, and the fact that the physical body IS made of earth, for it is the meaning of the word SALT. The different salts (12) build the body. "And God made man from the DUST OF THE EARTH." (Bible).

R. J. Campbell, in his Sermon, *The Tree of Knowledge*, writes understandingly on this subject and exactly from the viewpoint of this book. He claims the Bible is NOT history. He says: "I admit that the Genesis story (of the fall) as it stands can not be reasonably regarded as history: it is not history, it is something better; it is a symbolic statement of certain facts of experience."

There is no curse laid upon humanity for seeking self-preservation or the continuity of the race. This must be, as it is the only means whereby evolution may work out and perfection be attained. Generation is a step toward perfection, and an absolutely necessary preliminary phase. Review the interpretation of the word, and thoroughly understand what its true meaning is. NO COHABITATION EXCEPT FOR CHILDREN.

In the *Secret Doctrine*, by Madam Blavatsky, on page 410, Vol. II, we find the following clear-cut statement: "Nor was the curse of Karma called down upon them for seeking *natural* union, as all the mindless animal-world does in its proper seasons; but, for abusing the creative power, for desecrating the divine gift, and *wasting* the *life-essence* for no purpose except bestial personal gratification."

This is indeed emphatic language and there is absolutely no mistaking its meaning. And the statement in Genesis "multiply, replenish and subdue THE EARTH," has reference to one thing only, THE EARTHLY body of man.

Who has tamed the cyclone, who can prevent the appearance of lightning, who can stop an earthquake? The only earth that each one of us can subdue is that of our own bodies and animal passions. We CAN also multiply and replenish the cells of our own earthly bodies.

> "But a better land is there
> Where Olympus cleaved the air,
> The high still dell where the Muses dwell,
> Fairest of all things fair.
> O there is Grace, and there is Heart's Desire,
> And peace to adorn thee, thou Spirit of guiding fire."
>
> —*Eur. Bacch.* 409.

We will now consider the chemical side of the scorpion. Dr. Carey allocated it with Calcium sulph or lime sulphate, which is commonly known as Gypsum or plaster of Paris. The origin of the latter term is not known. To hide this fact, the dictionaries state that plaster of Paris derived its name from the fact that it was first discovered near Paris! No doubt the word Paris is derived from the Latin verb *pareo*, to become visible, to appear, to bring forth, to lay (as concerning eggs). This latter is very apropos, since eggs are protected by shells of this salt, plaster of Paris.

Calcium sulphate appears native as anhydrite, which means destitute of water. It is well known that when this salt is mixed with water to form plaster, the water quickly evaporates, leaving a hard surface which serves as a protection. Gypsum is another term for it. The root of this word means: to wander without a fixed purpose, to go around or gyrate—a circular motion. It is probably of eastern origin. The word gypsy is derived from the same root, and is very apropos, since this race or tribe of people is noted for its nomadic nature.

Nomas is the Latin word from which nomadic is derived, and means to distribute or allot. It will be observed that this characteristic also applies to this salt (Calcium sulph).

The gyri of the cerebrum are its convolutions, and it is easy to see that this salt must play an important part in forming them. Indeed, we are beginning to realize that all movement in nature is circular. In the building of all forms, cosmic and microscopic, this circular movement is necessary. The slang phrase "to gyp" means to swindle or cheat a person. As it is the root of the word gypsum or Calcium sulphate, we readily see that it is truly applicable to the sign Scorpio in a negative sense, since all who do not make the RIGHT USE of the procreative material are actually gyping themselves of their most precious possession, and are not aware of this fact.

It is said that the Romans marked with gypsum the feet of slaves put up for sale. This applies also to Scorpio, since human beings are yet enslaved and will be until sexual commerce and exchange ceases.

Calcium sulph or gypsum is used as a dressing for soil and also in making plaster casts and for stiff bandages.

We find that the word gypsy is related to the word Ægyptus, from which Egypt is derived—meaning a place of darkness and plagues. As a gypsy may be a vagrant and a fugitive, it is easy to see the analogy of this word to the procreative germs, for they float about and are driven to and fro without any certain direction. This is why most of us are vagabonds and fugitives, for we are traveling away from, instead of toward, HOME, our true destination. After a period of falling by the wayside, unable to travel further, and suffering tortures, we cry aloud for help. This is "knocking at the door" of self-knowledge. And that door opens a little or it opens wide, according to the strength and sincerity of that cry.

Applied to grape vines, Calcium sulph is said to improve the color and keeping qualities of the grapes. Biochemistry enables us to understand why. The skins are healthier and therefore furnish better protection for their contents. The same is true of egg shells, for they are formed from this same material.

In certain combinations, this salt may be made to take up and hold a certain quantity of water, or it may be made to release nearly all of it. Hydrous sulphate of lime is soft and easily scratched by the nails; but curiously enough, it is affected very little by acid. This is a fact which must be remembered in studying the association of this salt with the human body. It is well to state here that this salt has one very important use in the human body. It coats all its vascular surfaces. The surfaces must be *protected* from contact with fluids. Therefore the anhydrous form plays its part as well in physiological and anatomical well-being.

How many ever stop to think why the stomach lining is not itself digested? The reason is, that it is coated with plaster of Paris. When this salt becomes very deficient, naturally the coating on the stomach becomes thin, and easily abrased by irritating particles of any foreign substance. Also by the continued presence of acid. The fact that this lining is not *quickly* affected by acid is one of the wise provisions of beneficent Nature and Nature's God, otherwise we would not have the wonderful opportunities for recovering that we now have. Indeed we would not even have the time in which to recover.

The eyeballs, the nasal passages, mouth, throat, the passage way into the stomach, the bladder, in fact all parts contacting moisture must have a certain number of particles of this salt for protection.

Dr. Schuessler's treatise on biochemistry, as well as all works by subsequent writers on this subject, gives certain definite modalities by which anyone may at once recognize a symptom and its cause. One of the modalities concerned with lack of Calcium sulph, is a BURNING SENSATION. Even the skin may have this feeling. One occasionally contacts people who suffer from burning feet and are very uncomfortable in bed. They usually stick the feet out from under the covers. Great relief is felt when they contact any cold surface. This salt should be taken intensively—generously—for this trouble.

Ulcerated stomach is caused by deficiency in this salt, and there is no symptom that is more quickly relieved and cured; for, as soon as this salt is taken into the stomach, it can at once coat the surface, as it is not obliged to go into the blood before being carried to the surface or part requiring it.

When one realizes that Calcium sulph or plaster of Paris forms egg shells, without which the contents of eggs would not be preserved to fulfill their function, he understands the outstanding and curious relationship which this salt bears to the sign Scorpio.

This part of the body, the procreative glands, CREATES AND PRESERVES the procreative germ cells, until, of course, the spasmodic action of the nerves results in their prostration. These germ cells are little eggs—differentiated corpuscles—and must have *shells* to protect them. This enables their contents to be preserved intact. Science has named these shells CASTS. As yet, doctors have been unable to explain why casts are sometimes found in the blood. Schuessler's system is the only method which throws light on this subject.

When Calcium sulph becomes *very* deficient there is, naturally, insufficient to make the corpuscles or human egg-shells. The result is that their contents are unable to remain intact. They turn to *pus*. Loss of the casts, and disintegration of the organic substances in the corpuscles, is the *cause of pus*. Medical science has never explained this. This salt is one of the specifics in venereal diseases, and Kali mur, the LOWER MIND salt, is the other.

One of the three causes of barrenness in females, is lack of this salt, for the ova are unable to obtain sufficient Calcium sulph to complete their casts. Pus is frequently found in the ovaries or ovarian tubes. It is not uncommon for males to suffer from a collection of pus in the testes or prostate, although found more often in the latter.

Fistulas result from nature's efforts to rid the system of pus. She forces openings which remain until all pus has drained away, and Calcium sulph has been supplied. Long-continued suppuration is caused by starvation of the blood in this salt. Indeed it is one of the three causes of anemia. Disintegration of both creative and procreative corpuscles or cells result from an insufficient supply of this salt. People having yellowish or pasty-colored complexions require Calcium sulphate.

This remarkable salt is a *natural cement*, and it is no wonder that it is termed "POTTER'S STONE." Indeed, it is especially applicable to the sign Scorpio.

The Scriptures contain many references to clay, potter's wheel, etc., etc. In Isaiah 64:6, 7, 8 and 11th verses, we find the following: "But we are all as an unclean thing, and all our righteousnesses are as filthy rags; and we all do fade as a leaf; and our iniquities, like the wind, do take us away."

"But now, O Lord, thou art our father; we are the *clay*, and thou our *potter;* and we all are the work of thy hand."

"Our holy and our beautiful house, where our fathers praised thee, is BURNED UP WITH FIRE; and all our pleasant things are laid waste."

Recalling the interpretation given this period of the year by the ancients—that it is the gate of the abyss or bottomless pit, we find the above quotations very apropos. They also fit in well with the sign of Scorpio.

It is well to read over the chapter on Gemini in order to link up here with the Latin word *Cadus,* meaning vessel. This is analogous to the human form—made of earth or clay—and actually shaped by means of the gyrating motion of the cerebral currents following a path formed like the figure 8. This is a physiological fact.

Is it any wonder that the BURIAL GROUND FOR STRANGERS, PAUPERS AND CRIMINALS IS TERMED "THE POTTER'S FIELD?" It is based on the fact that the sign Scorpio is intimately related to death and burial. And it is also true that both are the result of *pauperizing ourselves,* becoming strangers to our higher selves and therefore criminals in the true sense of the word. We have sinned against the Most High.

The ancients made funeral urns of alabaster, a most beautiful form of Calcium sulph. A cadaver (dead body) was sealed in a sarcophagus by the ancients. These burial urns were of a form of lime (Calcium) which was believed slowly to consume the body.

How paradoxical it is that we make every effort (or have in the past) to PRESERVE DEAD BODIES *and are very little concerned in preserving the corpuscles of the living body.* It is a very good thing that cremation is coming more and more into use.

Some of the many other symptoms which are caused by

deficiency in this salt are: suppurations of yellow, purulent matter; abscess of the cornea; deep-seated ulcers of the eye; discharge of pus from the ear; third stage of cold, when the discharge is thick and yellow; chronic catarrh; mattery pimples on the face and especially at puberty; purulent secretions in the mouth; ulceration of the roots of the teeth; swollen gums and cheeks; third stage of sore throat and quinsy (suppuration); discharge of matter or blood and matter from the bowels; abscess of the liver; ulceration of the bowels; running off of the bowels; chronic inflammation of the bladder; suppurating abscess of the prostate in the male or the ovaries in the female; syphilis or gonorrhea, in the suppurative stage; yellow leucorrhea; inflammation of the breast; last stages of tuberculosis (indeed for all stages, since its inception is caused by lack of all forms of Calcium); cough with mattery sputa; burning of soles of the feet; skin festering easily, especially around the nails; neglected wounds which do not seem able to heal, due to a deficiency in this cast-making material. This salt should follow the use of Silicea, the surgeon which cleans out pus.

A marvelous change gradually takes place within the physical vessel, containing as it does the dead and dying cells. It will eventually become a beautiful alabaster vase from which not one drop of the precious oil of life is spilled. The ancient Greeks realized the imperfect condition of man's body and the cause, and Euripides, in his *Hippolytus,* makes his chorus sing:

> "In vain, in vain by old Alpheus' shore,
> The blood of many bulls doth stain the river,
> And all Greece bows on Phœbus' Pythian floor,
> Yet bring we to the Master of men no store,
> The Keybearer that standeth at the door
> Close barred, where hideth ever
> *Love's inmost jewel.* Yea, though he sacke man's life,
> Girt with calamity and strange ways of strife,
> Him have we worshipped never."

"For we must all appear before the judgment seat of Christ; that everyone may receive the things done in his body, according to that he hath done, whether it is good or bad."—2 Cor. 5:10.

CHAPTER IX

THE ANALYSIS AND SYNTHESIS OF SAGITTARIUS AND SILICEA

"And I saw and behold a WHITE HORSE, and he that sat on him had a BOW, and a crown was given unto him, and he went forth conquering and to conquer."—*Rev.* 6:2.

THE Sun enters the zodiacal sign Sagittarius on November 22, approximately, and remains until December 21. It relates to the higher mind and anatomically to the hips and thighs. It is also concerned with the formation of the first blood vessels. Jupiter is its ruler. As this period covers more of December than of November, it is associated with the vibration of ten, which is the perfect number expressing incessant equilibrium, will power and supremacy. Sagittarius is the third and last of the fire triplicity. Its symbol is the Centaur, a mythological being having the body of a horse, with the head, neck, and arms of a man. He holds a drawn bow, and points an arrow upward. This sign also deals with religion and law.

Referring to Greek mythology, we find that Jupiter or Zeus, when an infant, was concealed in the island of Crete in order to save him from following the fate of his other brothers and sisters. It seems that his father Chronos (Saturn) was told that he would be dethroned by one of his own children. To prevent this, he decided to swallow each as it was born. Jupiter was the sixth child. His mother covered a stone with swaddling clothes, and palmed it off on Chronos as his son Jupiter. In the Island of Crete, the latter was nurtured by the nymphs Adrastea and Ida, and fed on the milk of the goat Amalthea.

At maturity, Jupiter was chosen Sovereign of the World at the Council of the Gods. The name signifies the radiant light of heaven. In Classic Myths we find that "he was the supreme ruler of the universe, wisest of the divinities and most glorious. In the *Iliad,* he informs the other gods that their united strength would not budge him; that, on the contrary, he could *draw them,* and earth, and the seas to himself, and *suspend all from Olympus* by a golden chain. Throned in the high, clear heavens, Jupiter was the gatherer of clouds and snows, the dispenser of gentle rains and winds; the moderator of light and heat and the seasons; the thunderer and the wielder of the thunderbolt. Bodily strength and valor were dear to him and to him were sacred everywhere the loftiest trees and the grandest mountain peaks. He required of his worshipers cleanliness of surroundings and person and heart. Justice was his; his to repay violation of duty to the family, in social relations, and in the state. Prophecy was his; and his special messenger was the *eagle.*"

> "Jove said, and nodded with his shadowy brows;
> Waved on th' immortal head th' ambrosial locks,
> And all Olympus trembled at his nod."
>
> —*Iliad.*

"Juno was the wife of Jupiter, and the most worthy of the goddesses, queenly and ox-eyed, golden sandaled and golden-throned. Glorious beyond compare was her presence, when she had harnessed her horses, and driven forth the golden-wheeled chariot that Hebe made ready, and that the Hours set aside. She was wedded to Jupiter in the garden of the gods where ambrosial rivers flowed and where Earth sent up in honor of the rite a *tree of life,* heavy with *apples* golden like the sunset."

The above quotation is invaluable, as it gives us the meanings, qualities and attributes of the sign, as stated in books on astrology. Jupiter's power to draw all the gods to him clearly indicates the higher mind as the inevitable conqueror of all lesser powers, and their enthronement on high. He is truly Osiris of the Egyptians, and, with Juno or Isis, dwells in the Garden of Eden. We find that Greek mythology places them here, as do the Scriptures in dealing with Adam and Eve. We also find a Tree of Life on which hang golden apples.

It is evident that all nations and peoples have their sacred Scriptures which deal with the most intimate secrets. When these are studied and analyzed, they are all found to be identical.

It is interesting to note how many words in constant use are derived from the root words of both Jupiter and Sagittarius. They furnish us with indubitable proof that their interpretations as given in books on astrology are correct.

Sagitta means arrow, swift, fleet, sharp, and aimed at a mark. This is analogous to the higher mind and its processes. From the root of arrow, the word arrogance is obtained; it relates to exorbitant pride, exalting one's worth or importance to an undue degree. As Jupiter is the largest planet, and is interpreted positively as largess, abundance and generosity, "the giver of all good things," negatively it is associated with prodigality and wastefulness. Those who manifest proud contempt of others, who are insolent, overbearing, sharp and fault-finding in speech, represent the negative aspect of Jupiter.

The sagittal stone in an arch is termed the KEY STONE. It is the *voussoir* at the center of the *crown* of an arch, which, being the LAST SET IN PLACE, IS REGARDED AS BINDING THE WHOLE TOGETHER. *This is analogous to the completion of the forebrain association centers,* which are the *first* to atrophy in the average individual, and the *last* to develop.

We must pause a moment, in our interpretation of words, to note that, of the three cerebral association centers, the one in the forehead is the last to develop, if, indeed, it is *allowed* to. As this part of the head allocates with the third, and last, decan of Aries, it is under the co-rulership of Jupiter himself, "the giver of all good things." But it must also be remembered, as we review the chapter on Aries, that *Jupiter can not even develop or arrive at maturity unless he is nurtured* by the nymphs Adrastea and Ida, and it is absolutely necessary that he be fed on the milk of the *goat* Amalthea.

Adrastea and Ida are analogous to the pineal and pituitary glands in the cerebrum which are truly the real NURSES of the human body. They furnish the glandular fluids of positive and negative character, electrical and magnetic, without which no physical vehicle can be formed and without which it can not be sustained. The term *nymph* means a bride, or that which has been recently united, therefore a new or FRESH fluid. It may be said to relate to lymph, for these glands secrete albumin.

The fact that Jupiter was said to have been born on Mt. Olympus, and was nourished by a goat, is easy to interpret from its physiological standpoint, and certainly after studying the chapter on Scorpio. The electrical center which gives rise to the sacral and coccygeal nerves controlling the sexual glands, is placed within the neural canal or innermost tube of the spinal canal at the base of the spinal cord proper. It allocates with Capricorn, the goat. If this esse or milk is unable to RISE and return to the Father (Jupiter Pater), the cerebrum, then there is no material with which to develop and thus awaken the forebrain cells or association center having to do with INTUITION.

A study of *Gray's Anatomy* furnishes proof that these cells are the last to develop and the first to atrophy. Is it, then, any wonder that so many seem satisfied to live the way they do? When the intuition is not functioning, there is no way by which a person may be warned. If intuition were even a *little* active, the result of a *few* forebrain cells receiving some degree of nutriment, many accidents would be averted. One's affairs would run more smoothly, the result of more efficient planning. This would eventually result in all the fortune-tellers being forced out of business. One would begin to understand his own affairs, and know better what to do than others could tell him.

How to awaken dormant brain cells is a subject concerning which much curiosity will be aroused before Neptune has completed its journey through Virgo, the house of health, purity, regeneration and illumination.

We find, in the science of phrenology, a means whereby we can verify the above statement relative to the forebrain cells. The competent phrenologist states that the development of the forebrain indicates whether a person is a genius, mediocre or a moron. When two facts announced by two different savants of related sciences agree, it is conclusive proof of their correctness.

We find, by studying *Gray's Anatomy*, that the suture between the parietal bones of the skull constitutes the sagittal part of the head. As the top of the head is its crown, when all the cells are chemically and numerically perfect there will no longer be any danger of these walls falling down. Perfect material and perfect *thought* will bind or cement them together forevermore.

Metaphysically interpreted, sagitta means a thing having an analogous part or function. A part or force on which associated things depend for support. It is certainly true that mental process of the highest order are essential to the construction and preservation of both human forms and human affairs.

In Acts 14:12, we find reference to Jupiter. "And they called Barnabas Jupiter; and Paul, Mercurius, because he was the chief speaker."

In verse seventeen, there is evidence of Jupiter's connection with rain: "Nevertheless he left not himself without witness, in that he did good, and gave us rain from heaven, and fruitful seasons, filling our hearts with food and gladness."

Certain scientists who have "discovered" that there is nothing to astrology, that the planets have no connection with any of the affairs of mankind, would do well to endeavor to explain why all nations and peoples refer to them in their sacred writings. The word sagitta is derived from the root verb SAGIO, which means to perceive quickly, to feel keenly, all of which relates to mind.

From the root words of both Juno and Jupiter, are obtained the terms relating to law and religion. Jus is Latin for rights; juris-prudence for law. A jurant is one who takes an oath, who swears to the faithful performance of his duty.

The position of Neptune in Virgo, from which sign it is now operating SQUARE to Sagittarius, will work for the next twelve years to purify both religion and law. When the good law—the law of God—is obeyed, it constitutes the religious life.

In this age and time, both religion and law have become so perverted that the truth behind both has been almost entirely obliterated. Since Neptune entered Virgo, we have heard much more in regard to religious disturbances, particularly in Latin countries, than in the last hundred years. Uranus in Aries, the upsetter of *OLD* OPINIONS, is causing the minds of those who think, to discard any *OLD* BELIEFS which are contrary to reason and common sense. The correct interpretation of sacred and secret writings is now beginning to be demanded. Humanity is commencing to realize that it is responsible for its own salvation, and must therefore look around, *and endeavor to obtain the plan of the process.*

We must not make the mistake of pointing to the Catholic church as the only one where controversy is present, for all churches are concerned with this housecleaning. None are interpreting religion from its physiological and chemical analysis. This must be done before any light will be thrown on the subject. Ecclesiastics deal with a mediator exterior to man, whereas the real mediator actually is within the human brain, the SPIRIT in man.

Few people realize the true state of affairs in Russia. It is in reality an Aquarian nation. As such, it will continue to be forced along humanitarian lines, that of the greatest good for the greatest number. All false barriers of caste will be broken down. Nothing can prevent this taking place. Nobility of character, true worth, simplicity, modesty, and creative ability, are the true standards of measurement. The quicker we ourselves realize this, the sooner will our chaos lessen. If one truly lives in his own sanctuary, abiding in the secret place of the "Most High," he has no real need to enter any church constructed by human HANDS.

The real church is the perfected cerebrum. Here one dwells constantly, and forevermore, in his own special and private Holy of Holies. As the Scriptures state, "If a man can not rule his own house (Taurus) how can he TAKE CARE OF THE CHURCH OF GOD?" (Aries).

Jupiter is the River God, for he stands at the head of the spinal river Euphrates or Jordan. He is Jupiter Ammon of the Egyptians, and Bel-Moloch of the Chaldeans. The ancient Greeks considered him the divine personification of heaven itself, and the hurler of the lightning rays of thought.

Why did those who designed the first zodiac place Sagittarius in the ninth division of the circle, opposite Gemini? As the latter relates to the lower mind, the proper place for the study of the Higher is at a point opposite.

The hips and thighs, which relate physiologically to Sagittarius, constitute the ARCH of support in the earthly part or torso, while the forebrain is its analogy in the heavenly, or heaved-up part of man. As stated in the chapter on Scorpio, this natural arch weakens and eventually becomes unable to keep the frame erect and strong when sexual excesses are indulged in.

The hips and thighs also form a natural basin for the protection of the organs pertaining to excretion; also parturition and sexual activity. The condition of these organs naturally depends on whether Jupiter is the bountiful giver of all *good* things, or whether he is the prodigal son.

As Imperator he is ruler; as Invictus he is unconquerable;

as Opitulus he is helper; as Stator he is supporter, "guardian of law, defender of truth and protector of justice and virtue."

"Verospi's statue of Jupiter is in the Vatican; but one of the seven wonders of the world was the statue of Olympian Jove, by Phidias, destroyed by fire in Constantinople A.D. 475. It is said that this gigantic statue was nearly sixty feet high, made of ivory. The throne was of cedar wood, adorned with ivory, ebony, gold and precious stones. In his right hand was a golden statue of Victory, and his left hand rested on a long scepter surmounted by an eagle. The robe of the god was of gold, and so was his footstool supported by golden lions. This wonderful work of art was removed to Constantinople by Theodosius I."—*Classic Myths.*

There is much in this truly remarkable description which confirms the interpretation of the nature and purpose of Sagittarius. It may be termed a symposium of the three fire signs. The lions are made to serve as the supports of Jove's footstool. Recalling the interpretation of Leo, it is evident that the Lion is here the King of the tribe of Judah. It has become elevated, and is in its kingly place. Therefore the controlled emotions become the basis or foundation for the unlimited and positive creation of electrical energy. It has returned to the Father.

It is said that Hercules used the arrow of Jove to slay the vulture which was eating the liver of Prometheus. The days of the full moon were sacred to him, as also was the oak tree.

Encyclopædia Britannica states that "In this oldest Jupiter of the Latins and Romans, the god of light and the heaven, and the god invoked in taking the most solemn oaths, we may undoubtedly see not only the great protecting deity of the race, but one, and perhaps the only one, whose worship embodies a distinct moral conception. It was in the presence of his priest that the most ancient and sacred form of marriage, 'confarreatio,' took place. The Romans chose the name of Jupiter in almost every case, by which to indicate the chief deity of the peoples, proving that they continued to regard him, so long as his worship existed at all, as the god whom they themselves looked upon as greatest."

It must not be inferred that the Romans or Greeks worshiped idols. All so-called idols have merely been representations of that which the people wished to keep in mind. The golden calf stood for the regenerated animal man. We do the same thing, for we have created a tall man wearing striped trousers of red and white, and otherwise adorned with stars. We have named him "Uncle Sam" and he represents the spirit of Democracy. The statue of Liberty is another example. England also has her John Bull.

It is a curious fact that the cerebrum, when viewed from the pages of *Gray's Anatomy,* very closely resembles the English walnut. In fact it has been quite common to term one with unique or rather advanced ideas a "nut." There is also the expression "look out or the squirrels will get you." Insane asylums are termed "nut houses," in common vernacular. Therefore, one is not surprised to find that the English walnut is termed Jupiter's nut. It is interesting to learn that the walnut was known in ancient times. Its Latin name was Juglans Regia, meaning King Jove nut. I venture to say it was thus named because of its resemblance to the cerebrum, or two hemispheres of the brain.

As Sagittarius or Higher Mind is also related to speech, it would be associated, naturally, with the characters which are used to preserve the words and thoughts of our forebears. It is curious, but true, that the very first characters were cuneiform, wedge-shaped or arrowheaded.

Thought assuredly follows well-defined grooves down through the ages, for the reason that each thing has a definite and thus perpetual meaning.

Dr. Wakeman Ryno says, in *Amen the God of the Amonians:* "The Archer Sagitarrius stands with his bow bent ready to let fly an arrow across the river Eridanus, or Phlegethon, at the Scorpion (Beelzebub), whose poison tail is bent around the southern end of the Isle of Ææa, or Circe, of the Myth of Ulysses. Here on the Cimmerian shores of the fabled river of Hades, Sagittarius as Chiron or Charon ferries the Soul (Sol-Sun) over the fiery, starry stream of the Milky-way.

"The river of Hades is that part of the fiery or starry stream of the Milky-way which is *below* the equator, and which the Sun passes in October and November, represented by the Scorpion and Sagittarius. This part of the zodiac was called Hades by the ancient priests of the Sun, or the realm of the *dead* (the winter months)."

But there is a much better reason why it is termed Hades or realm of the dead. The bright and glorious nuclei or Keres from the cerebrum, have become souls in prison, chained within animal forms.

It is stated, in *Smith's Bible Dictionary,* that "Antiochus Epiphanes dedicated the Temple at Jerusalem to the service of Zeus (Jupiter) A. V." Here we have conclusive proof that the ancients knew of, and used, the name of Jupiter as analogous to the Almighty Father.

When Prometheus deceived Jupiter (the giver of all good things), and stole the celestial fire (fluidic electrical energy), he brought it down to (into) earth (the body), and concealed it in the narthex. A narthex is a box or receptacle of unguents, which are ointments for *consecration* or *medicinal* purposes.

The receptacle referred to, is naturally physiological in character, and much research into esoteric physiology will prove it to be the glands of Bartholin and, correspondingly, Cowper, for they are creators of oil (which is an unguent).

Modern science has no definite information relative to the gland of Bartholin in the female and Cowper in the male, but they are *supposed* to furnish a lubricating fluid. They contain a yellowish, oily substance, when in a healthy state. This is a special product. More information will be given in regard to it in *The Truth About Sex and Birth Control.*

Decharme writes, relative to Æsculapius stealing fire from heaven: "Now, according to Greek ideas 'identical in this with those of the occultists,' this possession forced from Jupiter, this *human trespassing upon the property of the gods, had to be followed by expiation."* It is indeed true that all have to pay the price, and will so continue until at last the celestial fire is no longer tampered with, but is free to return to its true home, its birth place on Mt. Olympus, the cerebrum.

Mr. Gaskell says of Olympus: "A symbol of the height of perfection and attainment; or the plane of Atma, the summit of manifestation."

"Homer was the first to divide the world into five portions. The three intermediate he has assigned to the three gods; the two extremes, Olympus the Earth, whereof the one is the boundary of things below, the other of things above, he has left common to all and unallotted to any."—Plutarch.

When will humanity realize that "immortal, transcendental facts" on the very highest planes of existence—facts which will explain the Divine scheme of attainment for man—are concealed in the embryonic cerebral cells? They are there, waiting, waiting, until the time arrives when humanity will realize that it has been blindly stealing from self; throwing away the food of efficiency, and blaming "luck" for lack of success.

As one ascends a mountain to obtain the first view of the sun, rising in all its glory and grandeur, so must we endeavor to center our thoughts in the highest part of our anatomy, the upper chamber, wherein each may eventually meet his Lord. Unlike Phaëton, we must guide the horses of mind *away* from the REGION OF THE SCORPION. We will then eventually reach the heights.

Job said "Is not my *help in me?*"

"And be not conformed to this world, but be ye *transformed* by the *renewing* of *your mind,* that ye may *prove* what is that good and acceptable and perfect will of God."—Romans 12:2.

Smythe writes, "The allegorical images of Jacob's blessing have been identified by several writers with the sign of the Via Solis, whence God, as bow-man, becomes Sagittarius." Certainly no real student will wish to differ, since God is truly Divine Mind. Miss Agnes M. Clarke says, "when Egypt adopted the Greek figures it was with various changes that effaced its character as a 'circle of *living things.*' " Most truly is the physical form a circle of living things, a mass of ever-productive corpuscles.

Richard Allen, in his *Star Names and Their Meanings,* informs us that the arrow of Sagittarius is always aimed at the scorpion's heart. As the star Antares occupies that position, it signifies that the scorpion must have a "change of heart" and no longer seek to do that which it *anti*-Ares.

Dupuis says that "Sagittarius was shown in Egypt as an Ibis or Swan, but the Denderah Zodiac has the customary Archer with the face of a lion added, so making it bi-faced." Since Leo is placed in trine to Sagittarius, it signifies that the Higher Mind or intuition is unable to manifest until the lion has become quiescent, for only thus is it capable of being the support of the footstool of Jove.

Some of the Semitic names for Sagittarius are: Udgudua or Smiting sun-face; Yuma-nahri or Day-of-dawn; Papilsak, Winged-fire-head; Ega, Crown; and Anunitum, Great-goddess-star.

R. Brown, in his *Primitive Constellations,* states that "An exceedingly old Babylonian tablet shows the Centaur with both hands grasping the Wild-beast." And Arator says:

> "But his right hand he ever seems to stretch
> Before the Altar's circle. The hand grasps
> Another creature, very firmly clutched,—
> The WILD-BEAST; so the men of old it named."

In Euphratean astrological lore, the original golden seed of heaven was the Sun. It was seized and swallowed up by the darkness in the form of different monsters. "Among the Jews, Sagittarius was the tribal symbol of Ephraim and Manasseh, from Jacob's last words to their father Joseph, 'his bow abode in strength.' "

"Cuneiform inscriptions," says Richard Allen, "designate Sagittarius as the Strong One, the Giant King of War, and as the Illuminator of the Great City. Upon some of the boundary stones of Sippara (Sepharvaim of the Old Testament), a solar city, Sagittarius appears sculptured in full glory." In Assyria it was always associated with the ninth month, Kislivu.

"Sagittarius is shown on a coin of Gallienus of about A.D. 260, with the legend Apollini Conservatori; and on those of King Stephen emblematic of his having landed in England in 1135 when the sun was in this sign." Again we have verification of the statement that the signs of the zodiac were known and studied back in the morning of time.

As the body is the "great city," it is evident that the Higher Mind, typified by the Centaur, is its illuminator. It is by means of the conflict between the Centaurs and the Lapithes (analogous to energy and substance) that the arrangement of matter and the creation of brain cells takes place.

The root of the word Lapithes gives us the word stone (lapis) and the original meaning of Centaur is a fiery steed. The Centaur is, then, analogous to creative energy.

There is a conflict eternally going on among the corpuscles of the brain (as well as in all other parts of the body), which may well be termed "the war of the cerebral cells." It will continue until such time as they receive all the material necessary to construct chemically perfect corpuscles. Now they suffer hourly from rapine and murder, because of the ignorance and thoughtlessness of mankind.

Warfare among nations and peoples, family quarrels, and

the attraction which *any* kind of a fight has for the average person, *is entirely due to the inharmonious state of the brain cells.* When they are better supplied with what is needful, man will no longer be "robbing God," for the Scriptures state "Can a man rob God? But ye have robbed me in tithes and offerings."

As "like attracts like"—we naturally respond to anything having a vibration corresponding to that which our brain cells create. There is, then, no immediate prospect of peace, either among nations or individuals. Differences in ideas and opinions are naturally the result of differences in brain power, in thought conception. Argument is of no avail, and only leads to still greater confusion and chaos.

The wonder is, that conditions are not worse. We are not astonished that so many die. The surprising thing is, that we live as long as we do. How terribly body and brain are abused—yet kindly Mother Nature struggles on to enable life to remain in the form a little longer.

The Centaur interpretation of Sagittarius seems to have been applied by the ancients to the savage or undeveloped manifestation of the Higher Mind. The half-animal and half-human mind is like an untamed and vicious horse. It must become capable of realizing that the Spirit is the master, and inevitable conqueror, otherwise the cruel bit (suffering resulting from experience) will wound the sensitive mouth, and blood-flecked foam cover the horse's bridle.

It is curious, and fascinating, to learn that the physiological term "hip" is derived from the Latin root of Hippo which means horse. This is particularly significant, since the hips and thighs were archaically assigned to Sagittarius.

There is an architectural rule applying to formation of the hips. "A hip is an external angle formed by the meeting of two sloping sides or skirts of a roof which have their wall plates running in different directions." It should not be difficult to realize that terms used in construction work were originally derived from the plan of the human body. Otherwise, the human brain would not have cognized them, having no conception of anything *exterior* unless possessing an *inner* prototype from which to pattern.

Indeed, we may be surprised to learn that the human brain CONTAINS a sea-horse, for this interpretation applies to the hippocampus, which is a curved, elongated eminence of gray matter extending throughout the floor of the descending horn of the lateral *ventricle*. As the cerebral substance is semi-fluidic, it may well be termed "the ocean of thought." The Bible refers to it as "the sea of glass." Moreover, it is a physiological fact that the eyes, which are "the windows of the Spirit," are directly connected with the cerebrum, the optic nerves actually being considered extensions of the cerebral substance itself.

When this substance is CLEAR AS CRYSTAL (quartz or Silicea) then will thought correspond, for no foreign particles will obstruct the view, and the mirror of mind will be without dust to confuse its reflections—Spiritual Light.

As the word medicine is derived from medeor or medicus, it means to heal or cure. It is obvious, then, that Hippocrates, who even today is looked upon as being "the Father of Medicine," is really the Higher Mind itself.

The Encyclopædia Britannica states that "he was born, according to Soranus, in Cos. He was a member of the family of Asclepiadæ and was believed to be a direct descendant of Æsculapius. It is also claimed for him that he was descended from Hercules. The incidents of his life are shrouded in uncertain tradition. He was supposed to have been of a family of priest-physicians. He cast superstition aside and based the practice of medicine on the principles of inductive philosophy. Hippocrates based his principle and practice on the theory of the existence of a spiritual restoring essence or principle, the VIS DEDICATRIX NATURÆ, in the management of which the art of the physician consisted. He had acuteness of observation in the manner in which occurrences of critical days in disease is enunciated."

Nothing is given concerning Soranus. Even the Latin lexicon mentions it only as "belonging to Sora, the most northerly town of the Volsci, in Latium." The word "Cos" is Latin for "any hard, *flinty* stone." Here we have verification of the association of flint or quartz with Sagittarius, for Dr. Carey allocated Silicea with this sign. Flint is a certain form of quartz or Silicea which is extremely hard and will emit sparks when struck with steel. As steel is iron, it is evident that there is a very close association between iron or Ferrum of Pisces and the Silicea of Sagittarius.

Biochemistry teaches us that sharp, clear-cut mental processes are impossible when Silicea is very deficient. And as a full supply of iron must be present in the blood in order to attract the Spirit-containing oxygen into the circulation, and to oxygenate the brain cells, the importance of these two salts in all mental activities must be emphasized.

As stated so many times, Greek mythology furnishes us with this complete plan expressed in poetical language. In the story of Pegasus we have an account of the initial appearance of that *esse* which is termed "dew" in the Hebrew sacred Scriptures. "The cranium is filled with crystalline (silicea) dew." The story goes that "Pegasus was the *winged-horse* which produced the fountain HIPPOCRENE (horse fountain) on Mt. Helicon (sacred to Apollo 'the sun,' and the muses), by a kick of his hoof against a flint." Pegasus was also "the winged-horse without whose aid it was impossible for Bellerophon to slay the monster called Chimæra."

The word Chimæra is Latin for *goat*. But it seems to have been a combination of several animals, which accounts for its terrible appearance. It was a fire-breathing monster, with the fore parts of a lion, the middle of a goat and the hind parts of a dragon. Bellerophon means "the slayer of the dragon or serpent," while the archaic symbol of Capricorn was originally part goat and part fish.

Pegasus was sacred to the Muses (goddesses of music, poetry and the fine arts). It must be remembered that the feminine always signifies *material*. Naturally FINE material is required in all FINE ARTS.

E. C. Brewer, in his *Dictionary of Phrase and Fable*, gives us an interesting interpretation of Pegasus: "The inspiration of poetry, or, according to Boiardo, the horse of the Muses. A poet speaks of his Pegasus, as 'My Pegasus will not go this morning,' meaning his brain will not work. 'I am mounting Pegasus,' i. e., going to write poetry. 'I am on my Pegasus,' *i. e.*, engaged in writing verses."

He also adds: "Pegasus or Pegasos, according to classic mythology, was the winged horse on which Bellerophon rode against the Chimæra. When the Muses contended with the daughters of Pieros (duty, or that which is due, a right by possession), Helicon rose heavenward with delight; but Pegasus gave it a kick, stopped its ascent, and brought out of the mountain the soul-inspiring waters of Hippocrene."

It is obvious that the latter refers to the semi-fluidic cerebral substance, which is a necessity in the creation of all fine arts.

Greek mythology informs us that Bellerophon was subjected to great trials and labors, but by the aid of Pegasus was able to triumph over all. The winged horse Pegasus is analogous to the balanced mind, while the common symbol used in astrology for Sagittarius plainly indicates the *three* mental stages which must become unified. These two symbols enable the student more thoroughly to analyze the subject.

It is interesting to note that the root word COS, which means any hard, flinty stone, is also the root of the word cosmic, which means the terrestrial or *earthly* world.

Many words in common use have been derived from the root of the word Pegasus. The consideration of a few of these will throw further light on Sagittarius, as well as the accurate method by which character may be analyzed, and the idiosyncrasies of those born under the different signs, accurately determined.

The word PEG is an interesting study. It means a pin, or piece of metal or wood, to hold things, to fasten them together. It also means a point of attainment, a step or degree; to hit or hammer, to work diligently, to labor constantly. Pego means pegging or beating—literally, to be *persistent.* It will be recalled that the beating or striking of the hoof of Pegasus on the flint stone resulted in the fountain of thought welling forth.

A curious correspondence is found in the word NAG, meaning HORSE. The verb to nag means to annoy by petty fault-finding, to irritate, to fret, to *persistently* urge, or scold, to be irritable and ill-natured. It is indeed true that those born in this sign are persistent in what they do. It is equally true that many are chronic naggers. Their sharp words are like mental *pegs,* constantly driven into the brain of the individual they are directed to, inevitably resulting in irritation and argument.

In Sanskrit mythology, Naga was a serpent. The Nagas were a race of human-faced serpents. The word nigger or nicker is an archaic expression signifying the neighing of a *horse,* while the old term NAGES means the buttocks, which allocate with the hips and thighs.

How many are sufficiently informed, relative to the subject of anatomy, to realize that the lower part of the lumbar region of the spine is called the cauda equina, or tail of the horse? Not only does anatomy verify astrology, but it proves it esoterically, through the fact that the roots of the upper sacral nerves (which are of great length because the spinal cord does not extend beyond the first lumbar vertebra) form a bundle within the spinal canal. This, when opened and spread out, is likened to a horse's tail. Lumbar means *loin,* which adds another verification to our list.

A nagus is a *skinflint* (silicea) or miser— a *niggard.* In stone cutting, *nig* means to dress (a stone) with a sharp-pointed (arrow) hammer. To hammer away, is to keep pegging. One "RIDES a hobby," meaning a subject or plan to which one is constantly referring. This constitutes NAGGING. The word hobby is derived from the Middle English word Hobyn, meaning a *nag* or active horse.

Mr. Mattieu Williams, the author of *The Fuel of the Sun* says of Jupiter, the ruler of this sign: "Recent observations justify us in regarding this as a miniature sun, with an external envelope of cloudy matter, apparently of partially-condensed water, but red-hot, or probably still hotter within. His vaporous atmosphere is evidently of enormous depth, and the force of gravitation being on his visible outer surface two-and-a-half times greater than that on our Earth's surface, the atmospheric pressure, in descending below this visible surface, must soon reach that at which the vapor of water would be brought to its *critical* condition. Therefore we may infer that *the oceans of Jupiter are neither frozen, liquid or gaseous water, but are oceans or atmospheres of critical water.*

"As the whole mass of Jupiter is 300 times greater than that of the Earth, and its compressing energy towards the center proportional to this, its materials, if similar to those of the earth, and no hotter, would be considerably more dense, and the whole planet would have a higher specific gravity; but we know by the movements of its satellites that, instead of this, its specific gravity is *less than one-fourth of that of the Earth.* This justifies the conclusion that it is intensely hot; for even hydrogen, if cold, would become denser than Jupiter under such pressure.

"As all elementary substances may exist as solids, liquids, or gases, or critically, according to the conditions of temperature and pressure, I am justified in hypothetically concluding that *Jupiter is neither a solid, a liquid nor a gaseous planet; but a critical planet, or an orb composed internally of associated elements in a critical state and surrounded by a dense atmos-*

phere of their vapors and those of some of their compounds, such as water."

A careful study of Mr. Williams' logic proves that the "MIND STUFF," which "the giver of all good things" bestows on mortals, is truly the magnet which attracts the electrical energy of thought. Thought at times has the power literally to sear the brain with anguish. The Higher Mind, the conscience, truly seems to SPEAK IN A VOICE OF THUNDER.

The "Critical point" which Mr. Williams mentions, refers to that state, condition or degree where a thing changes, merging into a different presentation. In other words, it is a point of transition, a point at which the gaseous and liquid conditions of a primary substance merge into each other; that is to say, when it is at its critical temperature and pressure. The pressure necessary to raise a substance in its liquid form to the boiling point, is the same as the critical temperature which will just liquify a gas. All of the foregoing is analogous to the CRITICAL POWER OF THOUGHT, WHICH ENABLES IT TO RAISE OR LOWER ITS OWN VIBRATIONS. Thought, substance, and mental power, are all of a CRITICAL nature.

It is obvious that Jupiter alone can hurl thunderbolts from Mt. Olympus, the home of the gods. Thunderbolts are truly arrows of thought.

It is very apropos, at this point, again to refer to the Scriptural injunction "Be ye transformed by the renewing of your minds."

Richard Allen informs us that the passage of the Sun through Sagittarius covers approximately 8.38 days. This is even less than the Scorpio period. These two facts serve to verify the *cosmic embryo* chart in this book.

Mr. G. A. Gaskell's metaphysical interpretation of this sign is splendid. He says: "It is a symbol of the ninth period of the cycle of life, in which the lower mind is perfected through evolution, and therefore 'dies.' The Higher Self seated on the intelligence (horse) destroys with the 'arrow' of the Spirit the lower qualities, thus enabling the lower consciousness to rise to the higher mind."

Good as the above statement is, it is evident that the chemical explanation of the CRITICAL state of mental substance, the pia mater (tender mother) of thought, is needed completely to clarify it.

"Dionysius proclaims: 'The Divine Goodness, this our great Sun, enlightens, nourishes, perfects, renews.' Even the pure can thus be made purer still. 'He, the Good, is called spiritual light; he cleanses the mental vision of the very angels; they taste, as it were, the light.' All this imagery goes back, in the first instance, to Proclus. For Proclus put in parallel 'sun' and 'God,' and 'to be enlightened' and 'to be deified' makes all purifying forces to *coalesce* in the activity of the Sun-God, Apollo Katharsios, the Purifier, who everywhere unifies multiplicity . . . . purifying the entire heaven and all living things throughout the world; and describes how 'from above, from his super-heavenly post, APOLLO SCATTERS THE ARROWS OF ZEUS—his rays upon all the world.' "—F. von Hugel, *Mystical Element*, Vol. II, p. 93.

Mr. Gaşkell also quotes from Mundaka Upanishad, II: "Having taken the Upanishad as the bow, as the great weapon, let him place on it the arrow, sharpened by devotion! Then having drawn it with a thought directed to that which is, hit the mark, O Friend, namely, that which is INDESTRUCTIBLE! Om is the bow, the Self is the arrow, Braham is called the aim. It is to be hit by a man who is not thoughtless, and then as the arrow becomes one with the target, he will become one with Brahman."

Mr. Gaskell's analysis of the above Sanskrit quotation is: "The soul is directed to rely upon the Word of God, *i. e.*, the expression of Truth within; and determine the will in accordance with the same. Then, with the mind aspiring toward the Highest, the soul is required to rest upon the Divine Reality which underlies the illusions of thought and sense. The expression of the indwelling Spirit (Om) is the energy outpoured in the soul; the spiritual Ego is the will, and union with the Higher Self is the aim. Union is to achieve by the mind, which is above the lower mind (thoughtless) and then as the will becomes one with the aim, so the lower self merges into the Higher Self."

There are many references in the Scriptures to the word arrow. In Psalms 45:5 we find the following: "Thine arrows are sharp in the heart of the king's enemies; whereby the people fall under thee." And in Psalms 64:7 are these words: "But God shall shoot at them with an arrow; suddenly shall they be wounded." No one can free himself from the arrow of conscience.

As Sagittarius is the ninth sign, it is "the number of perfection and completeness. Nine, which is three squared, refers to the attainment of perfection of the three lower planes."—G. A. Gaskell.

It is obvious that the attainment of chemical perfection (earthly) results automatically in perfection on *all* planes.

"Nine days through the army went the arrows of the god (Apollo); but on the *tenth, Achilles* called the people to an assembly."—*Iliad* Bk. 1.

"Yea, as a horse that bears to the gods; that which conveys to the gods is indeed the mind, for it is the mind which chiefly conveys the wise man to the gods."—*Sata. Brah.*, S. B. of E.

"Man does not rightly know the way to the heavenly world, but the horse does rightly know it."—*Ibid.*, 13:2, 3, I.

"An endeavor is made by the sorcerers to have the babe (Zoroaster) trampled to death by the horses, but the leading horse stands over the child and prevents it from perishing."—*Life of Zoroaster.* The Zoroastrians worshiped fire (Aries), and their story of the babe is the same as the Scriptural account of the infant Jesus.

Dr. Carey allocated Silicea with Sagittarius. It has been explained that Silicea is quartz. Flint, which has been utilized to produce sparks for fires from time immemorial, is a form of it. It constitutes a large part of the earth's crust. It does not occur free in nature and therefore must be separated by chemical means.

In its pure and crystallized form, it is rock crystal or quartz. In Inorganic Chemistry, we find that it stiffens the stems of cereal grains, and is also found in animal tissues. It occurs often in the form of hexagonal prisms, crowned by six-sided pyramids. As the triangle is the symbol of FIRE it will easily be seen how correct Dr. Carey's allocation is. No matter how small the particles of Silicea are broken up, all take the triangular form which is, of course, analogous to the arrowhead.

It is a scientific fact that practically all materials (and some say all) crystallize. When such is the case, the crystals may be easily seen. Quartz crystals are said to be the only ones *not* visible.

Domenico Guglielmini (Padova, 1706) asserted that the

crystals of each salt had a shape of their own with the plane angle of faces always the same. Modern scientists state that the angles between corresponding faces of all crystals of the same chemical substance, are always the same, and are characteristic of the substance. It is obvious, then, that the chemical element allocating with a certain zodiacal sign, *naturally* associates with it in order to accomplish a certain definite work in the body of the universe and of man.

Nearly all of the mineral salts crystallize under the hexakis-octahedron form. They have six scalene angles and forty-eight faces. This is the greatest number of faces possible for any simple form in crystals.

It is very interesting to note that Calcium fluoride crystals are used by opticians in the construction of certain lenses. It will be recalled that Calcium fluoride is the Cancer sign salt. As that sign is ruled by the Moon, it has a great deal to do with the brain, and hence, the eyes. Lack of this salt causes cataracts.

Calcium, Potassium and Silicea crystals rotate a beam of polarized light transmitted along the triad axis. Six kinds of primitive forms have been found in crystals. The older optical glasses, known as ordinary crown and flint glasses, are all of the nature of pure silicates, the basic constituents in the case of crown glass being lime, soda and lime, or potash (kali), or a mixture of both. Sometimes Magnesium is included. Manufacturers of glass inform us that a high Silicea content tends toward hardness and chemical *stability*. It is exactly for this reason that Silicea is used in making mortar. It is evident that the gem allocating with Sagittarius is the rock crystal.

Dr. Carey says of Silicea: "A deficiency of Silicea in the connective tissue between the cerebrum and the cerebellum produces a mental condition in which thinking is difficult." It is clear that there is insufficient FLINT upon which Pegasus' hoofs may strike. Therefore one is unable to woo the Muses.

In some of these chapters, I have referred to the use of slang phrases in which great truths are concealed. One in common use some years ago (and still occasionally heard) is "You have no sand" meaning no mental stamina. Since sand is nearly all silicea this expression is seen to be quite appropriate. Some occult works state that, as the cerebrum develops, very fine particles of mineral substance collect in the pineal gland.

Silicea is man's surgeon (the only absolutely safe one), his physical spade and electrical insulator. As it is not a conductor of electricity, its use as an insulator is invaluable.

The tiny particles of this salt travel here and there throughout the body, pushing in and around the cells congested with waste matter, actually digging it up, loosening it and pushing it on before them. These tiny but very active surgeon-workmen finally reach the surface with the heteroplasm or pus. If waste products are unable to follow natural channels of elimination, they do the next best thing. They take the avenues of least resistance. This is the cause of fistulas appearing around the rectum. Nature is sending her insistent message for Silicea, and all three Calcium combinations, and they must be taken intensively for many months.

Red eyelids constitute an outstanding modality which indicates need of Silicea. Also redness of the edges of the nostrils. There will be accompanying soreness. Other modalities are: acne, angry-red pimples; small red pimples on the scalp. When neither hot nor cold applications bring relief, and when one perspires very little, this salt is required. It is needed in connection with Ferrum, Kali mur and Kali sulph to break up a "cold." Large doses taken in hot water, in connection with a good hot bath, will break up a cold in short order if taken as soon as observed. It cleans out the pores. Naturally one must stop eating, and it is also necessary that the intestinal passage be thoroughly cleaned.

Some of the many symptoms arising from insufficient Silicea are: mental abstraction; despondency and disgust with life; lumps or nodules on the scalp; falling of hair or splitting of hair ends; sties on the eyelids; lachrymal fistula; boils and cystic tumors around the ears; cataract; dullness of hearing, with swelling and catarrh of the eustachian tubes (daily injections of Silicea are also needed); caries of the bones; mastoid process; catarrh, with discharge of thick, yellow matter; fetid, offensive discharge; caries and necrosis of the bones of face or jaw; gum-boils; pyorrhea; hardening of the tongue; ulcers on the tongue; ulceration of the throat; tonsilitis; abscess of the liver; suppuration of the kidneys; urine loaded with pus and mucus; chronic syphilis; prostatitis; chronic gonorrhea; leucorrhea; hard lumps in the breasts;

fistulous ulcers; tuberculosis; pneumonia; bronchitis; neglected injuries, festering and threatening to suppurate; hip-joint disease; carbuncles; fetid perspiration of feet; obstinate neuralgia, occurring at night, when neither heat nor cold gives relief; copious night sweats; insufficient perspiration; sleeplessness from orgasm of blood; jerking of limbs during sleep, etc., etc.

Symptoms are always worse at night and during the full moon, also worse in open air. They decrease in a warm room.

He who lives in the Higher Mind is insulated from all danger. The crystal-clear esse, the heavenly dew-drops, reflect without obstruction. Intuition is keen and clear-cut. He judges instantly and accurately. The arrow of thought flies straight to the mark.

The arrow of intuition cuts one entirely off from all that is base, unclean and unworthy. The Higher Mind is the bridge over which each one must cross to enter into paradise. The Higher Mind is Pegasus the horse, clothed with the wings of the eagle.

Guru Nanak says, in *The Sikh Religion,* Vol. I, by Macauliffe; "Let a man take the five arrows (the five virtues), put them on the bow of his brain, and KILL DEATH." What a stupendous and true admonition!

Max Müller quotes the following from *Selections from Buddha*, which is splendidly apropos, linking up, as it does, the signs Aries and Sagittarius:

"My *mind* is now athirst and longing for the draught of the fountain of sweet DEW, saddle then my horse, and quickly bring it here. I WISH TO REACH THE DEATHLESS CITY."

And matchless Shakespeare also knew the secret, as his words prove:

"Mount, eagle, to my palace crystalline!"

CHAPTER X

THE ANALYSIS AND SYNTHESIS OF CAPRICORN AND CALCIUM PHOSPHATE

"Janus am I; oldest of Potentates;
Forward I look, and backward and below;
I count, as god of avenues and gates
The years that through my portals come and go."
—*Longfellow's Poet's Calendar.*

THE Sun has now reached the southern "gate to heaven," from whence it must make ready to ascend. It is the goat, Capricorn, waiting at the foot of the mountain to begin its long climb.

From approximately December 21 to January 21, the sun is transiting the zodiacal sign Capricorn, and the nature of the work accomplished during this period pertains rather more to January than to December; for two weeks of the former, and only one of the latter, are affected.

January is derived from the Roman word Janus, who was an ancient Italian deity. "He was the god of all *beginnings* and who took precedence of all other gods. He was the Ancient of Days. He presided over the beginning of human life, of the day, of the agricultural year, over gateways and openings," all reference works inform us.

Under his archway the Roman armies marched to *war*. This archway in the Forum, afterwards replaced by a Temple with double doors, was closed only in times of *absolute peace*. In Hebrew the word Janum means *slumber*.

There is a mine of information available in the above statements. As Saturn is the ruler of Capricorn, its negative interpretation is Satan, who stands in the doorway of the Temple. He is the tempter who endeavors to stop those who would enter therein. Those who aspire to enter the sacred place have produced the mental vibrations causing the aspiration. In other words, they have not lost, or become deficient in, the MATERIAL necessary to produce these higher vibrations. They will succeed in effecting an entrance if Satan is unable to make them "look back."

Here it must be explained that the god Janus is pictured as having two faces looking in opposite directions. One face is that of an old man; the other, that of a youth. Therefore the necessity for the double doors of the Temple, for one opens into the *future,* while through the other one may still gaze into the past. One must decide which he will do. If past lessons have been sufficiently severe, and the prodigal son has learned them, the power of the tempter will have been lost. Then one is able to look in utter astonishment at the figure standing there. It has absolutely changed—it has taken on the form and the features of the CHRIST. Transmutation has been achieved, and one has at last entered into the STRAIT GATE WHICH IS STRAIGHT. "Enter ye in at the STRAIT gate, for wide is the gate that leadeth to destruction, and many there be which go in thereat;

"Because STRAIT is the gate, and narrow is the way, which leadeth unto *life,* and few there be that find it."—Matt. 7:13 and 14.

"And David said unto Gad, I am in a great STRAIT; let us fall now into the hands of the Lord; for his mercies are great; and let me not *fall* into the hand of man."—II Kings 24:14.

The straight gate opens into the "strait," which is a narrow passage connecting two bodies of fluid. It seems to wind around itself like a spiral stairway, or the curves in the horns of the goat. Capricorn is at the lower end, the entrance, while at the summit, or mountain top, is Aries. The body of fluid at the *bottom* is that of *procreation;* the body of fluid at the *top* is that of *creation* and *recreation.* It is obvious that one who seeks to recreate himself, aspires to fall into the hands of the Lord and not into the hands of man.

One of the popular fables of Greek mythology is the story of Jupiter, who was born on Mt. Olympus and suckled by the goat Amalthea. Pater Jupiter, or the Giver of all Good Things, would actually starve to death if the goat ceased to climb the mountain with his food.

This same mythology informs us that Nature was symbolized in the past by the figure of the goat-man whose name was Pan. Its esoteric meaning is FEEDER or nutriment. Pan is the root of many interesting words such as pantry (the place where food is kept), pan, a receptacle for containing food, water or any substance; also a process used in separating gold from sand. It is found in the word panacea, which is a "cure-all." *Food* may rightly be considered as the means of healing all diseases, since it contains the salts or mineral substances required by the cells of the body. It was originally intended to do this; but, for many reasons, this has become impossible. Gluttony, or living to eat, has replaced the plan of eating to live. In addition, the soil in different parts of the country has become so depleted that it is no longer possible to grow chemically perfect food. A third reason is the inability of the organs of digestion and assimilation to take care of the food.

Pan means ALL, while panis is Latin for *bread*. The Scriptures state that Jesus is "the BREAD OF LIFE," and they also refer to the LIVING BREAD which COMES DOWN from heaven (Aries—cerebrum). When this nutriment, or bread, is not used in PRO-creation or wasted, it may be laid on the table in the "upper chamber" and *become* the LORD'S SUPPER. This is the true explanation of the Scriptural statement.

Pan was termed the god of shepherds. As a shepherd is one who cares for sheep, or other flocks, it has a very esoteric interpretation. It must be recalled that this sign (Capricorn) is one of the four gates of heaven, out of which Spirits come, and into which they return. As Aries is the gate from which they come, Cancer is the gate through which Spirit enters into corpuscles, in forming the cells of the body. Libra is the gate of decision, the balance point which decides whether SPIRIT (ensouled in the corpuscles) WILL BE STRONG ENOUGH TO GO DOWN INTO THE PIT, THE GATE OF CAPRICORN, AND COME UP OUT OF IT —go down into hell, remain three days, and ON THE THIRD DAY RISE AGAIN.

The above are familiar words to readers of the Scriptures, but only astrology and physiology can explain them. The Sun, at this time of the year, is at its lowest declination—it seems actually to disappear below the earth. This occurs as the Sun enters the sign Capricorn. THREE DAYS AFTER, IT ENTERS THE THIRD DEGREE OF THE SIGN, WHICH DEGREE ALLOCATES WITH AQUARIUS AND THE SIGN OF THE SON OF MAN. NATURALLY JESUS IS BORN AT THIS TIME.

This is the period of the year when, if one had accomplished the task of allowing Jupiter to be fed—(himself automatically taking the Holy Sacrament)—the Divine Babe, the matrix of a *new man,* would be created within. But again, each one must WORK OUT HIS OWN SALVATION. It IS work!

The analysis of these two and one-half degree points will reveal everything concerning man and the universe. The twenty-fifth of December was the correct date chosen for the birth of Jesus, for the very good reason that at no other time can the proper creative vibration be produced.

As the carnal man disappears forever, when the Divine Son is born, it is natural that Greek mythology should thus express it: "Later, Pan came to be regarded as a representative of all Greek gods, and of Paganism itself. Indeed, according to an early Christian tradition, when the heavenly host announced the *birth of Christ* (Jesus) a deep groan, heard through the isles of Greece, told that great Pan was dead, that the dynasty of Olympus was dethroned, and several deities sent wandering in cold and darkness."

The earnest student will realize the irrefutable fact that the three days which creative energy spends in "hell," refer to the glands in the sacral region having to do with procreation, in other words the sexual glands. For here the corpuscles are changed into ANIMAL SEED. Thus a state of torment, misery and anguish results for the cabined Spirit, until such time as the long task of separating the human corpuscle from the animalized corpuscle begins. This is the Great Work and is referred to in the Scriptures as *"SEPARATING THE SHEEP FROM THE GOATS."*

As the real meaning of hell is TO CONCEAL, it verifies the above statement. The Divine Fire, and Celestial Esse, go down, and are concealed in the lower regions, which correspond cosmically to that period of darkness and coldness termed Winter. Winter is the season of the year when the sun shines MOST OBLIQUELY. Summer is the period of the year when the sun is directly overhead, which causes the rays to be hottest. It is the fire which Æsculapius stole from heaven and chained to earth.

It will be well to turn to the chart of The Cosmic Embryo, in this book, and note that the above statement relative to the rays of the sun in Winter being *most oblique,* furnishes further proof of the chart's correctness. Note that the path of the

Sun, under the vibration of Saturn, forms an absolutely oblique line from corner to corner, across that part of the heaven assigned to Capricorn.

It has been previously stated that, under the archway of Janus, the Roman armies marched to *war*, but that the gates were closed when there was *absolute peace*. This obviously refers to something out of the ordinary, since one would infer that any city gate would be opened at times, and would certainly not be closed in times of peace, but for protection in times of turmoil. It has a physiological interpretation.

The three decans of the zodiacal sign Capricorn allocate accurately with the first three vertebræ of the sacrum. The word sacrum is derived from the Latin *sacer,* meaning sacred, holy, consecrated. Recalling the fact that it is here where Æsculapius chained the Divine Fire, one understands why it has been given the name of sacrum. The CREATIVE FIRE of Aries (cerebrum) "falling from heaven" has become the PROCREATIVE FIRE.

Reviewing the information given in the previous chapters, one sees that this fire was never originally intended to be "chained" to earth (the earthly or carnal part). To be "chained" means to be unable to move away from the place. If the fire were not thus confined, it would be free AGAIN TO ASCEND and thus CIRCULATE in the body. Circulation is made impossible when the lower mind refuses to, or is unable to, raise its vibrations to those of the Higher. Freeing this energy or Serpent Power, and its allocating substance, enables it to RETURN TO THE FATHER. These two, being originally the product or progeny of the FATHER (cerebrum), must return and "become one with Him."

As stated many times, the student should make a study of the parts of the body under consideration. Thus he will find, in this case, that the sacrum and sacral vertebræ are the points of origin (within the spinal cord) of those nerves which form the sacral plexus, and which, in connection with the coccygeal nerves, control the functions of the sexual glands.

Humanity is not "bound" or in the clutches of any unseen being called Satan, but is hypnotized and enthralled by its passion for sensation. It will eventually, however, reach the heights when each and every one has "lifted up the serpent in the wilderness." Scorpio will have become the

FEATHERED OR WINGED SERPENT. Man will have ceased to be a centaur and will have mounted his Pegasus.

As this sign is said to pertain to beginnings (initial movements), gates, etc., since Capricorn is one of the four gates of heaven, the reason why *armies pass out* of this gate should be obvious. The armies refer to the *RAPACIOUS SPERMATOZOA*. It is a physiological fact that they represent countless hordes. WHEN THESE CEASE TO PASS OUT, THE GATE OR OPENING OUT OF WHICH THEY PASS WILL AUTOMATICALLY CLOSE. We understand, at last, why it is never shut except in times of ABSOLUTE PEACE.

The body is a "house divided against itself"—therefore it contains warring corpuscles—the procreative germ cells, for the SPIRIT within each one bitterly rebels against its martyrdom.

Ancient literature teems with this story. It should be plain to readers that the peculiar method of its wording is sufficient evidence that it refers wholly to the human body.

In the light of the above information, it is obvious why Janus "presides over the beginning of human life"—which is creation.

From the word pan, we derive brain-pan, which is the skull. The name Saturn allocates with brain-pan, for it is separated into Sat, which is a Latin word meaning enough or sufficient, and from which the word satiate (therefore full) is derived. An urn is a receptacle, pan, or pitcher for holding something. In ancient times it was used to hold the ashes of the dead. Since mineral salts are termed *ash,* it is obvious that the urn of Saturn (the Ancient of Days) held all the salts essential to life, before that god "fell from heaven." These are necessary in order to *satisfy* the need of creative energy. No one wishes to have his brain-pan become a funeral urn.

How a thing will "pan" out, is analogous to Saturn's natural power for rendering judgment on it. The law of cause and effect is here considered. Saturn is said to withhold from a person the result looked for, or desired, when that person has not actually *earned* it. It is also said that Saturn will pour into one's lap the fruits of legitimate *work.* But it must be forever realized that Saturn demands the very last farthing of what is due. When it is supplied, one is free of all bonds and restriction, for there is no longer any *danger* involved.

Without the vibration termed Saturn, in Nature, nothing could HOLD together. Cohesion would not exist. Saturn binds, and therefore limits *within a certain radius,* in order to create STABILITY. This implies support, a foundation.

The URN in the hands of Aquarius, the Heavenly Man, is Saturn himself, for it stands for labor and the FRUITS of that labor. Saturn is *within* each one. When the wholly natural vibrations of the cosmic Saturn find the corresponding material in the human body, then, and then only, will work in that body be properly executed. When King Saturn enters his kingdom, seeking to accomplish kingly work therein, and finds his material lacking, what is the result? Naturally the work can not be done. There is no other logical answer.

Calcium phosphate is Saturn's own particular material. One of its three special uses is to form the bones constituting the framework of the body. The foundation of any building is constructed first, and is, therefore, the *oldest* part of that building. This allocates with the nature of Saturn and his esoteric name of "Ancient of Days." He represents the *beginning.*

The bony framework of the body is its foundation. It is well known that it remains in the grave for a *long time* before it is converted into dust, its original particles. Saturn, then, is the MASTER MASON. When the initiatory process is perfected, Saturn has regained the mountain top with a FULL URN. The skull is the positive urn, while the pelvis is the negative urn, both being necessary for the function of circulation. As the fourteenth card of the *Tarot* pictures the essentials of the Great Work, we see the Spirit of Life (which is really Saturn) pouring the Water of Life from one urn into another WITHOUT SPILLING A DROP. And as the fourteenth card also symbolizes the letter N, which is literally Jesus, in Hebrew (the Divine Fruit of a regenerated body), the analogy is perfect.

To initiate means to GO-AT a thing, to make a beginning. It is said in astrclogical lore that Capricorn is the sign of the *initiate.* As Janus has two faces, it is evident that a "right-about face" is analogous to taking a *new step,* and therefore entering, as it were, another door. So it is, that one who has thought only of the lower or negative URN, at last realizes its utter poverty and the fact that he has been the prodigal son long enough. He *returns,* in thought, to his FATHER, and thereafter begins to make more material returns. Thus he is truly an ENTERED APPRENTICE, and prayerfully promises to endeavor, with all his strength, to BECOME A GOOD MASON, therefore AN ACCURATE BUILDER. He no longer tears down.

The true interpretation of Freemasonry is, that it is a *physio-chemical process* which will ultimately result in the metaphysical life. This, and this alone, is the TRUE SCIENCE OF CHRISTIANITY. Matter is teeming with life, and life can not manifest without matter.

One born with the Sun in Capricorn, may therefore be an initiate or still be "two-faced," which means to be CAPRICIOUS. This word is derived from the same root as Capella, which is the Latin name for the goat star. Caprice is "a movement of the mind as unaccountable as the springs and bounds of a goat," says Webster, while to caper means to frisk or prance about.

The Encyclopædia Britannica says of the goat: "Properly the name of the well-known domesticated European ruminant, which has *for all time* been regarded as the emblem of everything that is evil, in contradistinction to the sheep which is the symbol of excellence and purity."

Is it logical, then, for anyone to scoff at the fact that astrology has, from time immemorial, recognized and made use of the symbol of the goat? It has allocated the lamb or sheep with Aries, that part of the body having the highest vibration—the THINKER, the Fire of Life, while the negative pole, where humanity has kept that Fire chained, has been associated with the goat.

In Mediæval bestiary lore, the goat is the symbol of lechery or lustfulness. Shakespeare refers to a man of this nature, in the following terms:

"Thou damned and luxurious mountain goat."

It must be emphasized that this is the *negative* interpretation of this sign, for all signs have both positive and negative phases, the unregenerate representing one, and the entrants into the conditions of apprenticeship the other. The latter have young faces, while those worn with excesses may still be young in years but have aged faces.

The two Pans in the Scales of Libra allocate with Saturn. Both must be FULL OF SEED. The knee-pans are intimately associated with Saturn or Pan. One of the branches of the sciatic nerve ramifies to each knee pan, and reflex action is absent when the sacral center has become partially paralyzed because of sexual excesses. The word knee is *janu* in Sanskrit, and analogous to Janus and January. This is the reason for the knees being associated with Capricorn. It is true that this animal may kneel in feeding, but the first reason here given is the legitimate one.

Panathenæa was the name given by the ancient Greeks to two celebrations sacred to Pan, the goat, and Athena (wisdom), or the wise goat. The lesser was held every year, while the greater took place once in four years. The prizes for the victors consisted of urns of olive oil. This is analogous to Virgo the virgin, and also to Athena or wisdom. It is the basis for the expression "THE OIL OF GLADNESS." To be wise is to be happy and at peace.

Referring to the fact that in Hebrew the word Janus means *slumber,* or inactivity, we find this to be analogous to the fire *chained* to earth. The root of the word slumber is slum, which means a foul back street of a city, a low, squalid neighborhood. This is analogous to the lower part of the body, and the gates or openings, over which Janus or Capricorn is said to preside. The openings in the lower part of the body are for the passage of excrement and this region may well be termed the slums. A feeling of intense repugnance arises when one realizes that the procreative fluid finds exit via one of these passages.

To sleep means to be in a state of inactivity, sloth or supineness, caused by the cerebral nerves failing to keep the conscious part of the physical machinery at work. They have themselves become reduced in electrical power. Thus the nerves of the eyes (the electric eyes) become weary, and the eyes close. The pulley nerves contract, and let fall the curtains of sleep. In contradistinction to this state, due to loss of electrical power and vitality, is the vital, unwearied condition of the optic thalamus or All-Seeing Eye, as stated in Psalms 121:4: "He that keepeth Israel shall neither slumber nor sleep."

Bunyan, in *Pilgrim's Progress,* furnishes an example of the slothful condition which retards one's advancement: "At last he fell into a slumber, and thence into a fast sleep which *detained* him in that place." Lot's wife, it will be recalled "looked back and became a pillar of salt." In our present stage of evolution, a certain amount of rest is absolutely essential in order to enable one to work. There is yet *too much* waste, and one is subject to such a constant strain that the body can not become refreshed unless seven or eight hours of sleep are obtained.

It is interesting to note that the word *knee* is used in architecture. We are amazed to find, in its architectural analysis, the *actual geometrical plan of the sun's path through Capricorn,* for here knee means the *slope of a gable*—otherwise an oblique line. This statement is verified by noting the exactly oblique line connecting opposite corners of the space allotted to Capricorn in the chart of the Cosmic Embryo.

A study of the Sun's oblique or diagonal journey through the sign of the Goat gives us the metaphysical explanation of the faults of the unregenerate (not yet enlightened), born with the Sun in this sign. The meaning of diagonal or oblique is *not straightforward;* therefore *two-faced;* under-hand; sinister. Obliquity, derived from the same root, means DEVIATION FROM A RIGHT LINE, therefore deviation from moral rectitude and sound thinking. It is indeed gratifying to find in geometrical terms, another means of verifying these findings.

In following its oblique or diagonal path, energy (represented by the Sun) takes a *round-about* way—in other words seems to *waste time* (Saturn is Father Time) in addition to creative substance. This is because, in very truth, it *does not follow the straight and narrow path.* It is *chained* to earth and can not seem to start upward on its journey—it is stagnant, inactive, drowsy. As the *longest* side of the triangle is its oblique line, a longer time is required to cover the distance.

It is very apropos, at this writing, to refer to the state of PANIC which has existed for practically two years in the financial and industrial world. The ancients pointed to Pan as the cause of panic, and sudden, groundless fear. It is a fact that the word panic is derived from the same root. On referring to *Schuessler's Biochemic System,* we find that Calcium phos deficiency causes a state of fear and panic to exist in the mind. In the absence of *straightforwardness,* which means the inability of the mind to travel in a *straight line,* or path of wisdom (living the Satanic life—sinning), there is no moral support, hence no mental stamina. Naturally panic results.

The planet Saturn entered its own sign (Capricorn) in

March, 1929. Among other things, this sign pertains to occupation, profession, *honor,* and hence position; moral status and stability. Remember, Saturn or Æsculapius *stole* fire from heaven. In other words he became a perverter, which means to divert from a right use, to *corrupt,* to *misapply.* As the rock-bottom interpretation of Saturn is SEED, it is evident that the source of life and of all (pan means *all*) things including honor, have become corrupted; and decidedly wrong methods have been employed in handling the necessities of life. Innumerable Loan and Investment organizations have failed. The cause, in many instances, was the misappropriation of funds, or actual embezzlement. Very many have failed to stand the tremendous test of honor which is required by Saturn's position in his own sign. The brain cells have been incapable of setting up, or responding to, the high vibration corresponding to virtue. Therefore, crashes or falls have resulted.

So great has become the cupidity, covetousness and avariciousness of mankind, that altruism and honor have been almost entirely lost sight of. Humanity went mad over speculation. The pendulum may swing far in one direction, but it inevitably swings just as far in the opposite. The crash in Wall Street gave this pendulum of speculation a mighty blow. It was a "knockout" for many. If a position still existed, the wages earned began to find their way to the Savings Bank. It is true that during that orgy of speculation, spending and wasting in sexual excesses, humanity, as Mr. Ford aptly stated, was actually ill. The "knockout" was the blow that initiated recovery. But recovery is still a helpless infant, and will grow very slowly, for it is supplied at present with a poor quality of food that does not furnish much nutriment. Many of those who lost all of their savings, would stake all *again* if given the chance to double their money, for cupidity is not yet dead.

Saturn stands for truth, stability, honest values, honor and integrity. Where TRUST does not exist, there can be no stability. Uranus in Aries, the cerebrum, has been in a square position to Capricorn, and all relating thereto, since 1928; and when Saturn entered its own sign, this vibration became tremendously intensified. Spasms of fluctuation relative to Capricorn and Aries resulted. The little balance or harmony which existed disappeared, and chaos reigned.

Saturn will not leave Capricorn to enter the sign Aquarius,

until Feb. 24, 1932. But it does not advance far into it, for it begins to retrograde on May 15, 1932, and goes back into Capricorn, reaching the twenty-eighth degree before it moves forward again. It retrogrades for exactly the same reason that a school teacher returns to the schoolroom to see if the pupils are honorable, or are misbehaving on being left for a time to their own resources.

During the two and one-half years' stay of Saturn in his own sign, humanity is being tested relative to matters pertaining to honor. It is being called to an *accounting* of the money handled, it is being asked WHAT USE IT HAS MADE OF THE COIN OF THE REALM. The test will still continue when Saturn enters the sign Aquarius, but it will cause the conscience to begin to stir. Shame and repentance will gradually manifest. There is never any sudden remedying of any condition—years are required in which to bring it about. Education along all lines, desire for SELF-improvement and an honest effort toward right-living are absolutely essential factors for normal conditions. One must possess knowledge of the chemistry of life.

Jupiter, the "Giver of all Good Things," has been in Cancer for one year, but in July of this year (1931) left it to enter Leo. His position in Cancer was in opposition to Saturn in Capricorn, and square to Uranus in Aries. Interpreted, this means that the vibration of Saturn, which withholds, binds and constricts, was set against (pulled against) the vibration of the bountiful giver, Jupiter. As this was the condition of the cosmic ether waves, it was bound to have exactly the same effect on humanity and all that concerned it. To add to the confusion, the Dragon's Tail was in Libra, which produced the same rate of vibration as Saturn. We marvel that so many kept their reason and remained on their feet. It has been a terrible test of mental and physical stamina.

An outstanding indication of perversion relative to all that is worth while, has been inflated values. Beginning when Saturn was in Virgo, in 1919, land and real estate values (?) spasmodically soared skyward. The man who purchased property for $8000 at that time, asked and received double what he paid. The purchaser had the same experience. Thus avariciousness flourished unconfined. All material things developed artificial values, while things worth while—and having permanent or fixed value, such as virtue, honor and integrity—were entirely ignored.

This condition was naturally bound to become more or less fixed, because all else was forgotten in the mad orgy of money-getting, and in spending it in excesses of various kinds. It had apparently grown into a normal or natural condition, and was so considered by those concerned.

When the cosmic jolt came, it shook everything to its very *foundation* (Saturn), and panic resulted. With very little mental stability to depend on in the time of trial, it is no wonder that panic resulted.

Just, true, and honest valuations relative to ALL (Pan) things, will gradually bring about a readjustment, and ultimately a more or less harmonious condition.

In Biblical lore, Capricorn corresponds to Ephesus, the first of the Seven Churches of Asia mentioned in Revelation. It means in Hebrew to yield or surrender; which, in a sense, implies license. It is analogous to Sodom, which means LIME-PLACE. As lime is Calcium, this verifies Dr. Carey's allocation of Calcium to Capricorn. Sodom also means, a vineyard *burning*. "Sodomy" is the name of a common form of sexual perversion. The story of Sodom and Gomorrah (submersion) never referred to cities, but to localities or parts *in* physical real estate. It will be recalled that they were two of "the five wicked cities of the plain."—Genesis 13:10. Sodom is Hebrew for the BACK PASSAGE, the anus.

If it is such an unclean place, why is it termed a CHURCH in Revelation? Simply because it had become purified. It had at last reverted to its original status, which existed before the "fall."

Smith's Bible Dictionary states that the Temple of Diana which was erected at this place was one of the seven wonders of the world. "The building was raised on immense substructions, because of the *swampy* nature of the ground. The city of Ephesus was named the 'temple-keeper' or 'warden of Diana.'"

According to this same dictionary, "The first *seeds* of Christian truth were sown at Ephesus" which, physiologically, is a true statement. Saturn is the sower of seed—in fact, he IS SEED ITSELF. When Pan dies, Jesus is born. In other words, it is conservation of the souls IN these seeds (procreative) which constitutes their SAVING.

Diana was the Greek name for the Moon. It means virgin material, and refers to *FECUNDITY*.

A very curious statement concerning Ephesus is made by Mr. Smith. He says that "one of the most important officers of Ephesus was the 'TOWN-CLERK,' who was a person of very great influence and responsibility." It is not difficult to clarify the above when it is recalled that a town-clerk is one who keeps the records. In other words, he is Saturn or Father Time. Moreover, the Cosmic Records never will be seen by the Inner Eye (Aries) until its natural food—the bread of life—(Pan) is restored. Truly is Saturn's responsibility as town-clerk, or record-keeper, very great.

In the second chapter of Revelation, which deals with the Church of Ephesus, it says: "for thou hast left thy first love;" which is analogous to the "fall" of Saturn and to the Divine Fire.

The Bible dictionary states that there were "slime pits" at Sodom, and that the soil was a"fat, greasy loam." There is only one interpretation to the above—the physiological real estate contained oil.

There are many Scriptural references to an animal termed the unicorn. Uni means one, while corn has a number of old interpretations, among them being corn (seed), head, horn, cornucopia, and cerebrum. It is very curious and interesting to note how each of these is associated with Capricorn.

The word cornucopia is said to be associated with the *goat* Amalthæa (which nourished Jupiter on Mt. Olympus). According to Webster, its meaning is *abundance,* plenty, sufficient. Pan or bread has the same interpretation. It is, therefore, related to the conservation of that material which becomes the Lord's (Aries) supper. As bread is made of grain or seed, and as its inception is the cerebrum, the simile is obvious.

In Numbers 23:2, we find the following reference to the unicorn: "God brought them out of Egypt; he hath as it were the strength of an unicorn."

In Job 39:9 and 10, we read: "Will the unicorn be willing to serve thee, or abide by thy crib? Canst thou bind the unicorn with his band in the furrow; or will he harrow the valleys after thee?"

"Save me from the lion's (Leo) mouth; for thou hast heard me from the horns of the unicorns."—Psalms 92:10.

The dolphin is associated with the narwhal, the latter meaning corpse-whale, so-called because of its peculiar color, the top being gray and the under-side white, spotted with gray. No doubt its inner meaning was known in ancient times, also its association with the mysticism of the human body. By the allocation of the narwhal or unicorn with Capricorn, the fact is made clear that the procreative fish, or spermatozoa, are truly *corpse-fish,* for the very good reason that *death inevitably results from their creation.*

A description follows: "Narwhal is the Scandinavian name for a cetacean, characterized by the presence in the male of a long horn-like tusk. In the adult of both sexes there are only two teeth, both in the upper jaw, which lie horizontally side by side, and in the female remaining throughout life concealed in cavities of the bone. In the male the right tooth usually remains similarly concealed, but the left is immensely developed, attaining a length equal to more than half that of the entire animal. In a narwhal twelve feet long, from snout to tail, the exserted portion of the tusk may measure six, seven and occasionally eight feet in length. It projects horizontally forward from the head in the form of a cylindrical or slightly tapering, pointed tusk, composed of ivory, with the surface marked by spiral grooves and ridges, running in a sinistral direction.

"The head is short and rounded, the fore limbs or paddles are small and broad compared with those of most dolphins. Dorsal fins are wanting. *The name unicorn is sometimes applied to it.*"

The unicorn (horned goat or horse) has been made use of in heraldry from ancient times. It is employed to signify or represent *support.* It is quite apropos to state here that its horn, containing, as it does, a central cavity (which must be filled with marrow or oil), is analogous to the SPINAL VERTEBRÆ WHICH ALSO CONTAIN A CENTRAL CAVITY. These vertebræ are also OF THE NATURE OF A SUPPORT, as the backbone is the support of the torso. One having no CHARACTER is said to have no backbone.

Not only is the backbone the support of the body, but its strength and condition is, we may say, a barometer or gauge by which the mental and moral status may be judged. It is assuredly analogous. Again, the *quality of the oil* in the spinal canal corresponds to the general health and purity of the body. Its refination to the Nth degree is analogous to the Christ state, or that of the Christ consciousness. The horn of the unicorn thus contains the ANOINTING OIL.

In occult lore, the dolphin was considered sacred to Apollo, or the Sun—in other words ESSENTIAL TO ENERGY OR CREATIVE POWER.

Further proof of the correctness of this allocation is the following, from E. C. Brewer's *Dictionary of Phrase and Fable:* "According to the legends of the Middle Ages, the unicorn could be caught only by placing a virgin in his haunts; upon seeing the virgin, the creature would lose its fierceness and lie quiet at her feet. This is said to be an allegory of Jesus Christ, who willingly became man and entered the Virgin's womb, when he was taken by the hunters of blood. The one horn symbolizes the great Gospel doctrine that Christ is one with God." *(Guillaume, Clerc de Normandie Trouvère.)*

Mr. Brewer further states that: "According to a belief once popular, the unicorn by dipping its horn into a liquid could detect whether or not it contained poison. In the designs for gold and silver plates made for the Emperor Rudolph II, by Ottavio Strada, is a cup on which a unicorn stands as if to assay the liquid. James I. substituted a unicorn, one of the supporters of the Royal arms of Scotland, for the red dragon of Wales, introduced by Henry VII."

We find the analysis of the unicorn in the foregoing statement by Mr. Brewer rather confusing, as its allocation with Jesus Christ (the man) was according to the perverted interpretation and was not physiological. However, it is true of the *individual* and personal Jesus formed *in* each one, the result of Pan feeding Jupiter. The fact that the narwhal or unicorn could only be *tamed* by placing a virgin in his haunts, is analogous to the story of the VIRGIN, and the conservation and purification of the oil in the horn, the glands relating to Capricorn. It is a fact that only by a life of VIRGINITY is it possible to tame the animal.

A few facts relative to the association of stone and oil must be here given. Scripture states: "And I say unto thee that thou art Peter, and upon this rock I will build my church; and the gates of hell shall not prevail against it.

"And I will give unto thee the keys of the kingdom of

heaven, and whatsoever thou shalt bind upon earth shall be bound in heaven: and whatsoever thou shalt loose on earth shall be loosed in heaven."

As Peter is the same as Petra and means *stone,* it indeed is the stone (mineral) necessary in the construction of a perfect (holy) structure for the indwelling SPIRIT. Therefore the Peter referred to was stone. The "binding and loosening" no doubt refers to the unrefined and the refined oil.

The word Petroleum consists of two words, petra and oleum, meaning respectively, stone and oil, therefore mineral oil or oil formed from mineral. It is known to be a complex mixture of hydro-carbons, and varies much in appearance and properties. No doubt it represents a certain *critical* state resulting from the harmonious combination of all elements, for it is a fact that all substances may be analyzed out of it. In the form of naphtha is was known to the ancient Egyptians "who used it in their perpetual lamps." These lamps have been referred to in the first chapter.

It is a curious fact that the expression, "peter out," means to become exhausted, to fail, to run out. Peter is analogous to the sacral nerves controlling the sexual glands, while Paul is related to the cerebrum and is many times referred to as "the still small voice." It is indeed a fact that the strength of Paul is weakened when the creative force and substance "peters out."

It is well to here explain why saltpeter is often mixed with the food given to soldiers in times of war. The fact that it is done, is probably generally known, but few are aware of the reason or effect.

Due to excess mucous and glandular fluids (the result of chemical deficiency, acid, incorrect and excessive eating), the sexual glands of the average male are over-engorged with fluid. This, if understood, would be recognized as proof of a *diseased* condition. The pressure within the distended glands calls attention to them, creating desire, which becomes uncontrollable. As this part of the body is Ephesus, as before stated, the Biblical words "I have fought with wild beasts at Ephesus" (I Cor. 15. 32) may well apply to this condition of the sexual organs.

The action of saltpeter causes *relaxation of the involuntary fibers which depend upon spasms of the involuntary muscles.* In plain English, the muscles controlling the sexual organ are rendered incapable of contracting.

Encyclopædia Britannica says of saltpeter: "It was sometimes used by doctors in asthma and for many different diseases; but it is now never administered internally, as its extremely depressant action upon the heart is not compensated for by any useful properties which are not possessed by many other drugs." Comment on the above is unnecessary.

Robbing Peter to pay Paul is analogous to energizing the brain by means of continence.

Returning to the subject of the goat, it is said that the best wool is obtained from castrated Angora goats. The reason is, that the life force, and substance, is never wasted, but recreates the body.

"The Golden Age" was the name given by the ancients to the time of Saturn's reign, for this mighty angel had returned to heaven, his former fall having been forgotten.

The fish-tailed goat of the zodiac represents a close analogy to the Mexican calendar sign, which is a kind of marine monster resembling a narwhal.

Capricorn is the house of spiritual conception; and, if nine months are considered to be the period of spiritual gestation, Spiritual birth will be in Libra, meaning that balance is attained.

The facetious remark sometimes made by Freemasons, that a candidate is "to ride the goat" on a certain evening, literally means, whether he knows it or not, that he must learn to control his passions.

In the Babylonian creation-scheme, Capricorn was Abba-e, or "The Cave of the Rising," which is analogous to the birth of Jesus in the cave or manger. It was also Muna-kha, the Goat-fish.

In ancient times, a certain day was set aside as the Day of Atonement. The sins of the people were, metaphorically, cast upon a goat, which was then driven away into the wilderness. The familiar phrase "to be made the goat of," signifies to take the blame.

It is obvious, therefore, that something more than mere superstition has kept these expressions extant down through the ages.

It is said that "very ancient oriental legends which made Capricorn the nurse of the youthful son-god long anticipated the story of the infant Jupiter and the goat Amalthea."

Richard Allen says: "Very frequent mention was made of

this constellation in early days, for the Platonists held that the souls of men, when released from corporeity, ascended to heaven through the stars, whence it was called the GATE OF THE GODS; their road of descent having been through Cancer." Full explanation has been given in the fourth chapter of this book.

"Cæsius and Postellus are authority for its being Azazel, the Scapegoat of Leviticus. Manuscripts from the second to the fifteenth century show it with the head and body of a goat, or ibex, ending in a fish's tail. In the Aztec calendar it appeared as Cipactli, with a figure like that of a narwhal.

"Nashira is from Al Sa'd al Nashirah, the Fortunate One, or the Bringer of Good Tidings one of the stars in the constellation of Capricorn."

Madam Blavatsky states, on page 579 of the second part of the last edition of her work: "But the true sense of the word 'Makara' (Capricorn) does not mean 'crocodile,' in truth, at all, even when it is compared with the animal depicted on the Hindu Zodiac. For it has the head and fore-legs of an antelope and the body and tail of a fish. Hence the tenth sign of the Zodiac has been taken variously to mean a shark, a dolphin, etc.; as it is the VAHAN of VARUNA, the Ocean God, and is often called, for this reason, Jala-rupa or 'water-form.'" The procreative germs are the forms in the water.

Mr. G. A. Gaskell says of Capricorn: "A symbol of the tenth period of the cycle of life. It signifies the higher mind (white he-goat) which is attained by the ego climbing the mount of aspiration through the transmutation of the lower mind, in the cycle of evolution."

The glyph of Capricorn is very curious, and in close study will be found to be patterned after the sacral bone. The top is open, and the figure is in the form of a triangle pointed downward. Branching off from the right side is a curved line which circles to the right and downward. This is analogous of the sacral nerves branching off from the sacrum. A more esoteric interpretation is that of the Serpent Fire.

Dr. Carey allocated Calcium or lime phosphate with this sign. The body requires more of it than of any other mineral for the reason that a very great quantity is required for the bones alone. This fact proves it to be a correct chemical allocation. Saturn rules the bones, as mentioned heretofore. They are the OLDEST parts of the body, for they remain intact for long years after the flesh has disappeared. Not only is this salt essential to the growth and well-being of the framework, but, in addition, it forms the skeletal part of every cell. Limestone and mortar constitute the foundation stone of the body, the same as of any structure.

Mortar or mucus (albumin or pituitary substance) is created in Aries. Working "on the square," it combines with Calcium to form the basic parts of the body. No cells can be formed without it. In the proportion in which Calcium combines with albumin, is the resulting physical substance hard or soft. Both kinds are needed.

Any deficiency in lime results in excess mucus or albumin, for the latter has become non-functional. It works when it has sufficient lime to work with. Excess mucus is the cause of colds, the so-called "germ" for which science has so long been searching. A cold is Nature's method of housecleaning—she eradicates the mucus. Those who over-eat, and who consume large quantities of mucus-making foods, frequently have colds.

From lack of Calcium phosphate, mucus collects in the tonsils, thus causing them to enlarge. The tonsils should not be removed, for the free use of this salt, together with the assistance of the surgeon (Silicea), will eventually bring about a normal condition. Sometimes they become so diseased that they are tubercular, fall away in pieces and are raised with sputa. Nevertheless these two salts, with the addition of Calcium sulph, *will* restore them to health in about ten months.

Albumin or mucus (waste mortar) may collect in the thyroid gland. This is the cause of goiter. It may be intensified by nerve impingements in the cervical region. Manipulations and massage are very helpful because they stimulate the circulation.

Lack of iodine is not the cause of goiter, but Calcium phosphate deficiency. Iodine is not a constituent of the body, for the very good reason that it is an *irritant*. The Great Chemist and Architect never made use of irritants in the construction of the human body. It is man who has induced irritants into the Temple of God, and he continues doing this, no matter what is said. Iodine is no more a constituent of the body than is hydrochloric acid, for both are irritants. All the twelve chemical elements of the blood are alkaline; and, in addition, the Libra salt, Natrium phos, or sodium phosphate, is especially furnished in order that humanity may have some means of neutralizing the acid made by wrong eating, indigestion from worry, etc., etc.

A third and extremely important use of Calcium phos is by the digestive and assimilative organs; for, when Calcium phos is low, these organs are unable to do good work. When it is extremely deficient, scarcely any food digests. Cell starvation and anemia of the blood result. People do not seem to understand this statement, even when it is clearly explained; for they invariably ask: "What food shall I eat in order to obtain this form of Calcium?" When the digestive fluids are starved in this salt, it is utterly impossible to digest *any* food even though it contains Calcium salt. IT HAS FIRST TO BE RELEASED BY DIGESTION. Therefore, if the food is not digested, IT IS NOT RELEASED, AND THE ONLY MEANS OF OBTAINING IT IS TO TAKE THE CALCIUM PHOS TABLETS. This is the great mistake made by so many interested in the study of food chemistry, especially those who claim that the right kind of food and proper diet will cure anything. They are not informed relative to the nature of Calcium or to the absolutely necessary part it plays in the digestive fluids.

An outstanding example of the truth of the above, which is more or less world-wide knowledge, is the case of King George V of England. His was a case of semi-paralysis of the organs, and mal-nutrition. Many physicians of the old school were in attendance, but it remained for Dr. Dodds, Professor of Biochemistry in a London University, to find that his blood was very low in Calcium. On being given this salt, digestion improved, and through assimilating the food he began slowly to improve, where, previous to its administration, no improvement was noticeable. However, the King requires many more of the salts, to correct the symptoms to which he is subject. He is subject, among other symptoms, to pneumonia, bronchitis, and pleurisy; but his right lung, and especially the pleura of that lung, is much weaker than the left. His blood is watery, due to Natrium sulph need, and yet it also contains lumps of fibrin, due to his Kali mur deficiency. His system lacks oil, because of Kali sulph need, and he is subject to ptomaine poisoning, because of these two potassium combination deficiencies. He is also extremely deficient in the electrical salt, Kali phos, and because of this, tends to suffer from paralysis.

It can not be too often emphasized, that THESE SALTS ARE TAKEN INTO THE BLOOD AT ONCE, AS NO SEPARATIVE PROCESS IS NECESSARY. They are free salts, and instantly go about their work. Many, in commenting on the salts, say that the blood can not take them up. My sixteen years' experience with them in my own family, and with the thousands I have contacted, is sufficient proof that they are at once utilized by the blood. Indeed, I will make an even more emphatic statement and say that NOTHING ELSE WILL DO THE WORK THAT THESE LITTLE MINERAL WORKMEN, THE CELL SALTS, ACCOMPLISH IN THE BODY. THIS METHOD IS THE COMING SYSTEM. IT IS BEING HASTENED BY THE PRESENCE OF NEPTUNE, THE PURIFIER, IN VIRGO, THE HOUSE OF HEALTH. The perversion of health methods is slowly passing, together with all other perversions.

Only by means of astrology are we able to become cognizant of the relationship existing between the Macrocosm, or body of the universe, and the body of man. Thus we are at any time able to discover in what part of man Nature's forces are acting or operating, and just what effect is being produced. This also explains the presence and nature of epidemics.

Dr. Carey states, in his *Biochemic System of Medicine:* "Phosphate of lime is destined to play a prominent part in the treatment of the sick, when its range is understood by medical practitioners. This salt works with albumin, carries it to bone tissue or to any part of the body where it may be needed. It uses albumin as a cement to build up bone structure.

"Bone is fifty-seven percent phosphate of lime, the remainder gelatine, an albuminoid, gluey substance, carbonate of soda, magnesium phosphate and sodium chloride."

When non-functional albumin (due to lack of Calcium) is thrown off via the kidneys, Dr. Carey says "wise (?) men call it Bright's disease."

Acid naturally results when food is not properly digested, also when excess food is consumed. This salt will remedy it.

A few of the many symptoms arising from a deficiency in this salt are: poor memory; incapacity for concentrated thought; weak minds in those practicing or who have practiced self-abuse (Kali phos and other salts are also required); fear; panic; desire for solitude; cold feeling in the head, also tight sensation in the head; skull thin and soft; crawling sensation over head; dropsy of brain; loss of hair; inability to hold up the head; eyes sensitive to artificial light; aching of eyeballs; swelling of glands in scrofulous persons; nasal polypi; cold in the head and albuminous discharge; anæmic, dirty-looking face; pimples on the face; feeling of coldness and numbness; bad, disgusting taste in the mouth, especially in the morning, and very fetid breath; decay of teeth (Calcium phos will improve the teeth, hardening them. Dentists invariably comment on the improvement manifesting in this respect, in their patrons, and usually ask what has caused it); pale gums; tongue stiff and numb; enlargement of throat; goiter (other salts are also required); chronic enlargement of the tonsils; sticking pain in throat on swallowing; constant hoarseness; rough, hoarse voice in children; pain after eating —food seeming to lie in a lump; food causing distress; abnormal appetite; sinking or faint feeling in stomach; palpitation of the heart and weakness; pain in the bones; all bone troubles; articular spinal irritation; injuries to the base of the spine or coccyx; convulsions in teething children; bones easily broken; *stunted growth;* cellular disturbances; restless sleep, etc., etc.

A few words of comment on self-abuse are necessary. As this salt is required by the body in far greater quantities than any other, it will surprise the readers of this book to learn that it has recently been discovered, by actual analysis, that there is more Calcium in the *procreative fluid* than in the blood itself. The scientists responsible for this finding state that they are "non-plussed." They can not understand why there should be more lime in the semen than in the blood. Biochemistry alone enables one instantly to explain it. It is the chief *building* material. This proves, indubitably, that IT WAS NEVER CREATED TO BE THROWN AWAY—TO MAKE NOTHING OF.

In making this invaluable discovery, those responsible for it have unknowingly furnished still another means of verifying the statement made in Dr. Carey's writings and in my own, relative to the necessity for the conservation of the procreative fluid. In the present stage of the evolutionary process of humanity, it is solely for the purpose of procreation. EVENT-

UALLY IT WILL ALL REVERT TO THE USE ORIGINALLY INTENDED—BEFORE THE FALL. IT WILL ITSELF RECREATE THE HUMAN BODY.

In Latin, the word for Calcium is *calx*, meaning (in addition to lime) end or goal, and *attainment*. It also means heel. As the meaning of the latter is end, it also is apropos. How remarkable, then, Dr. Carey's allocation of this salt, which means end or attainment (the closing or concluding part), to Capricorn, which is the end of the old year and the beginning of the new. A Janus who "looks back," *wastes his Calcium*, but also the Janus who looks forward—who aspires—builds his Temple of God on LIVING LIME-STONE. The Great Pyramid of Gizeh is an age-long memorial of this fact.

"Each thing bears within itself the seed of its own regeneration.

"It is the Tincture or Medicine which is the LIFE of life in man, the seed of regeneration.

"Prithee, what madness binds you, when WITHIN NOT WITHOUT YOU is all that you seek outside instead of within you."—Sir Thomas Vaughan.

CHAPTER XI

THE ANALYSIS AND SYNTHESIS OF AQUARIUS AND NATRIUM MUR.

"And the Spirit of God moved upon the face of the waters. And God said, Let there be light; and there was light."

—*Genesis* 1:2-3

THE Sun enters the zodiacal sign Aquarius on approximately January 21, and remains until February 21. In its journey, it covers the last week in January and the first two weeks of February.

It is obvious that the work of Janus, which is the END of a process, and hence the commencement of another, must be followed by a cleansing or purification, since the Latin lexicon informs us that the latter is the meaning of the word February. In ancient times, the Romans held the festival of purification at the end of this month, symbolical of the fact that the process had been completed. The story however, is associated with the first decan of Pisces, and must therefore be considered in the next chapter.

February is derived from *februo*, a Sabine word. According to Mr. Brewer, "the Dutch used to term the month Spokkel-maand (vegetation month); the ancient Saxons, Sprote-cal (from the sprouting of pot-wort or kele); in the French Republican calendar it was called Pluviose (rain-month)."

The word Aquarius is derived from the same root as *aqua*, which is Latin for water. The meaning of Aquarius is Water-bearer or Cup-bearer. Its glyph is a very ancient symbol of water. The exoteric significance of this sign is, that when the Sun is transiting Aquarius, the moisture in the air is released and precipitated in the form of rain. The releasing Sodium sulphate vibrations in the Sun's rays offset those of the *retaining* Sodium chloride vibrations in the air. No more water can be retained, for the saturation point has been reached.

Synthesizing all of the interpretations that we have obtained thus far, we find no variation. It is obvious that the months of the year were named according to the particular and intimate work of Nature during these periods. It must also be remembered that the Sun's course through each sign is definite and unalterable, *following an established geometrical plan.* (See chart—Cosmic and Microcosmic Embryos).

Madam Blavatsky states that "the whole expanse of Heaven was called the 'Waters of Space' or the 'Celestial Ocean.' The name very likely comes from the Vedic Varuna, personified as the water god, and regarded as chief Aditya among the seven planetary deities. In Hesiod's *Theogony,* Ouranos (or Uranus) is the same as Cælus (Heavenly) the oldest of all the gods and the father of the divine Titans."

The Titans were analogous to the rays of the Sun, hence creative power. Greek mythology gives an account of the struggle or war between the Titans and the children of Kronos (Saturn), which is analogous to the everlasting contention going on today between the lower mind and the Higher Self. It is indeed one of Titanic proportion.

If the foregoing chapters have been understood, it will not be difficult for the reader to solve the following story from Greek mythology: "As Uranus destroyed his children by confining them in the *bosom* of the earth, Tythea, so Kronos at this *second stage* of *creation* destroyed his children from Rhea, by devouring them."

A few comments, however, will be helpful in refreshing the memory. The children of Uranus (heaven) are the Erotes, or electrical nuclei, the seed germs of life, which can not yet be seen with the microscope. They are the winged spirits of life. The belief is, that they are not destroyed, but retarded and restricted by being confined. For they take on human form as they enter Cancer—which pertains to the breast or bosom; also to the stomach and spleen. Then, at the *second stage,* these human corpuscles are taken *down* (fall) by Saturn into Tartarus (the Titans fell from heaven into Tartarus—hell). This means that in Scorpio they are conjoined with *animal* germs.

As Spirit is never LOST, the physical constituents of the animal corpuscles (procreative germ cells), if not USED in forming the body of a child, disintegrate. They go back to the earth from whence they came, while "the Spirit returns to God who gave it."

There is direct reference to this fact in the Scriptures, for, in John 3:5, we read: "Jesus answered, Verily, verily, I say unto thee, Except a man be born of water and of the Spirit, he can not enter into the kingdom of God."

And the sixth and seventh verses confirm our foregoing statements: "That which is born of the flesh is flesh; and that which is born of the Spirit is Spirit. Marvel not that I said unto thee, Ye must be born again."

No one can be born again until the MATERIAL IS FURNISHED WHICH IS NECESSARY IN THE PROCESS.

Additional information relative to the water glyph of Aquarius is available from many sources. It is curious that it is an *inverted* letter m. This is indicative of the fact that the waves of fluidic or humid air, intermixed with ether, are in *inverse position* in the heavens to the waves of water on the earth. This is esoteric.

A study of the letter m reveals the esoteric significance. The facts given relative to this letter in the chapter on Virgo, and again in that dealing with Scorpio, prove that its basic interpretation is Mare, or the Great Cosmic Mother. It is *fluid* containing all the chemical elements in solution.

In Aquarius we find them resolved back to a more etheric state than on the lower or earth plane. In other words, Mother has truly merged into her Son, for it is the "sign of the Son of Man." Mary has ascended *with* Jesus.

In the human body this has reference to the cleansed and chemically perfect BLOOD SERUM, for Aquarius, physiologically and anatomically relates to the saline solution of the blood, and also to the ankles. It likewise pertains to the last two vertebræ of the sacrum and the first coccygeal vertebræ. The only correspondence given to us in works on astrology, is its relation to the ankles. Its allocation with the SALINE solution of the blood and to the vertebræ is the result of much research work.

On page 269 of the second volume of the *Secret Doctrine*, we are informed that "Uranus was mutilated by his son Kronos, who thus condemned him to impotency." Naturally, when the Divine Fire was stolen from Heaven (Uranus), it was analogous to wounding him; and, if none were RETURNED, impotency, or the power to generate more winged electrons, eventually ceased.

"It is electricity, the one LIFE at the upper rung of Being, and Astral Fluid, the Athanor of the Alchemists, at its lowest; God and devil, good and evil," says Madam Blavatsky.

She further says of water: "For the Lotus and Water are among the oldest symbols, and in their origin are purely Aryan, though they became common property during the branching off of the fifth race. Let us give an example. Letters, as much as numbers, were all mystic, whether in combination or each taken separately. The most sacred of all is the letter M. It is both feminine and masculine, or androgynous, and is made to symbolize WATER, the great deep, in its origin. It is mystic in all the languages, Eastern and Western, and stands as a glyph for the waves, thus in the Aryan Esotericism, as in the Semitic, this letter has always stood for the waters, *e. g.*, in the Sanskrit MAKARA—the tenth sign of the zodiac (Aquarius) means a crocodile, or rather an aquatic monster associated always with water. The letter MA is equivalent to, and corresponds with, number 5—composed of a *binary,* the symbol of the two sexes separated, and of the *ternary,* symbol of the third life, the progeny of the *binary*. It is also the initial letter of the Greek Metis or Divine Wisdom; of Mimra, the Word or Logos; and of Mithras, the Monad, Mystery. All these are born in, and from, the great Deep, and are the Sons of Maya—the Mother; in Egypt, Mouth, in Greece Minerva (divine wisdom). Mary, or Miriam, Myrrha, etc.; of the Mother of the Christian Logos, and of Maya, the mother of Buddha. Madhava and Madhavi are the titles of the most important gods and goddesses of the Hindu Pantheon. Finally, Mandala is in Sanskrit 'a circle,' or an orb. The most sacred names in India begin with this letter generally—from Mahat, the first manifested intellect, and Mandara, the great mountain used by the gods to churn the OCEAN, down to Mandakin, the heavenly Ganga."

Madam Blavatsky also refers to the Biblical statement that Moses was "drawn from the water." Water is also a reminder of the three Marys. "This is why in Judaism and Christianity the Messiah is always connected with Water, Baptism, the *fishes* (the sign of the zodiac called Meenan in Sanskrit) and even with Matsya (fish) Avatar, and the Lotus."

In Hebrew, Ur, the root of Uranus, means *light;* also fortress or castle. Ur or Hur means the mother of bitumen, which would seem rather far-fetched, did we not know that bitumen is a form of petroleum, and hence a source of light and heat.

All the Hebrew names commencing with Ur have some interpretation relative to light. Uriel means the fire of God; Urijah, flame of Jehovah, the Uriah, light of Jehovah.

The uræus, which was the serpent emblem of Egyptian divinities and kings, was placed on head-dresses as a symbol of sovereignty. The positive interpretation of serpent is wisdom, therefore *mental light,* the light of intelligence.

The Romans gave the name Aquæ, "waters" to sites where mineral springs issued from the earth.

How many students of astrology have ever analyzed the fact that, of the twelve signs of the zodiac, eight are animal, three human and one inanimate? There is no work in existence, at least no translation of any old book or manuscript, dealing with this subject; for, together with everything else (except mathematics), the fundamental and esoteric analysis of the signs and all that pertains to them has been perverted. What little was known concerning them gradually faded from the race consciousness. And because the race consciousness *as a whole* does not yet wish to concern itself with *pure and unadulterated astrology, it will be seared and blinded by the lightning of Uranus.* For we are now in the Day of Uranus, and all that concerns the heavens and man will soon be uncovered. We may not look forward to it, but nothing can prevent it.

It will be recalled that the symbol of Gemini is the twins; that of Virgo the Virgin; that of Aquarius the heavenly man, the Son of Man, holding an urn from which the Water of Life is pouring upon the earth. The nature of the man is essentially heavenly—the LIGHT is being disseminated—etheric waves shortened, thus producing more powerful currents. The urn in the hand of Aquarius is Saturn. In astrological lore, Uranus and Saturn are co-rulers of this sign, another secret which has never been analyzed.

As Saturn is always concerned with SEED, the water in this urn must contain seed, and it does. Again the reader must be reminded of the necessity of studying anatomy and physiology. The blood serum, as before stated, is the *saline* (sea water) solution which vitalizes the blood corpuscles swimming in it. This serum is, therefore, the salt sea of the body in which live the physiological FISH, for the CORPUSCLES ARE FISH IN THE HUMAN SEA.

It is necessary at this point to state that Dr. Carey allocated Natrium mur or sodium chloride, with Aquarius. Most people are aware of the fact that it is what is commonly called *salt.* Dr Carey says: "A combination of sodium and chlorine forms the mineral known as common salt. This mineral absorbs water. The circulation or distribution of water in the human organism is due to the chemical action of the molecules of sodium chloride."

It is a fact that this salt does absorb water, but it is not its first or basic nature. Indeed, it possesses a far more subtle and portentous attribute. It has the power to ATTRACT water, therefore *actually to draw it to itself*—to become *one with it.* This is true of the SPIRIT, the LIGHT within the darkness of human ignorance. As long as the Spirit remains in the body, it is a candle shrouded in darkness. But it eventually draws to itself, if allowed to do so, *the materials with which to make a light.* Emphasis, then, must be placed on the *power of attraction* which this salt possesses.

When the cells in certain areas of the brain (cerebrum) are exceedingly deficient in this salt, and the corpuscles (fish) die, reason itself dies. Astrology proves itself, if given a chance to do so; for if the charts of the greatest criminals were studied in the light of astro-physio-chemistry, astrology would be acclaimed as a synthesizer of all sciences. Many of the world's noblest and most outstanding characters were born when the Sun was in Aquarius; while, on the other hand, terrible malefactors have acknowledged it as their Sun sign. The pairs of opposites is one of Nature's methods of displaying her wealth and her poverty.

The inanimate symbol of the Scales or Balance cries aloud to High Heaven that humanity MUST ATTAIN BALANCE—THE PERFECT OR NEUTER STATE.

In the maps of the heavens which have pictured these signs of the zodiac from remote times, we find that the Water of Life from the urn of Aquarius (the Heavenly Man) is being absorbed by the Southern Fish, one of the two constituting the sign Pisces. Humanity has never been left in the dark by the Great Architect of the universe, for in very truth He gave man His candle and said "LET there be LIGHT." He said, in effect, ALLOW, or ENABLE the light to be produced. This astounding picture of the fish eagerly drinking the Water of Life, is symbolical of the positive or human corpuscles being allowed (because furnished with it) to drink of the vitalizing and perfect blood serum. No further proof is needed.

In the blood stream are found the two fishes, the positive or GOLD FISH, and the negative or SILVER FISH. The former is analogous to the fish named John Dory, which is a corruption of *jaune adorée*, "the adorable or sacred yellow fish." Tradition says of it, that it was the fish from which St. Peter took the stater (a gold coin, therefore "coin of the realm"). In his *Dictionary of Phrase and Fable*, Mr. Brewer states that "this fish was called in French *le poisson de St. Pierre;* and, in Gascon, the golden or sacred cock, meaning St. Peter's cock. Like the haddock, it has a remarkable oval black spot on each side, said to be the fingermarks of St. Peter, when he held the fish to *extract* the coin."

Further information relative to these two fishes will be given in the next chapter.

As fish, which are natural habitants of salt water, cease living when removed from it, so do the physiological fish die when sodium chloride falls far below its normal quantity.

The word ewer is another synonym for urn, a jug to carry water. From its root is derived the word ewe, or adult female sheep. As the letter W is replaced in Hebrew by two V's, we find that Eve is derived from the same source. As she was the "mother of all living" and is analogous to Aries, the Lamb of God, the ewer as well as the ewe is truly the source and origin of the Water of Life. *"Feed* my sheep," Jesus longingly cries.

It is obvious that the urn of Aquarius (Sat-urn or urn of seed) is analogous to the pans or urns of the Scales of Libra. BOTH MUST BE FILLED WITH SEED.

A little-known expression is "ewe-neck" which is used in referring to horses having *thin,* insufficiently arched necks, suggesting those of sheep. How interesting to find that one of the outstanding modalities indicative of lack of Natrium mur, or sodium chloride, is *a thin, emaciated neck.* Many people having the Sun in Leo are examples of this fact, as anyone can prove by observation. The tissues of the neck do not contain sufficient fluid.

In Ecclesiastical History, the Aquarians were one of several sects of Christians, such as the Encratites in the primitive church, who used *water* in the Lord's Supper. An encratite, according to the Dictionary, means *self-disciplined,* one who abstains from *Marriage, Wine and Animal Food.* It is evident, therefore, that there have been, in times past, those who "made of themselves eunuchs for the Kingdom of Heaven's sake."

In the Babylonian Creation-Scheme, "Aquarius was As-a-an ('the Curse of Rain') and the story of the Flood is the legend especially connected with it". In Euphratean astronomy this region of the sky was actually called the *Sea.* Aquarius was also Gula ('The Urn') and Gusisa ('The Directing-urn').

In Sumerian and Akkadian lore, this sign was known as FISH-OF-THE-CANAL. As a canal is supposed to contain water or fluid, we have here verification of the statement previously made, that the corpuscles in the blood are truly the fish in the human canal.

Candlemas, the name for the ancient church festival, celebrated annually on the second of February, was in commemoration of the presentation of Christ in the Temple. In the Greek church, it is known as "the meeting of the Lord;" in the west, as the Purification of the Blessed Virgin. It is the most ancient of all the festivals in honor of the Virgin Mary. In the second half of the fourth century it was kept on February fourteenth. As Virgin Mary is analogous to pure fluid, Candlemas Day is no doubt analogous to the second of the three stages (beginning with Capricorn) in the premanifestation of Spirit, otherwise its journey from the invisible into the visible. The period from Capricorn to Aries covers this journey.

Richard Allen, in his *Star-Names and Their Meanings,* says of Aquarius: "New Testament Christians of the sixteenth and seventeenth centuries likened it appropriately enough to John the Baptist, and to Judas Thaddæus, the Apostle, although some went back to Naaman in the waters of the Jordan, and even to Moses taken out of the water."

He further states that "we find it, too, as Aristæus, their Elijah, who brought rain to the inhabitants of Ceos, the Cecrops, from the cicada nourished by the dew, whose eggs were hatched by the showers. The great Grecian lyric poet Pindar asserted that it symbolized the genius of the fountains of the Nile, the life-giving waters of the earth. Vergil called it FRIGIDUS, because it closed the year with moisture."

That astrology has been in evidence much longer than is

generally supposed, Richard Allen points out, continuing with Aquarius: "In Babylonia it was associated with the eleventh month Shabatu, the Curse of Rain; and the Epic of Creation has an account of the Deluge in its eleventh book, corresponding to this eleventh constellation; each of its other books numerically coinciding with the other zodiacal signs. In that country its URN seems to have been known as GU, a Water-jug overflowing, the Akkadian Ku-ur-ku, the Seat of the Flowing Waters; and it was also Rammān or Rammānu, the God of the Storm, the still earlier Imma, shown pouring water from a vase, the god, however, frequently being omitted. Some assert that Lord of Canals is the signification of the Akkadian word for Aquarius, given to it 15,000 years ago, when the Sun entered it and the Nile flood was at its height. And while this statement carries the beginning of astronomy very much further back than has generally been supposed, or will now be acknowledged, yet for many years we have seen Egyptian and Euphratean history continuously extended into the hitherto dim past; and this theory would easily solve the much discussed question of the origin of the zodiac figures if we are to regard either of these countries as their source, and the seasons and agricultural operations as giving them names.

"In China, with Capricornus, Pisces and a part of Sagittarius, it constituted the early Serpent, or Turtle, Tien Yuen; and later was known as Hiuen Ying, the Dark Warrior and Hero, or Darkly Flourishing One, the Hiuen Wu, or Hiuen Heaou, of the Han dynasty. It was a symbol of the emperor Tchoun Hin, in whose reign was a great deluge; but after the Jesuits came in, it became Paou Ping, the *Precious Vase.*"

Because Aquarius is heaven, it represents, naturally, the whole science of astronomy.

As the vibrations of Aquarius possess powerful virtue, influence and efficacy, it is evident that they alter the air and the seasons in a very strange and secret manner. Reference has been made in other chapters to the fact that our solar system has entered the sign of Aquarius. Therefore it naturally follows that great and drastic changes along all lines will slowly materialize. Beliefs and opinions, held because they were those of our forebears, are fast going into the scrap heap of old ideas. Study and concentration, a wish *to know,* brought about by the initial stirring of the *Inner Man,* will eventually present the *reasons for things* to the consciousness of mankind.

It is interesting to note here that Leo, the *beast,* is at the opposite end of this pole. In very truth are the Divine Man and the animal man antitheses of each other—one positive, the other negative.

Some astrologers attribute to Aquarius an aqueous blue. But, in the color chart presented in connection with this book, violet is allocated with it. As the blood serum is associated with this sign (as before stated), it is easy to understand whence came the expression "blue blood" or "royal blood," since the color of this sign is a kingly one. The sedative qualities of blue are well known.

Ganymede, the Cup-bearer of the gods, has ever been a symbol of Aquarius, in Greek mythology.

Mr. Spence says of Ganymedes, the cup-bearer of Jupiter: "He holds the cup or little urn in his hand, inclined downward; and is always pouring out of it; as indeed he ought to be, to be able from so small a source to form that river which you see running from his feet, and making so large a tour over all this part of the globe."

In Greek mythology we find the following interesting description of the cup-bearer of the Gods: "Ganymede was the son of Tros, King of Dardania and Callirrhöe. He was the most beautiful of mortals, and was carried off by the gods (by Zeus in the form of an eagle) to Olympus to serve as cup-bearer. By way of compensation, Zeus presented his father with a team of immortal horses (or a golden vine). Ganymede was afterwards regarded as the genius of the fountains of the Nile, the life-giving and fertilizing river, and identified by astronomers with the Aquarius of the zodiac. Thus the divinity who distributed drink to the gods in Heaven became the genius who presided over the due supply of water on earth."

We find in the name Ganymede the explanation of his office. Gany is derived from the same root as the Sanskrit Ganga or Ganges. The Ganges is the principal sacred river in India. The Sanskrit Glossary states that "There are two versions of its myth; one relates to Ganga (the goddess) having transformed herself into a river, flows through the big toe of

Vishnu;* the other, that the Ganga drops from the ear of Siva into the Anavatapta lake, thence passes out through the mouth of the *silver cow*, crosses all Eastern India, and falls into the Southern Ocean. 'An heretical superstition,' remarks Mr. Eitel, in his Sanskrit and Chinese Dictionary, 'ascribes to the waters of the Ganges *sin-cleansing power.*' No more a 'superstition,' one would say, than the belief that the waters of Baptism and the Jordan have 'sin-cleansing power.' "

The above statement goes to prove that all nations and people possess, in their literature and Sacred Scriptures, the same allegories and myths found in the Bible. Naturally so, as they refer to the same thing.

The first part of the name Ganymede, therefore, refers to a sacred river or cleansing stream. Mede is an old form of mead and refers to wine, honey, sweet drink or one made of *manna.* It is clearly analogous to the cerebral *esse* which forms the basis of all the fluids of the body.

The reward Zeus gave his father to compensate him for his son's removal to heaven, is analogous to the Higher Mind (horses) become awakened because of the return of the Wine of Life (son of the Father) to its heavenly (cerebral) source. In very truth, the fluid which waters the Garden of Eden (the head) goes down to water the earthly body. The Son of Man has often been termed "the Water of Life."

Ganymede was the son of Tros which word is identical with Tau-rus, for T in Hebrew is spelled TAU, and ros is really rus, which means DEW or manna. It must be noted that o and u have been used interchangeably in the past. The "son of dew" is the product of dew, in other words increased dew. Callirrhöe is a Latin word meaning beautiful flow, therefore PERFECT RHYTHM, while Dardanus means produce of Jupiter and Electra, or an electrical current. These two names are analogous to a beautiful or perfect fluid endowed with the fire of life. This is exactly the nature of the saline solution of the blood when in a perfect condition. Biochemistry (Schuessler's) informs us that this solution is a VITALIZING fluid, because Natrium mur is a vitalized (electric) salt. The latter has the power to increase vitality, and those in whom it is very deficient are devitalized. They arise in the morning tired, sometimes more weary than on retiring. Sleep has not refreshed them because of the fact

*Note: The water of Aquarius indeed flows into and through Vishnu, the Southern Fish of Pisces.

that the blood corpuscles themselves were unable to be revitalized during the cerebral rest.

Natrium mur is by nature a catalyst.

Some accounts state that Ganymede was Deucalion, son of Prometheus, who was translated to heaven in memory of the mighty deluge, from which only he and Pyrrha were saved. As Pyrrha means fire, and Deucalion means celestial stone, it is obvious that the blood stream is referred to, particularly since it is said that Deucalion and Pyrrha repeopled the earth after the deluge by throwing *stones* backward over their shoulders.

Aquarius is associated by the Kabbalists with the fourteenth letter N, or NUN. This letter literally means Jesus or fish, and is therefore apropos.

In Hebrew Scriptures this letter is allocated with *temperance.* This furnishes much food for thought. As Aquarius is concerned with the Heavenly Fluid, not only watery but fiery, *the fluid which tends to devitalize mankind,* it is evident that any *fluid* which tends to *devitalize him* is *bound to be banished.*

The following statement is not in the nature of a prophecy, but the scientific working out of a problem. The solar system has entered into the sphere or atmosphere of Aquarius, and therefore everything will be permeated with that atmosphere. As a result, all that is impregnated with it will slowly but surely commence to *vibrate with it.*

The generally accepted interpretation of temperance is *total abstinence from liquor.* An archaic meaning is SELF-CONTROL. Naturally this means that the lower self is subject to the Higher Self. One can not even imagine the God-Self in man suggesting that he drink intoxicating liquor.

The word intoxicant means that which POISONS WITHIN. Its use changes the *temper,* the nature, of man at once.

The *aqua pura* or purified and chemically perfect Water of Life, as stated before, is *vitalizing.* Fire water, which is the old Indian name for alcoholic beverages, is *devitalizing.* Under its effect mankind becomes helpless. The intelligence ceases to function; and, instead of acting as a human being endowed with the Spirit of God, man descends into the depths.

The clarion call of Nature and Nature's God to mankind has now gone forth. The Son of Man *in* man demands his own, and will no longer be denied. His cry is, "Cease torturing me, cease drying up the River of Life with products of fermentation. Cease wasting!"

When one realizes that the fluids of the body in the average person are poisoned with the toxic products of fermentation, the result of overeating and wrong diet, it is no wonder that the alcohol within the human body cries out for company. Few realize how they handicap themselves in this way. They actually create the *tempter* within their own bodies.

Alcohol is a poison because it is not a NATURAL constituent of the human body. The *best* medical practitioners are ceasing to use it. The other class advise its use.

The great trouble with mankind is, that with the brain cells chemically disorganized and filled with toxic poisons, it is mentally and nervously distraught, and finds itself utterly unable to raise its vibrations. As a result it deliberately lowers them.

It is encouraging to find many who are realizing this, and hence are doing everything in their power to improve the character of the body cells. As a result, they are assisting Nature to work out the salvation of mankind. Our brain cells are none too good—let us improve them, instead of doing that which injures them daily.

Lack of temperance means that the sword of character is not tempered to withstand—there is lack of self-control. Wars and strife, civic and national, can not entirely disappear until the very cells of the body cease their continual turmoil and warfare, fighting and struggling to get out of and away from the debilitating, disorganizing and devitalizing fluids surrounding them. These are truly the chemical result of man's ignorance.

And so the fiat has gone forth. Liquor MUST GO. It is not a matter of what any of us *wish,* it is the definite working out of a law. Nature is preparing now to specialize in a certain definite work which has not been done for twelve times 2160 years, not since the previous entrance of the entire solar system into the sign of Aquarius. Naturally this can not be accomplished in one generation. It can not be done until a sufficient number have suffered enough from the effects of the use of liquor, and until excessive eating ceases. This is why gluttony is given as the first obstacle to entrance into the kingdom of Heaven (harmony-health).

It is not liquor alone which must go, but everything that in any way is detrimental to the creation of the New Man. All will slowly but surely be removed.

As mechanical inventions pertaining to the air and unseen forces are constantly being brought forth, keen, clear, alert minds must direct them. Otherwise disaster results. Old Dobbin would see that his master arrived home safely, even though the reins were wound around the whip which never left its socket. But mechanical conveyances must be guided efficiently, otherwise physiological disorganization swiftly follows.

The Aquarian Age is that of aviation, and eventually we will find airships constructed of very light material, air tight and capable of rising far up beyond storm areas, where they will travel at far greater speed than is now imaginable. We do not yet dream of what is possible for the air-minded genius to create.

The consciousness of man *must* expand. His head *must* be lifted up, he *must* see the Sun, the stars, the *light*, at last. Note how the Spirit, cabined, confined and all but submerged, is nevertheless causing man to do the very thing which will eventually *create* the *habit* of looking upward! Even our perverted system of commercialism is not without its good points; for, acted on by the vibrations of Aquarius, man is becoming *Air-Minded.* He is using illuminated airplanes at night for advertising, and radio broadcasting from planes in the daytime. Handbills are dropped from planes, thus covering a wide area in a short time. Speed is demanded in all things, speed to keep pace with radio waves.

All this has come about since Uranus neared Aries, which it entered in 1928 and in which sign it will remain until 1935, its stay being seven years in each sign. Re-read the chapter on Aries in connection with this. Those who have hitherto thought and spoken disparagingly of astrology, should be convinced, after reading this book, that it is a legitimate science and a very noble one. They will not be blamed for their former opinions, since the esoteric side of astrology has been considered very little. This will be changed, however, as earnest astrologers become more and more air-minded.

In presenting the facts concerning which astrology alone furnishes explanation, another curious phase of advertising must not be omitted. The use of lighting effects, both white and colored, and especially the latter, has become general. This also owes its inception to the approach of Uranus into Aries. Buildings have been given HEAD lights, and their intriguing beauty has served and is serving to attract the attention. Thus color has been brought into prominence.

So penetrating and far-reaching are the vibrations of Uranus, that its effect is felt long before it enters a sign. That "Future events cast their shadows before," is quite true. The brilliant diamond of the white light of intelligence is broken up by mental processes and *angles* of thought, into all the colors of the spectrum. As Uranus literally shakes heaven and earth, so does it stir up the minds of men.

Who is there who does not love color? The less dull and heavy and the more clear and pure it is, the more it attracts.

As Pisces pertains (among other things) to the feet, when Uranus the great iconoclast and disturber of customs, beliefs and opinions (not of *truth*), entered the sign of Pisces in 1921, styles in footwear were subjected to a startling change. Shoes in all shades and colors resulted. Aside from a very few light colors for evening footwear, the standard colors up to that time were black, brown or gray. Never within the memory of the oldest person living has there been such colorful covering for feet.

And as Uranus neared Aries in 1928, a very unique change resulted. For, recalling the fact that the serpent with its tail in its mouth (thus forming a circle) is the ancient symbol of the cerebral hemispheres, serpent-skin shoes appeared and became very popular for a time, the use of this skin extending to bags, coats, etc., etc.

The explanation of all this is, that each sign of the zodiac is related to certain definite matters. A particular work is done, and as each planet enters the sign the work is done *in a certain way,* taking on various shades and colorings.

It is not difficult to realize that the effect of Uranus in Aries is to loosen, to shake up, to scatter. But it must be realized that it does not affect that which is heavenly, high, pure or true. So we are encouraged by the thought that, while at present humanity seems to be in a chaotic condition, it is merely because it is being shaken out of its former uncertain (because perverted) ideas. When we were mentally blind, we *thought* we were happy. Now that we are being aroused from our lethargy, we are beginning at last to dream of what PEACE is like.

All cycles of seven are potent. A common example is the Moon cycle, or period of 28 days (four times seven). Every woman is aware of this. Its influence, however, extends throughout all nature. The seven days of the week, and the seven planets, are examples. There are many more. The cycle of Uranus is seven years. The position of this planet in the horoscope of any individual, is the key whereby new and decided changes in his life may be studied. This can be done by noting the planet's position every seven years on the birthday.

This process of analysis can be brought down to a fine point by using the two and one-half degree divisions mentioned several times in these pages.

The following is the method:

Suppose the birthday falls on January 1, and the year of birth was 1880. The present age (1931) is 51. If the mind is clear and memory good, outstanding events may be recalled which occurred at the age of 21, and some may be able to think of much earlier happenings which made decided impressions on the mind. Begin by looking up the position of Uranus on January 1, 1929, which would be the seventh cycle. The seventh birthday represented the close of the first cycle, and the forty-ninth birthday the end of the seventh cycle. As the eighth occurs in 1936, the middle of the present year (1931) would represent half a cycle and a very gradual change in affairs would be noticeable.

Returning to the illustration, it is found that on January first, 1929, Uranus was in three and one-half degrees of Aries and in the Taurus vibration. (The first two and one-half degrees are decidedly those of Aries). As Taurus relates to possessions, not only concrete but abstract (mental), this analysis, allocation and synthesis of times, seasons and events, will be very interesting. It will invariably be found that the mental trend at that time was toward things of a Taurian nature. Physiologically, a disturbance in the fluidic content of the cerebral cells would be likely to occur, as well as other symptoms.

Those completing a seven year cycle this year will doubtless note disturbances and changes in respect to health, employment, relatives, partnerships and marriage; for Uranus has been traveling back and forth between the Virgo and Libra degree of Aries, causing decided upsets.

Whether these cycle recurrences will bring about positive and constructive, or negative and destructive, reactions, depends entirely, as before stated, on one's chemical condition. A deficiency in the mineral content of the blood prevents all parts, and any one part, of the physical machinery from being able to set up the same vibration which Uranus manifests. If no deficiency existed (which is true of none yet) great happiness, peace and true prosperity would manifest.

As Uranus means change, we need not fear, as many do, that the world is to be destroyed, which is the common interpretation of "the end of the world." The word world is derived from whorl, circle, or cycle.

It is indeed true that the earth itself is now changing, as anyone can see merely by reading the newspapers. But greater changes are in store. Uranus' journey through Aries is affecting the opposite sign Libra. The scale pans are wobbling, the balance point is quivering. At this time, the earth's balance is being checked by the mighty cosmic power. In its readjustment, some parts of the globe will go down, while at the same time islands will appear; new continents will rise; land will be purified, restored, refreshed. "And there shall be a new heaven and a new earth." This will be literally and physiologically true.

Since Heaven reflects all that takes place on earth, the minds of men and women are affected, unconsciously or otherwise. The result is, that their thoughts revert to old events and occurrences. An example, at the present time, is the fact that an expedition has started out to explore the region around the Azores, and to make extensive soundings with the express purpose of endeavoring to check the disappearance of a large continent called Atlantis. Plato referred to this continent in his writings, which proves that this myth is merely the ghost of something very substantial.

This is truly the time when we must choose whom we will serve, for we can not have two masters. One will be loved and the other denied.

To be capable of looking up, to be able to endure the brilliancy of highly vibrating colors, we must stand on our own feet, physically as well as mentally. Thus a clear brain, a clean and active liver, and a strong heart are absolutely necessary. Otherwise one will become faint and dizzy. Gluttony, drinking, drugs and sexuality are degenerating and devitalizing. We are dealing with physiological facts, not ideas nor opinions.

One of the interpretations of Aquarius is, that it has to do with *friends*. One's best friend is the Spirit of God within. The kind of treatment this Best Friend receives depends upon one's physical and mental reaction. Therefore, Shakespeare's splendid admonition, "to thine own self be true and then 'twill follow as the night the day, thou cans't not then be false to any man," is very apropos here. The statement that Aquarius relates to friends, refers first and foremost to this Friend within.

Hopes and wishes form another interpretation of this sign. Our hope is in Heaven, in the Holy of Holies within the cerebrum, the place of potential light and peace, the home of the Spirit. What each one wishes, is entirely in keeping with his mental ability to choose what is best for him. The popular slogan, "learn to get what you want" is a perversion of the real issue, and exceedingly misleading and pernicious. It eventually will be heard no more, along with many of its companion slogans.

Mr. G. A. Gaskell says of Aquarius: "It is a symbol of the eleventh period of the cycle of life. It signifies the buddhic vehicle of the Spirit, as the container of Truth (water) from the fountain of Divine Reality. It refers to the rise of consciousness through the lower buddhic plane, far advanced in the present period of evolution."

The same writer refers to the Fountain of Waters as "a symbol of the source of Life, as an outpouring of Truth from above."

John Milton, in *Areopagitica,* says: "Truth is compared in Scriptures to a streaming fountain; if her waters flow not in a perpetual progression, they sink into the muddy pool of conformity and tradition."

"In the beginning this (world) was water. Water produced the true, and the true is Brahman."—Brihad, *Upanishad,* V. 5, 1.

"I am the great God who created himself, that is to say, I am Water, that is to say, No, the father of the gods, or as others say, Ra, the creator of the names of his members which turned into the gods."—*Papyrus of Hunefer,* XVII.

"And the more learned among the priests think that Homer, like Thales, had learned from the Egyptians to lay down that Water was the beginning and origin of all things, for that his Ocean is Osiris, and his Tethys Isis, as nursing and helping to breed up all things."—Plutarch, *Isis and Osiris.*

"Water and earth—these were the two elements out of which the old inhabitants of Eridu believed the world to have been formed. It was the theory of Thales in its primitive shape."—Sayce, *Religion of Ancient Babylon,* p. 139.

"Water is the first element in the mundane system of the Chinese."—Kidd, *China,* p. 161.

"The emanation which produced the creation of the universe is like water gushing out from its source and spreading over everything near."—*The Geberol,* Myer, *Kabbalah,* p. 195.

"For the Man Regenerate is always the transmutation of the 'water' of his own Soul into the 'Wine of the Divine Spirit.' "—*The Perfect Way.*

The above quotation is the explanation of turning water into wine. The idea that Jesus wished to provide refreshment for the guests at the wedding in Galilee, and so manufactured wine on the spot, is absurd. What is more, it could not possibly have had any bearing on religion, or aided in any way whatsoever in purifying mind and body. On the other hand, when one understands that it refers to the cleansing and transmutation of body and mind, he sees the story's inestimable value.

In the light of all that has been here given relative to this sign, its ruling planets, etc., it should not be difficult to see why Aquarius has two rulers, Saturn and Uranus. For the former is analogous to seed, or the fertile corpuscles (fish); and the latter, Uranus, is the Spirit which vitalizes the water of Aquarius. Saturn rules the "night" or material side or interpretation of the sign, while Uranus rules the "day" or Spiritual nature. Charts must be studied with this in mind.

Dr. Carey's allocation of Natrium mur or sodium chloride to this sign, is at once seen to be correct. As stated before in this chapter, it must always be borne in mind that sodium chloride is the ATTRACTOR of water. As the physical body is practically 97 percent water (or to be accurate, watery or fluidic), it is evident that a large quantity of this salt is always required in order that the physiological functions may proceed as they were originally intended.

Dr. Carey says of this salt: "With the exception of phosphate of lime, the human system contains more sodium chloride than any other inorganic salt. The reason for this may be readily understood when we realize that our bodies are about 70 per cent water, which, in the absence of sodium chloride would be inert and useless. It is the power that this salt has to use water that renders it of any value to man. The same holds good in plants and vegetable life."

As the body must be flushed with water in order to carry off the waste products, it is necessary as a catalyst, and therefore is equally needed in tearing down as in construction.

Uranus rules vaporous or moist air in the head, so that this part of the anatomy becomes greatly disorganized when the sodium chloride content of the blood becomes very low. In whatever part of the body circulation is very slow (which may be determined by Saturn's position), either insufficient or excess fluid will be noted. When too little fluid is present, the brain tissues become dry, and one suffers from insomnia. The head is quickly affected by the hot rays of the sun, and this must be guarded against, for they draw what little water remains. Sodium chloride is, therefore, the remedy for sunstroke. The situation is similar in delirium tremens, for the water content is broken up by the great alcoholic content. Therefore sodium chloride must be administered in generous doses. When there is too little fluid in the head and the upper parts of the body, there is usually (although there are exceptions) too much in the extremities. The ankles and limbs are likely to swell, and dropsical tendencies may develop.

When the brain tissue contains too much fluid, it causes drowsiness, and tendency to fall asleep when the mind is not occupied with something interesting. The medical profession will learn, not long hence, that the mysterious disease termed "sleeping sickness" is not caused by any one of the following list of microbes kept on the physician's visiting list: distomum hepaticum; distomum lanceolatum; coccidium lanceolatum; coccidium oviform, echinococcic polymorphus; bothriocephalus latus; that "Freebooter of the highway" (as Dr. Carey terms it), ankylostomum duodenale; dochimus tringoncephalus and stenocephalus. There are others, constituting a long list of terrifying names for which Latin lexicons have been searched. The cause of "sleeping sickness" is easy to trace because of the clear light that astro-biochemistry throws on it. The brain contains a great excess of fluid, therefore THOUGHT IS ACTUALLY SUBMERGED, LITERALLY DROWNED.

Many of those deficient in Natrium mur (very frequently those born when the Sun is in Leo) either do not care for water, or are unable to retain it long after drinking it. This is easily explained by the fact that the cells of the body do not contain sufficient sodium chloride particles to *attract* water. Hence, when it enters the stomach, they are not present to seize upon and carry it around and distribute to the parts requiring it.

Lack of thirst—no desire to drink water—arises from the same cause. When a sufficient number of Natrium mur particles are present, their call for water manifests in thirst, and constitutes a decided *chemical pull.* It is easy to understand that a person whose blood is sufficiently supplied with this wonderful salt, would not succumb so easily to thirst when traveling in the desert and lacking a water supply. Some moisture would be drawn from the air, especially during the night.

The human body slowly becomes parched and dry when this much-needed salt diminishes in quantity. The brain fluids decrease, and this organ and gland becomes unreceptive to any downpour of heavenly dew.

So, too, with the soil which lacks this salt. The ground becomes arid and barren, for nothing can grow without absorption of water. In those parts of the country where irrigation is made necessary by lack of rain during the growing season, if the soil were supplied with sodium chloride in the proper proportion, much more moisture would be obtained at night from the atmosphere. The sodium chloride in the soil would actually aid condensation, and in the morning vegetation would be found to be quite damp. This would decrease the need for irrigation, which in itself constitutes quite a saving.

There is a soil food which has not been generally known but which has been in use many years, not only in this country, but abroad. It is called Stone Meal. It is obtained from a composite rock, which, by analysis, is found to contain all the mineral elements necessary for a chemically balanced soil. It is thus capable of producing chemically perfect food, perfectly to nourish mankind. It is ground to a very fine powder.

Insects and pests are conspicuous by their absence when

the mineral content of the soil is balanced, for healthy products result. Hence there is nothing to support the life of these scavengers of nature, and they disappear, or go to other fields where decaying matter exists.

Splendid endorsement is given Stone Meal by all who conscientiously test it. It is stated that, even in times of drought, gardens supplied with it flourish, while those not thus fortunate become parched and dry.

Those engaged in the business of supplying this Stone Meal to all who are interested in using it are real humanitarians. They are indeed benefactors of mankind. The late W. N. McCrillis, of Boston, Mass., was the original dispenser of this splendid product. The business has been recently reorganized under the name MENDERTH, INC., with offices at 126 State St., Boston. It is backed by F. H. Bennett, the altruistic founder of the Wheatsworth Line of real whole wheat products.

In addition to soil deficiencies practically over all this country (in itself a great calamity), humanity is still further handicapped because of the denatured food which has flooded the markets. So great is the greed and avariciousness of those who have no consideration for their fellow-men, that it is refreshing to find individuals not of this character. Many years ago the author heard of these two products, Stone Meal and Wheatsworth, and because of their similarity, in a way, to the work of Dr. Carey and herself, made it her business to investigate both.

Wheatsworth products, consisting of whole wheat flour, cereal and crackers, are made from the best hard wheat obtainable, cleaned and ground in the unique old mill which has been modernized by Mr. Bennett. The old water wheel is still used. The mill and Gingerbread Castle are interesting and instructive show-places in Hamburg, New Jersey.

The Gingerbread Castle of Hansel and Gretel, executed in poured concrete, is a New Age method of advertising, since the sole object of its construction is to assist in educating potential citizens (the coming generation), relative to their need for brain and body-building food. Mr. Bennett's products are all of this nature. The idea of building this unique castle occurred to him when he saw the original, designed by the famous architect, Joseph Urban, for the stage setting of the second act of the opera, "Hansel and Gretel."

The author offers this book not only as a memorial to Dr. Carey, but to Julius Hensel, to the author of Bread and Roses From Stones, to Mr. McCrillis, Mr. F. H. Bennett, and all others who are mineral-minded or altruistic chemists, for surely in no better way can humanity be helped to stand on its own feet. Mineral is MOTHER, and Spirit (energy) in Nature and in man, is unable to manifest without it.

Returning to the subject of the effect on the body due to Natrium mur deficiency, we find that a very prevalent symptom is eczema. This salt is almost a specific for this trouble, but the fact must never be lost sight of, that the astro-chemical analysis alone will furnish the accurate key to any condition; for, as stated before, there are always four salts which must be used for any symptom. The work on *The Biochemic System of Body Building and Astro-analysis,* which will be published in a few months, will deal with all phases of this subject.

Calcium sulph should be used in connection with Natrium mur to relieve the burning, which latter constitutes a modality indicative of deficiency in Calcium sulph. The intense itching is a Natrium mur modality. To the degree in which Ferrum phos is deficient, will inflammation and soreness accompany the other forms of irritation. Again, the flesh fibers themselves may be involved, and the "spinning salt" Kali mur be greatly needed to form the foundation fibers or threads of flesh.

A solution made of these salts, and applied to the irritated parts, soothes and heals miraculously. It must be remembered, however, that all skin troubles are caused by impure and therefore deficient blood, and that the exterior parts of the body will be unblemished when this is remedied. No outward application will serve to correct that which is caused by blood deficiencies. It is true, however, that the salts are actually pulled within, and greedily taken up by the starving cells.

Deficiency in Natrium mur causes one to feel very weary and tired on arising in the morning, sometimes more so than on retiring. This is likely to result in irritability. No pep or vitality manifests until long after the morning sun has dissipated the vapors of night. Rainy days are actually trouble-breeders for these people, and this holds good also for those needing another form of sodium, that of Natrium sulph. The entire body lacks tone and vitality.

All symptoms caused by lack of this salt are productive of either too little, or too much, water in certain parts. The following are some of them: too little saliva or too much, which will be frothy; mouth and tongue dry and parched, especially in the morning; delirium, with muttering and wandering; stupor and sleepiness; delirium tremens; despondent moods; sun-stroke; dull, heavy and hammering headaches; neuralgic pains in the eyes, and flow of tears; flow of tears when associated with cold in the head; dandruff; eruptions on the scalp, with watery contents; blisters anywhere on the body; smarting secretions from the eyes; fresh colds with transparent mucus and sneezing; hay fever, influenza. It must be stated here that hay fever and "rose" cold—any of these very unpleasant conditions which are supposed to be caused by the pollen of certain plants, are due solely to certain mineral deficiencies which naturally cause the vascular linings to be insufficiently protected. Thus any particles may cause irritation. But as for blaming plants for it, one might as unjustly blame the Sun for causing weak eyes to burn and water.

Other symptoms are: swelling of glands under the tongue; blisters on the tip of the tongue; constant spitting of frothy mucus; inflammation of the mucus lining of the throat (a common symptom); sore throat with excessive dryness; too much secretion; thin neck; all diseases of the stomach where watery vomit is present; very great craving for salt. It must be here stated that common table salt consists, for the most part, of particles too coarse to be taken up by the blood corpuscles. Therefore the blood is unable to obtain the quantity needed. These coarse particles often act as an irritant in the stomach and intestinal tract. Especially is this true of those with low Calcium sulphate content, for the vascular lining of the organs, including the intestinal tract, is quickly irritated by these salt particles, and "running off of the bowels" frequently results.

Other symptoms arising from this need are: stinging piles; catarrh of the bladder; diabetes; chronic gonorrhœa; chronic syphilis; itching skin; asthma; pleurisy; pulse rapid and intermittent heart beats felt all over the body; blood thin and watery; anemia; "fidgets"; joints cracking and creaking; hysterical spasms and debility; restlessness and twitching of the muscles; stings of insects; dropsy and many others too numerous to mention here.

CHAPTER XII

THE ANALYSIS AND SYNTHESIS OF PISCES AND FERRUM PHOS.

"Jesus is a fish that lives in the midst of the waters."
—*St. Augustine.*

ON approximately February 20, the Sun enters the zodiacal sign of Pisces to remain until March 21. This period covers the last week of February and the first two weeks of March. Therefore the process of purification covering the first two weeks of February is consummated in the last week, and the *Water of Life now becomes the Wine of Life.*

The sign Pisces is said, in astrological lore, to pertain to the feet, physiologically, and is concerned with the following matters: enemies, prisons, hospitals, limitations, the sea, water and all places of *confinement.* But while there are many old manuscripts in existence dealing with astrology, as Robert Brown informs us in his *Researches into the Origin of the Primitive Constellations of the Greeks, Phœnicians and Babylonians,* they have never been translated into the English language. No modern work on astrology has given the esoteric meaning of this sign, or explained WHY it has to do with prisons, hospitals, or with places of confinement, etc.

The reason is made plain in analyzing the word *March,* in which month the largest part of this sign falls. It is derived from the Latin word *margo,* meaning *boundary, confine, border, edge, limit, attainment, mark,* or *extremity.* Each of these interpretations supplies a vast amount of information relative to this sign.

Pisces is the LAST sign of the zodiac and MARKS the point or BOUNDARY where the circle of life is cemented together. It is even more than this—IT IS LIFE ITSELF.

"And God breathed into man the *Breath of Life* and he *became* a *Living Soul.*" An infant may be born with a seemingly perfect body, but unable to breathe. When a pulmotor is unable to initiate breath, it is because the chemical medium or contactor of oxygen is extremely deficient. The mother of the child is unable to furnish its blood with the required amount to start the breathing process. Ferrum phos or iron is the inorganic salt required to attract oxygen into the lungs; therefore Dr. Carey's allocation of this substance to Pisces, is a splendid proof of his intuition. It is a chemical fact that never can change.

To return to the analysis of the word March, we find that the word extremity is frequently used when speaking of the feet. The feet are the extremities. Pisces is the last sign, the foundation on which the entire body rests. If the feet give no trouble, one can stand on them without causing them to feel tired. One can also travel far, indulging in long walks.

Metaphysically, Pisces relates to *understanding*. When the understanding is active, one can travel far mentally.

In Pisces, we find the gauge by which all life is measured, the mental, moral and physical standing, or development. It is the *mark* (peg) which indicates the stage or place which one has reached on his journey. The three decans of this sign represent respectively DEGENERATION, GENERATION and REGENERATION. A very few are living the law necessary in the present phase of evolution. Spirits must return into physical bodies to work out salvation, which literally means to PERFECT THE VEHICLE—therefore, bodies must be supplied.

"Only one in 999,999," says Madam Blavatsky, "is really engaged in the GREAT WORK, that of endeavoring to become PERFECT."

The above statements prove that the words *mark, attainment,* or *goal* apply to Pisces. Therefore, when a life of degeneration is indicated, it is obvious that no ideal, no mark, no goal of attainment is considered. There is no foundation, no moral or physical stability by which and on which a strong, enduring, permanent structure may be erected. Instead of a mark or goal, it is THE END OF LIFE.

Astrological lore informs us that Pisces stands for the END OF THINGS. As *heel* means *end* (the heel of the loaf), this is the reason why the back part of the foot, which is the end of the body, is termed the heel. The head is the beginning of the body while the extremities constitute the end.

So man, in his *last extremity,* cries aloud to the Son of Man to save him, to Jesus, who (St. Augustine, one of the old Christian fathers, states) is "a FISH WHICH LIVES IN

THE MIDST OF THE WATERS." This will be dealt with further on in this chapter.

Pisces is interpreted as confinement. This is because it is analogous to the deep, the bottom, the pit. Below this, no one is able to go. When the depths have been reached, one is obliged (if life remains in his form) to place the feet on the first rung of the ladder, to raise the consciousness ever so little, and to endeavor to look up. Naturally his dull eyes can not bear the light yet, and indeed very little light is able to penetrate the darkness. But he is *going toward it*, which is the all-important fact.

The word march means to *set out*. This refers to a great mystery, for there are two journeys which may be considered. One is inevitably chosen. The first is the *setting out* of the Spirit into physical manifestation, from the realm of the invisible. Orders are received to enter again into the material body, and begin the *March of Life* once more—to begin again the work of *building* a better vehicle.

The combined vibrations produced by the planets in certain positions, are the means whereby the Spirit is once more drawn to earth. The previous form or instrument used in its last incarnation, is the means of deciding what the next must be. For the work must be taken up where it was left off. Nothing else is logical. Another school day has begun, and there are lessons to learn.

Thus from the realms of the unseen the Spirit prepares to manifest again, entering the arterial system of the mother through the breath. Unless the reincarnating Spirit is present, conception can not take place, for what is true of spiritual conception and birth is also true of physical conception and birth; the only difference being that one is on a higher plane or level.

The statement in Matthew 1:18, expresses the fact that the Spirit must be present. "Now the birth of Jesus Christ was on this wise: When as his mother Mary was espoused to Joseph, BEFORE THEY CAME TOGETHER, she was found with a child of the Holy Ghost." As Holy Ghost literally means *perfect breath*, the correctness of the above will be seen. In the Latin lexicon we find that the reference may be to the shade or ghost of a particular person.

Much research has revealed the fact that Pisces has to do with the ARTERIAL BLOOD, for it is the blood into which air or oxygen enters (this refers to the moist air of

Aquarius, the Water of Life). It is purified by both and has become transmuted into the WINE OF LIFE, the true blood of the grape. The entering of air into the blood via the lungs has been previously referred to as the miracle at the marriage feast, when Jesus turned water into wine.

Pisces, then, stands for the end of a cycle of Spiritual existence BEYOND THE VEIL, and the entrance of the Spirit into a new body.

It also refers to the fact that the Spirit leaves the body at death. Breath ceases—no more oxygen enters the blood through the lungs. The process of combustion and purification ceases, and, as a result, decomposition sets in. The Spirit which held the mineral particles together (the matrix or nucleus of each cell) departs, for it has not been supplied with sufficient material to enable it to remain. "Can a man rob God, but ye have robbed me in tithes and offerings."—Malachi 3:8.

"For the life of the flesh is in the blood; for it is the blood that maketh atonement for the soul."—Lev. 17:11. Here is a concrete statement, it is physiological and chemical. When all the mineral elements which constitute chemically perfect blood are present in the veins and arteries, the blood is in a state of at-one-ment and therefore is able to make *atonement* for the *soul,* which is the sum total of the etheric fluids, those of nerves and glands.

Disease (lack of at-one-ment) or deficiency (sin) is the cause of death. Otherwise none would die. To think one can step out of the picture and thus rid one's self of the task of perfecting the human body (which was planned to become a church), is to side-step the issue. It can not be done. Reincarnation will take place again and again until the task is completed. Then, as the Scriptures state, we shall "GO NO MORE OUT."

How little the majority think. The newspapers tell of a man's death. He was "in perfect health" up to that moment. God or Providence "called" him. These statements would be funny if they were not so pathetically lacking in logic. Barring accidents, it is utterly impossible for one in perfect health (if such exist) or even in moderate health, to pass on. The Creator made laws relative to right living; and, when they are disobeyed, the physical and mental processes deteriorate, the intake of vital electricity decreases, and death inevitably results.

Blood, composed as it is of chemical elements, IS MATTER. If the blood is the life of the flesh, how, then, can matter be dead and without life, as some claim? Such a viewpoint is contrary to actual scientific findings. When one considers that each kind of mineral may be seen vibrating with life, and emitting certain definite colors, the statement that there is no life in matter is absurd. That which is termed matter is the coarsest (per se) form of Spirit, while the latter is the finest of matter. Therefore there is only ONE THING. One may call it matter or Spirit, mother or father. They are, in essence, one and the same. In Latin, matter is *mater* or mother, the formative substance. The latter word is derived from the Latin *substare,* meaning *to stand under.* Matter is, then, the *foundation* of life. As matter *stands under* Spirit, it is its SUPPORT. Vice versa, Spirit supports matter.

As we look about us, we see trees, hills, mountains, valleys and rivers. We see moving objects. We observe, also, the handiwork of man, as well as that of God. What makes this possible? MATTER. Otherwise there would be nothing to look at AND NO EYES TO LOOK WITH.

How frequently we read this advertisement—"Come and learn how to breathe correctly and thus improve the health." It will be consigned to the mental scrap-heap after the study of life chemistry. "God breathed into man the breath of life, and he became a living soul." What does this mean, what is its interpretation? Divinity or Spirit enters man through the breath. Breath *is* Spirit.

It has been explained that Ferrum or iron is a powerfully magnetic salt which has a tremendous affinity for oxygen. Oxygen seeks to combine with iron wherever found. This is the explanation of the entrance of ether into the depths of earth. Iron is there to *pull it within.* And so, too, in the depths of the human or earthy body there must be the full quota of iron to attract sufficient Spirit fully to energize each atom. Otherwise they perish, one by one.

Man breathes easily, freely, fully, unconsciously, when there is no deficiency in iron (Ferrum). God (Spirit) in him does the breathing. On going out doors where there is more oxygen, the process at once becomes deeper. One never thinks of the breath until hampered by insufficient iron.

Here we have the scientific explanation for the feeling of depression and discouragement. There is a certain definite air pressure within the body, in health, and in the light of chemical knowledge we know it is due to the iron content in the body. When this remarkable salt is very deficient, it naturally follows that the air pressure ON the body far exceeds that within. This causes a feeling of oppression or depression. The psychologist is unable to explain the cause or to offer assistance in eliminating this symptom. To call it a "complex" buries it literally out of sight. Without biochemistry it IS too "complex" ever to be solved.

It is interesting to note that the word frontier, which is one of the interpretations of March, is derived from the Latin *frons,* meaning forehead or countenance. In architecture it has reference to the *face* of a building. Pisces is adjacent to Aries, which latter is the countenance.

A marcher is one who treads the pathway of life. Marcus means hammer of Thor. This is analogous to the function of iron, for it emits *sparks.* Here we link up with the spark of life which is Spirit. We connect the circle of synonyms with the statement that iron, which emits sparks, draws in oxygen to complete and close the circle of life. The 360 links of the circle must be *forged* together.

To march, means also to travel steadily, to advance, to progress. It is a steady onward movement.

Some of the poets have sensed what is meant by the march of life, for instance Pope, in the following:

> "The long, majestic, march, and energy divine."

while Bryant describes the month of March in these words:

> "The stormy March is come at last,
> With wind and cloud and changing skies."

Neptune is the positive ruler of Pisces. In other words, it represents the rate of vibration which alone is capable of performing *true* Piscean work.

In the Latin lexicon *nepa* means water-scorpion. It also refers to the three water (fluid) signs collectively—Pisces, Scorpio and Cancer. This implies that germs of life are to be found in water, or, more specifically, in fluid of which water forms a part.

Nephale means a cloud, which of course is watery vapor. A nephalist is a total abstainer from spiritous liquor. This is essential if one wishes eventually to be able to create, and to respond to, the vibration of Neptune, the highest and finest force in the universe.

Neptune is the most remote planet in our solar system. Fourteen (twice seven) years are required for it to transit each sign, thus making the circuit of the zodiac in one hundred and sixty-eight years. All things in existence have been said to originate from water. This makes the true origin or source of anything, remote. The highest and finest vibration is naturally the farthest away from one's conception. It is analogous, therefore, to concealment. The negative interpretation of Pisces is therefore deceit. The positive signification is perfection and purity. Comparing these two interpretations, we easily realize that we are not yet able to claim any close association with Neptune. Indeed, humanity, as a whole, has not yet even touched the hem of its pure garment.

In Greek mythology Neptune is the sea, the divine monarch of the ocean. The Saxons called Neptune BEN. This is interesting, for it at once calls to mind the Hebrew interpretation of Ben, which is SON, one of the carriers of the Ark. Benjamin was the *thirteenth* child, and was born near Bethlehem—the "house of bread." This is analogous to Virgo, the House of the Virgin, whence came the Bread of Life.

The sixth house of the zodiac, and the sixth division of the human body, are perfected only because *all twelve* function perfectly, after becoming chemically perfect. Thirteen is analogous to the perfect thing created therefrom—therefore the SON. Until we are able to perfect the circle, we are *unlucky* because unhealthy, imperfect, and unclean.

The ancients pictured Neptune as having his palace in the depths of the sea, but he made his home on Olympus when he chose. As Aries is Olympus, the close relationship of these two signs is indicated. It is also analogous to the circulation of fluid from head to feet.

The symbol of Neptune's power was the trident, or three-pronged spear, analogous to the three decans of Sagittarius, the higher mind. This trident was supposed to be used to catch fish. But there is a much better interpretation. An old word for spear is sprawn, which is a crustacean. Neptune's chariot was drawn by two horses (Hippocampos) each having only two legs, the hinder part of the body being that of a fish.

He was the son of Saturn (Cronus or Kronus), which is analogous to saying that he represented the water in the *Urn*. There were two dynasties of the sea, Neptune representing the younger. The older, which flourished during the time of

Saturn, refers to the fact that the first appearance of water or fluid was in the brain pan, or urn. Greek mythology informs us that from this older dynasty sprang three thousand rivers, and ocean-nymphs unnumbered. The brain pan or skull contains, and is the fountain-head of life, receiving the precipitated etheric vapors which constitute the cerebral *esse*.

Athens was the chosen seat of Neptune as well as Minerva, which literally means that fluid as well as wisdom has its source in Aries. It is said in mythology that "these two deities, during the reign of Cecrops (source of wisdom) the first king of Athens, had contended for the possession of the city (place of wisdom). The gods decreed that it should be awarded to the one who produced the gift most useful to mortals. Neptune gave the horse (Higher Mind); Minerva produced the olive. The gods awarded the city to the goddess, and after its Greek appellation it is named." As the olive is the source of oil (Christ), the true interpretation of Minerva is the same as Virgo.

Neptune invades territory belonging to all the other gods—meaning that water penetrates everywhere and is present in all parts of the human body. He rules both fresh and salt water. He both protects and shakes the earth. The continuous oscillation of the latter is caused by the tremendous push and pull of water. When Neptune's waters become foul, monsters are bred. This is analogous to impure blood. Neptune is the special ruler of the arterial blood. As earth-shaker, he causes convulsions of nature.

Orion, the Mighty Hunter (man), is the son of Neptune—literally brought forth from the water.

The ancients pictured the two fishes of Pisces bonded together, the bond or ribbon running to Cetus, the Sea Monster, with one foot of the Lamb tangled in its double end. Pisces is also the god Dagon of the Philistines. It is the two fishes with which Jesus fed five thousand people.

A legend of this sign is, that "Venus and her son, Cupid, while sitting on the bank of the Euphrates, suddenly saw Typhon, the enemy of the gods, approaching them. They leaped into the river, and were saved from drowning by two fishes, who were afterwards placed in the heavens by Venus in gratitude for their help."

At last Venus and Cupid ascend into heaven—they are themselves the fishes, and are thus analogous to Neptune, or purified lives. As Venus and Cupid, they no longer exist.

As the last decan of Aquarius is ruled by Venus, being the Libra division of the sign, it *joins* Pisces. Venus, in the legend, is thus sitting on the bank of the river. The sea monster, which is an *enemy* of the gods, is carnality or lust. The two fishes of regeneration save them, and the transportation to heaven results.

"He (God) had his dwelling in the Great Sea, and was a fish therein."—Zohar.

"So many fishes bred in the waters, and saved by one great fish," says Tertullian of the Christians. (Blavatsky, *S. D.*, Vol. II, p. 327). It is obvious that the "many fishes" referred to above are the corpuscles or life-germs. "One great fish" is the man-fish, or Jesus, the Divine germ which is the product of a purified and regenerated mind and body. This simply means *being born again of water and the Spirit,* Pisces and Aries. The circle of life is at last forged together with an adamantine link.

"Oannes was 'an animal endowed with reason . . . whose body was that of a fish's with feet also below, similar to those of a man, subjoined to the fish's tail, and whose voice and language too were articulate and human' (Polhhistor and Apollodorus). The fish's head was simply a head-gear, the MITER worn by priests and gods, made in the form of a fish's head, and which in a very little modified form is what we see even now on the heads of the high Lamas and Romanish Bishops. The fish's tail is simply the train of a long, stiff mantle as depicted on some Assyrian tablets, the form being seen reproduced in the sacerdotal gold cloth garment worn during service by the modern Greek priests."—Madam Blavatsky in *S. D.*

The meaning of the foregoing is evident. The "fish" is an old and sacred symbol, frequently used in the Mystery-language. It always refers to the Divine germ, Jesus, the new man who is born of water and Spirit. The story of Jonah being swallowed by a fish (not whale) is symbolical of the real man submerged, swallowed up by the waters of DEGENERATION. IT LITERALLY MEANS THAT NO USE IS MADE OF THE CREATIVE FLUID.

In Smith's *Bible Dictionary,* we find that the word Dagon means "dear little fish, apparently the masculine correlative of Atargatis and the national god of the Philistines. Dagon was represented with the face and hands of a man and the tail of a fish. In the Babylonian mythology the name Dagon (Odakon) is applied to a fish-like being who rose from the waters of the Red Sea as one of the great benefactors of man. The fish-like form was a national emblem of fruitfulness."

Humanity is never truly fruitful until the Divine Son is born.

Fürst says: "The spiritual inspiration of God in man, gives spiritual power and physical life." The word inspiration means *to breathe in.* What better proof can be found of the correctness of Dr. Carey's allocations; for iron attracts oxygen, in which is the breath of life, that which elevates, lifts up, inspires.

Smith says, in his *Bible Dictionary*: "The secret of a true life is that a man should consecrate the vigor of his *youth* to God. It is well to do that before the night comes, before the slow decay of age benumbs all the faculties of sense." For, as the fluid of the body becomes depleted in iron, the corpuscles (fish-germs) slowly suffocate, and eventually putrefy. THIS IS THE TRUE CAUSE OF CANCER. Without iron, combustion can not go on. Kali sulph and Ferrum are, then, the legitimate cure for this putrid and virulent disease. This statement can not be found elsewhere.

It is very interesting to note that *Smith's Bible Dictionary* gives the definition of iron in Hebrew as *piety.* As piety is holiness and true godliness, it is very apropos. Religion is derived from the Latin word *religio* and means *to tie, to fasten behind, to bind back.* This is clearly seen as analogous to the joining of the circle, the forging of the link between Pisces and Aries. When the waters are perfected, purified, the cerebral fluids will become as crystalline dew.

In Latin, the word Ferrum is derived from the word *fero,* meaning to bear, to bring, to carry, and this is the true nature of this magnetic salt. It bears, brings, carries *Oxygen,* the breath of life, the Spirit of God in man.

Where strength and firmness are required, iron is used. Our strongest machinery is made of it. Iron and steel are used for the framework of buildings. Its use in the body is exactly the same—for *Strength.* Therefore, in attracting oxygen —SPIRIT—into the body, humanity is supplied with strength to endure, and to fight for the right.

The following information from the Encyclopædia Britannica verifies Dr. Schuessler's statement in his *Biochemic Sys-*

tem, that Ferrum (iron) as well as the other eleven salts ARE absorbed by the blood.

"Whether inorganic salts are directly absorbed has been a matter of much discussion; it has, however, been directly proved by the experiments of Kunkel and Gaule (*Archiv fur die gesamte Physiologie des Menchen und der Tiere,* lxi)." This should be read by those who, without testing conscientiously or taking the trouble to inform themselves relative to the findings of others, strenuously, and even angrily, deny that the salts are, or can be, absorbed by the blood. Certainly the extensive practice of Schuessler, whose work is known in many countries, and who has been honored in his own country by the erection of a splendid memorial, is evidence of the value of the science of biochemistry. He rediscovered and made it available to the people of this age.

Pisces corresponds to the tribe of Naphtali in Biblical lore. Smith's *Bible Dictionary* states that "Naphtali occupied a position north of the Sacred Tent." As it is obvious that this Tent is none other than Aries, we may rest assured that the allocation is correct. But we have another means of checking. Naphtha is derived from the same root as Naphtali, and as it means *a cleansing,* it is obvious that the arterial blood (which is the oxygenated blood) must contain a highly refined oil. As the word for oil in Greek is Christ, it is clear what is meant by the statement that "the blood of Jesus Christ cleanseth us from all sin." In very truth, the *great work* is for each one to so purify and perfect his blood that it *becomes the Christ blood.*

There is much Scriptural evidence to prove that the female is unclean during the period of the menstrual discharge. As long as generation persists, so does impurity, therefore adulteration. In this phase of evolution, humanity may be correctly termed "an adulterous nation." For as "without the shedding of blood there is no remission of sin," so until the female of the race ceases to shed the menstrual blood, and the necessity for furnishing forms for incarnating egos exists no longer, sin or deficiency, and hence adulteration, will not be done away with.

The menstrual or monthly blood is for THE HEALING OF THE NATION, the twelve tribes or twelve parts of the body. One of the most pernicious of modern-day teachings by certain cults, is the practice of endeavoring to bring about the continuance of this function, and to cause its recurrence after the menopause has taken place.

When no blood is shed there will be no sin to remit (forgive, give for, make good, return, supply).

The last two signs of the zodiac are the only ones having two rulers. While Neptune is the positive or spiritual ruler of Pisces, Jupiter rules its negative interpretation, and stands for the prodigal son (prodigality). In Biblical lore, the prodigal son had descended into the depths among the swine with nothing but husks for food. Eventually he said, as all will say: "I will *arise* and return to my father."

In the Babylonian Creation Scheme, we find that Pisces has several interpretations, such as: pregnant-woman, cord-place, fish, dusky-one, and great-dragon. In the Euphratean Planisphere, Pisces is Se-Kisil, and means: "The Sowing of Seed." This section of the heavens is termed the great deep, and many mythological denizens of the sea are found therein, such as the Sea-goat, the Dolphin, the Sea-monster, the Fishes and the Sea-horse. It will be noted that these cover the last three signs of the zodiac, and may be interpreted as moist earth, humid air and magnetized or vitalized water. In Semitic, Pisces was Nunu, which reminds us that Nun is fish, in Hebrew.

In the terminology of Catholicism, a Nun is the bride of Jesus, and may therefore be termed a female fish. She lives only to exemplify in herself that perfection which alone is responsible for the creation of the perfect being. She represents absolute purity of body and mind. Eventually all women and all men will realize that this is the ultimate ideal, and begin, at least, TO THINK about it.

It is interesting to note that the sign Aries lies within the boundaries of the sign Pisces, which is indubitable proof of their esoteric interrelation and the indissoluble tie existing between them. Even the Lamb must be nourished with fish. Aries must receive the food which is necessary for the Lord's supper, else there is no supper. The SHEWBREAD must be laid upon the table in the upper chamber.

This is the region of the vernal equinox, the exact position of which is a comparatively starless area. The Fishes are termed The Leaders of the Celestial Host. This expression will be better understood if the fact is recalled that the corpuscles are physiological fish and therefore the *multitude* (of cells) must be fed with them. Otherwise anemia and ultimate starvation will result.

According to Richard Allen, some of the early titles of Pisces are: The Fishes of Hea or Ia, Nuni and Zib, the latter name meaning boundary, as Pisces is the end of the zodiac. As Ia and Ja or Ya are synonymous, and represent the first syllable of the name Jehovah, the name Ia refers to the origin of life—the *beginning*.

Smith's *Bible Dictionary* states that "Zia was one of the Gadites" which links up again with Aries. Again, Zibiah is Hebrew for ROE, meaning the eggs of fishes. Atl was the Aztecs' name for Pisces. This reminds us that the name Atlantic is of ancient origin, and is derived from the Latin word *atlas*, meaning *to bear*, therefore to create or support. The Divine Fish or life germ within each corpuscle is its support. This is substantiated by the interpretation of Piscis Hori, the Coptic term for this sign, which Brown translated as protection.

It is appropriate to explain at this point why astrology has assigned enemies to Pisces. No explanation is given in any work on astrology. If the reader has given much time and thought to the consideration of these pages, a definite conclusion will have been reached. On being told that Pisces has to do with enemies many people ask: "If I am born in this sign am I supposed to make enemies?" It is regrettable that there are so few works on esoteric astrology at present available.

The true explanation of the word enemy in relation to this sign is, that an enemy is one who is hostile, an adversary, someone or something inharmonious. A true friend is exactly the opposite. Aquarius deals with friends—those who are humanitarian, altruistic, good. In respect to its physiological interpretation, Aquarius is the helpful, vitalizing saline solution of the blood, the Water of Life.

As Pisces is a female and therefore negative sign, it has to do with the basic creative *substance*. The corpuscles or fish in the blood are either harmonious (healthy), therefore friendly, or they are not. The diseased, unhealthy fish or corpuscles in the blood stream constitute true enemies of the body. The greater the number, the more pronounced will be the negative action of the brain. One's acts will therefore be such as to create enemies without. The true Piscean is gentle, kindly, Christ-like in thought and deed. It is obviously impossible for such a one to create an enemy.

When the blood stream consists of a majority of "enemies," it naturally follows that the cells of the body are inharmonious. Is it not logical that the mental activities will be *limited* and *confined?* One is capable of understanding very little, and therefore is unable to take any extensive mental journeys.

The more deficient and diseased the brain cells are, the more distorted and chaotic the actions. Is it, then, any wonder that confinement must inevitably result? Hence the need for prisons, hospitals and sanitariums. When the former are eliminated, the latter will be automatically done away with.

The Dark Warrior, as a name for Pisces, is appropriate, since the life or contending force is hidden within the germ cells.

Richard Allen says that the sign in ancient times meant only one fish, and this no doubt has to do with the "one and only," Jesus, THE "fish in the midst of the waters." When the positive and negative or male and female become harmonized or perfected, this long desired consummation will take place.

Revati, meaning Abundant or Wealthy, and Kwei or Koei —Striding Legs—are other ancient names for this sign.

Richard Allen also states that "The Greeks confounded this divinity with another Syrian goddess, Astarte, identified with Venus; who precipitated herself, with her son Cupid, into the Euphrates when frightened by the attack of the monster Typhon; these *becoming* two fishes that afterwards were placed in the zodiac. Latin classical authors, with the same groundwork of the story, make Pisces the fish that carried Venus and her boy *out of danger,* so that, as Manilius said,

"'Venus ow'd her Safety to their Shape.'"

The constellation was thus known as Venus et Cupido, Venus Syria cum Cupidine, Venus cum Adone, Dione and Veneris Mater, and also Urania, the Sarmatian Aphrodite. All this, perhaps, was the foundation of the Syrian's idea that fish were divine. They actually abstained from them as an article of food. Ovid repeats this in the Fasti, in Gower's rendering:

"Hence Syrians hate to eat that kind of fishes;
Nor is it fit to make their gods their dishes."

In the light of the information given in the preceding chapters, it is obvious that the above refers not only to fish as food, BUT MORE ESPECIALLY TO "EATING" OR CONSUMING, UNWORTHILY, THOSE GERMS OF LIFE WHOSE SOLE PURPOSE IS TO NOURISH THE GODS IN MAN.

This also explains why, in astrological lore, Venus is said to be *exalted* in Pisces, for this vibration has entered the waters and emerges purified. It is, therefore, at the point of mergence that Venus BECOMES NEPTUNE, for the latter is the HIGHER OCTAVE OF VENUS.

Venus is said to be in her *fall* in Virgo because it is the place of her *labor,* which she has entered as Mary Magdalene. She must *wash the feet of (Pisces) Jesus.* She thus begins the task which she consummates in Pisces. *Here She Ascends, is one with Jesus.*

The thinker, the earnest student and searcher for truth can not help but realize what this story is all about, and how inseparable are chemistry, physiology, religion and astrology.

The first decan of Pisces contains the cord or band holding the fishes and *held* by the Lamb, its double end fast to the neck of Cetus the Dolphin, which is sacred to the Sun.

In the second decan of this sign is Cepheus, a crowned King, as the great victor and lord, holding a band or scepter, and with his foot planted on the Pole Star.

The third and last decan of Pisces contains Andromeda, a woman in chains and threatened by the serpents in the head of Medusa. In the next, which is the first of Aries, we find Cassieopia. Here a few words of explanation must be given.

In Euphratean star-lore, Cassieopia, as she is termed, is Kasseba, or Lady-of-corn. In Semetic, she is Zir-banitu, the Creatress-of-seed. Both are easy to understand in the light of esoteric astrology. Corn and seed are synonymous, and in this instance are analogous to the cerebral seed, or electrical nuclei. Elsewhere in Euphratean star-lore, Andromeda is termed the Pregnant Woman, which is not difficult to interpret, since Neptune is the Virgin and thus truly becomes THE MOTHER OF GOD—ARIES.

The cord binding the two fishes is symbolical of the fact that they must not be separated, and that male and female must *become one* in order that the Lamb shall no longer be slain.

Piscis Australia, the Southern Fish, is seen "drinking," as Richard Allen states, "the whole outflow from the Urn. The idea of the Fish drinking the Stream is an ancient one, and may have given rise to the title Piscis aquosus, found with Ovid and in the fourth Georgic, which has commonly been referred to this constellation; Vergil mentioning it in his directions as to the time for gathering the honey harvest."

It is unfortunate that no information relative to the esoteric interpretation of the above is available. But those who have awakened to the true meaning of Aquarius and the Son of Man, will be able to analyze it correctly. The germ of life is no longer thirsty, because he has drunk the Living Water. As the bee is a symbol in ancient writings for *Spirit*, this water becomes the nectar and ambrosia prepared especially to nourish the indwelling gods, those having their habitation on Mt. Olympus.

In early legend, this fish (Australis) is the parent of the other two. Since it lies so close to Aquarius this may be true, but it is just as logical that it may be the progeny of the harmonized Northern and Western fishes. There is evidence of the latter in the fact that it was adored in Egypt, and has even been associated with the greater Oannes, the Fish God or Savior. Our poet Longfellow called it the Golden Fish.

"The Mosaicists held the asterism to represent the Barrel of Meal belonging to Sarephtha's widow; but Schickard pronounces it to be the Fish taken by St. Peter with a piece of money in its mouth," says Richard Allen.

The above will be seen as analogous to the Biblical account of the widow who took meal and mixed it with oil to make her cake. This is symbolical of the Virgin (pure material), mixing the refined oil with the meal or earth dust to make the Bread of Life (the fish or Divine Germ), which is, at one and the same time, both the Supper and the Lord Himself.

How curious that the Chinese termed it Tien Tsien, Heavenly Cash, which is logical and not far-fetched, since the perfected corpuscles or life germs *are true coin of the realm*, real treasure, which must be constantly laid up in heaven (cerebrum).

Mr. Gaskell says of this sign: "A symbol of the twelfth period of the cycle of life, which is the final period of evolution on the buddhic plane. At the close of the cycle, the Christ-soul (Jesus the 'Fish') becomes one with the Christ (Higher Self the 'FISH') or the redeemed souls become one with the Redeemer,—the lower consciousness unites with the higher."

"Possibly the 'Fish' symbol of early Christianity may be explained by Pisces. On the catacomb lamps there are two fish, one swallowing the other."—A Jeremias, *The Old Test.* Vol. I, p. 76.

"Pisces, the last of the signs, is represented by two fishes bound by a cord. Love and deep compassion is the real nature of Pisces."—Vanstone.

"Jesus as the Fish is a symbol of the Higher Self as the Savior of the human soul. The 'Great Sea' is the primeval 'water,' the symbol of Truth—Reality which outpours from the Absolute. The Higher Self abides and manifests in that Ocean of Truth; hence the symbol of the Fish, as the spiritual Life within the reality of Being."

Is it strange that the Scriptures refer to Jesus as the Lamb? Why does it also say "Jesus is a fish in the midst of the waters?" Is it not easy to understand that astrology alone has the great key to the mystery?

Here it is necessary again to mention Aries, for while Pisces relates to Jesus the Fish, the first sign of the Zodiac is concerned with the Christed-Jesus, the "Lamb of God which taketh away the sins of the world." "A symbol of Christ as the Divine sacrifice for the benefit of humanity. The young ram (Aries) is a world-wide symbol of the sacrifice of the Higher Self in entering upon the cycle of manifestation," says Mr. Gaskell.

To explain more fully, the Higher Self is cabined and confined. It is in this vehicle simply because the latter must become perfect. It has not made an adequate machine for Spirit to use. The meaning is not clear until explained physiologically and chemically. The Spirit sacrifices its *time,* so to speak, waiting for the body to be made perfect. A better understanding may be gained by likening the Spirit in the body to the power which runs a machine. If anything is wrong with the latter, the work can not be done properly. Power is not to blame. The machine must be attended to. It must be repaired.

Mr. Gaskell further says that "Jesus being a generic name, with varieties such as Joshua and Jehoshua, it is requisite that it should be allocated to a particular described type before it may bear a symbolical meaning."

"Who shall descend into the deep? (that is, to bring Christ up from the dead). Romans 10:7. All are dead until Christ is risen—Christ in each and all."

In order to rise, a higher vibration—that of expansion—is necessary. In order to breathe, oxygen must enter the body. It has already been proved that Dr. Carey correctly allocated Ferrum phos or iron with Pisces.

The beginning of form is in Aries. As the Sun passes through the signs of the zodiac, a certain form of construction work goes on in each, and eventually the twelve parts are completed. After nine months' gestation, the child is born, and if there is sufficient iron in the blood cells of the lungs it will breathe, otherwise not.

It is said of iron that it is one of the most important, and one of the most abundant, metals in nature. It has been known from the earliest times. Tubal-cain was said to be an artificer in metal. The iron found in the earth generally contains nickel, and is said to be of meteoric origin. The author feels certain that it was the presence of this type of iron in the water, which led to the discovery of the new energy ray by Dr. Milliken, and it should have been named "the Ariean-Ironic Ray."

Where experiments concerning this ray take place in lake water fed by glaciers, much better results will be obtained, for the reason that meteoric iron, which the author prefers to term etheric iron, for such it must be, is naturally precipitated in snow. This is the explanation back of the statement that "snow is the poor man's fertilizer."

It is logical and, with astrology and biochemistry as means of proof, irrefutable, to believe that the air and especially the higher stratas are filled with invisible specks or atoms of Ferrum. Many people can even see them, but have thought it some defect of vision.

The geometrical plan of man within the circle, places the feet over the head. This is also true of the child in utero. It must naturally follow, since all that is true of the macrocosm is true of the microcosm, the latter being of small proportion only. Therefore the watery ether above is filled with the smallest particles of iron, the same as the iron in the earth and in man's body.

Without iron there would be no means whereby ether could penetrate either into man's body or the body of the earth. Let us analyze the word iron or Ferrum, and find the solution of its secret. Its Latin term is Ferrum and it is derived from the root of the verb *fero,* meaning *to create, to form, to bear, therefore to give birth to.* Is any further proof required that it is the salt necessary for the existence of all things? *It actually bears life—carries life.*

The word fervor is derived from the same root, and means boiling heat. Ferocious means fierce, rough, rude, uncontrolled energy. Ferox is Latin for courage, good sense, high *Spirit.* This latter definition verifies the explanation previously given in this chapter relative to the fact that one is weak, low-spirited, discouraged and disheartened when the iron content of the blood is low; and strong, high-spirited, energetic and *alive* when the blood is well supplied.

As energy must be *tempered* with gentleness, so must iron become tempered, in order that it may be elastic, not hard and unyielding. "Steel resembles iron very closely, being distinguished from it only by the remarkable property it possesses of being extremely hard and brittle when heated and suddenly cooled. By cautious re-heating, the brittleness thus acquired may be diminished, the steel becoming highly *elastic;* this process is termed tempering." (*Inorganic Chemistry,* by George F. Barker, M.D.)

It should not be difficult to understand why many of the symptoms which will be given forthwith arise from deficiency in iron. Nor does it require much thought to realize that a good disposition is the result of a nature which has been tempered like steel. With the *natural* quota of iron in the blood, and hence in the cells of the brain, one is not upset by anything. One does not become angry with another. The feelings and emotions are not aroused to *fever* heat—and, by the way, the word fever is derived from the same root. Is it, then, curious that Dr. Schuessler should credit Ferrum or iron with being a specific for fever? Its use produces marvelous results. And why not, since it actually brings an increased supply of Spirit or Cosmic Energy into the blood, and from thence into all parts of the body to make it *more alive.*

How great the wisdom of the Great Architect in planning that the earth (collection of various salts) should contain a very large proportion of this remarkable salt. Sir Thomas Vaughan states, in his work, that it has a very great attraction for Magnesium, that they work together. This is very easy to understand. Magnesium, it will be remembered, is a *moving* or magnetic salt, but there must be something *within* or accompanying it, to enable it to move. As Ferrum means *to bear,* and Magnesium means *to move,* it is obvious that they must work together.

One lacking in strength, power, firmness and endurance is very deficient in iron. "Complexes" can all be eliminated by furnishing more Ferrum for the blood. Indeed the word "complex" can be consigned to the scrap heap and never be missed.

A smith is one who *works* in metals, especially in iron. His particular occupation is to FORGE. Therefore his work is required here between Pisces and Aries, where the circle of life is forged together. Is it not evident, then, how great is the importance of iron in the blood?

The Encyclopædia Britannica states that the archaic interpretation of smith as one who smites, is far-fetched and not applicable. How can this possibly be true, since the root words of both are identical? A smith must smite in order to assist in forging. Moreover, the word smite is most illuminating, for *it is the Smiting that Produces the Sparks.* The *Sparks* of life actually fly off the forge of Vulcan. They are iron particles.

A smith is also one who shapes and fashions, an artificer. In Greek, the word for smith means a GRAVER'S TOOL. In its original or archaic sense (the source of its meaning) it refers to SPIRIT, which is the Cosmic Sculptor. How deftly Spirit guides and turns the diamond-pointed tool by which man's form is created.

The word fabric is derived from the same root as forge. How interesting to learn that the *Burin,* which is the cutting tool of the engraver, is made of tempered steel.

In the ancient but much perverted story, Jesus is said to have been a CARPENTER. How confused all this has become, simply because people have never taken the trouble to look up the derivation of words. They have all been applied *without* instead of *within.*

The word carpenter is derived from the Latin verb *carpere,* and means an artificer, also to speak. A curious but revealing definition is obtained from the Sanskrit word for speech—SPHURJ—which means *A Spark of Fire.* It will be recalled that the first chapter, Aries, describes speech as the HISSING NAGA, which is Sanskrit for serpent. Mind (functioning through the brain and nerves) directs the energy, moving the muscles of the mouth, tongue and throat, and a hissing sound is emitted.

Therefore, back of the word carpenter or artificer, we find the idea of creator or producer. There is no historical work in existence about a MAN named Jesus, who was a carpenter. The Bible is NOT a historical work.

But every corpuscle of the blood—therefore every fish—is a potential Jesus, and is, therefore, A CARPENTER OR ARTIFICER. And more especially may this be said of the iron magnet within each one, SINCE SPIRIT, OR ETHERIC OXYGEN, IS THE ENSOULING LIFE.

In Hebrew, Cain or Kain means A SMITH, while Tabul or Tupal actually means IRON SLAG. As slag is "Scoria" or REFUSE, it is obvious that the refuse in the blood must be consumed in a combustion which the presence of iron alone can create.

It is well known that phosphate of iron colors the blood corpuscles red. It carries (bears) oxygen to all parts of the body. It is the vital force which SUSTAINS (strength) life. Dr. Carey says of this salt:

"Without a proper balance of iron in the blood, health can not be sustained. When a deficiency in this cell-salt occurs, the circulation is increased, for the blood tries to carry enough oxygen to all the tissues of the body with the limited amount of iron at hand, and in order to do so must move more rapidly; exactly as seven men must move faster in order to accomplish as much work as could ten, moving at a slower pace.

"This increased motion being changed to heat, by the law of the conservation of energy, is called FEVER. Search all the medical writings, from Hippocrates to Koch, and you will not find so good and true a definition of 'fever' as the one offered by the biochemic pathology. It is not the fever or heat alone that causes the condition of 'not at ease' in the patient, but the deficiencies in iron molecules, and a consequent lack of oxygen. This molecular disturbance soon breaks up the continuity of other cell-salts. A deficiency in potassium chloride nearly always follows a deficiency in iron, unless the missing links be quickly supplied."

One of the "bugbears" of life is the common cold, the supposed germ or microbe of which scientists have sought long and vainly. This they admit. They will never find it, for it does not exist. A cold is the housecleaning process by which kindly Mother Nature rids the body of the mucus or non-functional albumin (phlegm or pituitary) which has accumulated because of the great Calcium deficiency. Recalling the chapter on Capricorn and Calcium phos, we note this salt is required in greater quantities than any other. Sufficient is never obtained, unless the diet is supplemented with the Calcium tablets.

To the extent that iron is deficient will fever accompany the "cold;" and the character and color of the mucus eliminated via the nostrils and mouth depend on the consensus of deficiencies, according to biochemic pathology.

There are two forms of "colds": stuffy and watery. Kali mur and Calcium fluoride, Kali sulph, Silicea and Ferrum phos are all very deficient, as well as Calcium phos, in the former instance. One will feel stiff, lame, sometimes feverish, and the mucus will be thick, tough, and difficult to raise. In the latter case the sodium combinations are very deficient, which causes the mucus to take on a very watery character, with accompanying sneezing and running of water from the eyes.

A few of the many symptoms due to lack of Ferrum are: rush of blood to the head causing delirium; congestion of the brain from any cause; injury to the brain; wakefulness due to the walls of the blood vessels in the head being unable to disgorge the blood so that sleep may result (they lose their tonicity and do not support normal circulation); cerebritis; dizziness; emotional unbalance or insanity; headache with rush of blood to the head; headache of a dull, throbbing, bruising, beating character; head very sore to touch, pain on pulling the hair; congestion (nose-bleeding relieves, and many times is the means of lives being saved); all fevers; erysipelas; inflamed gums (apply locally); hemorrhage; *very* red tongue (like beefsteak) indicating inflammation; sore throat; vomiting of bright red blood; first stages of all inflammations; incontinence of urine when from WEAKNESS of the sphincter muscle; cystitis; burning, sore pain over kidneys; lumbago; sore muscles, tenderness and soreness of the skin; weak, sore ligaments; menstrual discharge bright red; palpitation of the heart; anemia (*one* form); hyperæmia—accumulation of blood in any of the blood vessels; stiff back.

Fractures and injuries of all kinds call for the free use of this salt to induce more of the healing oxygen, and to enable the waste and poison to be carried off. IN FACT THIS SALT IS ALWAYS REQUIRED, NO MATTER WHAT OTHER DEFICIENCIES ARE PRESENT. THE

REASON FOR THIS IS OBVIOUS, SINCE IRON IS THE MEANS OF THE HEALING SPIRIT ENTERING THE BLOOD.

It is marvelous what the application of iron to the surface of the body, when injured, will accomplish. A cut or bruise covered with a cream made from slightly moistened iron is all that is required. It will heal beautifully and leave no scar. Scars are Nature's method of reminding us that she did not have sufficient material to renew the part and leave no marks.

"Most of the ailments under this salt," says Dr. Carey, "are of a congestive nature, and are, therefore, relieved by *cold* and aggravated by motion. The cold should be applied directly to the congestion, or the relief will not be felt. If the inflammation is deep-seated, heat should be applied to relieve the engorgement of the deeper vessels."

Lack of iron, as we have previously stated, causes depression, discouragement, and a feeling as if one were absolutely crushed, since the air pressure ON the body is much greater than that *within*. The blood is thus poisoned and will eventually become very putrid, especially as potassium deficiency *always* accompanies lack of iron.

A few words relative to Neptune's present position are absolutely essential in closing this chapter and completing this book.

Neptune, the Spiritual ruler of Pisces, entered Virgo in October of 1928, and fourteen years are required to transit the sign. After mentally digesting what has been given in the chapter on Pisces, review the chapters on Virgo, Sagittarius, and Gemini. Their nature and activities and the parts of the body of man, and the universe with which they allocate, are definitely concerned in the passage of this Spiritual planet through Virgo. A MACROCOSMIC AND MICROCOSMIC HOUSECLEANING HAS BEGUN; THEREFORE, AN UNCOVERING AND ELIMINATION OF FILTH, UNTRUTH, AND WRONG METHODS, HAS BEEN INITIATED BY THE POWERS THAT BE.

This is accentuated by the presence of Uranus in Aries, which is vitally assisting in overthrowing all erroneous ideas and opinions, as well as in many instances demolishing the brain cells of non-thinkers. The youth of the world are utterly dissatisfied with the interpretations of religion and law (Sagittarius), with educational methods (Gemini), with so-called medical science, health and hygiene, labor and employment conditions, subtle caste differences between rich and poor (Virgo), and last, but not by any means least, with MORALS (Pisces), and the wholly inadequate and entirely perverted explanations relative to them which have been given in the past. THEY HAVE SCRAPPED THEM ALL, and are making a new start. They are learning for themselves by means of *experience,* as they go along. Because a person may not go to church is no proof that he is not religious—that he is not seeking to find God, to learn what is right and DO IT.

If people are unable to obtain a logical explanation of salvation, and how and why science and religion are twin-brothers, they will lose interest in attending church. There is plenty of evidence that the churches are already obliged to exert every means, and employ many curious methods in order to attract attendance.

No matter what has been concealed, and no matter how long—Neptune will now reveal it. All that can not bear the light of day must be done away with; for the depth of the earth, the matrix of the Virgin, is now being vibrated by the Divine Ray. If it finds enough to work with, it will begin to create the germ of the new man.

And as Neptune is the spiritual ruler of the depths of both the ocean and the earth, we have now to prepare for the SHAKING which will inevitably result. We have already had proof that the ocean bed is changing, and new continents are preparing to arise. Naturally some of those now standing will be depressed and submerged. Neptune in Virgo *opposite* its own sign Pisces, will therefore PULL the water of the ocean upon the earth and tidal waves will result. Tides will tend to be higher during the period of the transit of this planet through Virgo, and especially so at those times when the moon is also in this sign. At the time of the new moon tides will be very high.

When the powerful planet Jupiter enters Virgo in the summer of next year (1932), this will be intensified. There have been many complaints of lack of water, but too much is as bad as too little. Even the Indians living near the valley of the Mississippi are moving to higher ground—"the Great Spirit has told them," they say, "that WATER IS COMING."

We need not smile at these people who have lived so close to Nature, and are so far removed from all that is artificial.

Nature has revealed herself to them, and they observe all her moods. They know that when the squirrels begin to lay in their winter supply of food early, the season is approaching quickly. This is but one of the many keys they use. Nature's God communes intimately with those who live close to her, those who endeavor to find out what her laws are, and to obey them.

"I say unto you, Love your enemies."—Matt. 5:44. As love means understanding, it is obvious that the reason for the *presence* of enemy cells or corpuscles within us (which in the brain create thoughts of enmity) must be found out. Therefore, astro-biochemistry is the key. Perfect obedience to the law results in safety, as the Scriptures state, for "the law of the wise is a fountain of life."—Proverbs 13:14. This is the astrological reason why Sagittarius (law) is square to Pisces (the fountain of life—the blood).

"Unwearied thus for years on years the Fish propelled the ship across the heaped up waters, till at length it bore the vessel to the *peak* of Himavan (the personified Himalayas—the source of water); then softly smiling, thus the FISH addressed the sage—HASTE THEE TO BIND THY SHIP TO THIS HIGH CRAG."

♈ ♓

CHART of COSMIC & MICROCOSMIC EMBRYOS.

THE PATH of THE SUN in BOTH HEMISPHERES

COSMIC EMBRYOS

THE TRUE PATH OF THE SUN IN THE UNIVERSE.

THE PATH WHICH ENERGY (THE SUN) FOLLOWS IN MAN.

THE PATH WHICH ENERGY FOLLOWS IN SHAPING THE FORM OF THE EMBRYO IN UTERO.

LEGEND

THE COSMIC AND MICROCOSMIC EMBRYOS

THE Chart of the Cosmic and Microcosmic Embryos owes its inception to an idea that it would be interesting to make twelve concentric circles corresponding to the number of zodiacal signs. Then, to place each zodiacal symbol on the circle corresponding in number to that of the sign. Thus the glyph of Aries was placed in its usual position in the East, on the equator.

The symbol for Taurus, the second sign, was placed on the second circle and on the line forming the cusp between Aries and Taurus. The Gemini symbol fell on the third circle (it being the third sign); Cancer's glyph on the fourth, and so on until Pisces, the twelfth and last sign, was reached. Its symbol was placed on the circumference of the innermost circle forming the matrix.

The idea of drawing a line connecting these symbols was next conceived. When it was done, the result was astounding. It was instantly obvious that this line constituted THE OUTLINE OF AN EMBRYO, and furnished conclusive proof that *creative (cosmic) energy follows a path of curvature forming at one and the same time an ellipse and the figure of the embryo.*

These findings seem to explain why the climate, as well as the seasons, in the Northern Hemisphere differs from those in the Southern.

While meditating on the fact that the human body is egg-shaped or ellipsoidal, it was recalled that science had already discovered that life-currents in the brain follow a path shaped like the figure 8. (See *Gray's Anatomy*, p. 845, 1924 Edition.)

Madam Blavatsky adds further proof in her statement (on page 433 of *S. D.* Vol. I), that "man represents the figure X within the circle." The cerebrum is patterned after the triangle, and when drawn correctly proportioned, the *pyramid* can be erected within it. An imaginary line drawn between the upper and lower brain, forms the base of the pyramid. Sad to say, we have no really correct anatomical charts. Neither do accurate geographical maps exist, more especially those covering large areas.

After completing the plan of the embryos, it was found possible to fill in the geometrical figure of an ellipse without having to make a single correction, a truly unusual procedure.

Of still further interest is the fact that the formation of a double pyramid whose point of contact fell on the seed point within the innermost circle, also proved to be the pyramid formed in the head of each embryo; and, most wonderful to relate, the embryonic eye fell exactly on the middle point of the pyramid, which corresponds with the location of the All-Seeing Eye in the triangle as set forth in the lore of Masonry.

Thus geometry furnishes unusual information relative to embryology.

Again, each inorganic salt allocates with a certain sign, simply because it is capable of setting up a rate of motion which moves in a certain direction, *thus creating a particular pattern*. In other words, it covers a certain angular area.

The author earnestly hopes that this chart will furnish food for much thought.

It is quite possible that it will eventually be discovered that maps of the earth, as presented on globes, are not based on facts. When the author was a very young student, the mere sight of one of these globes caused a mental irritation and feeling of dissatisfaction which the research work of recent years has fully explained.

A partial description of a map which is much more reason-satisfying to the author is here presented for the consideration of the reader.

ASTRO-CHEMICO-PHYSIOLOGICAL AND CHROMATIC CHART

LEGEND

The only point relative to this chart which is necessary to explain, is its color allocation.

Earnest students of astrology have endeavored to allocate color with the zodiacal signs, never realizing that it could be quickly accomplished by merely bending the spectrum and placing it over the zodiac.

The zero point, where Aries and Pisces join and link the circle of life together, harmonizes with that part of the spectrum where violet-cerise or "royal purple" merges into pure cerise.

It will be noted that the primary signs in astrology are the FIRE SIGNS: Aries, Leo, and Sagittarius. As the *primary colors,* cerise (termed red), yellow, and blue, automatically place themselves OVER these signs when the spectrum is placed on the zodiac, no further proof that my chart is correct, is required.

However, additional proof is present on all sides. Aries is the complement of Libra, whose allocating color is green. Red and green are complementary colors.

As the zodiacal signs opposite each other are natural complements, it is equally true that their corresponding colors are also complementary.

Color is the visible manifestation of invisible molecular action, otherwise the electrical field of energy enveloping its area.

The North Pole is really the pole or center of the universe or earth, its navel, so to speak. It is to the earth, what the solar plexus is to the physical body. Around it, on a more or less concave surface, the continents and islands are grouped.

The South Pole will never be visited by anyone, as it lies deep within the foundation of the earth. If this idea is difficult to visualize, study a child's top for an example. It is spun or twirled by means of its upper (north pole) end. It rests or spins on the opposite pole or end. But it must be constantly recalled that IT HAS A FOUNDATION UNDER IT.

The surface of the earth changes during certain cycles, a gradual submergence taking place in definite areas, while at the same time new continents slowly rise from the ocean bed.

The earth may be pictured as an enormous egg in a tub of water. The under portion is submerged. A partly inflated rubber ball is a still better example to use. Pressure on the center causes the sides to bulge up while pressure on one side results in the other rising still higher. It is evident to the student that something of the sort is taking place in the middle of the North American continent.

It seems within the bounds of reason to assume that Richard E. Byrd's explorations were concerned with the matrix or pivotal point of the earth, and the region very far south.

The points farthest north, south, east and west of the Pole naturally form the four points of the compass. These connected by an imaginary line form the circumference or ice-barrier which no human being has ever seen.

It does not seem unreasonable to assume that this circumference is met by the *arch* of the sky (since energy never fails to take a circular course), for it constitutes a very good reason for the formation of the immeasurable and insurmountable ice barrier which MAY one day be discovered to be LIQUEFIED AIR.

It is a scientific fact that the icy waters of the so-called "polar seas" contain an immense quantity of Kali mur or chloride of potassium. As this salt is chemically capable of producing great cold, we have further evidence of the possibility that the supposed ice-barrier is really liquefied air. On re-reading the chapter on Gemini, which is an AIR sign, it will not be difficult to understand the points above given, and especially when it is recalled that Kali mur is an AIR salt. Kali or potassium (the carrier of fire), and chlorine (a heavy gaseous element), combine to precipitate and thus materialize what was heretofore invisible.

Order will eventually appear out of the chaos of perversion.

INDEX

INDEX

D

Index

Index

INDEX

INDEX

T